BASIC
MATHEMATICS

MARVIN L. BITTINGER

CUSTOM EDITION FOR SULLIVAN UNIVERSITY

Taken from:
Basic Mathematics, Tenth Edition
by Marvin L. Bittinger

Custom Publishing

New York   Boston   San Francisco
London   Toronto   Sydney   Tokyo   Singapore   Madrid
Mexico City   Munich   Paris   Cape Town   Hong Kong   Montreal

Cover Art: Illustration by Pearson Custom Publishing

Taken from:

Basic Mathematics, Tenth Edition
by Marvin L. Bittinger
Copyright © 2007 by Pearson Education, Inc.
Published by Addison-Wesley
Boston, Massachusetts 02116

This special edition published in cooperation with Pearson Custom Publishing.

Printed in the United States of America

10   9   8   7   6   5   4

2008360994

LR

Pearson
Custom Publishing
is a division of

www.pearsonhighered.com

ISBN 10: 0-558-03171-4
ISBN 13: 978-0-558-03171-8

Contents

DATA, GRAPHS, AND STATISTICS

REAL NUMBERS

ALGEBRA: SOLVING EQUATIONS AND PROBLEMS

Index of Applications

Index of Study Tips

Preface

It is with great pride and excitement that we present to you the tenth edition of *Basic Mathematics*. The text has evolved dramatically over the past 36 years through your comments, responses, and opinions. This feedback, combined with our overall objective of presenting the material in a clear and accurate manner, drives each revision. It is our hope that *Basic Mathematics*, Tenth Edition, and the supporting supplements will help provide an improved teaching and learning experience by matching the needs of instructors and successfully preparing students for their future.

This text is the first in a series that includes the following:

Bittinger: *Basic Mathematics,* Tenth Edition

Bittinger: *Fundamental Mathematics,* Fourth Edition

Bittinger: *Introductory Algebra,* Tenth Edition

Bittinger: *Intermediate Algebra,* Tenth Edition

Bittinger/Beecher: *Introductory and Intermediate Algebra,* Third Edition

Building Understanding through an Interactive Approach

The pedagogy of this text is designed to provide an interactive learning experience between the student and the exposition, annotated examples, art, margin exercises, and exercise sets. This unique approach, which has been developed and refined over ten editions and is illustrated at the right, provides students with a clear set of learning

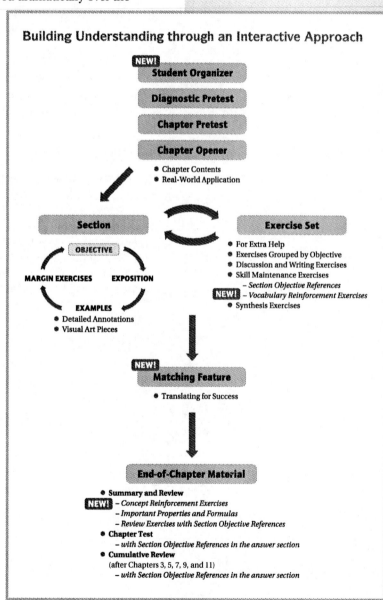

Building Understanding through an Interactive Approach

NEW! **Student Organizer**

Diagnostic Pretest

Chapter Pretest

Chapter Opener
- Chapter Contents
- Real-World Application

Section

OBJECTIVE

MARGIN EXERCISES — EXPOSITION

EXAMPLES
- Detailed Annotations
- Visual Art Pieces

Exercise Set
- For Extra Help
- Exercises Grouped by Objective
- Discussion and Writing Exercises
- Skill Maintenance Exercises
  – *Section Objective References*
  NEW! – *Vocabulary Reinforcement Exercises*
- Synthesis Exercises

NEW! **Matching Feature**
- Translating for Success

End-of-Chapter Material
- **Summary and Review**
  NEW! – *Concept Reinforcement Exercises*
  – *Important Properties and Formulas*
  – *Review Exercises with Section Objective References*
- **Chapter Test**
  – *with Section Objective References in the answer section*
- **Cumulative Review**
  (after Chapters 3, 5, 7, 9, and 11)
  – *with Section Objective References in the answer section*

objectives, involves them with the development of the material, and provides immediate and continual reinforcement and assessment through the margin exercises.

Let's Visit the Tenth Edition

The style, format, and approach of the ninth edition have been strengthened in this new edition in a number of ways. However, the accuracy that the Bittinger books are known for has not changed. This edition, as with all editions, has gone through an exhaustive checking process to ensure accuracy in the problem sets, mathematical art, and accompanying supplements. We know what a critical role the accuracy of a book plays in student learning and we value the reputation for accuracy that we have earned.

NEW! IN THE TENTH EDITION

Each revision gives us the opportunity to incorporate new elements and refine existing elements to provide a better experience for students and teachers alike. Below are four new features designed to help students succeed.

- Student Organizer
- Translating for Success matching exercises
- Vocabulary Reinforcement exercises
- Concept Reinforcement exercises

These features, along with the hallmark features of this book, are discussed in the pages that follow.

In addition, the tenth edition has been designed to be open and flexible, helping students focus their attention on details that are critical at this level through prominent headings, boxed definitions and rules, and clearly labeled objectives. *Chapter Pretests*, now located along with the Diagnostic Pretest in the *Printed Test Bank* and in MyMathLab, diagnose at the section and objective level and can be used to place students in a specific section, or objective, of the chapter, allowing them to concentrate on topics with which they have particular difficulty. Answers to these pretests are available in the *Printed Test Bank* and in MyMathLab.

NEW! STUDENT ORGANIZER

Along with the study tips found throughout the text, we have provided a pull-out card that will help students stay organized and increase their ability to be successful in this course. Students can use this card to keep track of important dates and useful contact information and to access information for technology and to plan class time, study time, work time, travel time, family time, and, sometimes most importantly, relaxation time.

CHAPTER OPENERS

To engage students and prepare them for the upcoming chapter material, gateway chapter openers are designed with exceptional artwork that is tied to a motivating real-world application. (See pages 1, 89, and 149.)

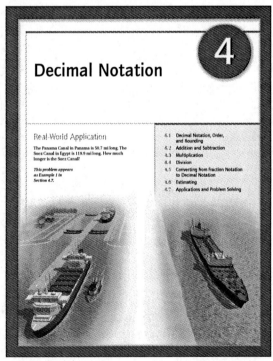

OBJECTIVE BOXES

At the beginning of each section, a boxed list of objectives is keyed by letter not only to section subheadings, but also to the exercises in the Pretest (located in the *Printed Test Bank* and MyMathLab), the section exercise sets, and the Summary and Review exercises, as well as to the answers to the questions in the Chapter Tests and Cumulative Reviews. This correlation enables students to easily find appropriate review material if they need help with a particular exercise or skill at the objective level. (See pages 90, 165, and 218.)

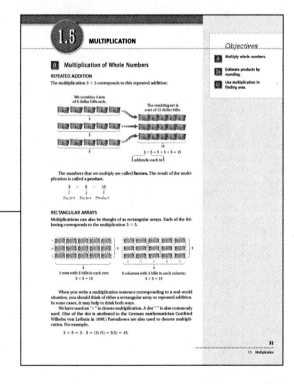

ANNOTATED EXAMPLES

Detailed annotations and color highlights lead the student through the structured steps of the examples. The level of detail in these annotations is a significant reason for students' success with this book. (See pages 168, 192, and 314.)

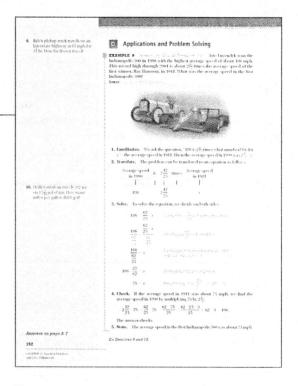

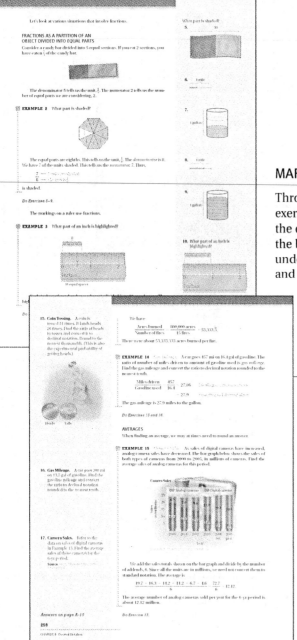

MARGIN EXERCISES

Throughout the text, students are directed to numerous margin exercises that provide immediate practice and reinforcement of the concepts covered in each section. Answers are provided at the back of the book so students can immediately self-assess their understanding of the skill or concept at hand. (See pages 91, 250, and 292.)

REAL-DATA APPLICATIONS

This text encourages students to see and interpret the mathematics that appears every day in the world around them. Throughout the writing process, an extensive and energetic search for real-data applications was conducted, and the result is a variety of examples and exercises that connect the mathematical content with the real world. A large number of the applications are new to this edition, and many are drawn from the fields of business and economics, life and physical sciences, social sciences, and areas of general interest such as sports and daily life. To further encourage students to understand the relevance of mathematics, many applications are enhanced by graphs and drawings similar to those found in today's newspapers and magazines, and feature source lines as well. (See pages 164, 239, and 301.)

NEW! TRANSLATING FOR SUCCESS

Translating for Success The goal of the matching exercises in this new feature is to practice step two, *Translate*, of the five-step problem-solving process. Students translate each of ten problems to an equation and select the correct translation from fifteen given equations. This feature appears once in each chapter and reviews skills and concepts with problems from all preceding chapters. (See pages 195, 277, and 319.)

ART PROGRAM

Today's students are often visually oriented and their approach to a printed page is no exception. The art program is designed to improve the visualization of the mathematical concepts and to enhance the real-data applications. (See pages 107, 270, and 320.)

The use of color is carried out in a methodical and precise manner so that it conveys a consistent meaning, which enhances the readability of the text. For example, when perimeter is considered, figures have a red border to emphasize the perimeter. When area is considered, figures are outlined in black and screened with amber to emphasize the area. Similarly, when volume is considered, figures are three-dimensional and airbrushed blue. When fractional parts are illustrated, those parts are shown in purple.

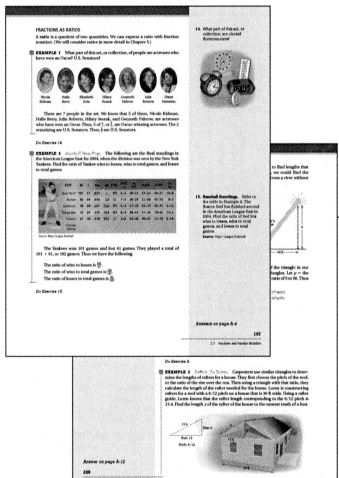

PHOTOGRAPHS

Often, an application becomes relevant to students when the connection to the real world is illustrated with a photograph. This text has numerous photographs throughout in order to help students see the relevance and visualize the application at hand. (See pages 104, 219, and 303.)

CAUTION BOXES

Found at relevant points throughout the text, boxes with the "Caution!" heading warn students of common misconceptions or errors made in performing a particular mathematics operation or skill. (See pages 125, 190, and 224.)

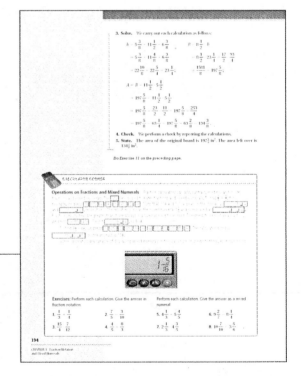

CALCULATOR CORNERS

Where appropriate throughout the text, students will find optional Calculator Corners. Popular in the ninth edition, these Calculator Corners have been revised to be more accessible to students and to represent current calculators. (See pages 194, 230, and 310.)

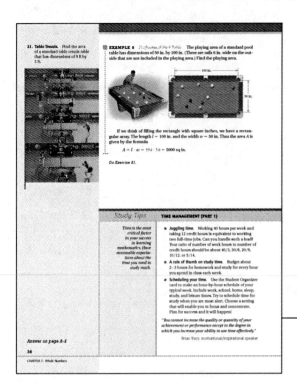

STUDY TIPS

A variety of Study Tips throughout the text give students pointers on how to develop good study habits as they progress through the course. At times short snippets and at other times more lengthy discussions, these Study Tips encourage students to get involved in the learning process. (See pages 155, 295, and 308.)

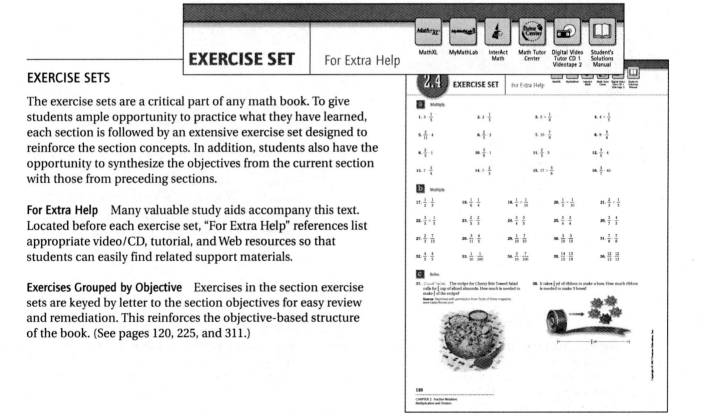

EXERCISE SETS

The exercise sets are a critical part of any math book. To give students ample opportunity to practice what they have learned, each section is followed by an extensive exercise set designed to reinforce the section concepts. In addition, students also have the opportunity to synthesize the objectives from the current section with those from preceding sections.

For Extra Help Many valuable study aids accompany this text. Located before each exercise set, "For Extra Help" references list appropriate video/CD, tutorial, and Web resources so that students can easily find related support materials.

Exercises Grouped by Objective Exercises in the section exercise sets are keyed by letter to the section objectives for easy review and remediation. This reinforces the objective-based structure of the book. (See pages 120, 225, and 311.)

Discussion and Writing Exercises Designed to help students develop a deeper comprehension of critical concepts, Discussion and Writing exercises (indicated by D_W) are suitable for individual or group work. These exercises encourage students to both think and write about key mathematical ideas in the chapter. (See pages 121, 189, and 283.)

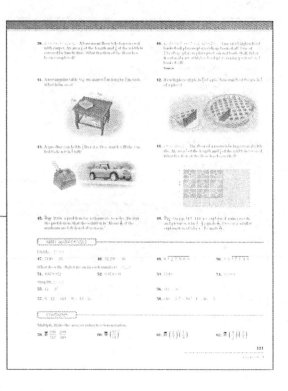

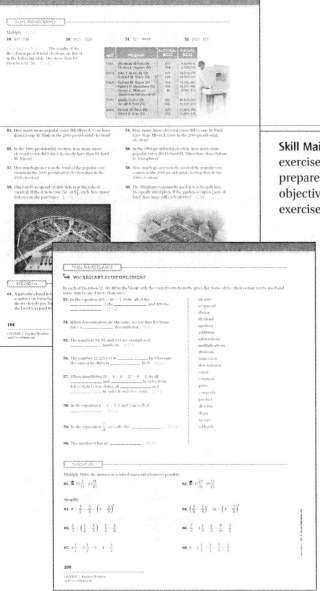

Skill Maintenance Exercises Found in each exercise set, these exercises review concepts from other sections in the text to prepare students for their final examination. Section and objective codes appear next to each Skill Maintenance exercise for easy reference. (See pages 164, 172, and 284.)

NEW! **Vocabulary Reinforcement Exercises** This new feature checks and reviews students' understanding of the vocabulary introduced throughout the text. It appears once in every chapter, in the Skill Maintenance portion of an exercise set, and is intended to provide a continuing review of the terms that students must know in order to be able to communicate effectively in the language of mathematics. (See pages 143, 200, and 269.)

Synthesis Exercises In most exercise sets, Synthesis exercises help build critical-thinking skills by requiring students to synthesize or combine learning objectives from the current section as well as from preceding text sections. (See pages 114, 208, and 332.)

END-OF-CHAPTER MATERIAL

At the end of each chapter, students can practice all they have learned as well as tie the current chapter content to material covered in earlier chapters.

SUMMARY AND REVIEW

A three-part *Summary and Review* appears at the end of each chapter. The first part includes the Concept Reinforcement Exercises described below. The second part is a list of important properties and formulas, when applicable, and the third part provides an extensive set of review exercises.

NEW! **Concept Reinforcement Exercises** Found in the Summary and Review of every chapter, these true/false exercises are designed to increase understanding of the concepts rather than merely assess students' skill at memorizing procedures. (See pages 209, 285, and 333.)

Important Properties and Formulas A list of the important properties and formulas discussed in the chapter is provided for students in an organized manner to help them prioritize topics learned and prepare for chapter tests. This list is only provided in those chapters in which new properties or formulas are presented. (See pages 410, 510, and 569.)

Review Exercises At the end of each chapter, students are provided with an extensive set of review exercises. Reference codes beside each exercise or direction line allow students to easily refer back to specific, objective-level content for remediation. (See pages 144, 209, and 285.)

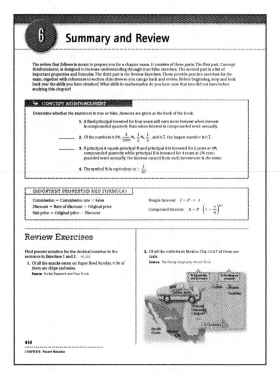

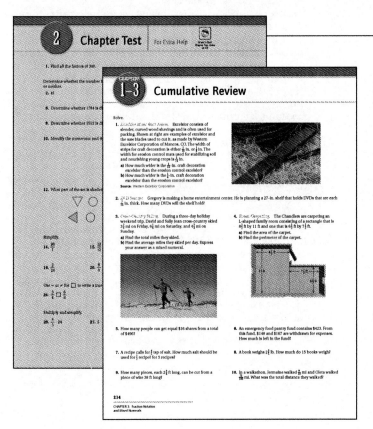

CHAPTER TEST

Following the Review Exercises, a sample Chapter Test allows students to review and test comprehension of chapter skills prior to taking an instructor's exam. Answers to all questions in the Chapter Test are given at the back of the book. Section and objective references for each question are included with the answers. (See pages 147, 212, and 288.)

CUMULATIVE REVIEW

Following Chapters 3, 5, 7, 9, and 11, students encounter a Cumulative Review. This exercise set reviews skills and concepts from all preceding chapters to help students recall previously learned material and prepare for a final exam. At the back of the book are answers to all Cumulative Review exercises, together with section and objective references, so that students know exactly what material to study if they miss a review exercise. Additional Cumulative Review Tests for every chapter are available in the *Printed Test Bank*. (See pages 214, 338, and 671.)

Ancillaries

The following ancillaries are available to help both instructors and students use this text more effectively.

Student Supplements

Student's Solutions Manual (ISBN 0-321-29607-9)

- By Judith A. Penna, *Indiana University Purdue University Indianapolis*
- Contains completely worked-out solutions with step-by-step annotations for all the odd-numbered exercises in the text, with the exception of the discussion and writing exercises, as well as completely worked-out solutions to all the exercises in the Chapter Reviews, Chapter Tests, and Cumulative Reviews.

Collaborative Learning Activities Manual
(ISBN 0-321-29604-4)

- Features group activities tied to text sections and includes the focus, time estimate, suggested group size and materials, and background notes for each activity.
- Available as a stand-alone supplement sold in the bookstore, as a textbook bundle component for students, or as a classroom activity resource for instructors.

Videotapes (ISBN 0-321-30569-8)

- Include new chapter openers presented by author Marvin Bittinger.
- Present a series of lectures correlated directly to the content of each section of the text.
- Feature an engaging team of instructors who present material in a format that stresses student interaction, often using examples and exercises from the text.

Digital Video Tutor (ISBN 0-321-29605-2)

- Complete set of digitized videos (as described above) on CD-ROMs for student use at home or on campus.
- Ideal for distance learning or supplemental instruction.
- Are available with captioning on request. Contact your local Addison-Wesley representative for details.

NEW! Work It Out! Chapter Test Video on CD
(ISBN 0-321-41985-5)

- Presented by Judith A. Penna and Barbara Johnson
- Provides step-by-step solutions to every exercise in each Chapter Test from the text.
- Helps students prepare for chapter tests and synthesize content.

Math Study Skills for Students Video on CD
(ISBN 0-321-29745-8)

- Presented by author Marvin Bittinger
- Designed to help students make better use of their math study time and improve their retention of concepts and procedures taught in classes from basic mathematics through intermediate algebra.
- Through carefully crafted graphics and comprehensive on-camera explanation, focuses on study skills that are commonly overlooked.

Instructor Supplements

Annotated Instructor's Edition (ISBN 0-321-30553-1)

- Includes answers to all exercises printed in blue on the same page as those exercises.

Instructor's Solutions Manual (ISBN 0-321-30556-6)

- By Judith A. Penna, *Indiana University Purdue University Indianapolis*
- Contains brief solutions to the even-numbered exercises in the exercise sets, answers to all of the Discussion and Writing exercises, and the completely worked-out solutions to all the exercises in the Chapter Reviews, Chapter Tests, and Cumulative Reviews.

Online Answer Book

- By Judith A. Penna, *Indiana University Purdue University Indianapolis*
- Available in electronic form from the instructor resource center. Contact your local Addison-Wesley representative for details.
- Contains answers to all the section exercises in the text.

Printed Test Bank (ISBN 0-321-30557-4)

- By Laurie Hurley
- Contains one diagnostic test.
- Contains one pretest for each chapter.
- Provides 13 new test forms for every chapter and 8 new test forms for the final exam.
- For the chapter tests, 5 test forms are modeled after the chapter tests in the text, 3 test forms are organized by topic order following the text objectives, 3 test forms are designed for 50-minute class periods and organized so that each objective in the chapter is covered on one of the tests, and 2 test forms are multiple-choice. Chapter tests also include more challenging synthesis questions.
- Contains 2 cumulative tests per chapter beginning with Chapter 2.
- For the final exam, 3 test forms are organized by chapter, 3 test forms are organized by question type, and 2 test forms are multiple-choice.

NEW! Instructor and Adjunct Support Manual
(ISBN 0-321-30554-X)

- Includes Adjunct Support Manual material.
- Features resources and teaching tips designed to help both new and adjunct faculty with course preparation and classroom management.
- Resources include chapter reviews, extra practice sheets, conversion guide, video index, audio index, and transparency masters.
- Also available electronically so course/adjunct coordinators can customize material specific to their schools.

Student Supplements

Audio Recordings

- By Bill Saler
- Lead students through the material in each section of the text, explaining solution steps to examples, pointing out common errors, and focusing on margin exercises and solutions.
- Audio files are available to download in MP3 format. Contact your local Addison-Wesley representative for details.

Addison-Wesley Math Tutor Center

www.aw-bc.com/tutorcenter

- The Addison-Wesley Math Tutor Center is staffed by qualified mathematics instructors who provide students with tutoring on examples and odd-numbered exercises from the textbook. Tutoring is available via toll-free telephone, toll-free fax, e-mail, or the Internet. White Board technology allows tutors and students to actually see problems worked while they "talk" in real time over the Internet during tutoring sessions.

MathXL® Tutorials on CD   (ISBN 0-321-29747-4)

- Provides algorithmically generated practice exercises that correlate at the objective level to the content of the text.
- Includes an example and a guided solution to accompany every exercise and video clips for selected exercises.
- Recognizes student errors and provides feedback; generates printed summaries of students' progress.

Instructor Supplements

TestGen with Quizmaster   (ISBN 0-321-30567-1)

- Enables instructors to build, edit, print, and administer tests.
- Features a computerized bank of questions developed to cover all text objectives.
- Algorithmically based content allows instructors to create multiple but equivalent versions of the same question or test with a click of a button.
- Instructors can also modify test-bank questions or add new questions by using the built-in question editor, which allows users to create graphs, input graphics, and insert math notation, variable numbers, or text.
- Tests can be printed or administered online via the Internet or another network. Quizmaster allows students to take tests on a local area network.
- Available on a dual-platform Windows/Macintosh CD-ROM.

MathXL®   www.mathxl.com

MathXL is a powerful online homework, tutorial, and assessment system that accompanies Addison-Wesley textbooks in mathematics or statistics. With MathXL, instructors can create, edit, and assign online homework and tests using algorithmically generated exercises correlated at the objective level to the textbook. They can also create and assign their own online exercises and import TestGen tests for added flexibility. All student work is tracked in MathXL's online gradebook. Students can take chapter tests in MathXL and receive personalized study plans based on their test results. The study plan diagnoses weaknesses and links students directly to tutorial exercises for the objectives they need to study and retest. Students can also access supplemental animations and video clips directly from selected exercises. MathXL is available to qualified adopters. For more information, visit our Web site at www.mathxl.com or contact your Addison-Wesley sales representative.

MyMathLab   www.mymathlab.com

MyMathLab is a series of text-specific, easily customizable online courses for Addison-Wesley textbooks in mathematics and statistics. Powered by CourseCompass™ (Pearson Education's online teaching and learning environment) and MathXL® (our online homework, tutorial, and assessment system), MyMathLab gives instructors the tools they need to deliver all or a portion of their course online, whether students are in a lab setting or working from home. MyMathLab provides a rich and flexible set of course materials, featuring free-response exercises that are algorithmically generated for unlimited practice and mastery. Students can also use online tools, such as video lectures, animations, and a multimedia textbook, to independently improve their understanding and performance. Instructors can use MyMathLab's homework and test managers to select and assign online exercises correlated directly to the textbook, and they can also create and assign their own online exercises and import TestGen tests for added flexibility. MyMathLab's online gradebook—designed specifically for mathematics and statistics—automatically tracks students' homework and test results and gives the instructor control over how to calculate final grades. Instructors can also add offline (paper-and-pencil) grades to the gradebook. MyMathLab is available to qualified adopters. For more information, visit our Web site at www.mymathlab.com or contact your Addison-Wesley sales representative.

InterAct Math® Tutorial Web site   www.interactmath.com

Get practice and tutorial help online! This interactive tutorial Web site provides algorithmically generated practice exercises that correlate directly to the exercises in the textbook. Students can retry an exercise as many times as they like with new values each time for unlimited practice and mastery. Every exercise is accompanied by an interactive guided solution that provides helpful feedback for incorrect answers, and students can also view a worked-out sample problem that steps them through an exercise similar to the one they're working on.

ADDISON-WESLEY MATH ADJUNCT SUPPORT CENTER

The Addison-Wesley Math Adjunct Support Center is staffed by qualified mathematics instructors with over 50 years of combined experience at both the community college and university level. Assistance is provided for faculty in the following areas:

- Suggested syllabus consultation
- Tips on using materials packaged with your book
- Book-specific content assistance
- Teaching suggestions including advice on classroom strategies

For more information, visit www.aw-bc.com/tutorcenter/math-adjunct.html

Acknowledgments and Reviewers

Many of you helped to shape the tenth edition by reviewing and spending time with us on your campuses. Our deepest appreciation to all of you and in particular to the following:

Sally Clark, *Ozarks Technical Community College*

Penny Deggelman, *Lane Community College*

Molly Misko, *Gadsden State Community College*

Cassonda Thompson, *York Technical College*

Mary Woestman, *Broome Community College*

We wish to express our heartfelt appreciation to a number of people who have contributed in special ways to the development of this textbook. Our editor, Jennifer Crum, and marketing manager, Jay Jenkins, encouraged our vision and provided marketing insight. Kari Heen, the project manager, deserves special recognition for overseeing every phase of the project and keeping it moving. The unwavering support of the Developmental Math group, including Katie Nopper, project editor, Elizabeth Bernardi and Alison Macdonald, editorial assistants, Ron Hampton, managing editor, Dennis Schaefer, cover designer, and Sharon Smith and Ceci Fleming, media producers, and the endless hours of hard work by Kathy Diamond and Geri Davis have led to products of which we are immensely proud.

We also want to thank Judy Penna for writing the *Student's* and *Instructor's Solutions Manuals* and for her strong leadership in the preparation of the printed supplements, videotapes, and MyMathLab. Other strong support has come from Laurie Hurley for the *Printed Test Bank,* Bill Saler for the audio recordings, and Barbara Johnson, Michelle Lanosga, and Jennifer Rosenberg for their accuracy checking of the manuscript. We also wish to recognize those who wrote scripts, presented lessons on camera, and checked the accuracy of the videotapes.

To the Student

As your author, I would like to welcome you to this study of *Basic Mathematics.* Whatever your past experiences, I encourage you to look at this mathematics course as a fresh start. Approach this course with a positive attitude about mathematics. Mathematics is a base for life, for many majors, for personal finances, for most careers, or just for pleasure.

You are the most important factor in the success of your learning. In earlier experiences, you may have allowed yourself to sit back and let the instructor "pour in" the learning, with little or no follow-up on your part. But now you must take a more assertive and proactive stance. This may be the first adjustment you make in college. As soon as possible after class, you should thoroughly read the textbook and the supplements and do all you can to learn on your own. In other words, rid yourself of former habits and take responsibility for your own learning. Then, with all the help you have around you, your hard work will lead to success.

One of the most important suggestions I can make is to allow yourself enough *time* to learn. You can have the best book, the best instructor, and the best supplements, but if you do not give yourself time to learn, how can they be of benefit? Many other helpful suggestions are presented in the Study Tips that you will find throughout the book. You may want to read through all the Study Tips before you begin the text. An Index of Study Tips can be found at the front of the book.

M.L.B.

Bittinger Student Organizer

Study Tips

Throughout this text, you will find a feature called *Study Tips*. We discuss these in the Preface of this text. They are intended to help improve your math study skills. An index of all the *Study Tips* can be found at the front of the book.

For Extra Help

 MyMathLab

 MathXL

 Student's Solutions Manual

 Digital Video Tutor CD Videotape

 Math Tutor Center

 InterAct Math

Additional Resources

Basic Math Review Card
(ISBN 0-321-39476-3)

Algebra Review Card
(ISBN 0-321-39473-9)

Math for Allied Health Reference Card
(ISBN 0-321-39474-7)

Graphing Calculator Reference Card
(ISBN 0-321-39475-5)

Math Study Skills for Students Video on CD
(ISBN 0-321-29745-8)

Go to
www.aw-bc.com/math
for more information.

On the first day of class, complete this chart and the weekly planner that follows on the reverse page.

Instructor Information:

Name _____

Office Hours and Location _____

_____

Phone Number _____

Fax Number _____

E-mail Address _____

Find the names of two students whom you could contact for class information or study questions:

1. Name _____

   Phone Number _____

   Fax Number _____

   E-mail Address _____

2. Name _____

   Phone Number _____

   Fax Number _____

   E-mail Address _____

Math Lab on Campus:

Location _____

Hours _____

Phone Number _____

Tutoring:

Campus Location _____

Hours _____

 To order the Addison-Wesley Math Tutor Center, call 1-888-777-0463.

(*See the Preface for important information concerning this tutoring.*)

Important Supplements: (*See the Preface for a complete list of available supplements.*)

Supplements recommended by the instructor _____

_____

Online Log-in Information (*include access code, password, Web address, etc.*)

_____

_____

For more information about this text or any of its supplements, visit www.aw-bc.com/math

Bittinger Student Organizer

WEEKLY PLANNER

Success is planned. On this page, plan a typical week. Consider time allotments for class, study, work, travel, family, and relaxation.

Important Dates

Midterm Exam

_____

Final Exam

_____

Holidays

_____

_____

_____

_____

Other

_____

_____

_____

TIME	Sun.	Mon.	Tues.	Wed.	Thurs.	Fri.	Sat.
6:00 A.M.							
6:30							
7:00							
7:30							
8:00							
8:30							
9:00							
9:30							
10:00							
10:30							
11:00							
11:30							
12:00 P.M.							
12:30							
1:00							
1:30							
2:00							
2:30							
3:00							
3:30							
4:00							
4:30							
5:00							
5:30							
6:00							
6:30							
7:00							
7:30							
8:00							
8:30							
9:00							
9:30							
10:00							
10:30							
11:00							
11:30							
12:00 A.M.							

For more information about this text or any of its supplements, visit www.aw-bc.com/math

Ratio and Proportion

5

Real-World Application

The number of women attending Purdue University's veterinary school of medicine has grown to surpass the number of men in the past three decades. In 1971, 53 men and 12 women were enrolled. In 1979, 36 men and 36 women were enrolled, and in 2004, there were 58 women and 12 men. What was the ratio of women to men in 1971, in 1979, and in 2004? What was the ratio of men to total enrollment in 2004?

Source: Purdue University School of Veterinary Medicine, *Indianapolis Star*

This problem appears as Example 7 in Section 5.1.

Objectives

a Find fraction notation for ratios.

b Simplify ratios.

1. Find the ratio of 5 to 11.

2. Find the ratio of 57.3 to 86.1.

3. Find the ratio of $6\frac{3}{4}$ to $7\frac{2}{5}$.

4. **Rainfall.** The greatest amount of rainfall ever recorded for a 12-month period was 739 in. in Kukui, Maui, Hawaii, from December 1981 to December 1982. Find the ratio of rainfall to time in months.

Source: *The Handy Science Answer Book*

Answers on page A-11

a Ratios

> **RATIO**
>
> A **ratio** is the quotient of two quantities.

In the 2004–2005 season, the Detroit Pistons basketball team averaged 93.3 points per game and allowed their opponents an average of 89.5 points per game. The *ratio* of points earned to points allowed is given by the fraction notation

$$\text{Points earned} \longrightarrow \frac{93.3}{89.5} \quad \text{or by the colon notation} \quad 93.3 : 89.5.$$
$$\text{Points allowed} \longrightarrow$$

We read both forms of notation as "the ratio of 93.3 to 89.5," listing the numerator first and the denominator second.

> **RATIO NOTATION**
>
> The **ratio** of a to b is given by the fraction notation $\frac{a}{b}$, where a is the numerator and b is the denominator, or by the colon notation $a : b$.

EXAMPLE 1 Find the ratio of 7 to 8.

The ratio is $\frac{7}{8}$, or $7 : 8$.

EXAMPLE 2 Find the ratio of 31.4 to 100.

The ratio is $\frac{31.4}{100}$, or $31.4 : 100$.

EXAMPLE 3 Find the ratio of $4\frac{2}{3}$ to $5\frac{7}{8}$. You need not simplify.

The ratio is $\frac{4\frac{2}{3}}{5\frac{7}{8}}$, or $4\frac{2}{3} : 5\frac{7}{8}$.

Do Exercises 1–3.

In most of our work, we will use fraction notation for ratios.

EXAMPLE 4 *Wind Speeds.* The average wind speed in Chicago is 10.4 mph. The average wind speed in Boston is 12.5 mph. Find the ratio of the wind speed in Chicago to the wind speed in Boston.

Source: *The Handy Geography Answer Book*

The ratio is $\frac{10.4}{12.5}$.

EXAMPLE 5 *Batting.* In the 2004 season, Vladimir Guerrero of the Anaheim Angels got 206 hits in 612 at-bats. What was the ratio of hits to at-bats? of at-bats to hits?

Source: Major League Baseball

The ratio of hits to at-bats is

$$\frac{206}{612}.$$

The ratio of at-bats to hits is

$$\frac{612}{206}.$$

5. **Fat Grams.** In one serving ($\frac{1}{2}$-cup) of fried scallops, there are 12 g of fat. In one serving ($\frac{1}{2}$-cup) of fried oysters, there are 14 g of fat. What is the ratio of grams of fat in one serving of scallops to grams of fat in one serving of oysters?

Source: *Better Homes and Gardens: A New Cook Book*

6. **Earned Runs.** In the 2004 season, Roger Clemens of the Houston Astros gave up 71 earned runs in 214.1 innings pitched. What was the ratio of earned runs to innings pitched? of innings pitched to earned runs?

Source: Major League Baseball

Do Exercises 4–6. (Exercise 4 is on the preceding page.)

EXAMPLE 6 Refer to the triangle below.

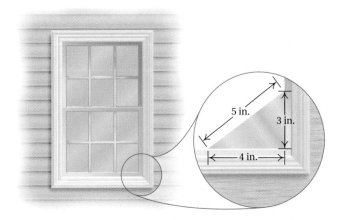

a) What is the ratio of the length of the longest side to the length of the shortest side?

$$\frac{5}{3}$$

b) What is the ratio of the length of the shortest side to the length of the longest side?

$$\frac{3}{5}$$

Do Exercise 7.

7. In the triangle below, what is the ratio of the length of the shortest side to the length of the longest side?

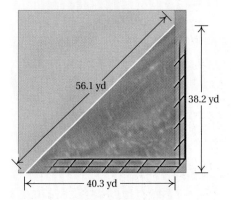

Answers on page A-11

8. Soap Box Derby. Participation in the All-American Soap Box Derby World Championship has increased by more than 300 competitors since 1985. In 2004, there were 483 participants, 278 boys and 205 girls. What was the ratio of girls to boys? of boys to girls? of boys to total number of participants?

Source: All-American Soap Box Derby

EXAMPLE 7 *Veterinary Medicine.* The number of women attending Purdue University's veterinary school of medicine has grown to surpass the number of men in the past three decades.

Enrollment in Veterinary Medicine: Purdue University

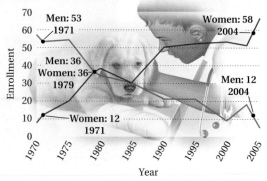

Sources: Purdue University School of Veterinary Medicine; *Indianapolis Star*

a) What was the ratio of women to men in 1971? in 1979? in 2004?

b) What was the ratio of men to women in 1971? in 1979? in 2004?

c) What was the ratio of women to total enrollment in 2004?

d) What was the ratio of men to total enrollment in 2004?

a) The ratio of women to men

$$\text{in 1971: } \frac{12}{53}; \quad \text{in 1979: } \frac{36}{36}; \quad \text{in 2004: } \frac{58}{12}.$$

b) The ratio of men to women

$$\text{in 1971: } \frac{53}{12}; \quad \text{in 1979: } \frac{36}{36}; \quad \text{in 2004: } \frac{12}{58}.$$

c) The ratio of women to total enrollment

$$\text{in 2004: } \frac{58}{70}.$$

d) The ratio of men to total enrollment

$$\text{in 2004: } \frac{12}{70}.$$

Do Exercise 8.

b · Simplifying Notation for Ratios

Sometimes a ratio can be simplified. This provides a means of finding other numbers with the same ratio.

EXAMPLE 8 Find the ratio of 6 to 8. Then simplify and find two other numbers in the same ratio.

Answer on page A-11

CHAPTER 5: Ratio and Proportion

We write the ratio in fraction notation and then simplify:

$$\frac{6}{8} = \frac{2 \cdot 3}{2 \cdot 4} = \frac{2}{2} \cdot \frac{3}{4} = 1 \cdot \frac{3}{4} = \frac{3}{4}.$$

Thus, 3 and 4 have the same ratio as 6 and 8. We can express this by saying "6 is to 8" as "3 is to 4."

Do Exercise 9.

EXAMPLE 9 Find the ratio of 2.4 to 10. Then simplify and find two other numbers in the same ratio.

We first write the ratio in fraction notation. Next, we multiply by 1 to clear the decimal from the numerator. Then we simplify.

$$\frac{2.4}{10} = \frac{2.4}{10} \cdot \frac{10}{10} = \frac{24}{100} = \frac{4 \cdot 6}{4 \cdot 25} = \frac{4}{4} \cdot \frac{6}{25} = \frac{6}{25}$$

Thus, 2.4 is to 10 as 6 is to 25.

Do Exercises 10 and 11.

EXAMPLE 10 A standard HDTV screen with a width of 40 in. has a height of $22\frac{1}{2}$ in. Find the ratio of width to height and simplify.

The ratio is

$$\frac{40}{22\frac{1}{2}} = \frac{40}{22.5} = \frac{400}{225}$$

$$= \frac{25 \cdot 16}{25 \cdot 9} = \frac{25}{25} \cdot \frac{16}{9}$$

$$= \frac{16}{9}.$$

Thus we can say the ratio of width to height is 16 to 9, which can also be expressed as 16:9.

Do Exercise 12.

9. Find the ratio of 18 to 27. Then simplify and find two other numbers in the same ratio.

10. Find the ratio of 3.6 to 12. Then simplify and find two other numbers in the same ratio.

11. Find the ratio of 1.2 to 1.5. Then simplify and find two other numbers in the same ratio.

12. In Example 10, find the ratio of the height of the HDTV screen to the width and simplify.

Answers on page A-11

Study Tips   TIME MANAGEMENT (PART 2)

Here are some additional tips to help you with time management. (See also the Study Tips on time management in Sections 1.5 and 5.5.)

■ **Avoid "time killers."** We live in a media age, and the Internet, e-mail, television, and movies all are time killers. Allow yourself a break to enjoy some college and outside activities. But keep track of the time you spend on such activities and compare it to the time you spend studying.

■ **Prioritize your tasks.** Be careful about taking on too many college activities that fall outside of academics. Examples of such activities are decorating a homecoming float, joining a fraternity or sorority, and participating on a student council committee. Any of these is important but keep your involvement to a minimum to be sure that you have enough time for your studies.

■ **Be aggressive about your study tasks.** Instead of worrying over your math homework or test preparation, do something to get yourself started. Work a problem here and a problem there, and before long you will accomplish the task at hand. If the task is large, break it down into smaller parts, and do one at a time. You will be surprised at how quickly the large task can then be completed.

5.1 EXERCISE SET

For Extra Help

MathXL MyMathLab InterAct Math Math Tutor Center Digital Video Tutor CD 3 Videotape 5 Student's Solutions Manual

---

a   Find fraction notation for the ratio. You need not simplify.

1. 4 to 5

2. 3 to 2

3. 178 to 572

4. 329 to 967

5. 0.4 to 12

6. 2.3 to 22

7. 3.8 to 7.4

8. 0.6 to 0.7

9. 56.78 to 98.35

10. 456.2 to 333.1

11. $8\dfrac{3}{4}$ to $9\dfrac{5}{6}$

12. $10\dfrac{1}{2}$ to $43\dfrac{1}{4}$

---

13. *Corvette Accidents.*   Of every 5 fatal accidents involving a Corvette, 4 do not involve another vehicle. Find the ratio of fatal accidents involving just a Corvette to those involving a Corvette and at least one other vehicle.

Source: *Harper's Magazine*

14. *Price of a Book.*   The recent paperback book *A Short History of Nearly Everything* by Bill Bryson had a list price of $15.95 but was sold by Amazon.com for $10.85. What was the ratio of the sale price to the list price? of the list price to the sale price?

Source: www.amazon.com

---

15. *Physicians.*   In 2001, there were 356 physicians in Connecticut per 100,000 residents. In Wyoming, there were 173 physicians per 100,000 residents. Find the ratio of the number of physicians to residents in Connecticut and in Wyoming.

Source: U.S. Census Bureau, American Medical Association

16. *Silicon in the Earth's Crust.*   Of every 100 tons of the earth's crust, there will be about 28 tons of silicon in its content. What is the ratio of silicon to the weight of crust? of the weight of crust to the weight of silicon?

Source: *The Handy Science Answer Book*

---

17. *Heart Disease.*   In the state of Minnesota, of every 1000 people, 93.2 will die of heart disease. Find the ratio of those who die of heart disease to all people.

Source: "Reforming the Health Care System; State Profiles 1999," AARP

18. *Cancer Deaths.*   In the state of Texas, of every 1000 people, 122.8 will die of cancer. Find the ratio of those who die of cancer to all people.

Source: "Reforming the Health Care System; State Profiles 1999," AARP

CHAPTER 5: Ratio and Proportion

19. *Batting.* In the 2004 season, Todd Helton of the Colorado Rockies got 190 hits in 547 at-bats. What was the ratio of hits to at-bats? of at-bats to hits?

Source: Major League Baseball

20. *Batting.* In the 2004 season, Manny Ramirez of the Boston Red Sox got 175 hits in 568 at-bats. What was the ratio of hits to at-bats? of at-bats to hits?

Source: Major League Baseball

21. *Field Hockey.* A diagram of the playing area for field hockey is shown below. What is the ratio of width to length? of length to width?

Source: *Sports: The Complete Visual Reference*

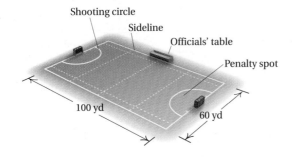

22. *The Leaning Tower of Pisa.* At the time of this writing, the Leaning Tower of Pisa is still standing. It is 184.5 ft tall but leans about 17 ft out from its base. What is the ratio of the distance it leans to its height? its height to the distance it leans?

Source: *The Handy Science Answer Book*

---

b Find the ratio of the first number to the second and simplify.

23. 4 to 6

24. 6 to 10

25. 18 to 24

26. 28 to 36

27. 4.8 to 10

28. 5.6 to 10

29. 2.8 to 3.6

30. 4.8 to 6.4

31. 20 to 30

32. 40 to 60

33. 56 to 100

34. 42 to 100

35. 128 to 256

36. 232 to 116

37. 0.48 to 0.64

38. 0.32 to 0.96

39. In this rectangle, find the ratios of length to width and of width to length.

478 ft

213 ft

40. In this right triangle, find the ratios of shortest length to longest length and of longest length to shortest length.

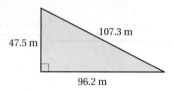

47.5 m

107.3 m

96.2 m

41. **Dw** Can every ratio be written as the ratio of some number to 1? Why or why not?

42. **Dw** What can be concluded about a rectangle's width if the ratio of length to perimeter is 1 to 3? Make some sketches and explain your reasoning.

SKILL MAINTENANCE

Use = or ≠ for ☐ to write a true sentence.   [2.5c]

43. $\frac{12}{8}$ ☐ $\frac{6}{4}$

44. $\frac{4}{7}$ ☐ $\frac{5}{9}$

45. $\frac{7}{2}$ ☐ $\frac{31}{9}$

46. $\frac{17}{25}$ ☐ $\frac{68}{100}$

Divide. Write decimal notation for the answer.   [4.4a]

47. 200 ÷ 4

48. 95 ÷ 10

49. 232 ÷ 16

50. 342 ÷ 2.25

Solve.   [3.5c]

51. Rocky is $187\frac{1}{10}$ cm tall and his daughter is $180\frac{3}{4}$ cm tall. How much taller is Rocky?

52. Aunt Louise is $168\frac{1}{4}$ cm tall and her son is $150\frac{7}{10}$ cm tall. How much taller is Aunt Louise?

SYNTHESIS

53. Find the ratio of $3\frac{3}{4}$ to $5\frac{7}{8}$ and simplify.

Fertilizer.   Exercises 54 and 55 refer to a common lawn fertilizer known as "5, 10, 15." This mixture contains 5 parts of potassium for every 10 parts of phosphorus and 15 parts of nitrogen (this is often denoted 5 : 10 : 15).

54. Find the ratio of potassium to nitrogen and of nitrogen to phosphorus.

55. Simplify the ratio 5 : 10 : 15.

5.2 RATES AND UNIT PRICES

Objectives

a Give the ratio of two different measures as a rate.

b Find unit prices and use them to compare purchases.

a Rates

A 2005 Kia Sportage EX 4WD can go 414 miles on 18 gallons of gasoline. Let's consider the ratio of miles to gallons:

Source: Kia Motors America, Inc.

$$\frac{414 \text{ mi}}{18 \text{ gal}} = \frac{414}{18} \frac{\text{miles}}{\text{gallon}} = \frac{23}{1} \frac{\text{miles}}{\text{gallon}}$$

$$= 23 \text{ miles per gallon} = 23 \text{ mpg}.$$

"per" means "division," or "for each."

The ratio

$$\frac{414 \text{ mi}}{18 \text{ gal}}, \quad \text{or} \quad \frac{414}{18} \frac{\text{mi}}{\text{gal}}, \quad \text{or} \quad 23 \text{ mpg}$$

is called a **rate.**

> **RATE**
>
> When a ratio is used to compare two different kinds of measure, we call it a **rate.**

Suppose David says his car goes 392.4 mi on 16.8 gal of gasoline. Is the mpg (mileage) of his car better than that of the Kia Sportage above? To determine this, it helps to convert the ratio to decimal notation and perhaps round. Then we have

$$\frac{392.4 \text{ miles}}{16.8 \text{ gallons}} = \frac{392.4}{16.8} \text{ mpg} \approx 23.357 \text{ mpg}.$$

Since $23.357 > 23$, David's car gets better mileage than the Kia Sportage does.

EXAMPLE 1 It takes 60 oz of grass seed to seed 3000 sq ft of lawn. What is the rate in ounces per square foot?

$$\frac{60 \text{ oz}}{3000 \text{ sq ft}} = \frac{1}{50} \frac{\text{oz}}{\text{sq ft}}, \quad \text{or} \quad 0.02 \frac{\text{oz}}{\text{sq ft}}$$

EXAMPLE 2 A cook buys 10 lb of potatoes for $3.69. What is the rate in cents per pound?

$$\frac{\$3.69}{10 \text{ lb}} = \frac{369 \text{ cents}}{10 \text{ lb}}, \quad \text{or} \quad 36.9 \frac{\text{cents}}{\text{lb}}$$

Study Tips

RECORDING YOUR LECTURES

Consider recording your lectures and playing them back when convenient, say, while commuting to campus. (Be sure to get permission from your instructor before doing so, however.) Important points can be emphasized verbally. We consider this idea so worthwhile that we provide a series of audio recordings that accompany the book. (See the Preface for more information.)

A ratio of distance traveled to time is called *speed*. What is the rate, or speed, in miles per hour?

1. 45 mi, 9 hr

2. 120 mi, 10 hr

3. 89 km, 13 hr (Round to the nearest hundredth.)

What is the rate, or speed, in feet per second?

4. 2200 ft, 2 sec

5. 52 ft, 13 sec

6. 242 ft, 16 sec

7. Ratio of Home Runs to Strikeouts. Referring to Example 4, determine Rolen's home-run to strikeout rate.

Source: Major League Baseball

EXAMPLE 3 A pharmacy student working as a pharmacist's assistant earned $3690 for working 3 months one summer. What was the rate of pay per month?

The rate of pay is the ratio of money earned per length of time worked, or

$$\frac{\$3690}{3 \text{ mo}} = 1230 \frac{\text{dollars}}{\text{month}}, \quad \text{or}$$

$1230 per month.

EXAMPLE 4 *Ratio of Strikeouts to Home Runs.* In the 2004 season, Scott Rolen of the St. Louis Cardinals had 92 strikeouts and 34 home runs. What was his strikeout to home-run rate?

Source: Major League Baseball

$$\frac{92 \text{ strikeouts}}{34 \text{ home runs}} = \frac{92}{34} \frac{\text{strikeouts}}{\text{home runs}} = \frac{92}{34} \text{ strikeouts per home run}$$

$$\approx 2.71 \text{ strikeouts per home run}$$

Do Exercises 1–8. (Exercise 8 is on the following page.)

b Unit Pricing

> **UNIT PRICE**
>
> A **unit price,** or **unit rate,** is the ratio of price to the number of units.

EXAMPLE 5 *Unit Price of Pears.* A consumer bought a $15\frac{1}{4}$-oz can of pears for $1.07. What is the unit price in cents per ounce?

Often it is helpful to change the cost to cents so we can compare unit prices more easily:

$$\text{Unit price} = \frac{\text{Price}}{\text{Number of units}}$$

$$= \frac{\$1.07}{15\frac{1}{4} \text{ oz}} = \frac{107 \text{ cents}}{15.25 \text{ oz}} = \frac{107}{15.25} \frac{\text{cents}}{\text{oz}}$$

$$\approx 7.016 \text{ cents per ounce.}$$

Do Exercise 9 on the following page.

To do comparison shopping, it helps to compare unit prices.

EXAMPLE 6 *Unit price of Heinz Ketchup.* Many factors can contribute to determining unit pricing in food, such as variations in store pricing and special discounts. Heinz produces ketchup in containers of various sizes. The table below lists several examples of pricing for these packages from a Meijer store. Starting with the price given for each package, compute the unit prices and decide which is the best purchase on the basis of unit price per ounce alone.

Source: Meijer Stores

PACKAGE	PRICE	UNIT PRICE
14 oz	$1.29	9.214¢/oz
24 oz	$1.47	6.125¢/oz
36 oz	$2.49	6.917¢/oz
64 oz	$4.45	6.953¢/oz
101-oz twin pack (two $50\frac{1}{2}$-oz packages)	$5.69	5.634¢/oz Lowest unit price

We compute the unit price for the 24-oz package and leave the remaining prices to the student to check. The unit price for the 24-oz, $1.47 package is given by

$$\frac{\$1.47}{24\text{ oz}} = \frac{147\text{ cents}}{24\text{ oz}} = \frac{147}{24}\frac{\text{cents}}{\text{oz}} = 6.125 \text{ cents per ounce} = 6.125 \text{ ¢/oz}.$$

On the basis of unit price alone, we see that the 101-oz twin pack is the best buy.

Sometimes, as you will see in Margin Exercise 10, a larger size may not have the lower unit price. It is also worth noting that "bigger" is not always "cheaper." (For example, you may not have room for larger packages or the food may go to waste before it is used.)

Do Exercise 10.

8. **Babe Ruth.** In his entire career, Babe Ruth had 1330 strikeouts and 714 home runs. What was his home-run to strikeout rate? How does it compare to Rolen's?

   Source: Major League Baseball

9. **Unit Price of Mustard.** A consumer bought a 20-oz container of French's yellow mustard for $1.49. What is the unit price in cents per ounce?

10. **Meijer Brand Olives.** Complete the following table of unit prices for Meijer Brand olives. Which package has the better unit price?

    Source: Meijer Stores

PACKAGE	PRICE	UNIT PRICE
7 oz	$1.69	
10 oz	$2.59	
$5\frac{3}{4}$ oz	$1.39	

Answers on page A-11

5.2 EXERCISE SET — For Extra Help

MathXL   MyMathLab   InterAct Math   Math Tutor Center   Digital Video Tutor CD 3 Videotape 5   Student's Solutions Manual

a In Exercises 1–4, find the rate, or speed, as a ratio of distance to time. Round to the nearest hundredth where appropriate.

1. 120 km, 3 hr

2. 18 mi, 9 hr

3. 217 mi, 29 sec

4. 443 m, 48 sec

5. *Chevrolet Cobalt LS—City Driving.* A 2005 Chevrolet Cobalt LS will go 300 mi on 12.5 gallons of gasoline in city driving. What is the rate in miles per gallon?
Source: *Car and Driver,* April 2005, p. 104

6. *Audi A6 4.2 Quattro—City Driving.* A 2005 Audi A6 4.2 Quattro will go 246.5 miles on 14.5 gallons of gasoline in city driving. What is the rate in miles per gallon?
Source: *Car and Driver,* May 2005, p. 52

7. *Audi A6 4.2 Quattro—Highway Driving.* A 2005 Audi A6 4.2 Quattro will go 448.5 miles on 19.5 gallons of gasoline in highway driving. What is the rate in miles per gallon?
Source: *Car and Driver,* May 2005, p. 52

8. *Chevrolet Cobalt LS—Highway Driving.* A 2005 Chevrolet Cobalt LS will go 432 miles on 13.5 gallons of gasoline in highway driving. What is the rate in miles per gallon?
Source: *Car and Driver,* April 2005, p. 104

9. *Population Density of Monaco.* Monaco is a tiny country on the Mediterranean coast of France. It has an area of 0.75 square mile and a population of 32,270 people. What is the rate of number of people per square mile? The rate per square mile is called the *population density.* Monaco has the highest population density in the world.
Source: *Time Almanac, 2005*

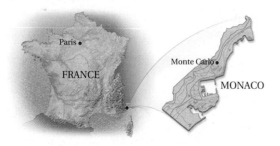

10. *Population Density of Australia.* The continent of Australia, with the island state of Tasmania, has an area of 2,967,893 sq mi and a population of 19,913,144 people. What is the rate of number of people per square mile? The rate per square mile is called the *population density.* Australia has one of the lowest population densities in the world.
Source: *Time Almanac, 2005*

11. A car is driven 500 mi in 20 hr. What is the rate in miles per hour? in hours per mile?

12. A student eats 3 hamburgers in 15 min. What is the rate in hamburgers per minute? in minutes per hamburger?

13. *Points per Game.* In the 2004–2005 season, Yao Ming of the Houston Rockets scored 1465 points in 80 games. What was the rate in points per game?
Source: National Basketball Association

14. *Points per Game.* In the 2004–2005 season, Tayshaun Prince of the Detroit Pistons scored 1206 points in 82 games. What was the rate in points per game?
Source: National Basketball Association

15. *Lawn Watering.* To water a lawn adequately requires 623 gal of water for every 1000 ft^2. What is the rate in gallons per square foot?

16. A car is driven 200 km on 40 L of gasoline. What is the rate in kilometers per liter?

17. *Speed of Light.* Light travels 186,000 mi in 1 sec. What is its rate, or speed, in miles per second?
Source: *The Handy Science Answer Book*

18. *Speed of Sound.* Sound travels 1100 ft in 1 sec. What is its rate, or speed, in feet per second?
Source: *The Handy Science Answer Book*

19. Impulses in nerve fibers travel 310 km in 2.5 hr. What is the rate, or speed, in kilometers per hour?

20. A black racer snake can travel 4.6 km in 2 hr. What is its rate, or speed, in kilometers per hour?

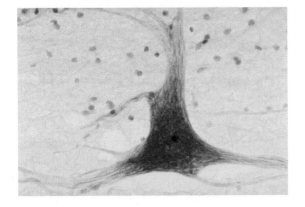

21. *Elephant Heartbeat.* The heart of an elephant, at rest, will beat an average of 1500 beats in 60 min. What is the rate in beats per minute?

Source: *The Handy Science Answer Book*

22. *Human Heartbeat.* The heart of a human, at rest, will beat an average of 4200 beats in 60 min. What is the rate in beats per minute?

Source: *The Handy Science Answer Book*

b Find each unit price in each of Exercises 23–32. Then determine which size has the lowest unit price.

23. *Pert Plus Shampoo.*

PACKAGE	PRICE	UNIT PRICE
13.5 oz	$2.59	
25.4 oz	$3.99	

24. *Roll-on Deodorant.*

PACKAGE	PRICE	UNIT PRICE
2.25 oz	$2.49	
3.5 oz	$3.98	

25. *Miracle Whip.*

PACKAGE	PRICE	UNIT PRICE
16-oz jar	$1.84	
18-oz squeezable	$2.49	

26. *Bush's Homestyle Baked Beans.*

PACKAGE	PRICE	UNIT PRICE
16 oz	$0.99	
28 oz	$1.44	

27. *Meijer Coffee.*

PACKAGE	PRICE	UNIT PRICE
11.5 oz	$2.09	
34.5 oz	$5.27	

28. *Maxwell House Coffee.*

PACKAGE	PRICE	UNIT PRICE
13 oz	$3.74	
34.5 oz	$6.36	

29. *Jif Creamy Peanut Butter.*

PACKAGE	PRICE	UNIT PRICE
18 oz	$1.89	
28 oz	$3.25	
40 oz	$4.99	
64 oz	$7.99	

30. *Downy Fabric Softener.*

PACKAGE	PRICE	UNIT PRICE
40 oz	$3.23	
60 oz	$4.79	
80 oz	$7.99	
120 oz	$10.69	

31. *Tide Liquid Laundry Detergent.*

PACKAGE	PRICE	UNIT PRICE
50 fl oz	$4.29	
100 fl oz	$5.29	
200 fl oz	$10.49	
300 fl oz	$15.79	

32. *Del Monte Green Beans.*

PACKAGE	PRICE	UNIT PRICE
8 oz	$0.59	
14.5 oz	$0.69	
28 oz	$1.19	

Use the unit prices listed in Exercises 23–32 when doing Exercises 33 and 34.

33. **D**w Look over the unit prices for each size package of Downy fabric softener. What seems to violate common sense about these unit prices? Why do you think the products are sold this way?

34. **D**w Compare the prices and unit prices for the 16-oz jar of Miracle Whip and the 18-oz squeezable container of Miracle Whip. What seems unusual about these prices? Explain why you think this has happened.

SKILL MAINTENANCE

Solve.

35. There are 20.6 million people in this country who play the piano and 18.9 million who play the guitar. How many more play the piano than the guitar?   [4.7a]

36. A serving of fish steak (cross section) is generally $\frac{1}{2}$ lb. How many servings can be prepared from a cleaned $18\frac{3}{4}$-lb tuna?   [3.6c]

37. *Surf Expo.*   In a swimwear showing at Surf Expo, a trade show for retailers of beach supplies, each swimsuit test takes 8 minutes (min). If the show runs for 240 min, how many tests can be scheduled?   [1.8a]

38. *Eating Habits.*   Each year, Americans eat 24.8 billion hamburgers and 15.9 billion hot dogs. How many more hamburgers than hot dogs do Americans eat?   [4.7a]

Multiply.   [4.3a]

39. $\begin{array}{r} 4\,5.6\,7 \\ \times \qquad 2.4 \\ \hline \end{array}$

40. $\begin{array}{r} 6\,7\,8.1\,9 \\ \times \qquad 1\,0\,0 \\ \hline \end{array}$

41. 84.3×69.2

42. 1002.56×465

SYNTHESIS

43. Recently, certain manufacturers have been changing the size of their containers in such a way that the consumer thinks the price of a product has been lowered when, in reality, a higher unit price is being charged.

Some aluminum juice cans are now concave (curved in) on the bottom. Suppose the volume of the can in the figure has been reduced from a fluid capacity of 6 oz to 5.5 oz, and the price of each can has been reduced from 65¢ to 60¢. Find the unit price of each container in cents per ounce.

$\frac{5}{16}$ in.

$1\frac{13}{16}$ in.

$2\frac{1}{16}$ in.

Objectives

a Determine whether two pairs of numbers are proportional.

b Solve proportions.

5.3 PROPORTIONS

During the 2004 season, Peyton Manning of the Indianapolis Colts completed 336 passes out of 497 attempts. His pass-completion rate was

$$\text{Completion rate} = \frac{336 \text{ completions}}{497 \text{ attempts}} = \frac{336}{497} \frac{\text{completion}}{\text{attempt}}$$

$$\approx 0.676 \frac{\text{completion}}{\text{attempt}}.$$

The rate was 0.676 completion per attempt.

Ben Roethlisberger of the Pittsburgh Steelers completed 196 passes out of 295 attempts. His pass-completion rate was

$$\text{Completion rate} = \frac{196 \text{ completions}}{295 \text{ attempts}} = \frac{196}{295} \frac{\text{completion}}{\text{attempt}}$$

$$\approx 0.664 \frac{\text{completion}}{\text{attempt}}.$$

The rate was 0.664 completion per attempt. We can see that the rates are not equal.

Source: National Football League

Instead of comparing the rates in decimal notation, we can compare the ratios

$$\frac{336}{497} \quad \text{and} \quad \frac{196}{295}$$

using the test for equality considered in Section 2.5. We compare cross products.

$$= \begin{array}{c} 336 \cdot 295 \\ 99{,}120 \end{array} \quad \frac{336}{497} \overset{?}{=} \frac{196}{295} \quad \begin{array}{c} 497 \cdot 196 \\ 97{,}412 \end{array}$$

Since

$$99{,}120 \neq 97{,}412, \text{ we know that}$$

$$\frac{336}{497} \neq \frac{196}{295}.$$

Thus the ratios are not equal. If the ratios had been equal, we would say they are proportional.

a Proportions

When two pairs of numbers (such as 3, 2 and 6, 4) have the same ratio, we say that they are **proportional.** The equation

$$\frac{3}{2} = \frac{6}{4}$$

states that the pairs 3, 2 and 6, 4 are proportional. Such an equation is called a **proportion.** We sometimes read $\frac{3}{2} = \frac{6}{4}$ as "3 is to 2 as 6 is to 4."

EXAMPLE 1 Determine whether 1, 2, and 3, 6 are proportional.

We can use cross products:

$$1 \cdot 6 = 6 \qquad \overset{?}{\underset{}{\frac{1}{2} = \frac{3}{6}}} \qquad 2 \cdot 3 = 6.$$

Since the cross products are the same, $6 = 6$, we know that $\frac{1}{2} = \frac{3}{6}$, so the numbers are proportional.

EXAMPLE 2 Determine whether 2, 5 and 4, 7 are proportional.

We can use cross products:

$$2 \cdot 7 = 14 \qquad \overset{?}{\underset{}{\frac{2}{5} = \frac{4}{7}}} \qquad 5 \cdot 4 = 20.$$

Since the cross products are not the same, $14 \neq 20$, we know that $\frac{2}{5} \neq \frac{4}{7}$, so the numbers are not proportional.

Do Exercises 1–3.

EXAMPLE 3 Determine whether 3.2, 4.8 and 0.16, 0.24 are proportional.

We can use cross products:

$$3.2 \times 0.24 = 0.768 \qquad \overset{?}{\underset{}{\frac{3.2}{4.8} = \frac{0.16}{0.24}}} \qquad 4.8 \times 0.16 = 0.768.$$

Since the cross products are the same, $0.768 = 0.768$, we know that $\frac{3.2}{4.8} = \frac{0.16}{0.24}$, so the numbers are proportional.

Do Exercises 4 and 5.

EXAMPLE 4 Determine whether $4\frac{2}{3}, 5\frac{1}{2}$ and $8\frac{7}{8}, 16\frac{1}{3}$ are proportional.

We can use cross products:

$$4\frac{2}{3} \cdot 16\frac{1}{3} = \frac{14}{3} \cdot \frac{49}{3} \qquad \overset{?}{\underset{}{\frac{4\frac{2}{3}}{5\frac{1}{2}} = \frac{8\frac{7}{8}}{16\frac{1}{3}}}} \qquad 5\frac{1}{2} \cdot 8\frac{7}{8} = \frac{11}{2} \cdot \frac{71}{8}$$

$$= \frac{686}{9} \qquad\qquad\qquad\qquad\qquad = \frac{781}{16}$$

$$= 76\frac{2}{9} \qquad\qquad\qquad\qquad\qquad = 48\frac{13}{16}.$$

Since the cross products are not the same, $76\frac{2}{9} \neq 48\frac{13}{16}$, we know that the numbers are not proportional.

Do Exercise 6.

b Solving Proportions

Let's now look at solving proportions. Consider the proportion

$$\frac{x}{3} = \frac{4}{6}.$$

One way to solve a proportion is to use cross products. Then we can divide on

Determine whether the two pairs of numbers are proportional.

1. 3, 4 and 6, 8

2. 1, 4 and 10, 39

3. 1, 2 and 20, 39

Determine whether the two pairs of numbers are proportional.

4. 6.4, 12.8 and 5.3, 10.6

5. 6.8, 7.4 and 3.4, 4.2

6. Determine whether $4\frac{2}{3}, 5\frac{1}{2}$ and 14, $16\frac{1}{2}$ are proportional.

Answers on page A-11

12. Solve:

$$\frac{8\frac{1}{3}}{x} = \frac{10\frac{1}{2}}{3\frac{3}{4}}.$$

EXAMPLE 9 Solve: $\dfrac{4\frac{2}{3}}{5\frac{1}{2}} = \dfrac{14}{x}$. Write a mixed numeral for the answer.

We have

$$\frac{4\frac{2}{3}}{5\frac{1}{2}} = \frac{14}{x}$$

$$4\frac{2}{3} \cdot x = 14 \cdot 5\frac{1}{2} \qquad \text{Equating cross products}$$

$$\frac{14}{3} \cdot x = 14 \cdot \frac{11}{2} \qquad \text{Converting to fraction notation}$$

$$\frac{\frac{14}{3} \cdot x}{\frac{14}{3}} = \frac{14 \cdot \frac{11}{2}}{\frac{14}{3}} \qquad \text{Dividing by } \frac{14}{3}$$

$$x = 14 \cdot \frac{11}{2} \div \frac{14}{3}$$

$$x = \cancel{14} \cdot \frac{11}{2} \cdot \frac{3}{\cancel{14}} \qquad \text{Multiplying by the reciprocal of the divisor}$$

$$x = \frac{11 \cdot 3}{2} \qquad \text{Simplifying by removing a factor of 1: } \frac{14}{14} = 1$$

$$x = \frac{33}{2}, \text{ or } 16\frac{1}{2}.$$

The solution is $16\frac{1}{2}$.

Answer on page A-11

Do Exercise 12.

CALCULATOR CORNER

Solving Proportions Note in Examples 5–9 that when we solve a proportion, we equate cross products and then we divide on both sides to isolate the variable on one side of the equation. We can use a calculator to do the calculations in this situation. In Example 8, for instance, after equating cross products and dividing by 3.4 on both sides, we have

$$n = \frac{4.93 \times 10}{3.4}.$$

To find n on a calculator, we can press [4] [·] [9] [3] [×] [1] [0] [÷] [3] [·] [4] [=]. The result is 14.5, so $n = 14.5$.

Exercises

1. Use a calculator to solve each of the proportions in Examples 5–7.

2. Use a calculator to solve each of the proportions in Margin Exercises 7–11.

Solve each proportion.

3. $\dfrac{15.75}{20} = \dfrac{a}{35}$

4. $\dfrac{32}{x} = \dfrac{25}{20}$

5. $\dfrac{t}{57} = \dfrac{17}{64}$

6. $\dfrac{71.2}{a} = \dfrac{42.5}{23.9}$

7. $\dfrac{29.6}{3.15} = \dfrac{x}{4.23}$

8. $\dfrac{a}{3.01} = \dfrac{1.7}{0.043}$

a Determine whether the two pairs of numbers are proportional.

1. 5, 6 and 7, 9

2. 7, 5 and 6, 4

3. 1, 2 and 10, 20

4. 7, 3 and 21, 9

5. 2.4, 3.6 and 1.8, 2.7

6. 4.5, 3.8 and 6.7, 5.2

7. $5\frac{1}{3}, 8\frac{1}{4}$ and $2\frac{1}{5}, 9\frac{1}{2}$

8. $2\frac{1}{3}, 3\frac{1}{2}$ and 14, 21

Pass-Completion Rates. The table below lists the records of four NFL quarterbacks from the 2000 season.

PLAYER	TEAM	NUMBER OF PASSES COMPLETED	NUMBER OF PASSES ATTEMPTED	NUMBER OF COMPLETIONS PER ATTEMPT (completion rate)
Tom Brady	New England Patriots	288	474	
Drew Brees	San Diego Chargers	262	400	
Daunte Culpepper	Minnesota Vikings	379	548	
Ben Roethlisberger	Pittsburgh Steelers	196	295	

Source: National Football League

9. Find each pass-completion rate rounded to the nearest hundredth. Are any the same?

10. Use cross products to determine whether any quarterback completion rates are the same.

b Solve.

11. $\dfrac{18}{4} = \dfrac{x}{10}$

12. $\dfrac{x}{45} = \dfrac{20}{25}$

13. $\dfrac{x}{8} = \dfrac{9}{6}$

14. $\dfrac{8}{10} = \dfrac{n}{5}$

15. $\dfrac{t}{12} = \dfrac{5}{6}$

16. $\dfrac{12}{4} = \dfrac{x}{3}$

17. $\dfrac{2}{5} = \dfrac{8}{n}$

18. $\dfrac{10}{6} = \dfrac{5}{x}$

19. $\dfrac{n}{15} = \dfrac{10}{30}$

20. $\dfrac{2}{24} = \dfrac{x}{36}$

21. $\dfrac{16}{12} = \dfrac{24}{x}$

22. $\dfrac{7}{11} = \dfrac{2}{x}$

23. $\dfrac{6}{11} = \dfrac{12}{x}$

24. $\dfrac{8}{9} = \dfrac{32}{n}$

25. $\dfrac{20}{7} = \dfrac{80}{x}$

26. $\dfrac{5}{x} = \dfrac{4}{10}$

27. $\dfrac{12}{9} = \dfrac{x}{7}$

28. $\dfrac{x}{20} = \dfrac{16}{15}$

29. $\dfrac{x}{13} = \dfrac{2}{9}$

30. $\dfrac{1.2}{4} = \dfrac{x}{9}$

31. $\dfrac{t}{0.16} = \dfrac{0.15}{0.40}$

32. $\dfrac{x}{11} = \dfrac{7.1}{2}$

33. $\dfrac{100}{25} = \dfrac{20}{n}$

34. $\dfrac{35}{125} = \dfrac{7}{m}$

35. $\dfrac{7}{\frac{1}{4}} = \dfrac{28}{x}$

36. $\dfrac{x}{6} = \dfrac{1}{6}$

37. $\dfrac{\frac{1}{4}}{\frac{1}{2}} = \dfrac{\frac{1}{2}}{x}$

38. $\dfrac{1}{7} = \dfrac{x}{4\frac{1}{2}}$

39. $\dfrac{1}{2} = \dfrac{7}{x}$

40. $\dfrac{x}{3} = \dfrac{0}{9}$

41. $\dfrac{\frac{2}{7}}{\frac{3}{4}} = \dfrac{\frac{5}{6}}{y}$

42. $\dfrac{\frac{5}{4}}{\frac{5}{8}} = \dfrac{\frac{3}{2}}{Q}$

43. $\dfrac{2\frac{1}{2}}{3\frac{1}{3}} = \dfrac{x}{4\frac{1}{4}}$

44. $\dfrac{5\frac{1}{5}}{6\frac{1}{6}} = \dfrac{y}{3\frac{1}{2}}$

45. $\dfrac{1.28}{3.76} = \dfrac{4.28}{y}$

46. $\dfrac{10.4}{12.4} = \dfrac{6.76}{t}$

47. $\dfrac{10\frac{3}{8}}{12\frac{2}{3}} = \dfrac{5\frac{3}{4}}{y}$

48. $\dfrac{12\frac{7}{8}}{20\frac{3}{4}} = \dfrac{5\frac{2}{3}}{y}$

49. D_W Instead of equating cross products, a student solves $\frac{x}{7} = \frac{5}{3}$ (see Example 5) by multiplying on both sides by the least common denominator, 21. Is his approach a good one? Why or why not?

50. D_W An instructor predicts that a student's test grade will be proportional to the amount of time the student spends studying. What is meant by this? Write an example of a proportion that involves the grades of two students and their study times.

 VOCABULARY REINFORCEMENT

In each of Exercises 51–58, fill in the blank with the correct term from the given list. Some of the choices may not be used.

51. A ratio is the _____ of two quantities.   [5.1a]

52. A number is divisible by 9 if the _____ of the digits is divisible by 9.   [2.2a]

53. To compute a(n) _____ of a set of numbers, we add the numbers and then divide by the number of addends.   [3.7a]

54. To convert from _____ to _____ , move the decimal point two places to the right and change the $ sign in front to the ¢ sign at the end.   [4.3b]

55. In the equation $103 - 13 = 90$, the _____ is 13.   [1.3a]

56. The decimal 0.125 is an example of a(n) _____ decimal.   [4.5a]

57. The sentence $\frac{2}{5} \cdot \frac{4}{9} = \frac{4}{9} \cdot \frac{2}{5}$ illustrates the _____ law of multiplication.   [1.5a]

58. To solve $\frac{x}{a} = \frac{c}{d}$, equate the _____ and divide on both sides to get x alone.   [5.3b]

cross products

cents

dollars

terminating

repeating

sum

difference

minuend

subtrahend

associative

commutative

average

product

quotient

 Solve.

59. $\dfrac{1728}{5643} = \dfrac{836.4}{x}$

60. $\dfrac{328.56}{627.48} = \dfrac{y}{127.66}$

61. *Strikeouts per Home Run.*   Baseball Hall-of-Famer Babe Ruth had 1330 strikeouts and 714 home runs in his career. Hall-of-Famer Mike Schmidt had 1883 strikeouts and 548 home runs in his career.

   a) Find the unit rate of each player in terms of strikeouts per home run. (These rates were considered among the highest in the history of the game and yet each made the Hall of Fame.)
   b) Which player had the higher rate?

Objective

a Solve applied problems involving proportions.

1. Calories Burned. Your author generally exercises for 2 hr each day. The readout on an exercise machine tells him that if he exercises for 24 min, he will burn 356 calories. How many calories will he burn if he exercises for 30 min?

Source: Star Trac Treadmill

5.4 APPLICATIONS OF PROPORTIONS

a Applications and Problem Solving

Proportions have applications in such diverse fields as business, chemistry, health sciences, and home economics, as well as to many areas of daily life. Proportions are useful in making predictions.

EXAMPLE 1 *Predicting Total Distance.* Donna drives her delivery van 800 mi in 3 days. At this rate, how far will she drive in 15 days?

1. Familiarize. We let d = the distance traveled in 15 days.

2. Translate. We translate to a proportion. We make each side the ratio of distance to time, with distance in the numerator and time in the denominator.

$$\text{Distance in 15 days} \rightarrow \frac{d}{15} = \frac{800}{3} \leftarrow \text{Distance in 3 days}$$
$$\text{Time} \rightarrow \qquad\qquad \leftarrow \text{Time}$$

It may help to verbalize the proportion above as "the unknown distance d is to 15 days as the known distance 800 miles is to 3 days."

3. Solve. Next, we solve the proportion:

$$3 \cdot d = 15 \cdot 800 \qquad \text{Equating cross products}$$

$$\frac{3 \cdot d}{3} = \frac{15 \cdot 800}{3} \qquad \text{Dividing by 3 on both sides}$$

$$d = \frac{15 \cdot 800}{3}$$

$$d = 4000. \qquad \text{Multiplying and dividing}$$

4. Check. We substitute into the proportion and check cross products:

$$\frac{4000}{15} = \frac{800}{3};$$

$$4000 \cdot 3 = 12,000; \qquad 15 \cdot 800 = 12,000.$$

The cross products are the same.

5. State. Donna will drive 4000 mi in 15 days.

Do Exercise 1.

Problems involving proportion can be translated in more than one way. In Example 1, any one of the following is a correct translation:

$$\frac{800}{3} = \frac{d}{15}, \qquad \frac{15}{d} = \frac{3}{800}, \qquad \frac{15}{3} = \frac{d}{800}, \qquad \frac{800}{d} = \frac{3}{15}.$$

Equating the cross products in each equation gives us the equation $3 \cdot d = 15 \cdot 800$.

Answer on page A-12

EXAMPLE 2 *Recommended Dosage.* To control a fever, a doctor suggests that a child who weighs 28 kg be given 320 mg of Tylenol. If the dosage is proportional to the child's weight, how much Tylenol is recommended for a child who weighs 35 kg?

2. Determining Paint Needs.
Lowell and Chris run a summer painting company to support their college expenses. They can paint 1600 ft^2 of clapboard with 4 gal of paint. How much paint would be needed for a building with 6000 ft^2 of clapboard?

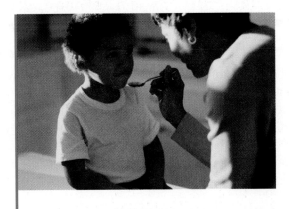

1. **Familiarize.** We let t = the number of milligrams of Tylenol.

2. **Translate.** We translate to a proportion, keeping the amount of Tylenol in the numerators.

$$\text{Tylenol suggested} \rightarrow \frac{320}{28} = \frac{t}{35} \leftarrow \text{Tylenol suggested}$$
$$\text{Child's weight} \rightarrow \qquad\qquad \leftarrow \text{Child's weight}$$

3. **Solve.** Next, we solve the proportion:

$$320 \cdot 35 = 28 \cdot t \qquad \text{Equating cross products}$$

$$\frac{320 \cdot 35}{28} = \frac{28 \cdot t}{28} \qquad \text{Dividing by 28 on both sides}$$

$$\frac{320 \cdot 35}{28} = t$$

$$400 = t. \qquad \text{Multiplying and dividing}$$

4. **Check.** We substitute into the proportion and check cross products:

$$\frac{320}{28} = \frac{400}{35};$$

$$320 \cdot 35 = 11{,}200; \qquad 28 \cdot 400 = 11{,}200.$$

The cross products are the same.

5. **State.** The dosage for a child who weighs 35 kg is 400 mg.

Do Exercise 2.

EXAMPLE 3 *Purchasing Tickets.* Carey bought 8 tickets to an international food festival for $52. How many tickets could she purchase with $90?

1. **Familiarize.** We let n = the number of tickets that can be purchased with $90.

2. **Translate.** We translate to a proportion, keeping the number of tickets in the numerators.

$$\text{Tickets} \rightarrow \frac{8}{52} = \frac{n}{90} \leftarrow \text{Tickets}$$
$$\text{Cost} \rightarrow \qquad\qquad \leftarrow \text{Cost}$$

Answer on page A-12

3. Purchasing Shirts. If 2 shirts can be bought for $47, how many shirts can be bought with $200?

3. Solve. Next, we solve the proportion:

$$52 \cdot n = 8 \cdot 90 \qquad \text{Equating cross products}$$

$$\frac{52 \cdot n}{52} = \frac{8 \cdot 90}{52} \qquad \text{Dividing by 52 on both sides}$$

$$n = \frac{8 \cdot 90}{52}$$

$$n \approx 13.8. \qquad \text{Multiplying and dividing}$$

Because it is impossible to buy a fractional part of a ticket, we must round our answer *down* to 13.

4. Check. As a check, we use a different approach: We find the cost per ticket and then divide $90 by that price. Since $52 \div 8 = 6.50$ and $90 \div 6.50 \approx 13.8$, we have a check.

5. State. Carey could purchase 13 tickets with $90.

Do Exercise 3.

EXAMPLE 4 *Women's Hip Measurements.* For improved health, it is recommended that a woman's waist-to-hip ratio be 0.85 (or lower). Marta's hip measurement is 40 in. To meet the recommendation, what should Marta's waist measurement be?

Source: David Schmidt, "Lifting Weight Myths," *Nutrition Action Newsletter* 20, no. 4, October 1993

4. Men's Hip Measurements. It is recommended that a man's waist-to-hip ratio be 0.95 (or lower). Malcolm's hip measurement is 40 in. To meet the recommendation, what should Malcolm's waist measurement be?

Source: David Schmidt, "Lifting Weight Myths," *Nutrition Action Newsletter* 20, no. 4, October 1993

Waist measurement is the smallest measurement below the ribs but above the navel.

Hip measurement is the largest measurement around the widest part of the buttocks.

1. Familiarize. Note that $0.85 = \frac{85}{100}$. We let $w =$ Marta's waist measurement.

2. Translate. We translate to a proportion as follows:

$$\begin{array}{c} \text{Waist measurement} \rightarrow \\ \text{Hip measurement} \rightarrow \end{array} \frac{w}{40} = \frac{85}{100} . \begin{array}{c} \nwarrow \text{Recommended} \\ \swarrow \text{waist-to-hip ratio} \end{array}$$

3. Solve. Next, we solve the proportion:

$$100 \cdot w = 40 \cdot 85 \qquad \text{Equating cross products}$$

$$\frac{100 \cdot w}{100} = \frac{40 \cdot 85}{100} \qquad \text{Dividing by 100 on both sides}$$

$$w = \frac{40 \cdot 85}{100}$$

$$w = 34. \qquad \text{Multiplying and dividing}$$

Answers on page A-12

4. Check. As a check, we divide 34 by 40: $34 \div 40 = 0.85$. This is the desired ratio.

5. State. Marta's recommended waist measurement is 34 in. (or less).

Do Exercise 4 on the preceding page.

EXAMPLE 5 *Construction Plans.* Architects make blueprints of projects being constructed. These are scale drawings in which lengths are in proportion to actual sizes. The Hennesseys are constructing a rectangular deck just outside their house. The architectural blueprints are rendered such that $\frac{3}{4}$ in. on the drawing is actually 2.25 ft on the deck. The width of the deck on the drawing is 4.3 in. How wide is the deck in reality?

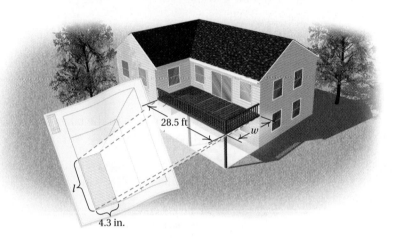

28.5 ft   w

l

4.3 in.

1. Familiarize. We let $w =$ the width of the deck.

2. Translate. Then we translate to a proportion, using 0.75 for $\frac{3}{4}$ in.

$$\begin{matrix} \text{Measure on drawing} \rightarrow \\ \text{Measure on deck} \rightarrow \end{matrix} \frac{0.75}{2.25} = \frac{4.3}{w} \begin{matrix} \leftarrow \text{Width of drawing} \\ \leftarrow \text{Width of deck} \end{matrix}$$

3. Solve. Next, we solve the proportion:

$$0.75 \times w = 2.25 \times 4.3 \qquad \text{Equating cross products}$$

$$\frac{0.75 \times w}{0.75} = \frac{2.25 \times 4.3}{0.75} \qquad \text{Dividing by 0.75 on both sides}$$

$$w = \frac{2.25 \times 4.3}{0.75}$$

$$w = 12.9.$$

4. Check. We substitute into the proportion and check cross products:

$$\frac{0.75}{2.25} = \frac{4.3}{12.9};$$

$$0.75 \times 12.9 = 9.675; \qquad 2.25 \times 4.3 = 9.675.$$

The cross products are the same.

5. State. The width of the deck is 12.9 ft.

Do Exercise 5.

5. Construction Plans. In Example 5, the length of the actual deck is 28.5 ft. What is the length of the deck on the blueprints?

Answer on page A-12

6. Estimating a Deer Population.
To determine the number of deer in a forest, a conservationist catches 612 deer, tags them, and releases them. Later, 244 deer are caught, and it is found that 72 of them are tagged. Estimate how many deer are in the forest.

EXAMPLE 6 *Estimating a Wildlife Population.* To determine the number of fish in a lake, a conservationist catches 225 fish, tags them, and throws them back into the lake. Later, 108 fish are caught, and it is found that 15 of them are tagged. Estimate how many fish are in the lake.

1. **Familiarize.** We let F = the number of fish in the lake.

2. **Translate.** We translate to a proportion as follows:

Fish tagged originally $\rightarrow$ $\dfrac{225}{F} = \dfrac{15}{108}$. $\leftarrow$ Tagged fish caught later
Fish in lake $\rightarrow$ $\leftarrow$ Fish caught later

3. **Solve.** Next, we solve the proportion:

$$225 \cdot 108 = F \cdot 15 \qquad \text{Equating cross products}$$

$$\frac{225 \cdot 108}{15} = \frac{F \cdot 15}{15} \qquad \text{Dividing by 15 on both sides}$$

$$\frac{225 \cdot 108}{15} = F$$

$$1620 = F. \qquad \text{Multiplying and dividing}$$

4. **Check.** We substitute into the proportion and check cross products:

$$\frac{225}{1620} = \frac{15}{108};$$

$$225 \cdot 108 = 24{,}300; \qquad 1620 \cdot 15 = 24{,}300.$$

The cross products are the same.

5. **State.** We estimate that there are 1620 fish in the lake.

Do Exercise 6.

Answer on page A-12

Translating for Success

1. **Calories in Cereal.** There are 140 calories in a $1\frac{1}{2}$-cup serving of Brand A cereal. How many calories are there in 6 cups of the cereal?

2. **Calories in Cereal.** There are 140 calories in 6 cups of Brand B cereal. How many calories are there in a $1\frac{1}{2}$-cup serving of the cereal?

3. **Gallons of Gasoline.** Jared's SUV traveled 310 miles on 15.5 gallons of gasoline. At this rate, how many gallons would be needed to travel 465 miles?

4. **Gallons of Gasoline.** Elizabeth's new fuel-efficient car traveled 465 miles on 15.5 gallons of gasoline. At this rate, how many gallons will be needed to travel 310 miles?

5. **Perimeter.** Find the perimeter of a rectangular field that measures 83.7 m by 62.4 m.

The goal of these matching questions is to practice step (2), *Translate*, of the five-step problem-solving process. Translate each word problem to an equation and select a correct translation from equations A–O.

A. $\dfrac{310}{15.5} = \dfrac{465}{x}$

B. $180 = 1\frac{1}{2} \cdot x$

C. $x = 71\frac{1}{8} - 76\frac{1}{2}$

D. $71\frac{1}{8} \cdot x = 74$

E. $74 \cdot 71\frac{1}{8} = x$

F. $x = 83.7 + 62.4$

G. $71\frac{1}{8} + x = 76\frac{1}{2}$

H. $x = 1\frac{2}{3} \cdot 180$

I. $\dfrac{140}{6} = \dfrac{x}{1\frac{1}{2}}$

J. $x = 2(83.7 + 62.4)$

K. $\dfrac{465}{15.5} = \dfrac{310}{x}$

L. $x = 83.7 \cdot 62.4$

M. $x = 180 \div 1\frac{2}{3}$

N. $\dfrac{140}{1\frac{1}{2}} = \dfrac{x}{6}$

O. $x = 1\frac{2}{3} \div 180$

Answers on page A-12

6. **Electric Bill.** Last month Todd's electric bills for his two rentals were $83.70 and $62.40. What was the total electric bill for the two properties?

7. **Package Tape.** A postal service center uses rolls of package tape that each contain 180 feet of tape. If it takes an average of $1\frac{2}{3}$ ft per package, how many packages can be taped with one roll?

8. **Online Price.** Jane spent $180 for an area rug in a department store. Later she saw the same rug for sale online and realized she had paid $1\frac{1}{2}$ times the online price. What was the online price?

9. **Heights of Sons.** Henry's three sons play basket-ball on three different college teams. Jeff, Jason, and Jared's heights are 74 in., $71\frac{1}{8}$ in., and $76\frac{1}{2}$ in., respectively. How much taller is Jared than Jason?

10. **Total Investment.** An investor bought 74 shares of stock at $71\frac{1}{8}$ per share. What was the total investment?

MathXL MyMathLab InterAct Math Math Tutor Center Digital Video Tutor CD 3 Videotape 5 Student's Solutions Manual

a   Solve.

1. *Study Time and Test Grades.*   An English instructor asserted that students' test grades are directly proportional to the amount of time spent studying. Lisa studies 9 hr for a particular test and gets a score of 75. At this rate, how many hours would she have had to study to get a score of 92?

2. *Study Time and Test Grades.*   A mathematics instructor asserted that students' test grades are directly proportional to the amount of time spent studying. Brent studies 15 hr for a particular test and gets a score of 85. At this rate, what score would he have received if he had studied 16 hr?

3. *Cap'n Crunch's Peanut Butter Crunch® Cereal.*   The nutritional chart on the side of a box of Quaker Cap'n Crunch's Peanut Butter Crunch® Cereal states that there are 110 calories in a $\frac{3}{4}$-cup serving. How many calories are there in 6 cups of the cereal?

4. *Rice Krispies® Cereal.*   The nutritional chart on the side of a box of Kellogg's Rice Krispies® Cereal states that there are 120 calories in a $1\frac{1}{4}$-cup serving. How many calories are there in 5 cups of the cereal?

Nutrition Facts

Serving Size 3/4 Cup (27g)
Servings Per Container about 15

Amount Per Serving	Cereal Alone	with 1/2 Cup Vitamin A&D Fortified Skim Milk
Calories	110	150
Calories from Fat	25	25
	% Daily Value	
Total Fat 2.5g	4%	4%
Saturated Fat 0.5g	3%	3%
Polyunsaturated Fat 0.5g		
Monounsaturated Fat 1g		
Cholesterol 0mg	0%	0%
Sodium 200mg	8%	11%
Potassium 65mg	2%	8%
Total Carbohydrate 21g	7%	9%
Dietary Fiber 1g	3%	3%
Sugars 9g		
Other Carbohydrate 12g		
Protein 2g		

Nutrition Facts

Serving Size $1\frac{1}{4}$ Cups (33g/1.2oz)
Servings Per Container about 12

Amount Per Serving	Cereal	Cereal with 1/2 Cup Vitamins A&D Fat Free Milk
Calories	120	160
Calories from Fat	0	0
	% Daily Value	
Total Fat 0g	0%	0%
Saturated Fat 0g	0%	0%
Trans Fat 0g		
Cholesterol 0mg	0%	0%
Sodium 320mg	13%	16%
Potassium 40mg	1%	7%
Total Carbohydrate 29g	10%	11%
Dietary Fiber 0g	0%	0%
Sugars 3g		
Other Carbohydrate 26g		
Protein 2g		

5. *Overweight Americans.*   A study recently confirmed that of every 100 Americans, 60 are considered overweight. There were 295 million Americans in 2005. How many would be considered overweight?
Source: U.S. Centers for Disease Control

6. *Cancer Death Rate in Illinois.*   It is predicted that for every 1000 people in the state of Illinois, 130.9 will die of cancer. The population of Chicago is about 2,721,547. How many of these people will die of cancer?
Source: *2001 New York Times Almanac*

7. *Gasoline Mileage.*   Nancy's van traveled 84 mi on 6.5 gal of gasoline. At this rate, how many gallons would be needed to travel 126 mi?

8. *Bicycling.*   Roy bicycled 234 mi in 14 days. At this rate, how far would Roy travel in 42 days?

9. *Quality Control.* A quality-control inspector examined 100 lightbulbs and found 7 of them to be defective. At this rate, how many defective bulbs will there be in a lot of 2500?

11. *Painting.* Fred uses 3 gal of paint to cover 1275 ft^2 of siding. How much siding can Fred paint with 7 gal of paint?

13. *Publishing.* Every 6 pages of an author's manuscript corresponds to 5 published pages. How many published pages will a 540-page manuscript become?

15. *Exchanging Money.* On 26 April 2005, 1 U.S. dollar was worth about 0.52521 British pound.
a) How much would 45 U.S. dollars be worth in British pounds?
b) How much would a car cost in U.S. dollars that costs 8640 British pounds?

17. *Exchanging Money.* On 26 April 2005, 1 U.S. dollar was worth about 106.03 Japanese yen.
a) How much would 200 U.S. dollars be worth in Japanese yen?
b) Dan was traveling in Japan and bought a skateboard that cost 3180 Japanese yen. How much would it cost in U.S. dollars?

10. *Grading.* A professor must grade 32 essays in a literature class. She can grade 5 essays in 40 min. At this rate, how long will it take her to grade all 32 essays?

12. *Waterproofing.* Bonnie can waterproof 450 ft^2 of decking with 2 gal of sealant. How many gallons should Bonnie buy for a 1200-ft^2 deck?

14. *Turkey Servings.* An 8-lb turkey breast contains 36 servings of meat. How many pounds of turkey breast would be needed for 54 servings?

16. *Exchanging Money.* On 26 April 2005, 1 U.S. dollar was worth about 1.1894 Swiss francs.
a) How much would 360 U.S. dollars be worth in Swiss francs?
b) How much would a pair of jeans cost in U.S. dollars that costs 80 Swiss francs?

18. *Exchanging Money.* On 26 April 2005, 1 U.S. dollar was worth about 11.059 Mexican pesos.
a) How much would 120 U.S. dollars be worth in Mexican pesos?
b) Jackie was traveling in Mexico and bought a watch that cost 3600 Mexican pesos. How much would it cost in U.S. dollars?

19. *Gas Mileage.* A 2005 Ford Mustang GT Convertible will go 372 mi on 15.5 gal of gasoline in highway driving.

   a) How many gallons of gasoline will it take to drive 2690 mi from Boston to Phoenix?

   b) How far can the car be driven on 140 gal of gasoline?

Source: Ford

20. *Gas Mileage.* A 2005 Volkswagen Passat will go 462 mi on 16.5 gal of gasoline in highway driving.

   a) How many gallons of gasoline will it take to drive 1650 mi from Pittsburgh to Albuquerque?

   b) How far can the car be driven on 130 gal of gasoline?

Source: Volkswagen of America, Inc.

21. *Lefties.* In a class of 40 students, on average, 6 will be left-handed. If a class includes 9 "lefties," how many students would you estimate are in the class?

22. *Sugaring.* When 38 gal of maple sap are boiled down, the result is 2 gal of maple syrup. How much sap is needed to produce 9 gal of syrup?

23. *Mileage.* Jean bought a new car. In the first 8 months, it was driven 9000 mi. At this rate, how many miles will the car be driven in 1 yr?

24. *Coffee Production.* Coffee beans from 14 trees are required to produce the 17 lb of coffee that the average person in the United States drinks each year. How many trees are required to produce 375 lb of coffee?

25. *Metallurgy.* In a metal alloy, the ratio of zinc to copper is 3 to 13. If there are 520 lb of copper, how many pounds of zinc are there?

26. *Class Size.* A college advertises that its student-to-faculty ratio is 14 to 1. If 56 students register for Introductory Spanish, how many sections of the course would you expect to see offered?

27. *Painting.* Helen can paint 950 ft^2 with 2 gal of paint. How many 1-gal cans does she need in order to paint a 30,000-ft^2 wall?

28. *Snow to Water.* Under typical conditions, $1\frac{1}{2}$ ft of snow will melt to 2 in. of water. To how many inches of water will $5\frac{1}{2}$ ft of snow melt?

29. *Grass-Seed Coverage.* It takes 60 oz of grass seed to seed 3000 ft² of lawn. At this rate, how much would be needed for 5000 ft² of lawn?

30. *Grass-Seed Coverage.* In Exercise 29, how much seed would be needed for 7000 ft² of lawn?

31. *Estimating a Deer Population.* To determine the number of deer in a game preserve, a forest ranger catches 318 deer, tags them, and releases them. Later, 168 deer are caught, and it is found that 56 of them are tagged. Estimate how many deer are in the game preserve.

32. *Estimating a Trout Population.* To determine the number of trout in a lake, a conservationist catches 112 trout, tags them, and throws them back into the lake. Later, 82 trout are caught, and it is found that 32 of them are tagged. Estimate how many trout there are in the lake.

33. *Map Scaling.* On a road atlas map, 1 in. represents 16.6 mi. If two cities are 3.5-in. apart on the map, how far apart are they in reality?

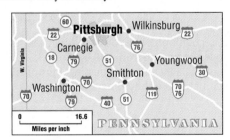

34. *Map Scaling.* On a map, $\frac{1}{4}$ in. represents 50 mi. If two cities are $3\frac{1}{4}$-in. apart on the map, how far apart are they in reality?

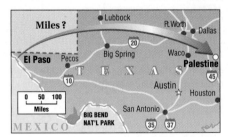

35. *Points per Game.* At one point in the 2000–2001 NBA season, Allen Iverson of the Philadelphia 76ers had scored 884 points in 33 games.

a) At this rate, how many games would it take him to score 1500 points?

b) There are 82 games in an entire NBA season. At this rate, how many points would Iverson score in the entire season?

Source: National Basketball Association

36. *Points per Game.* At one point in the 2000–2001 NBA season, Shaquille O'Neal, then of the Los Angeles Lakers, had scored 826 points in 32 games.

a) At this rate, how many games would it take him to score 2000 points?

b) There are 82 games in an entire NBA season. At this rate, how many points would O'Neal score in the entire season?

37. **D**W Can unit prices be used to solve proportions that involve money? Explain why or why not.

38. **D**W *Earned Run Average.* In baseball, the average number of runs given up by a pitcher in nine innings is his *earned run average,* or *ERA.* Set up a formula for determining a player's ERA. Then verify it using the fact that in the 2000 season, Daryl Kile of the St. Louis Cardinals gave up 101 earned runs in $232\frac{1}{3}$ innings to compile an ERA of 3.91. Then use your formula to determine the ERA of Randy Johnson of the Arizona Diamondbacks, who gave up 73 earned runs in $248\frac{2}{3}$ innings. Is a low ERA considered good or bad?

Source: Major League Baseball

Determine whether each number is prime, composite, or neither. [2.1c]

39. 1   **40.** 28   **41.** 83   **42.** 93   **43.** 47

Find the prime factorization of each number. [2.1d]

44. 808   **45.** 28   **46.** 866   **47.** 93   **48.** 2020

49. Carney College is expanding from 850 to 1050 students. To avoid any rise in the student-to-faculty ratio, the faculty of 69 professors must also increase. How many new faculty positions should be created?

50. In recognition of her outstanding work, Sheri's salary has been increased from $26,000 to $29,380. Tim is earning $23,000 and is requesting a proportional raise. How much more should he ask for?

51. *Baseball Statistics.* Cy Young, one of the greatest baseball pitchers of all time, gave up an average of 2.63 earned runs every 9 innings. Young pitched 7356 innings, more than anyone in the history of baseball. How many earned runs did he give up?

52. *Real-Estate Values.* According to Coldwell Banker Real Estate Corporation, a home selling for $189,000 in Austin, Texas, would sell for $665,795 in San Francisco. How much would a $450,000 home in San Francisco sell for in Austin? Round to the nearest $1000.

Source: Coldwell Banker Real Estate Corporation

53. The ratio 1:3:2 is used to estimate the relative costs of a CD player, receiver, and speakers when shopping for a stereo. That is, the receiver should cost three times the amount spent on the CD player and the speakers should cost twice as much as the amount spent on the CD player. If you had $900 to spend, how would you allocate the money, using this ratio?

5.5 GEOMETRIC APPLICATIONS

a Proportions and Similar Triangles

Look at the pair of triangles below. Note that they appear to have the same shape, but their sizes are different. These are examples of **similar triangles.** By using a magnifying glass, you could imagine enlarging the smaller triangle to get the larger. This process works because the corresponding sides of each triangle have the same ratio. That is, the following proportion is true.

$$\frac{a}{d} = \frac{b}{e} = \frac{c}{f}$$

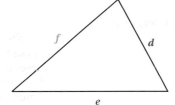

Objectives

a Find lengths of sides of similar triangles using proportions.

b Use proportions to find lengths in pairs of figures that differ only in size.

1. This pair of triangles is similar. Find the missing length x.

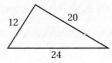

SIMILAR TRIANGLES

Similar triangles have the same shape. The lengths of their corresponding sides have the same ratio—that is, they are proportional.

EXAMPLE 1 The triangles below are similar triangles. Find the missing length x.

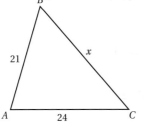

The ratio of x to 9 is the same as the ratio of 24 to 8 or 21 to 7. We get the proportions

$$\frac{x}{9} = \frac{24}{8} \quad \text{and} \quad \frac{x}{9} = \frac{21}{7}.$$

We can solve either one of these proportions. We use the first:

$$\frac{x}{9} = \frac{24}{8}$$

$x \cdot 8 = 24 \cdot 9$ Equating cross products

$\dfrac{x \cdot 8}{8} = \dfrac{24 \cdot 9}{8}$ Dividing by 8 on both sides

$x = 27.$ Simplifying

The missing length x is 27. Other proportions could also be used.

Do Exercise 1.

Answer on page A-12

2. How high is a flagpole that casts a 45-ft shadow at the same time that a 5.5-ft woman casts a 10-ft shadow?

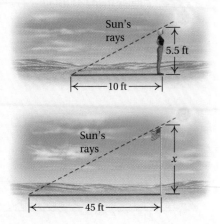

Similar triangles and proportions can often be used to find lengths that would ordinarily be difficult to measure. For example, we could find the height of a flagpole without climbing it or the distance across a river without crossing it.

EXAMPLE 2   How high is a flagpole that casts a 56-ft shadow at the same time that a 6-ft man casts a 5-ft shadow?

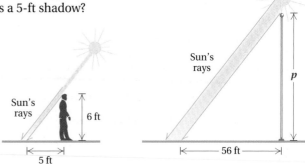

If we use the sun's rays to represent the third side of the triangle in our drawing of the situation, we see that we have similar triangles. Let $p =$ the height of the flagpole. The ratio of 6 to p is the same as the ratio of 5 to 56. Thus we have the proportion

Height of man $\rightarrow$ $\dfrac{6}{p} = \dfrac{5}{56}$. $\leftarrow$ Length of shadow of man
Height of pole $\rightarrow$ $\phantom{\dfrac{6}{p} = }$ $\leftarrow$ Length of shadow of pole

Solve: $6 \cdot 56 = 5 \cdot p$ Equating cross products

$\dfrac{6 \cdot 56}{5} = \dfrac{5 \cdot p}{5}$ Dividing by 5 on both sides

$\dfrac{6 \cdot 56}{5} = p$ Simplifying

$67.2 = p$

The height of the flagpole is 67.2 ft.

Do Exercise 2.

EXAMPLE 3   *Rafters of a House.*   Carpenters use similar triangles to determine the lengths of rafters for a house. They first choose the pitch of the roof, or the ratio of the rise over the run. Then using a triangle with that ratio, they calculate the length of the rafter needed for the house. Loren is constructing rafters for a roof with a 6/12 pitch on a house that is 30 ft wide. Using a rafter guide, Loren knows that the rafter length corresponding to the 6/12 pitch is 13.4. Find the length x of the rafter of the house to the nearest tenth of a foot.

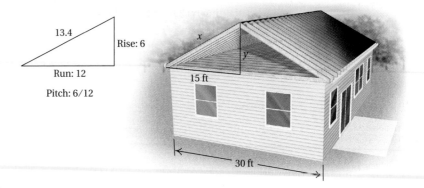

Answer on page A-12

Thus we have the proportion

Length of rafter
in 6/12 triangle → $\dfrac{13.4}{x} = \dfrac{12}{15}$ ← Run in 6/12 triangle
Length of rafter →
on the house ← Run in similar triangle on the house

Solve: $13.4 \cdot 15 = x \cdot 12$ Equating cross products

$\dfrac{13.4 \cdot 15}{12} = \dfrac{x \cdot 12}{12}$ Dividing by 12 on both sides

$\dfrac{13.4 \cdot 15}{12} = x$

$16.8 \text{ ft} \approx x$ Rounding to the nearest tenth of a foot

The length of the rafter x of the house is about 16.8 ft.

Do Exercise 3.

b Proportions and Other Geometric Shapes

When one geometric figure is a magnification of another, the figures are similar. Thus the corresponding lengths are proportional.

EXAMPLE 4 The sides in the negative and photograph below are proportional. Find the width of the photograph.

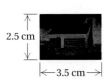

We let x = the width of the photograph. Then we translate to a proportion.

Photo width → $\dfrac{x}{2.5} = \dfrac{10.5}{3.5}$ ← Photo length
Negative width → ← Negative length

Solve: $3.5 \times x = 2.5 \times 10.5$ Equating cross products

$\dfrac{3.5 \times x}{3.5} = \dfrac{2.5 \times 10.5}{3.5}$ Dividing by 3.5 on both sides

$x = \dfrac{2.5 \times 10.5}{3.5}$ Simplifying

$x = 7.5$

Thus the width of the photograph is 7.5 cm.

Do Exercise 4.

3. Rafters of a House. Referring to Example 3, find the length y in the rafter of the house to the nearest tenth of a foot.

4. The sides in the photographs below are proportional. Find the width of the larger photograph.

6 cm
|←10 cm→|

Answers on page A-12

5. Refer to the figures in Example 5. If a model skylight is 3 cm wide, how wide will the actual skylight be?

EXAMPLE 5 A scale model of an addition to an athletic facility is 12 cm wide at the base and rises to a height of 15 cm. If the actual base is to be 116 ft, what will be the actual height of the addition?

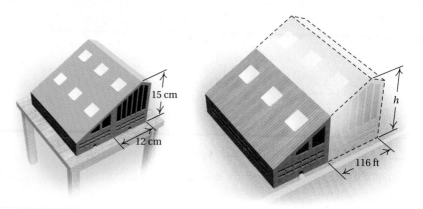

We let h = the height of the addition. Then we translate to a proportion.

$$\begin{array}{c} \text{Width in model} \rightarrow \\ \text{Actual width} \rightarrow \end{array} \frac{12}{116} = \frac{15}{h} \begin{array}{c} \leftarrow \text{Height in model} \\ \leftarrow \text{Actual height} \end{array}$$

Solve: $12 \cdot h = 116 \cdot 15$ Equating cross products

$$\frac{12 \cdot h}{12} = \frac{116 \cdot 15}{12}$$ Dividing by 12 on both sides

$$h = \frac{116 \cdot 15}{12} = 145$$

Thus the height of the addition will be 145 ft.

Do Exercise 5.

Answer on page A-12

Study Tips

TIME MANAGEMENT (PART 3)

Here are some additional tips to help you with time management. (See also the Study Tips on time management in Sections 1.5 and 5.1.)

■ **Are you a morning or an evening person?** If you are an evening person, it might be best to avoid scheduling early-morning classes. If you are a morning person, do the opposite, but go to bed earlier to compensate. Nothing can drain your study time and effectiveness like fatigue.

■ **Keep on schedule.** Your course syllabus provides a plan for the semester's schedule. Use a write-on calendar, daily planner, laptop computer, or personal digital assistant to outline your time for the semester. Be sure to note deadlines involving term papers and exams so you can begin a task early, breaking it down into smaller segments that can be accomplished more easily.

■ **Balance your class schedule.** You may be someone who prefers large blocks of time for study on the off days. In that case, it might be advantageous for you to take courses that meet only three days a week. Keep in mind, however, that this might be a problem when tests in more than one course are scheduled for the same day.

5.5

EXERCISE SET

For Extra Help

MathXL   MyMathLab   InterAct   Math Tutor   Digital Video   Student's
                        Math   Center   Tutor CD 3   Solutions
                                                 Videotape 5   Manual

a   The triangles in each exercise are similar. Find the missing lengths.

1.

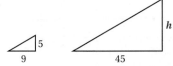

2.

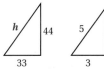

3.

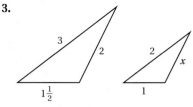

4.

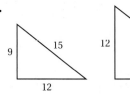

5.

6.

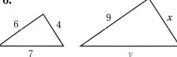

7.

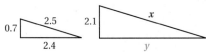

8.

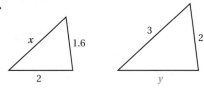

9. When a tree 8 m high casts a shadow 5 m long, how long a shadow is cast by a person 2 m tall?

10. How high is a flagpole that casts a 42-ft shadow at the same time that a $5\frac{1}{2}$-ft woman casts a 7-ft shadow?

11. How high is a tree that casts a 27-ft shadow at the same time that a 4-ft fence post casts a 3-ft shadow?

12. How high is a tree that casts a 32-ft shadow at the same time that an 8-ft light pole casts a 9-ft shadow?

13. Find the height h of the wall.

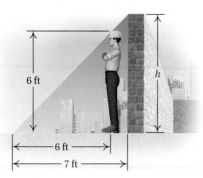

6 ft

6 ft

7 ft

h

14. Find the length L of the lake. Assume that the ratio of L to 120 yd is the same as the ratio of 720 yd to 30 yd.

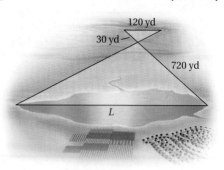

120 yd

30 yd

720 yd

L

15. Find the distance across the river. Assume that the ratio of d to 25 ft is the same as the ratio of 40 ft to 10 ft.

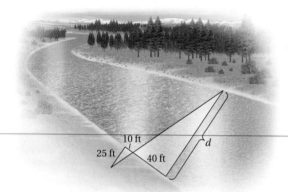

10 ft

25 ft

40 ft

d

16. To measure the height of a hill, a string is drawn tight from level ground to the top of the hill. A 3-ft stick is placed under the string, touching it at point P, a distance of 5 ft from point G, where the string touches the ground. The string is then detached and found to be 120 ft long. How high is the hill?

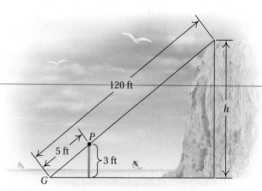

120 ft

h

P

5 ft

3 ft

G

b   In each of Exercises 17–26, the sides in each pair of figures are proportional. Find the missing lengths.

17.

6

9

x

6

18.

5

7

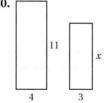

x

14

19.

7

4

x

6

20.

11

4

x

3

21.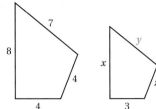

22.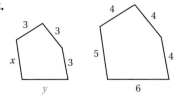

23.

24.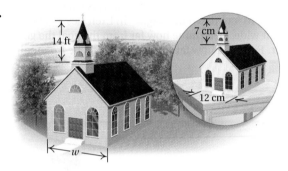

25.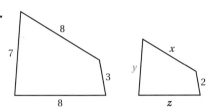

26.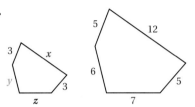

27. A scale model of an addition to an athletic facility is 15 cm wide at the base and rises to a height of 19 cm. If the actual base is to be 120 ft, what will be the height of the addition?

28. Refer to the figures in Exercise 27. If a model skylight is 3 cm wide, how wide will the actual skylight be?

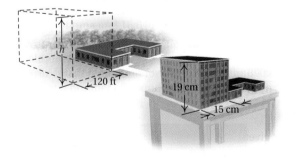

29. **D**_W_ Is it possible for two triangles to have two pairs of sides that are proportional without the triangles being similar? Why or why not?

30. **D**_W_ Design for a classmate a problem involving similar triangles for which

$$\frac{18}{128.95} = \frac{x}{789.89}.$$

13. *Pillsbury Orange Breakfast Rolls.* The price for these breakfast rolls is $1.97 for 13.9 oz. Find the unit price in cents per ounce. [5.2b]

In each of Exercises 14 and 15, find the unit prices. Then determine in each case which has the lowest unit price. [5.2b]

14. *Paper Towels.*

PACKAGE	PRICE	UNIT PRICE PER SHEET
8 rolls, 60 (2 ply) sheets per roll	$6.38	
15 rolls, 60 (2 ply) sheets per roll	$13.99	
6 big rolls, 165 (2 ply) sheets per roll	$10.99	

15. *Crisco Oil.*

PACKAGE	PRICE	UNIT PRICE
32 oz	$2.19	
48 oz	$2.49	
64 oz	$3.59	
128 oz	$7.09	

Determine whether the two pairs of numbers are proportional. [5.3a]

16. 9, 15 and 36, 59

17. 24, 37 and 40, 46.25

Solve. [5.3b]

18. $\dfrac{8}{9} = \dfrac{x}{36}$

19. $\dfrac{6}{x} = \dfrac{48}{56}$

20. $\dfrac{120}{\frac{3}{7}} = \dfrac{7}{x}$

21. $\dfrac{4.5}{120} = \dfrac{0.9}{x}$

Solve. [5.4a]

22. If 3 dozen eggs cost $2.67, how much will 5 dozen eggs cost?

23. *Quality Control.* A factory manufacturing computer circuits found 39 defective circuits in a lot of 65 circuits. At this rate, how many defective circuits can be expected in a lot of 585 circuits?

24. *Exchanging Money.* On 5 August 2005, 1 U.S. dollar was worth about 0.808 European Monetary Unit (Euro).

a) How much would 250 U.S. dollars be worth in Euros?
b) Jamal was traveling in France and saw a sweatshirt that cost 50 Euros. How much would it cost in U.S. dollars?

25. A train travels 448 mi in 7 hr. At this rate, how far will it travel in 13 hr?

26. Fifteen acres are required to produce 54 bushels of tomatoes. At this rate, how many acres are required to produce 97.2 bushels of tomatoes?

27. *Garbage Production.*   It is known that 5 people produce 13 kg of garbage in one day. San Diego, California, has 1,266,753 people. How many kilograms of garbage are produced in San Diego in one day?

28. *Snow to Water.*   Under typical conditions, $1\frac{1}{2}$ ft of snow will melt to 2 in. of water. To how many inches of water will $4\frac{1}{2}$ ft of snow melt?

29. *Lawyers in Michigan.*   In Michigan, there are 2.3 lawyers for every 1000 people. The population of Detroit is 911,402. How many lawyers would you expect there to be in Detroit?

Source: U.S. Bureau of the Census

Each pair of triangles in Exercises 30 and 31 is similar. Find the missing length(s).   [5.5a]

30.

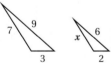

31.

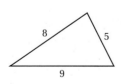 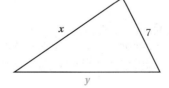

32. How high is a billboard that casts a 25-ft shadow at the same time that an 8-ft sapling casts a 5-ft shadow? [5.5a]

33. The lengths in the figures below are proportional. Find the missing lengths.   [5.5b]

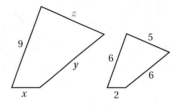

34. **D**w If you were a college president, which would you prefer: a low or high faculty-to-student ratio? Why? [5.1a]

35. **D**w Write a proportion problem for a classmate to solve. Design the problem so that the solution is "Leslie would need 16 gal of gasoline in order to travel 368 mi." [5.4a]

SYNTHESIS

36. It takes Yancy Martinez 10 min to type two-thirds of a page of his term paper. At this rate, how long will it take him to type a 7-page term paper?   [5.4a]

37. ▦ The following triangles are similar. Find the missing lengths.   [5.5a]

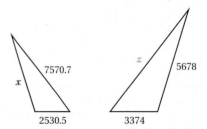

38. Shine-and-Glo Painters uses 2 gal of finishing paint for every 3 gal of primer. Each gallon of finishing paint covers 450 ft². If a surface of 4950 ft² needs both primer and finishing paint, how many gallons of each should be purchased?   [5.4a]

Write fraction notation for the ratio. Do not simplify.

1. 85 to 97

2. 0.34 to 124

Find the ratio of the first number to the second number and simplify.

3. 18 to 20

4. 0.75 to 0.96

5. What is the rate in feet per second?

      10 feet,   16 seconds

6. *Ham Servings.* A 12-lb shankless ham contains 16 servings. What is the rate in servings per pound?

7. *Gas Mileage.* The 2005 Chevrolet Malibu Maxx will go 319 mi on 14.5 gal of gasoline in city driving. What is the rate in miles per gallon?
Source: General Motors Corporation

8. *Laundry Detergent.* A box of Cheer laundry detergent powder sells at $6.29 for 81 oz. Find the unit price in cents per ounce.

9. The following table lists prices for various packages of Tide laundry detergent powder. Find the unit price of each package. Then determine which has the lowest unit price.

PACKAGE	PRICE	UNIT PRICE
33 oz	$3.69	
87 oz	$6.22	
131 oz	$10.99	
263 oz	$17.99	

Determine whether the two pairs of numbers are proportional.

10. 7, 8 and 63, 72

11. 1.3, 3.4 and 5.6, 15.2

Solve.

12. $\dfrac{9}{4} = \dfrac{27}{x}$

13. $\dfrac{150}{2.5} = \dfrac{x}{6}$

14. $\dfrac{x}{100} = \dfrac{27}{64}$

15. $\dfrac{68}{y} = \dfrac{17}{25}$

Solve.

16. *Distance Traveled.* An ocean liner traveled 432 km in 12 hr. At this rate, how far would the boat travel in 42 hr?

17. *Time Loss.* A watch loses 2 min in 10 hr. At this rate, how much will it lose in 24 hr?

18. *Map Scaling.* On a map, 3 in. represents 225 mi. If two cities are 7 in. apart on the map, how far are they apart in reality?

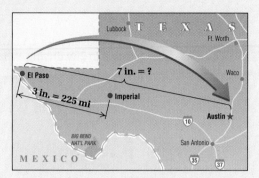

19. *Tower Height.* A birdhouse built on a pole that is 3 m high casts a shadow 5 m long. At the same time, the shadow of a tower is 110 m long. How high is the tower?

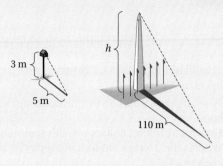

20. *Exchanging Money.* On 5 August 2005, 1 U.S. dollar was worth about 7.775 Hong Kong dollars.

a) How much would 450 U.S. dollars be worth in Hong Kong dollars?

b) Mitchell was traveling in Hong Kong and saw a DVD player that cost 795 Hong Kong dollars. How much would it cost in U.S. dollars?

21. *Automobile Violations.* In a recent year, the Indianapolis Police Department employed 1088 officers and made 37,493 arrests. At this rate, how many arrests could be made if the number of officers were increased to 2500?

Source: *Indianapolis Star,* 12-31-00

The lengths in each pair of figures are proportional. Find the missing lengths.

22.

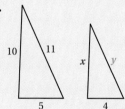

23.

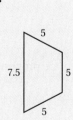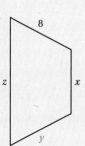

24. Nancy Morano-Smith wants to win a season football ticket from the local bookstore. Her goal is to guess the number of marbles in an 8-gal jar. She knows that there are 128 oz in a gallon. She goes home and fills an 8-oz jar with 46 marbles. How many marbles should she guess are in the jar?

1. *Baseball Salaries.* Alex Rodriguez now plays with the New York Yankees under a 10-yr contract for $252 million that he originally signed with the Texas Rangers in 2000.

    a) Find standard notation for the dollar amount of this contract.
    b) How many billion dollars was this contract?
    c) What is the average amount of money he makes each year?
    d) In 2000, Rodriguez had 554 at-bats. How much money did he average for each at-bat?

    Source: Major League Baseball

2. *Gas Mileage.* The 2005 Volkswagen Jetta 2.5 L will go 319 mi on 14.5 gal of gasoline in city driving. What is the rate in miles per gallon?

    Source: Volkswagen of America, Inc.

Add and simplify.

3. $\begin{array}{r} 2\ 7.6\ 8 \\ 3.0\ 1\ 9 \\ +\ 4\ 8\ 3.2\ 9\ 7 \\ \hline \end{array}$

4. $\begin{array}{r} 2\frac{1}{3} \\ +4\frac{5}{12} \\ \hline \end{array}$

5. $\dfrac{6}{35} + \dfrac{5}{28}$

Subtract and simplify.

6. $\begin{array}{r} 4\ 0.2 \\ -\ \ \ 9.7\ 0\ 9 \\ \hline \end{array}$

7. $73.82 - 0.908$

8. $\dfrac{4}{15} - \dfrac{3}{20}$.

Multiply and simplify.

9. $\begin{array}{r} 3\ 7.6\ 4 \\ \times\ \ \ \ \ 5.9 \\ \hline \end{array}$

10. 5.678×100

11. $2\dfrac{1}{3} \cdot 1\dfrac{2}{7}$

Divide and simplify.

12. $2.3\,\overline{)\,9\,8.9}$

13. $5\ 4\,\overline{)\,4\,8,5\,4\,6}$

14. $\dfrac{7}{11} \div \dfrac{14}{33}$

15. Write expanded notation: 30,074.

16. Write a word name for 120.07.

Which number is larger?

17. 0.7,   0.698

18. 0.799,   0.8

19. Find the prime factorization of 144.

20. Find the LCM of 28 and 35.

21. What part is shaded?

22. Simplify: $\dfrac{90}{144}$.

Calculate.

23. $\dfrac{3}{5} \times 9.53$

24. $\dfrac{1}{3} \times 0.645 - \dfrac{3}{4} \times 0.048$

25. Write fraction notation for the ratio 0.3 to 15.

26. Determine whether the pairs 3, 9 and 25, 75 are proportional.

27. What is the rate in meters per second?

660 meters,   12 seconds

28. The following table lists prices for various brands of liquid dish soap. Find the unit price of each brand. Then determine which has the lowest unit price.

BRAND	PACKAGE	PRICE	UNIT PRICE
Palmolive	13 oz	$1.53	
Dawn	42.7 oz	$3.99	
Dawn	14.7 oz	$1.43	
Joy	28 oz	$1.78	
Joy	42.7 oz	$2.99	

Solve.

29. $\dfrac{14}{25} = \dfrac{x}{54}$

30. $423 = 16 \cdot t$

31. $\dfrac{2}{3} \cdot y = \dfrac{16}{27}$

32. $\dfrac{7}{16} = \dfrac{56}{x}$

33. $34.56 + n = 67.9$

34. $t + \dfrac{7}{25} = \dfrac{5}{7}$

Solve.

35. A particular kind of fettuccini Alfredo has 520 calories in 1 cup. How many calories are there in $\frac{3}{4}$ cup?

36. *Exchanging Money.*   On 26 April 2005, 1 U.S. dollar was worth about 6.085 South African Rand.

a) How much would 220 U.S. dollars be worth in Rand?
b) Monica was traveling in South Africa and saw a camera that cost 2050 Rand. How much would it cost in U.S. dollars?

37. *Gas Mileage.*   A Greyhound tour bus traveled 347.6 mi, 249.8 mi, and 379.5 mi on three separate trips. What was the total mileage of the bus?

38. A machine can stamp out 925 washers in 5 min. The company owning the machine needs 1295 washers by the end of the morning. How long will it take to stamp them out?

39. A 46-oz juice can contains $5\frac{3}{4}$ cups of juice. A recipe calls for $3\frac{1}{2}$ cups of juice. How many cups are left over?

40. It takes a carpenter $\frac{2}{3}$ hr to hang a door. How many doors can the carpenter hang in 8 hr?

41. *The Leaning Tower of Pisa.* At the time of this writing, the Leaning Tower of Pisa was still standing. It is 184.5 ft tall but leans about 17 ft out from its base. Each year, it leans about an additional $\frac{1}{20}$ in., or $\frac{1}{240}$ ft.
   a) After how many years will it lean the same length as it is tall?
   b) At most how many years do you think the Tower will stand?

42. *Airplane Tire Costs.* A Boeing 747-400 jumbo jet has 2 nose tires and 16 rear tires. Each tire costs about $20,000.
   a) What is the total cost of a new set of tires for such a plane?
   b) Suppose an airline has a fleet of 400 such planes. What is the total cost of a new set of tires for all the planes?
   c) Suppose the airline has to change tires every month. What would be the total cost for tires for the airline for an entire year?

   Source: *World-Traveler,* October 2000

43. *Car Travel.* A car travels 337.62 mi in 8 hr. How far does it travel in 1 hr?

44. *Shuttle Orbits.* A recent space shuttle made 16 orbits a day during an 8.25-day mission. How many orbits were made during the entire mission?

For each of Exercises 45–47, choose the correct answer from the selections given.

45. How many even prime numbers are there?
   a) 5   **b)** 3   **c)** 2
   d) 1   **e)** None

46. The gas mileage of a car is 28.16 miles per gallon. How many gallons per mile is this?
   a) $\dfrac{704}{25}$ **b)** $\dfrac{25}{704}$ **c)** $\dfrac{2816}{100}$
   d) $\dfrac{250}{704}$ **e)** None

47. By what number do you multiply the side s of a square to find its perimeter?
   a) s itself   **b)** 4   **c)** 2
   d) 8   **e)** None

SYNTHESIS

48. A soccer goalie wishing to block an opponent's shot moves toward the shooter to reduce the shooter's view of the goal. If the goalie can only defend a region 10 ft wide, how far in front of the goal should the goalie be? (See the figure at right.)

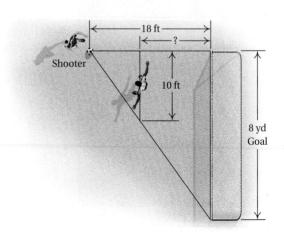

Percent Notation

Real-World Application

There are 1,168,195 people in the United States in active military service. The numbers in the four armed services are as follows: Air Force, 314,477; Army, 391,126; Marine Corps, 135,324; Navy, 327,268. What percent of the total does each branch represent? Round the answers to the nearest tenth of a percent.

Source: U.S. Department of Defense

This problem appears as Exercise 2 in Section 6.5.

Objectives

a Write three kinds of notation for a percent.

b Convert between percent notation and decimal notation.

Write three kinds of notation as in Examples 1 and 2.

1. 70%

2. 23.4%

3. 100%

It is thought that the Roman emperor Augustus began percent notation by taxing goods sold at a rate of $\frac{1}{100}$. In time, the symbol "%" evolved by interchanging the parts of the symbol "100" to "0/0" and then to "%."

a Understanding Percent Notation

Of all the surface area of the earth, 70% of it is covered by water. What does this mean? It means that of every 100 square miles of the earth's surface area, 70 square miles are covered by water. Thus, 70% is a ratio of 70 to 100, or $\frac{70}{100}$.

Source: *The Handy Geography Answer Book*

70 of 100 squares are shaded.

70% or $\frac{70}{100}$ or 0.70 of the large square is shaded.

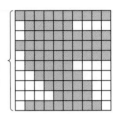

Percent notation is used extensively in our everyday lives. Here are some examples:

44% of all Americans use at least one prescribed medicine.

35.5% of Massachusetts residents age 25 and over have a bachelor's degree.

18% of household personal vehicles are pickup trucks.

50.3% of all paper used in the United States is recycled.

54% of all kids prefer white bread.

0.08% blood alcohol level is a standard used by some states as the legal limit for drunk driving.

Percent notation is often represented in pie charts to show how the parts of a quantity are related. For example, the circle graph below illustrates the percentage of vehicles manufactured in the most popular car colors during 2003 in North America.

Most Popular Car Colors, 2003 (SUV/Truck/Van)

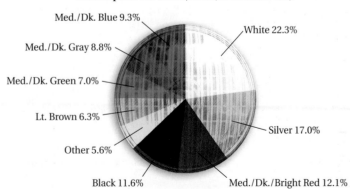

Med./Dk. Blue 9.3%
White 22.3%
Med./Dk. Gray 8.8%
Med./Dk. Green 7.0%
Lt. Brown 6.3%
Silver 17.0%
Other 5.6%
Black 11.6%
Med./Dk./Bright Red 12.1%

Source: DuPont Herberts Automotive Systems, Troy, Michigan, 2003, DuPont Automotive Color Survey Results

Answers on page A-13

PERCENT NOTATION

The notation **n%** means "n per hundred."

This definition leads us to the following equivalent ways of defining percent notation.

NOTATION FOR n%

Percent notation, n%, can be expressed using:

ratio $\rightarrow$ $n\% = $ the ratio of n to $100 = \dfrac{n}{100}$,

fraction notation $\rightarrow$ $n\% = n \times \dfrac{1}{100}$, or

decimal notation $\rightarrow$ $n\% = n \times 0.01$.

From 1998 to 2008, the number of jobs for professional chefs will increase by 13.4%.

Source: *Handbook of U.S. Labor Statistics*

EXAMPLE 1 Write three kinds of notation for 35%.

Using ratio: $35\% = \dfrac{35}{100}$ A ratio of 35 to 100

Using fraction notation: $35\% = 35 \times \dfrac{1}{100}$ Replacing % with $\times \dfrac{1}{100}$

Using decimal notation: $35\% = 35 \times 0.01$ Replacing % with $\times 0.01$

EXAMPLE 2 Write three kinds of notation for 67.8%.

Using ratio: $67.8\% = \dfrac{67.8}{100}$ A ratio of 67.8 to 100

Using fraction notation: $67.8\% = 67.8 \times \dfrac{1}{100}$ Replacing % with $\times \dfrac{1}{100}$

Using decimal notation: $67.8\% = 67.8 \times 0.01$ Replacing % with $\times 0.01$

Do Exercises 1–3 on the preceding page.

b Converting Between Percent Notation and Decimal Notation

Consider 78%. To convert to decimal notation, we can think of percent notation as a ratio and write

$78\% = \dfrac{78}{100}$ Using the definition of percent as a ratio

$ = 0.78.$ Dividing

Similarly,

$4.9\% = \dfrac{4.9}{100}$ Using the definition of percent as a ratio

$ = 0.049.$ Dividing

We could also convert 78% to decimal notation by replacing "%" with "$\times 0.01$" and write

$78\% = 78 \times 0.01$ Replacing % with $\times 0.01$

$ = 0.78.$ Multiplying

CALCULATOR CORNER

Converting from Percent Notation to Decimal Notation Many calculators have a [%] key that can be used to convert from percent notation to decimal notation. This is often the second operation associated with a particular key and is accessed by first pressing a [2nd] or [SHIFT] key. To convert 57.6% to decimal notation, for example, you might press

[5] [7] [.] [6] [2nd] [%] or
[5] [7] [.] [6] [SHIFT] [%] .

The display would read

[0.576] , so

57.6% = 0.576. Read the user's manual to determine whether your calculator can do this conversion.

Exercises: Use a calculator to find decimal notation.

1. 14%   2. 0.069%
3. 43.8%   4. 125%

343

Find decimal notation.

4. 34%

5. 78.9%

6. $6\frac{5}{8}\%$

Find decimal notation for the percent notation in the sentence.

7. Pickup Trucks. Of all household personal vehicles in the United States, 18% are pickup trucks.

Source: Department of Transportation, 2001 National Household Travel Survey

8. Blood Alcohol Level. A blood alcohol level of 0.08% is a standard used by some states as the legal limit for drunk driving.

Answers on page A-13

Similarly,

$$4.9\% = 4.9 \times 0.01 \quad \text{Replacing \% with} \times 0.01$$
$$= 0.049. \quad \text{Multiplying}$$

Dividing by 100 amounts to moving the decimal point two places to the left, which is the same as multiplying by 0.01. This leads us to a quick way to convert from percent notation to decimal notation—we drop the percent symbol and move the decimal point two places to the left.

To convert from percent notation to decimal notation,	36.5%
a) replace the percent symbol % with × 0.01, and	36.5×0.01
b) multiply by 0.01, which means move the decimal point two places to the left.	0.36.5 Move 2 places to the left.
	36.5% = 0.365

EXAMPLE 3 Find decimal notation for 99.44%.

a) Replace the percent symbol with × 0.01. 99.44×0.01

b) Move the decimal point two places to the left.   0.99.44

Thus, 99.44% = 0.9944.

EXAMPLE 4 The interest rate on a $2\frac{1}{2}$-year certificate of deposit is $6\frac{3}{8}\%$. Find decimal notation for $6\frac{3}{8}\%$.

a) Convert $6\frac{3}{8}$ to decimal notation and replace the percent symbol with × 0.01. $6\frac{3}{8}\%$ 6.375×0.01

b) Move the decimal point two places to the left.   0.06.375

Thus, $6\frac{3}{8}\% = 0.06375$.

Do Exercises 4–8.

To convert 0.38 to percent notation, we can first write fraction notation, as follows:

$$0.38 = \frac{38}{100} \quad \text{Converting to fraction notation}$$
$$= 38\%. \quad \text{Using the definition of percent as a ratio}$$

Note that $100\% = 100 \times 0.01 = 1$. Thus to convert 0.38 to percent notation, we can multiply by 1, using 100% as a symbol for 1.

$$0.38 = 0.38 \times 1$$
$$= 0.38 \times 100\%$$
$$= 0.38 \times 100 \times 0.01 \quad \text{Replacing 100\% with } 100 \times 0.01$$
$$= (0.38 \times 100) \times 0.01 \quad \text{Using the associative law of multiplication}$$

Then

$$38 \times 0.01 = 38\%. \qquad \text{Replacing "} \times 0.01 \text{" with the \% symbol}$$

Even more quickly, since $0.38 = 0.38 \times 100\%$, we can simply multiply 0.38 by 100 and write the % symbol.

To convert from decimal notation to percent notation, we multiply by 100%—that is, we move the decimal point two places to the right and write a percent symbol.

To convert from decimal notation to percent notation, multiply by 100%. That is,	$0.675 = 0.675 \times 100\%$
a) move the decimal point two places to the right, and	0.67.5 Move 2 places to the right.
b) write a % symbol.	67.5% $0.675 = 67.5\%$

EXAMPLE 5 Find percent notation for 1.27.

a) Move the decimal point two places to the right.   1.27.

b) Write a % symbol.   127%

Thus, $1.27 = 127\%$.

EXAMPLE 6 Of the time that people declare as sick leave, 0.21 is actually used for family issues. Find percent notation for 0.21.
Source: CCH Inc.

a) Move the decimal point two places to the right.   0.21.

b) Write a % symbol.   21%

Thus, $0.21 = 21\%$.

EXAMPLE 7 Find percent notation for 5.6.

a) Move the decimal point two places to the right, adding an extra zero.   5.60.

b) Write a % symbol.   560%

Thus, $5.6 = 560\%$.

EXAMPLE 8 Of those who play golf, 0.149 play 8–24 rounds per year. Find percent notation for 0.149.
Source: U.S. Golf Association

a) Move the decimal point two places to the right.   0.14.9

b) Write a % symbol.   14.9%

Thus, $0.149 = 14.9\%$.

Do Exercises 9–13.

Find percent notation.

9. 0.24

10. 3.47

11. 1

Find percent notation for the decimal notation in the sentence.

12. High School Graduate. The highest level of education for 0.321 of persons 25 and over in the United States is high school graduation.

    Source: U.S. Department of Commerce, Bureau of the Census, *Current Population Survey*

13. Golf. Of those who play golf, 0.253 play 25–49 rounds per year.

    Source: U.S. Golf Association

Answers on page A-13

a Write three kinds of notation as in Examples 1 and 2 on p. 343.

1. 90%

2. 58.7%

3. 12.5%

4. 130%

b Find decimal notation.

5. 67%

6. 17%

7. 45.6%

8. 76.3%

9. 59.01%

10. 30.02%

11. 10%

12. 80%

13. 1%

14. 100%

15. 200%

16. 300%

17. 0.1%

18. 0.4%

19. 0.09%

20. 0.12%

21. 0.18%

22. 5.5%

23. 23.19%

24. 87.99%

25. $14\frac{7}{8}\%$

26. $93\frac{1}{8}\%$

27. $56\frac{1}{2}\%$

28. $61\frac{3}{4}\%$

Find decimal notation for the percent notation(s) in the sentence.

29. *Pediatricians.* By 2020, the population of children in the United States is expected to increase by about 9% while the number of pediatricians will leap 58%.

Source: Study by Dr. Scott Shipman, an Oregon Health and Science University pediatrician

30. *Cancer Survival.* In 2005, 78.9% of children with cancer survive at least 5 years compared to about 60% in 1975.

Source: National Cancer Institute

31. *Eating Out.* On a given day, 44% of all adults eat in a restaurant.

Source: *AARP Bulletin,* November 2004

32. Of those who play golf, 18.6% play 100 or more rounds per year.

Source: U.S. Golf Association

33. *Knitting and Crocheting.* Of all women ages 25 to 34, 36% know how to knit or crochet.

Source: Research Inc. for Craft Yarn Council of America

34. According to a recent survey, 95.1% of those asked to name what sports they participate in chose swimming.

Source: Sporting Goods Manufacturers

Find percent notation.

35. 0.47	**36.** 0.87	**37.** 0.03	**38.** 0.01	**39.** 8.7
40. 4	**41.** 0.334	**42.** 0.889	**43.** 0.75	**44.** 0.99
45. 0.4	**46.** 0.5	**47.** 0.006	**48.** 0.008	**49.** 0.017
50. 0.024	**51.** 0.2718	**52.** 0.8911	**53.** 0.0239	**54.** 0.00073

Find percent notation for the decimal notation(s) in the sentence.

55. *Hours of Sleep.* In 2005, only 0.26 of people get eight or more hours of sleep a night on weekdays. This rate has declined from 0.38 in 2001.

Source: National Sleep Foundation's 2005 Sleep in America Poll

56. According to a recent survey, 0.526 of those asked to name what sports they participate in chose bowling.

Source: Sporting Goods Manufacturers

57. *Bachelor's Degrees.* For 0.177 of the United States population 25 and over, the bachelor's degree is the highest level of educational attainment.

Source: U.S. Department of Commerce, Bureau of the Census, *Current Population Survey*; National Center for Educational Statistics, *Digest of Education Statistics*, 2003

58. About 0.69 of all newspapers are recycled.

Sources: American Forest and Paper Association; Newspaper Association of America

59. *65 and Over.* In Clearwater, Florida, 0.215 of the residents are 65 or over.

Source: U.S. Census Bureau

60. Of those people living in North Carolina, 0.1134 will die of heart disease.

Source: American Association of Retired Persons

61. **D_W** *Winning Percentage.* During the 2004 regular baseball season, the Boston Red Sox won 98 of 162 games and went on to win the World Series. Find the ratio of number of wins to total number of games played in the regular season and convert it to decimal notation. Such a rate is often called a "winning percentage." Explain why.

62. **D_W** Athletes sometimes speak of "giving 110%" effort. Does this make sense? Explain.

SKILL MAINTENANCE

Convert to a mixed numeral. [3.4a]

63. $\dfrac{100}{3}$

64. $\dfrac{75}{2}$

65. $\dfrac{75}{8}$

66. $\dfrac{297}{16}$

67. $\dfrac{567}{98}$

68. $\dfrac{2345}{21}$

Convert to decimal notation. [4.5a]

69. $\dfrac{2}{3}$

70. $\dfrac{1}{3}$

71. $\dfrac{5}{6}$

72. $\dfrac{17}{12}$

73. $\dfrac{8}{3}$

74. $\dfrac{15}{16}$

6.2 PERCENT AND FRACTION NOTATION

a Converting from Fraction Notation to Percent Notation

Consider the fraction notation $\frac{7}{8}$. To convert to percent notation, we use two skills we already have. We first find decimal notation by dividing:

$$\frac{7}{8} = 0.875$$

$$
\begin{array}{r}
0.8\ 7\ 5 \\
8\ )\overline{\ 7.0\ 0\ 0} \\
\underline{6\ 4} \\
6\ 0 \\
\underline{5\ 6} \\
4\ 0 \\
\underline{4\ 0} \\
0
\end{array}
$$

Then we convert the decimal notation to percent notation. We move the decimal point two places to the right

$$0.8\ 7.5$$

and write a % symbol:

$$\frac{7}{8} = 87.5\%, \text{ or } 87\frac{1}{2}\%.$$

To convert from fraction notation to percent notation,

$\frac{3}{5}$ Fraction notation

a) find decimal notation by division, and

$$
\begin{array}{r}
0.6 \\
5\ )\overline{\ 3.0} \\
\underline{3\ 0} \\
0
\end{array}
$$

b) convert the decimal notation to percent notation.

$0.6 = 0.60 = 60\%$ Percent notation

$$\frac{3}{5} = 60\%$$

EXAMPLE 1   Find percent notation for $\frac{9}{16}$.

a) We first find decimal notation by division.

$$
\begin{array}{r}
0.5\ 6\ 2\ 5 \\
1\ 6\ )\overline{\ 9.0\ 0\ 0\ 0} \\
\underline{8\ 0} \\
1\ 0\ 0 \\
\underline{9\ 6} \\
4\ 0 \\
\underline{3\ 2} \\
8\ 0 \\
\underline{8\ 0} \\
0
\end{array}
$$

$$\frac{9}{16} = 0.5625$$

349

Find fraction notation.

7. 60%

8. 3.25%

9. $66\frac{2}{3}\%$

10. Complete this table.

FRACTION NOTATION	$\frac{1}{5}$		
DECIMAL NOTATION		$0.83\overline{3}$	
PERCENT NOTATION			$37\frac{1}{2}\%$

Answers on page A-13

Do Exercises 7–10.

EXAMPLE 6 Find fraction notation for 62.5%.

$$62.5\% = \frac{62.5}{100} \qquad \text{Using the definition of percent}$$

$$= \frac{62.5}{100} \times \frac{10}{10} \qquad \text{Multiplying by 1 to eliminate the decimal point in the numerator}$$

$$= \frac{625}{1000}$$

$$\left. \begin{array}{l} = \frac{5 \cdot 125}{8 \cdot 125} = \frac{5}{8} \cdot \frac{125}{125} \\[2mm] = \frac{5}{8} \end{array} \right\} \quad \text{Simplifying}$$

EXAMPLE 7 Find fraction notation for $16\frac{2}{3}\%$.

$$16\frac{2}{3}\% = \frac{50}{3}\% \qquad \text{Converting from the mixed numeral to fraction notation}$$

$$= \frac{50}{3} \times \frac{1}{100} \qquad \text{Using the definition of percent}$$

$$\left. \begin{array}{l} = \frac{50 \cdot 1}{3 \cdot 50 \cdot 2} = \frac{1}{6} \cdot \frac{50}{50} \\[2mm] = \frac{1}{6} \end{array} \right\} \quad \text{Simplifying}$$

The table on the inside back cover lists decimal, fraction, and percent equivalents used so often that it would speed up your work if you memorized them. For example, $\frac{1}{3} = 0.\overline{3}$, so we say that the **decimal equivalent** of $\frac{1}{3}$ is $0.\overline{3}$, or that $0.\overline{3}$ has the **fraction equivalent** $\frac{1}{3}$.

EXAMPLE 8 Find fraction notation for $16.\overline{6}\%$.

We can use the table on the inside back cover or recall that $16.\overline{6}\% = 16\frac{2}{3}\% = \frac{1}{6}$. We can also recall from our work with repeating decimals in Chapter 4 that $0.\overline{6} = \frac{2}{3}$. Then we have $16.\overline{6}\% = 16\frac{2}{3}\%$ and can proceed as in Example 7.

Do Exercises 7–10.

Study Tips

MEMORIZING

Memorizing is a very helpful tool in the study of mathematics. Don't underestimate its power as you memorize the table of decimal, fraction, and percent notation on the inside back cover. We will discuss memorizing more later.

CALCULATOR CORNER

Applications of Ratio and Percent: The Price–Earnings Ratio and Stock Yields

The Price–Earnings Ratio   If the total earnings of a company one year were $5,000,000 and 100,000 shares of stock were issued, the earnings per share were $50. At one time, the price per share of Coca-Cola was $58.125 and the earnings per share were $0.76. The **price-earnings ratio,** P/E, is the price of the stock divided by the earnings per share. For the Coca-Cola stock, the price-earnings ratio, P/E, is given by

$$\frac{P}{E} = \frac{58.125}{0.76} \approx 76.48. \qquad \text{Dividing, using a calculator, and rounding to the nearest hundredth}$$

Stock Yields   At one time, the price per share of Coca-Cola stock was $58.125 and the company was paying a yearly dividend of $0.68 per share. It is helpful to those interested in stocks to know what percent the dividend is of the price of the stock. The percent is called the **yield.** For the Coca-Cola stock, the yield is given by

$$\text{Yield} = \frac{\text{Dividend}}{\text{Price per share}} = \frac{0.68}{58.125} \approx 0.0117 \qquad \text{Dividing and rounding to the nearest ten-thousandth}$$

$$= 1.17\% \qquad \text{Converting to percent notation}$$

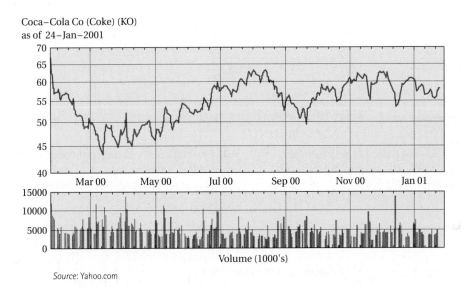

Coca–Cola Co (Coke) (KO)
as of 24–Jan–2001

Volume (1000's)

Source: Yahoo.com

Exercises: Compute the price–earnings ratio and the yield for each stock listed below.

	STOCK	PRICE PER SHARE	EARNINGS	DIVIDEND	P/E	YIELD
1.	Pepsi (PEP)	$42.75	$1.40	$0.56		
2.	Pearson (PSO)	$25.00	$0.78	$0.30		
3.	Quaker Oats (OAT)	$92.375	$2.68	$1.10		
4.	Texas Insts (TEX)	$42.875	$1.62	$0.43		
5.	Ford Motor Co (F)	$27.5625	$2.30	$1.19		
6.	Wendy's Intl (WEN)	$25.75	$1.47	$0.23		

6.2 EXERCISE SET

For Extra Help

MathXL   MyMathLab   InterAct Math   Math Tutor Center   Digital Video Tutor CD 3 Videotape 6   Student's Solutions Manual

a Find percent notation.

1. $\frac{41}{100}$ 2. $\frac{36}{100}$ 3. $\frac{5}{100}$ 4. $\frac{1}{100}$ 5. $\frac{2}{10}$ 6. $\frac{7}{10}$

7. $\frac{3}{10}$ 8. $\frac{9}{10}$ 9. $\frac{1}{2}$ 10. $\frac{3}{4}$ 11. $\frac{7}{8}$ 12. $\frac{1}{8}$

13. $\frac{4}{5}$ 14. $\frac{2}{5}$ 15. $\frac{2}{3}$ 16. $\frac{1}{3}$ 17. $\frac{1}{6}$ 18. $\frac{5}{6}$

19. $\frac{3}{16}$ 20. $\frac{11}{16}$ 21. $\frac{13}{16}$ 22. $\frac{7}{16}$ 23. $\frac{4}{25}$ 24. $\frac{17}{25}$

25. $\frac{1}{20}$ 26. $\frac{31}{50}$ 27. $\frac{17}{50}$ 28. $\frac{3}{20}$

Find percent notation for the fraction notation in the sentence.

29. *Driving While Drowsy.* Almost half of U.S. drivers say they have driven while drowsy. Of this group, $\frac{2}{5}$ fight off sleep by opening a window, and $\frac{9}{50}$ drink a caffeinated beverage.

Source: Harris Interactive for Tylenol PM

30. *Paved Roads.* About $\frac{13}{20}$ of the roads and streets in the United States are paved.

Source: U.S. Department of Transportation, *Highway Statistics*

In Exercises 31–36, write percent notation for the fractions in this pie chart.

Time Workers Spend Sorting Unsolicited e-mail and Spam

Less than 5 minutes $\frac{59}{100}$

$\frac{11}{50}$ 5–15 minutes

$\frac{9}{100}$ 15–30 minutes

$\frac{1}{20}$ 30–60 minutes

$\frac{1}{50}$ More than 1 hour

$\frac{3}{100}$ Did not know/ not sure

Source: Data from InsightExpress

31. $\frac{11}{50}$ **32.** $\frac{3}{100}$

33. $\frac{1}{20}$ **34.** $\frac{59}{100}$

35. $\frac{9}{100}$ **36.** $\frac{1}{50}$

Find fraction notation. Simplify.

37. 85%

38. 55%

39. 62.5%

40. 12.5%

41. $33\frac{1}{3}$%

42. $83\frac{1}{3}$%

43. $16.\overline{6}$%

44. $66.\overline{6}$%

45. 7.25%

46. 4.85%

47. 0.8%

48. 0.2%

49. $25\frac{3}{8}$%

50. $48\frac{7}{8}$%

51. $78\frac{2}{9}$%

52. $16\frac{5}{9}$%

53. $64\frac{7}{11}$%

54. $73\frac{3}{11}$%

55. 150%

56. 110%

57. 0.0325%

58. 0.419%

59. $33.\overline{3}$%

60. $83.\overline{3}$%

Find fraction notation for the percent notation in the following bar graph.

**Organ Transplants
in the United States, 2003**

Source: National Organ Procurement and Transplantation Network

61. 8%

62. 22%

63. 60%

64. 4%

65. 2%

66. 3%

Find fraction notation for the percent notation in the sentence.

67. A 1.9-oz serving of Raisin Bran Crunch® cereal with $\frac{1}{2}$ cup of skim milk satisfies 35% of the minimum daily requirements for Vitamin B$_{12}$.
Source: Kellogg's USA, Inc.

68. A 1-cup serving of Wheaties® cereal with $\frac{1}{2}$ cup of skim milk satisfies 15% of the minimum daily requirements for calcium.
Source: General Mills Sales, Inc.

69. Of all those who are 85 or older, 47% have Alzheimer's disease.
Source: Alzheimer's Association

70. In 2003, 24.4% of Americans 18 and older smoked cigarettes.
Source: U.S. Centers for Disease Control and Prevention

Complete the table.

71.

FRACTION NOTATION	DECIMAL NOTATION	PERCENT NOTATION
$\frac{1}{8}$		12.5%, or $12\frac{1}{2}$%
$\frac{1}{6}$		
		20%
	0.25	
		33.$\overline{3}$%, or $33\frac{1}{3}$%
		37.5% or $37\frac{1}{2}$%
		40%
$\frac{1}{2}$		

72.

FRACTION NOTATION	DECIMAL NOTATION	PERCENT NOTATION
$\frac{3}{5}$		
	0.625	
$\frac{2}{3}$		
	0.75	75%
$\frac{4}{5}$		
$\frac{5}{6}$		83.$\overline{3}$%, or $83\frac{1}{3}$%
$\frac{7}{8}$		87.5%, or $87\frac{1}{2}$%
		100%

73.

FRACTION NOTATION	DECIMAL NOTATION	PERCENT NOTATION
	0.5	
$\frac{1}{3}$		
		25%
		16.$\overline{6}$%, or $16\frac{2}{3}$%
	0.125	
$\frac{3}{4}$		
	0.8$\overline{3}$	
$\frac{3}{8}$		

74.

FRACTION NOTATION	DECIMAL NOTATION	PERCENT NOTATION
		40%
		62.5%, or $62\frac{1}{2}$%
	0.875	
$\frac{1}{1}$		
	0.6	
	0.$\overline{6}$	
$\frac{1}{5}$		

75. DW What do the following have in common? Explain.

$$\frac{23}{16}, \quad 1\frac{875}{2000}, \quad 1.4375, \quad \frac{207}{144}, \quad 1\frac{7}{16}, \quad 143.75\%, \quad 1\frac{4375}{10,000}$$

76. DW Is it always best to convert from fraction notation to percent notation by first finding decimal notation? Why or why not?

SKILL MAINTENANCE

Solve.

77. $13 \cdot x = 910$ [1.7b]

78. $15 \cdot y = 75$ [1.7b]

79. $0.05 \times b = 20$ [4.4b]

80. $3 = 0.16 \times b$ [4.4b]

81. $\frac{24}{37} = \frac{15}{x}$ [5.3b]

82. $\frac{17}{18} = \frac{x}{27}$ [5.3b]

83. $\frac{9}{10} = \frac{x}{5}$ [5.3b]

84. $\frac{7}{x} = \frac{4}{5}$ [5.3b]

Convert to a mixed numeral.   [3.4a]

85. $\frac{100}{3}$

86. $\frac{75}{2}$

87. $\frac{250}{3}$

88. $\frac{123}{6}$

89. $\frac{345}{8}$

90. $\frac{373}{6}$

91. $\frac{75}{4}$

92. $\frac{67}{9}$

Convert from a mixed numeral to fraction notation.   [3.4a]

93. $1\frac{1}{17}$

94. $20\frac{9}{10}$

95. $101\frac{1}{2}$

96. $32\frac{3}{8}$

SYNTHESIS

Write percent notation.

97. $\frac{41}{369}$

98. $\frac{54}{999}$

99. $2.5\overline{74631}$

100. $3.2\overline{93847}$

Write decimal notation.

101. $\frac{14}{9}\%$

102. $\frac{19}{12}\%$

103. $\frac{729}{7}\%$

104. $\frac{637}{6}\%$

Objectives

a Translate percent problems to percent equations.

b Solve basic percent problems.

Translate to an equation. Do not solve.

1. 12% of 50 is what?

2. What is 40% of 60?

Translate to an equation. Do not solve.

3. 45 is 20% of what?

4. 120% of what is 60?

a Translating to Equations

To solve a problem involving percents, it is helpful to translate first to an equation. To distinguish the method in Section 6.3 from that of Section 6.4, we will call these *percent equations*.

EXAMPLE 1 Translate:

$$
\begin{array}{ccccc}
23\% & \text{of} & 5 & \text{is} & \text{what?} \\
\downarrow & \downarrow & \downarrow & \downarrow & \downarrow \\
23\% & \cdot & 5 & = & a
\end{array}
$$

This is a *percent equation*.

KEY WORDS IN PERCENT TRANSLATIONS	
"**Of**" translates to "·", or "×".	"**Is**" translates to "=".
"**What**" translates to any letter.	"**%**" translates to "$\times \frac{1}{100}$" or "$\times 0.01$".

EXAMPLE 2 Translate:

$$
\begin{array}{ccccc}
\text{What} & \text{is} & 11\% & \text{of} & 49? \\
\downarrow & \downarrow & \downarrow & \downarrow & \downarrow \\
a & = & 11\% & \cdot & 49
\end{array}
$$

Any letter can be used.

Do Exercises 1 and 2.

EXAMPLE 3 Translate:

$$
\begin{array}{ccccc}
3 & \text{is} & 10\% & \text{of} & \text{what?} \\
\downarrow & \downarrow & \downarrow & \downarrow & \downarrow \\
3 & = & 10\% & \cdot & b
\end{array}
$$

EXAMPLE 4 Translate:

$$
\begin{array}{ccccc}
45\% & \text{of} & \text{what} & \text{is} & 23? \\
\downarrow & \downarrow & \downarrow & \downarrow & \downarrow \\
45\% & \times & b & = & 23
\end{array}
$$

Do Exercises 3 and 4.

EXAMPLE 5 Translate:

$$
\begin{array}{cccc}
10 & \text{is} & \text{what percent} & \text{of} \quad 20? \\
\downarrow & \downarrow & \downarrow & \downarrow \quad \downarrow \\
10 & = & p & \times \quad 20
\end{array}
$$

EXAMPLE 6 Translate:

$$\underbrace{\text{What percent}}_{p} \quad \underset{\cdot}{\text{of}} \quad \underset{50}{50} \quad \underset{=}{\text{is}} \quad \underset{7}{7?}$$

Do Exercises 5 and 6.

b | Solving Percent Problems

In solving percent problems, we use the *Translate* and *Solve* steps in the problem-solving strategy used throughout this text.

Percent problems are actually of three different types. Although the method we present does *not* require that you be able to identify which type you are solving, it is helpful to know them.

We know that

15 is 25% of 60,   or $15 = 25\% \times 60$.

We can think of this as:

> Amount = Percent number × Base.

Each of the three types of percent problems depends on which of the three pieces of information is missing.

1. **Finding the *amount* (the result of taking the percent)**

   Example: $\quad$ What $\quad$ is $\quad$ 25% $\quad$ of $\quad$ 60?

   Translation: $\quad a \quad = \quad 25\% \quad \cdot \quad 60$

2. **Finding the *base* (the number you are taking the percent of)**

   Example: $\quad$ 15 $\quad$ is $\quad$ 25% $\quad$ of $\quad$ what number?

   Translation: $\quad$ 15 $\quad = \quad 25\% \quad \cdot \quad b$

3. **Finding the *percent number* (the percent itself)**

   Example: $\quad$ 15 $\quad$ is $\quad$ what percent $\quad$ of $\quad$ 60?

   Translation: $\quad$ 15 $\quad = \quad p \quad \cdot \quad 60$

FINDING THE AMOUNT

EXAMPLE 7 What is 4.6% of 105,000,000?

Translate: $a = 4.6\% \times 105,000,000$.

Solve: The letter is by itself. To solve the equation, we just convert 4.6% to decimal notation and multiply:

$$a = 4.6\% \times 105,000,000$$
$$= 0.046 \times 105,000,000 = 4,830,000.$$

Thus, 4,830,000 is 4.6% of 105,000,000. The answer is 4,830,000.

Do Exercise 7.

Translate to an equation. Do not solve.

5. 16 is what percent of 40?

6. What percent of 84 is 10.5?

7. Solve:

What is 12% of 50?

Answers on page A-14

There are 105,000,000 households in the United States and approximately 4.6% own a pet bird. How many households own at least one pet bird?

6.3 Solving Percent Problems
Using Percent Equations

8. Solve:

64% of $55 is what?

In a survey of a group of people, it was found that 5%, or 20 people, chose strawberry as their favorite ice cream. How many people were surveyed?

Source: International Ice Cream Association

Solve.

9. 20% of what is 45?

10. $60 is 120% of what?

EXAMPLE 8   120% of $42 is what?

Translate: $120\% \times 42 = a$.

Solve: The letter is by itself. To solve the equation, we carry out the calculation:

$$a = 120\% \times 42$$
$$= 1.2 \times 42 \qquad 120\% = 1.2$$
$$= 50.4.$$

Thus, 120% of $42 is $50.40. The answer is $50.40.

Do Exercise 8.

FINDING THE BASE

EXAMPLE 9   5% of what is 20?

Translate: $5\% \times b = 20$.

Solve: This time the letter is *not* by itself. To solve the equation, we divide by 5% on both sides:

$$\frac{5\% \times b}{5\%} = \frac{20}{5\%} \qquad \text{Dividing by 5\% on both sides}$$

$$b = \frac{20}{0.05} \qquad 5\% = 0.05$$

$$b = 400.$$

Thus, 5% of 400 is 20. The answer is 400.

EXAMPLE 10 $3 is 16% of what?

Translate: $3 \quad \text{is} \quad 16\% \quad \text{of what?}$

$$3 \quad = \quad 16\% \quad \times \quad b.$$

Solve: Again, the letter is *not* by itself. To solve the equation, we divide by 16% on both sides:

$$\frac{3}{16\%} = \frac{16\% \times b}{16\%} \qquad \text{Dividing by 16\% on both sides}$$

$$\frac{3}{0.16} = b \qquad 16\% = 0.16$$

$$18.75 = b.$$

Thus, $3 is 16% of $18.75. The answer is $18.75.

Do Exercises 9 and 10.

Answers on page A-14

FINDING THE PERCENT NUMBER

In solving these problems, you *must* remember to convert to percent notation after you have solved the equation.

EXAMPLE 11   13 is what percent of 260?

Translate: 13   is   what percent   of   260?

$$13 \quad = \quad p \quad \times \quad 260.$$

Solve: To solve the equation, we divide by 260 on both sides and convert the result to percent notation:

$$p \cdot 260 = 13$$

$$\frac{p \cdot 260}{260} = \frac{13}{260} \qquad \text{Dividing by 260 on both sides}$$

$$p = 0.05 \qquad \text{Converting to decimal notation}$$

$$p = 5\%. \qquad \text{Converting to percent notation}$$

Thus, 13 is 5% of 260. The answer is 5%.

Do Exercise 11.

EXAMPLE 12   What percent of $50 is $16?

Translate: What percent   of $50   is $16?

$$p \quad \times \quad 50 \quad = \quad 16.$$

Solve: To solve the equation, we divide by 50 on both sides and convert the answer to percent notation:

$$\frac{p \times 50}{50} = \frac{16}{50} \qquad \text{Dividing by 50 on both sides}$$

$$p = \frac{16}{50}$$

$$p = 0.32$$

$$p = 32\%. \qquad \text{Converting to percent notation}$$

Thus, 32% of $50 is $16. The answer is 32%.

Do Exercise 12.

> **Caution!**
>
> When a question asks "what percent?", be sure to give the answer in percent notation.

Workers in the United States on the average get 13 vacation days per year. What percent of the 260 work days per year are vacation days?

11. Solve:

16 is what percent of 40?

12. Solve:

What percent of $84 is $10.50?

Answers on page A-14

CALCULATOR CORNER

Using Percents in Computations   Many calculators have a $\boxed{\%}$ key that can be used in computations. (See the Calculator Corner on page 343.) For example, to find 11% of 49, we press $\boxed{1}\ \boxed{1}\ \boxed{\text{2nd}}\ \boxed{\%}\ \boxed{\times}$ $\boxed{4}\ \boxed{9}\ \boxed{=}$ or $\boxed{4}\ \boxed{9}\ \boxed{\times}\ \boxed{1}\ \boxed{1}\ \boxed{\text{SHIFT}}\ \boxed{\%}$. The display reads $\boxed{\quad 5.39}$, so 11% of 49 is 5.39.

In Example 9, we perform the computation 20/5%. To use the $\boxed{\%}$ key in this computation, we press $\boxed{2}\ \boxed{0}\ \boxed{\div}\ \boxed{5}\ \boxed{\text{2nd}}\ \boxed{\%}\ \boxed{=}$, or $\boxed{2}\ \boxed{0}\ \boxed{\div}\ \boxed{5}\ \boxed{\text{SHIFT}}\ \boxed{\%}$. The result is 400.

We can also use the $\boxed{\%}$ key to find the percent number in a problem. In Example 11, for instance, we answer the question "13 is what percent of 260?" On a calculator, we press $\boxed{1}\ \boxed{3}\ \boxed{\div}\ \boxed{2}\ \boxed{6}\ \boxed{0}\ \boxed{\text{2nd}}\ \boxed{\%}\ \boxed{=}$, or $\boxed{1}\ \boxed{3}\ \boxed{\div}\ \boxed{2}\ \boxed{6}\ \boxed{0}\ \boxed{\text{SHIFT}}\ \boxed{\%}$. The result is 5, so 13 is 5% of 260.

Exercises: Use a calculator to find each of the following.

1. What is 5% of 24?
2. What is 12.6% of $40?
3. What is 19% of 256?
4. 140% of $16 is what?
5. 0.04% of 28 is what?
6. 33% of $90 is what?
7. 8% of what is 36?
8. $45 is 4.5% of what?
9. 23 is what percent of 920?
10. What percent of $442 is $53.04?

6.3

EXERCISE SET
For Extra Help

MathXL MyMathLab InterAct Math Tutor Digital Video Student's
Math Center Tutor CD 3 Solutions
Videotape 6 Manual

a Translate to an equation. Do not solve.

1. What is 32% of 78?

2. 98% of 57 is what?

3. 89 is what percent of 99?

4. What percent of 25 is 8?

5. 13 is 25% of what?

6. 21.4% of what is 20?

b Translate to an equation and solve.

7. What is 85% of 276?

8. What is 74% of 53?

9. 150% of 30 is what?

10. 100% of 13 is what?

11. What is 6% of $300?

12. What is 4% of $45?

13. 3.8% of 50 is what?

14. $33\frac{1}{3}\%$ of 480 is what?
$\left(Hint:\ 33\frac{1}{3}\% = \frac{1}{3}.\right)$

15. $39 is what percent of $50?

16. $16 is what percent of $90?

17. 20 is what percent of 10?

18. 60 is what percent of 20?

19. What percent of $300 is $150?

20. What percent of $50 is $40?

21. What percent of 80 is 100?

22. What percent of 60 is 15?

23. 20 is 50% of what?

24. 57 is 20% of what?

25. 40% of what is $16?

26. 100% of what is $74?

27. 56.32 is 64% of what?

28. 71.04 is 96% of what?

29. 70% of what is 14?

30. 70% of what is 35?

31. What is $62\frac{1}{2}\%$ of 10?

32. What is $35\frac{1}{4}\%$ of 1200?

33. What is 8.3% of $10,200?

34. What is 9.2% of $5600?

35. **D**_{**W**} Write a question that could be translated to the equation

$$25 = 4\% \times b.$$

36. **D**_{**W**} Suppose we know that 40% of 92 is 36.8. What is a quick way to find 4% of 92? 400% of 92? Explain.

Write fraction notation.   [4.1b]

37. 0.09

38. 1.79

39. 0.875

40. 0.125

41. 0.9375

42. 0.6875

Write decimal notation.   [4.1b]

43. $\dfrac{89}{100}$

44. $\dfrac{7}{100}$

45. $\dfrac{3}{10}$

46. $\dfrac{17}{1000}$

Solve.

47. 🖩 What is 7.75% of $10,880?
Estimate _____
Calculate _____

48. 🖩 50,951.775 is what percent of 78,995?
Estimate _____
Calculate _____

49. 🖩 $2496 is 24% of what amount?
Estimate _____
Calculate _____

50. 🖩 What is 38.2% of $52,345.79?
Estimate _____
Calculate _____

51. 40% of $18\frac{3}{4}\%$ of $25,000 is what?

6.4 SOLVING PERCENT PROBLEMS USING PROPORTIONS*

Objectives

a Translate percent problems to proportions.

b Solve basic percent problems.

a Translating to Proportions

A percent is a ratio of some number to 100. For example, 47% is the ratio $\frac{47}{100}$. The numbers 68,859,700 and 146,510,000 have the same ratio as 47 and 100.

$$\frac{47}{100} = \frac{68,859,700}{146,510,000}$$

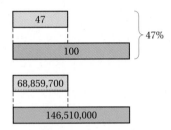

To solve a percent problem using a proportion, we translate as follows:

Number → $\dfrac{N}{100} = \dfrac{a}{b}$ ← Amount
100 ──→ $\phantom{\dfrac{N}{100}}$ ← Base

> You might find it helpful to read this as "part is to whole as part is to whole."

For example, 60% of 25 is 15 translates to

$$\frac{60}{100} = \frac{15}{25}. \quad \begin{array}{l} \leftarrow \text{Amount} \\ \leftarrow \text{Base} \end{array}$$

A clue in translating is that the base, b, corresponds to 100 and usually follows the wording "percent of." Also, $N\%$ always translates to $N/100$. Another aid in translating is to make a comparison drawing. To do this, we start with the percent side and list 0% at the top and 100% near the bottom. Then we estimate where the specified percent—in this case, 60%—is located. The corresponding quantities are then filled in. The base—in this case, 25—always corresponds to 100% and the amount—in this case, 15—corresponds to the specified percent.

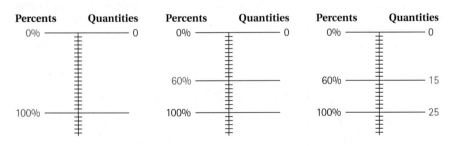

The proportion can then be read easily from the drawing: $\dfrac{60}{100} = \dfrac{15}{25}$.

In the United States, 47% of the labor force are women. In 2003, there were 146,510,000 people in the labor force. This means that 68,859,700 were women.

Sources: U.S. Department of Labor, Bureau of Labor Statistics

> *Note: This section presents an alternative method for solving basic percent problems. You can use either equations or proportions to solve percent problems, but you might prefer one method over the other, or your instructor may direct you to use one method over the other.

Translate to a proportion. Do not solve.

1. 12% of 50 is what?

EXAMPLE 1 Translate to a proportion.

23% of 5 is what?

$$\frac{23}{100} = \frac{a}{5}$$

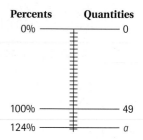

Percents	Quantities
0%	0
23%	a
100%	5

2. What is 40% of 60?

EXAMPLE 2 Translate to a proportion.

What is 124% of 49?

$$\frac{124}{100} = \frac{a}{49}$$

Percents	Quantities
0%	0
100%	49
124%	a

Do Exercises 1–3.

3. 130% of 72 is what?

EXAMPLE 3 Translate to a proportion.

3 is 10% of what?

$$\frac{10}{100} = \frac{3}{b}$$

Percents	Quantities
0%	0
10%	3
100%	b

Translate to a proportion. Do not solve.

4. 45 is 20% of what?

EXAMPLE 4 Translate to a proportion.

45% of what is 23?

$$\frac{45}{100} = \frac{23}{b}$$

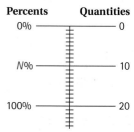

Percents	Quantities
0%	0
45%	23
100%	b

Do Exercises 4 and 5.

5. 120% of what is 60?

EXAMPLE 5 Translate to a proportion.

10 is what percent of 20?

$$\frac{N}{100} = \frac{10}{20}$$

Percents	Quantities
0%	0
N%	10
100%	20

Answers on page A-14

EXAMPLE 6   Translate to a proportion.

What percent of 50 is 7?

$$\frac{N}{100} = \frac{7}{50}$$

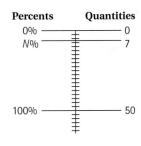

Translate to a proportion. Do not solve.

6. 16 is what percent of 40?

Do Exercises 6 and 7.

b   Solving Percent Problems

After a percent problem has been translated to a proportion, we solve as in Section 5.3.

7. What percent of 84 is 10.5?

EXAMPLE 7   5% of what is $20?

Translate: $\dfrac{5}{100} = \dfrac{20}{b}$

Solve: $5 \cdot b = 100 \cdot 20$ Equating cross products

$\dfrac{5 \cdot b}{5} = \dfrac{100 \cdot 20}{5}$ Dividing by 5

$b = \dfrac{2000}{5}$

$b = 400$ Simplifying

Thus, 5% of $400 is $20. The answer is $400.

8. Solve:

20% of what is $45?

Do Exercise 8.

EXAMPLE 8   120% of 42 is what?

Translate: $\dfrac{120}{100} = \dfrac{a}{42}$

Solve: $120 \cdot 42 = 100 \cdot a$ Equating cross products

$\dfrac{120 \cdot 42}{100} = \dfrac{100 \cdot a}{100}$ Dividing by 100

$\dfrac{5040}{100} = a$

$50.4 = a$ Simplifying

Thus, 120% of 42 is 50.4. The answer is 50.4.

Solve.
9. 64% of 55 is what?

10. What is 12% of 50?

Do Exercises 9 and 10.

Answers on page A-14

11. Solve:

60 is 120% of what?

12. Solve:

$12 is what percent of $40?

13. Solve:

What percent of 84 is 10.5?

EXAMPLE 9 3 is 16% of what?

Translate: $\dfrac{3}{b} = \dfrac{16}{100}$

Solve: $3 \cdot 100 = b \cdot 16$ Equating cross products

$\dfrac{3 \cdot 100}{16} = \dfrac{b \cdot 16}{16}$ Dividing by 16

$\dfrac{300}{16} = b$ Multiplying and simplifying

$18.75 = b$ Dividing

Thus, 3 is 16% of 18.75. The answer is 18.75.

Percents		Quantities
0%		0
16%		3
100%		b

Do Exercise 11.

EXAMPLE 10 $10 is what percent of $20?

Translate: $\dfrac{10}{20} = \dfrac{N}{100}$

Solve: $10 \cdot 100 = 20 \cdot N$ Equating cross products

$\dfrac{10 \cdot 100}{20} = \dfrac{20 \cdot N}{20}$ Dividing by 20

$\dfrac{1000}{20} = N$ Multiplying and simplifying

$50 = N$ Dividing

Thus, $10 is 50% of $20. The answer is 50%.

Percents		Quantities
0%		0
N%		$10
100%		$20

Do Exercise 12.

EXAMPLE 11 What percent of 50 is 16?

Translate: $\dfrac{N}{100} = \dfrac{16}{50}$

Solve: $50 \cdot N = 100 \cdot 16$ Equating cross products

$\dfrac{50 \cdot N}{50} = \dfrac{100 \cdot 16}{50}$ Dividing by 50

$N = \dfrac{1600}{50}$ Multiplying and simplifying

$N = 32$ Dividing

Thus, 32% of 50 is 16. The answer is 32%.

Percents		Quantities
0%		0
N%		16
100%		50

Do Exercise 13.

Answers on page A-14

a   Translate to a proportion. Do not solve.

1. What is 37% of 74?

2. 66% of 74 is what?

3. 4.3 is what percent of 5.9?

4. What percent of 6.8 is 5.3?

5. 14 is 25% of what?

6. 133% of what is 40?

b   Translate to a proportion and solve.

7. What is 76% of 90?

8. What is 32% of 70?

9. 70% of 660 is what?

10. 80% of 920 is what?

11. What is 4% of 1000?

12. What is 6% of 2000?

13. 4.8% of 60 is what?

14. 63.1% of 80 is what?

15. $24 is what percent of $96?

16. $14 is what percent of $70?

17. 102 is what percent of 100?

18. 103 is what percent of 100?

19. What percent of $480 is $120?

20. What percent of $80 is $60?

21. What percent of 160 is 150?

22. What percent of 33 is 11?

23. $18 is 25% of what?

24. $75 is 20% of what?

25. 60% of what is 54?

26. 80% of what is 96?

27. 65.12 is 74% of what?

28. 63.7 is 65% of what?

29. 80% of what is 16?

30. 80% of what is 10?

31. What is $62\frac{1}{2}$% of 40?

32. What is $43\frac{1}{4}$% of 2600?

33. What is 9.4% of $8300?

34. What is 8.7% of $76,000?

35. D_W In your own words, list steps that a classmate could use to solve any percent problem in this section.

36. D_W In solving Example 10, a student simplifies $\frac{10}{20}$ before solving. Is this a good idea? Why or why not?

SKILL MAINTENANCE

Solve. [5.3b]

37. $\dfrac{x}{188} = \dfrac{2}{47}$

38. $\dfrac{15}{x} = \dfrac{3}{800}$

39. $\dfrac{4}{7} = \dfrac{x}{14}$

40. $\dfrac{612}{t} = \dfrac{72}{244}$

41. $\dfrac{5000}{t} = \dfrac{3000}{60}$

42. $\dfrac{75}{100} = \dfrac{n}{20}$

43. $\dfrac{x}{1.2} = \dfrac{36.2}{5.4}$

44. $\dfrac{y}{1\frac{1}{2}} = \dfrac{2\frac{3}{4}}{22}$

Solve.

45. A recipe for muffins calls for $\frac{1}{2}$ qt of buttermilk, $\frac{1}{3}$ qt of skim milk, and $\frac{1}{16}$ qt of oil. How many quarts of liquid ingredients does the recipe call for? [3.2b]

46. The Ferristown School District purchased $\frac{3}{4}$ ton (T) of clay. If the clay is to be shared equally among the district's 6 art departments, how much will each art department receive? [2.7d]

SYNTHESIS

Solve.

47. 🖩 What is 8.85% of $12,640?

Estimate _____

Calculate _____

48. 🖩 78.8% of what is 9809.024?

Estimate _____

Calculate _____

370

6.5 APPLICATIONS OF PERCENT

Objectives

a Solve applied problems involving percent.

b Solve applied problems involving percent of increase or decrease.

a Applied Problems Involving Percent

Applied problems involving percent are not always stated in a manner easily translated to an equation. In such cases, it is helpful to rephrase the problem before translating. Sometimes it also helps to make a drawing.

EXAMPLE 1 *Presidential Deaths in Office.* George W. Bush was inaugurated as the 43rd President of the United States in 2001. Since Grover Cleveland was both the 22nd and the 24th presidents, there have been only 42 different presidents. Of the 42 presidents, 8 have died in office: William Henry Harrison, Zachary Taylor, Abraham Lincoln, James A. Garfield, William McKinley, Warren G. Harding, Franklin D. Roosevelt, and John F. Kennedy. What percent have died in office?

Harrison   Taylor   Garfield   McKinley

Harding   Roosevelt   Kennedy

1. **Familiarize.** The question asks for a percent of the presidents who have died in office. We note that 42 is approximately 40 and 8 is $\frac{1}{5}$, or 20%, of 40, so our answer is close to 20%. We let p = the percent who have died in office.

2. **Translate.** There are two ways in which we can translate this problem.

Percent equation (see Section 6.3):

8   is   what percent   of   42?
↓   ↓   ↓   ↓   ↓
8   =   p   ·   42

Proportion (see Section 6.4):

$$\frac{N}{100} = \frac{8}{42}$$

For proportions, $N\% = p$.

Percents	Quantities
0%	0
N%	8
100%	42

Study Tips

MAKING APPLICATIONS REAL

Newspapers and magazines are full of mathematical applications. Some of the easiest ones to find in the area of Basic Mathematics are about percent. Find such an application and share it with your class. As you obtain more skills in mathematics, you will find yourself observing the world from a different perspective, seeing mathematics everywhere. Math courses become more interesting when we connect the concepts to the real world.

1. Presidential Assassinations in Office. Of the 42 U.S. presidents, 4 have been assassinated in office. These were Garfield, McKinley, Lincoln, and Kennedy. What percent have been assassinated in office?

3. Solve. We now have two ways in which to solve this problem.

Percent equation (see Section 6.3):

$$8 = p \cdot 42$$

$$\frac{8}{42} = \frac{p \cdot 42}{42} \qquad \text{Dividing by 42 on both sides}$$

$$\frac{8}{42} = p$$

$$0.190 \approx p \qquad \text{Finding decimal notation and rounding to the nearest thousandth}$$

$$19.0\% \approx p \qquad \text{Remember to find percent notation.}$$

Note here that the solution, p, includes the % symbol.

Proportion (see Section 6.4):

$$\frac{N}{100} = \frac{8}{42}$$

$$N \cdot 42 = 100 \cdot 8 \qquad \text{Equating cross products}$$

$$\frac{N \cdot 42}{42} = \frac{800}{42} \qquad \text{Dividing by 42 on both sides}$$

$$N = \frac{800}{42}$$

$$N \approx 19.0 \qquad \text{Dividing and rounding to the nearest tenth}$$

We use the solution of the proportion to express the answer to the problem as 19.0%. Note that in the proportion method, $N\% = p$.

4. Check. To check, we note that the answer 19.0% is close to 20%, as estimated in the *Familiarize* step.

5. State. About 19.0% of the U.S. presidents have died in office.

Do Exercise 1.

EXAMPLE 2 *Transportation to Work.* In the 15 largest cities in the United States, there are about 130,000,000 workers 16 years and over. Approximately 76.3% drive to work alone. How many workers in these 15 cities drive to work alone?

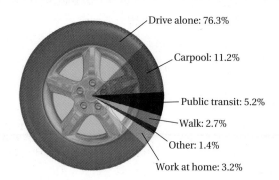

Transportation to Work (in the 15 Largest Cities in the United States)

Drive alone: 76.3%

Carpool: 11.2%

Public transit: 5.2%

Walk: 2.7%

Other: 1.4%

Work at home: 3.2%

Source: U.S. Bureau of the Census

Answer on page A-14

1. **Familiarize.** We can make a drawing of a pie chart to help familiarize ourselves with the problem. We let b = the total number of workers who drive to work alone.

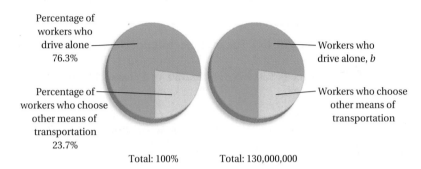

Transportation to Work

Percentage of workers who drive alone 76.3%

Percentage of workers who choose other means of transportation 23.7%

Workers who drive alone, b

Workers who choose other means of transportation

Total: 100% Total: 130,000,000

2. **Transportation to Work.** There are about 130,000,000 workers 16 years or over in the 15 largest cities in the United States. Approximately 11.2% carpool to work. How many workers in these 15 cities carpool to work?

Source: U.S. Bureau of the Census

2. **Translate.** There are two ways in which we can translate this problem.

Percent equation:

What number is 76.3% of 130,000,000?

$b \quad = \quad 76.3\% \quad \cdot \quad 130,000,000$

Proportion:

$$\frac{76.3}{100} = \frac{b}{130,000,000}$$

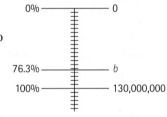

Percents   Quantities
0% —— 0

76.3% —— b
100% —— 130,000,000

3. **Solve.** We now have two ways in which to solve this problem.

Percent equation:

$b = 76.3\% \cdot 130,000,000$

We convert 76.3% to decimal notation and multiply:

$b = 0.763 \times 130,000,000 = 99,190,000.$

Proportion:

$$\frac{76.3}{100} = \frac{b}{130,000,000}$$

$76.3 \times 130,000,000 = 100 \cdot b$ \qquad Equating cross products

$$\frac{76.3 \cdot 130,000,000}{100} = \frac{100 \cdot b}{100}$$ \qquad Dividing by 100

$$\frac{9,919,000,000}{100} = b$$

$99,190,000 = b$ \qquad Simplifying

4. **Check.** To check, we can repeat the calculations. We can also do a partial check by estimating. Since 76.3% is about 80%, or $\frac{4}{5}$, and $\frac{4}{5}$ of 130,000,000 is 104,000,000 and 104,000,000 is close to 99,190,000, our answer is reasonable.

5. **State.** The number of workers in the 15 largest cities who drive to work alone is 99,190,000.

Answer on page A-14

Do Exercise 2.

3. Percent of Increase. The value of a car is $36,875. The price is increased by 4%.

a) How much is the increase?

b) What is the new price?

b   Percent of Increase or Decrease

Percent is often used to state increase or decrease. Let's consider an example of each, using the price of a car as the original number.

PERCENT OF INCREASE

One year a car sold for $20,455. The manufacturer decides to raise the price of the following year's model by 6%. The increase is $0.06 \times$ $20,455, or $1227.30. The new price is $20,455 + $1227.30, or $21,682.30. The *percent of increase* is 6%.

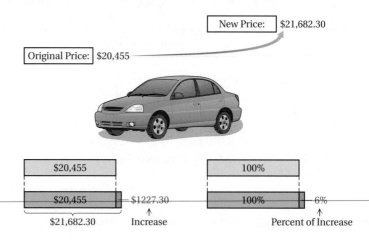

PERCENT OF DECREASE

4. Percent of Decrease. The value of a car is $36,875. The car depreciates in value by 25% after one year.

a) How much is the decrease?

b) What is the depreciated value of the car?

Lisa buys the car listed above for $20,455. After one year, the car depreciates in value by 25%. This is $0.25 \times$ $20,455, or $5113.75. This lowers the value of the car to

$$20,455 - $5113.75, \quad \text{or} \quad $15,341.25.$$

Note that the new price is thus 75% of the original price. If Lisa decides to sell the car after a year, $15,341.25 might be the most she could expect to get for it. The *percent of decrease* is 25%, and the decrease is $5113.75.

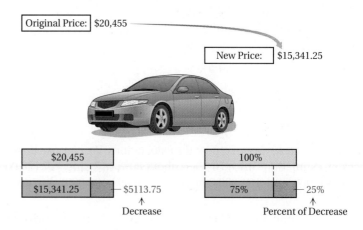

Answers on page A-14

Do Exercises 3 and 4.

When a quantity is decreased by a certain percent, we say we have **percent of decrease.**

EXAMPLE 3 *Chain Link Fence.* For one week only, Sam's Farm Supply had 4 ft × 50 ft rolls of galvanized chain link fence on sale for $39.99. The regular price was $49.99 per roll. What was the percent of decrease?

1. Familiarize. We find the amount of decrease and then make a drawing.

$$\begin{array}{r} 4\ 9.9\ 9 \\ -\ 3\ 9.9\ 9 \\ \hline 1\ 0.0\ 0 \end{array}$$ Retail price / Sale price / Decrease

$49.99		100%	
$39.99	—$10.00		—?%

2. Translate. There are two ways in which we can translate this problem.

Percent equation:

$$\underbrace{10.00}\ \underbrace{\text{is}}\ \underbrace{\text{what percent}}\ \underbrace{\text{of}}\ \underbrace{49.99?}$$
$$10.00\ =\ p\ \times\ 49.99$$

Proportion:

$$\frac{N}{100} = \frac{10.00}{49.99}$$

For proportions, $N\% = p$.

3. Solve. We have two ways in which to solve this problem.

Percent equation:

$$10.00 = p \times 49.99$$

$$\frac{10.00}{49.99} = \frac{p \times 49.99}{49.99} \qquad \text{Dividing by 49.99 on both sides}$$

$$\frac{10.00}{49.99} = p$$

$$0.20 \approx p$$

$$20\% \approx p \qquad \text{Converting to percent notation}$$

Proportion:

$$\frac{N}{100} = \frac{10.00}{49.99}$$

$$49.99 \times N = 100 \times 10 \qquad \text{Equating cross products}$$

$$\frac{49.99 \times N}{49.99} = \frac{100 \times 10}{49.99} \qquad \text{Dividing by 49.99 on both sides}$$

$$N = \frac{1000}{49.99}$$

$$N \approx 20$$

We use the solution of the proportion to express the answer to the problem as 20%.

Percents — **Quantities**
0% — 0
N% — 10.00
100% — 49.99

5. Volume of Mail. The volume of U.S. mail decreased from about 208 billion pieces of mail in 2000 to 202 billion pieces in 2003. What was the percent of decrease?
Source: U.S. Postal Service

Answer on page A-14

4. Check. To check, we note that, with a 20% decrease, the reduced (or sale) price should be 80% of the retail (or original) price. Since

$$80\% \times 49.99 = 0.80 \times 49.99 = 39.992 \approx 39.99,$$

our answer checks.

5. State. The percent of decrease in the price of the roll of fence was 20%.

Do Exercise 5 on the preceding page.

When a quantity is increased by a certain percent, we say we have **percent of increase.**

EXAMPLE 4 *Motor Vehicle Production.* The number of motor vehicles produced worldwide increased from approximately 57.5 million in 2000 to 60.3 million in 2003. What was the percent of increase in motor vehicle production?

Source: Ward's Communications, *Ward's Motor Vehicle Facts & Figures,* 2004

1. Familiarize. We first note that the increase in the number of vehicles produced was 60.3 − 57.5 million, or 2.8 million. A drawing can help us visualize the situation.

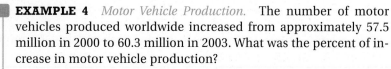

We are asking this question: The increase is what percent of the *original* amount? We let p = the percent of increase.

2. Translate. There are two ways in which we can translate this problem.

Percent equation:

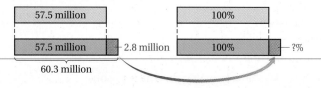

Proportion:

$$\frac{N}{100} = \frac{2.8}{57.5}$$

For proportions, $N\% = p$.

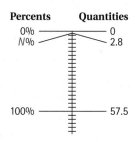

3. Solve. We have two ways in which to solve this problem.

Percent equation:

$$2.8 = p \cdot 57.5$$

$$\frac{2.8}{57.5} = \frac{p \times 57.5}{57.5} \qquad \text{Dividing by 57.5 on both sides}$$

$$\frac{2.8}{57.5} = p$$

$$0.049 \approx p$$

$$4.9\% \approx p \qquad \text{Converting to percent notation}$$

Proportion:

$$\frac{N}{100} = \frac{2.8}{57.5}$$

$$57.5 \times N = 100 \times 2.8 \qquad \text{Equating cross products}$$

$$\frac{57.5 \times N}{57.5} = \frac{100 \times 2.8}{57.5} \qquad \text{Dividing by 57.5 on both sides}$$

$$N = \frac{280}{57.5}$$

$$N \approx 4.9$$

We use the solution of the proportion to express the answer to the problem as 4.9%.

4. Check. To check, we take 4.9% of 57.5:

$$4.9\% \times 57.5 = 0.049 \times 57.5 = 2.8175.$$

Since we rounded the percent, this approximation is close enough to 2.8 to be a good check.

5. State. The percent of increase in the number of motor vehicles produced is 4.9%.

Do Exercise 6.

6. Patents Issued. The number of patents issued per year by the U.S. government increased from 107,332 in 1993 to 189,597 in 2003. What was the percent of increase over the ten-year period?

Source: U.S. Patent and Trademark Office

Answer on page A-14

Translating
for Success

The goal of these matching questions is to practice step (2), *Translate*, of the five-step problem-solving process. Translate each word problem to an equation and select a correct translation from equations A–O.

1. *Distance Walked.* After knee replacement, Alex walked $\frac{1}{8}$ mi each morning and $\frac{1}{5}$ mi each afternoon. How much farther did he walk in the afternoon?

2. *Stock Prices.* A stock sold for $5 per share on Monday and only $2\frac{1}{8}$ per share on Friday. What was the percent of decrease from Monday to Friday?

3. *SAT Score.* After attending a class titled *Improving Your SAT Scores,* Jacob raised his total score from 884 to 1040. What was the percent of increase?

4. *Change in Population.* The population of a small farming community decreased from 1040 to 884. What was the percent of decrease?

5. *Lawn Mowing.* During the summer, brothers Steve and Rob earned money for college by mowing lawns. The largest lawn they mowed was $2\frac{1}{8}$ acres. Steve can mow $\frac{1}{5}$ acre per hour, and Rob can mow only $\frac{1}{8}$ acre per hour. Working together, how many acres did they mow per hour?

6. *Land Sale.* Cole sold $2\frac{1}{8}$ acres from the 5 acres he inherited from his uncle. What percent did he sell?

7. *Travel Expenses.* A magazine photographer is reimbursed 16.25¢ per mile for business travel up to 1000 miles per week. In a recent week, he traveled only 250 miles. What was the total reimbursement for travel?

8. *Trip Expenses.* The total expenses for Claire's recent business trip were $1040. She put $884 on her charge card and paid the balance in cash. What percent did she place on her charge card?

9. *Cost of Copies.* During the first summer session at a community college, the campus copy center advertised 250 copies for $16.25. At this rate, what is the cost of 1000 copies?

10. *Cost of Insurance.* Following a raise in the cost of health insurance, 250 of a company's 1040 employees dropped their health coverage. What percent of the employees canceled their insurance?

A. $x + \dfrac{1}{5} = \dfrac{1}{8}$

B. $250 = x \cdot 1040$

C. $884 = x \cdot 1040$

D. $\dfrac{250}{16.25} = \dfrac{1000}{x}$

E. $156 = x \cdot 1040$

F. $16.25 = 250 \cdot x$

G. $\dfrac{1}{5} + \dfrac{1}{8} = x$

H. $2\dfrac{1}{8} = x \cdot 5$

I. $5 = 2\dfrac{7}{8} \cdot x$

J. $\dfrac{1}{8} + x = \dfrac{1}{5}$

K. $1040 = x \cdot 884$

L. $\dfrac{250}{16.25} = \dfrac{x}{1000}$

M. $2\dfrac{7}{8} = x \cdot 5$

N. $x \cdot 884 = 156$

O. $x = 16.25 \cdot 250$

Answers on page A-14

6.5

EXERCISE SET

For Extra Help

MathXL MyMathLab InterAct Math Tutor Center Math Tutor Center Digital Video Tutor CD 3 Videotape 6 Student's Solutions Manual

a Solve.

1. *Wild Horses.*   There are 27,369 wild horses on land managed by the Federal Bureau of Land Management. It is estimated that 48.4% of this total is in Nevada. How many wild horses are in Nevada?

Source: Bureau of Land Management, 2005

2. *U.S. Armed Forces*   There are 1,168,195 people in the United States in active military service. The numbers in the four armed services are listed in the table below. What percent of the total does each branch represent? Round the answers to the nearest tenth of a percent.

U.S. ARMED FORCES WORLDWIDE, 2004	
Total	1,168,195
Air Force	314,477
Army	391,126
Marine Corps	135,324
Navy	327,268

Source: U.S. Department of Defense

3. *Car Value.*   The base price of a Nissan 350Z is $34,000. This vehicle is expected to retain 62% of its value at the end of three years and 52% at the end of five years. What is the value of a Nissan 350Z after three years? after five years?

Source: November/December *Kelley Blue Book Residual Values Guide*

4. *Panda Survival.*   Breeding the much-loved panda bear in captivity has been quite difficult for zookeepers.

a) From 1964 to 1997, of 133 panda cubs born in captivity, only 90 lived to be one month old. What percent lived to be one month old?

b) In 1999, Mark Edwards of the San Diego Zoo developed a nutritional formula on which 18 of 20 newborns lived to be one month old. What percent lived to be one month old?

5. *Overweight and Obese.*   Of the 294 million people in the United States, 60% are considered overweight and 25% are considered obese. How many are overweight? How many are obese?

Source: U.S. Centers for Disease Control

6. *Smoking and Diabetes.*   Of the 294 million people in the United States, 26% are smokers. How many are smokers?

Source: SAMHSA, Office of Applied Studies, National Survey on Drug Use and Health

7. A lab technician has 680 mL of a solution of water and acid; 3% is acid. How many milliliters are acid? water?

8. A lab technician has 540 mL of a solution of alcohol and water; 8% is alcohol. How many milliliters are alcohol? water?

9. *Mississippi River.* The Mississippi River, which extends from Minneapolis, Minnesota, to the Gulf of Mexico, is 2348 miles long. Approximately 77% of the river is navigable. How many miles of the river are navigable?

Source: National Oceanic and Atmospheric Administration

Mississippi River

10. *Immigrants.* In 2003, 705,827 immigrants entered the United States. Of this total, 16.4% were from Mexico and 7.1% were from India. How many immigrants came from Mexico? from India?

Source: U.S. Department of Justice, *2003 Yearbook of Immigration Statistics*

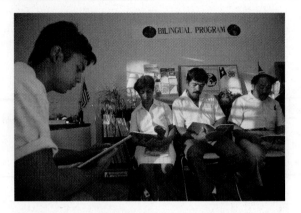

11. *Hispanic Population.* The Hispanic population is growing rapidly in the United States. In 2003, the population of the United States was about 291,000,000 and 13.7% of this total was Hispanic. How many Hispanic people lived in the United States in 2003?

Source: U.S. Bureau of the Census

12. *Age 65 and Over.* By 2010, it is predicted that 13.2% of the U.S. population will be 65 and over. If the population of the United States in 2010 is 307,000,000, how many people will be 65 and over?

Source: U.S. Bureau of the Census

13. *Test Results.* On a test of 40 items, Christina got 91% correct. (There was partial credit on some items.) How many items did she get correct? incorrect?

14. *Test Results.* On a test of 80 items, Pedro got 93% correct. (There was partial credit on some items.) How many items did he get correct? incorrect?

15. *Test Results.* On a test, Maj Ling got 86%, or 81.7, of the items correct. (There was partial credit on some items.) How many items were on the test?

16. *Test Results.* On a test, Juan got 85%, or 119, of the items correct. How many items were on the test?

17. *TV Usage.* Of the 8760 hr in a year, most television sets are on for 2190 hr. What percent is this?

18. *Colds from Kissing.* In a medical study, it was determined that if 800 people kiss someone who has a cold, only 56 will actually catch a cold. What percent is this?

Source: U.S. Centers for Disease Control

19. *Maximum Heart Rate.* Treadmill tests are often administered to diagnose heart ailments. A guideline in such a test is to try to get you to reach your *maximum heart rate,* in beats per minute. The maximum heart rate is found by subtracting your age from 220 and then multiplying by 85%. What is the maximum heart rate of someone whose age is 25? 36? 48? 55? 76? Round to the nearest one.

20. It costs an oil company $40,000 a day to operate two refineries. Refinery A accounts for 37.5% of the cost, and refinery B for the rest of the cost.
a) What percent of the cost does it take to run refinery B?
b) What is the cost of operating refinery A? refinery B?

b Solve.

21. *Savings Increase.* The amount in a savings account increased from $200 to $216. What was the percent of increase?

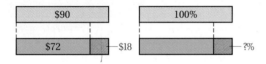

22. *Population Increase.* The population of a small mountain town increased from 840 to 882. What was the percent of increase?

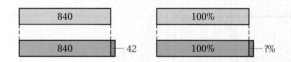

23. During a sale, a dress decreased in price from $90 to $72. What was the percent of decrease?

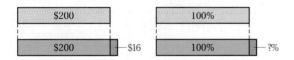

24. A person on a diet goes from a weight of 125 lb to a weight of 110 lb. What is the percent of decrease?

25. *Population Increase.* The population of the state of Nevada increased from 1,201,833 in 1990 to 2,241,154 in 2003. What is the percent of increase?
Source: U.S. Bureau of the Census

26. *Population Increase.* The population of the state of Utah increased from 1,722,850 in 1990 to 2,351,467 in 2003. What is the percent of increase?
Source: U.S. Bureau of the Census

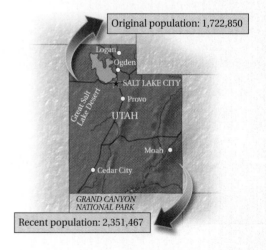

Original population: 1,722,850

Recent population: 2,351,467

27. A person earns $28,600 one year and receives a 5% raise in salary. What is the new salary?

28. A person earns $43,200 one year and receives an 8% raise in salary. What is the new salary?

29. *Car Depreciation.* Irwin buys a car for $21,566. It depreciates 25% each year that he owns it. What is the depreciated value of the car after 1 yr? after 2 yr?

30. *Car Depreciation.* Janice buys a car for $22,688. It depreciates 25% each year that she owns it. What is the depreciated value of the car after 1 yr? after 2 yr?

31. *Doormat.* A bordered coir doormat 42 in. × 24 in. × $1\frac{1}{2}$ in. has a retail price of $89.95. Over the holidays it is on sale for $65.49. What is the percent of decrease?

32. *Business Tote.* A leather business tote retails for $239.99. An insurance company bought 30 totes for its sales staff at a reduced price of $184.95. What was the percent of decrease in the price?

33. *Two-by-Four.* A cross-section of a standard or nominal "two-by-four" board actually measures $1\frac{1}{2}$ in. by $3\frac{1}{2}$ in. The rough board is 2 in. by 4 in. but is planed and dried to the finished size. What percent of the wood is removed in planing and drying?

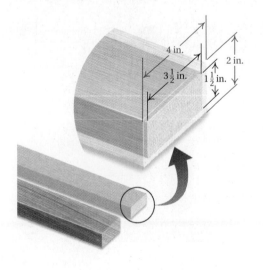

34. *Tipping.* Diners frequently add a 15% tip when charging a meal to a credit card. What is the total amount charged if the cost of the meal, without tip, is $18? $34? $49?

35. 🖩 *Population Decrease.* Between 1990 and 2000, the population of Detroit, Michigan, decreased from 1,028,000 to 951,000.

a) What is the percent of decrease?

b) If this percent of decrease over a 10-yr period repeated itself in the following decade, what would the population be in 2010?

Source: U.S. Bureau of the Census

36. 🖩 *World Population.* World population is increasing by 1.14% each year. In 2004, it was 6.39 billion. How much will it be in 2006? 2010? 2015?

Source: *The World Factbook,* 2004

Life Insurance Rates for Smokers and Nonsmokers. The following table provides data showing how yearly rates (premiums) for a $500,000 term life insurance policy are increased for smokers. Complete the missing numbers in the table.

TYPICAL INSURANCE PREMIUMS (DOLLARS)

	AGE	RATE FOR NONSMOKER	RATE FOR SMOKER	PERCENT INCREASE FOR SMOKER
	35	$ 345	$ 630	83%
37.	40	$ 430	$ 735	
38.	45	$ 565		84%
39.	50	$ 780		100%
40.	55	$ 985		117%
41.	60	$1645	$2955	
42.	65	$2943	$5445	

Source: Pacific Life PL Protector Term Life Portfolio, OYT Rates

---

Population Increase. The following table provides data showing how the populations of various states increased from 1990 to 2003. Complete the missing numbers in the table.

	STATE	POPULATION IN 1990	POPULATION IN 2003	CHANGE	PERCENT CHANGE
43.	Alaska	550,043	648,818		
44.	Connecticut	3,287,116		196,256	
45.	Montana		917,621	118,556	
46.	Texas		22,118,509	5,131,999	
47.	Colorado	3,294,394		1,256,294	
48.	Pennsylvania	11,881,643	12,365,455		

Source: U.S. Bureau of the Census

49. *Car Depreciation.* A car generally depreciates 25% of its original value in the first year. A car is worth $27,300 after the first year. What was its original cost?

50. *Car Depreciation.* Given normal use, an American-made car will depreciate 25% of its original cost the first year and 14% of its remaining value in the second year. What is the value of a car at the end of the second year if its original cost was $36,400? $28,400? $26,800?

51. *Strike Zone.* In baseball, the *strike zone* is normally a 17-in. by 30-in. rectangle. Some batters give the pitcher an advantage by swinging at pitches thrown out of the strike zone. By what percent is the area of the strike zone increased if a 2-in. border is added to the outside?

Source: Major League Baseball

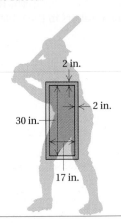

52. Tony has planted grass seed on a 24-ft by 36-ft area in his back yard. He has also installed a 6-ft by 8-ft garden. By what percent does the garden reduce the area he will have to mow?

53. $\mathbf{D_W}$ Which is better for a wage earner, and why: a 10% raise followed by a 5% raise a year later, or a 5% raise followed by a 10% raise a year later?

54. $\mathbf{D_W}$ A worker receives raises of 3%, 6%, and then 9%. By what percent has the original salary increased? Explain.

Convert to decimal notation. [4.1b], [4.5a]

55. $\dfrac{25}{11}$ **56.** $\dfrac{11}{25}$ **57.** $\dfrac{27}{8}$ **58.** $\dfrac{43}{9}$ **59.** $\dfrac{23}{25}$

60. $\dfrac{20}{24}$ **61.** $\dfrac{14}{32}$ **62.** $\dfrac{2317}{1000}$ **63.** $\dfrac{34,809}{10,000}$ **64.** $\dfrac{27}{40}$

---

65. *Adult Height.* It has been determined that at the age of 10, a girl has reached 84.4% of her final adult growth. Cynthia is 4 ft, 8 in. at the age of 10. What will be her final adult height?

Source: *Dunlop Illustrated Encyclopedia of Facts.* New York: Sterling Publishing, 1970.

66. *Adult Height.* It has been determined that at the age of 15, a boy has reached 96.1% of his final adult height. Claude is 6 ft, 4 in. at the age of 15. What will be his final adult height?

Source: *Dunlop Illustrated Encyclopedia of Facts.* New York: Sterling Publishing, 1970.

67. If p is 120% of q, then q is what percent of p?

68. A coupon allows a couple to have dinner and then have $10 subtracted from the bill. Before subtracting $10, however, the restaurant adds a tip of 15%. If the couple is presented with a bill for $44.05, how much would the dinner (without tip) have cost without the coupon?

6.6 SALES TAX, COMMISSION, AND DISCOUNT

Objectives

a Solve applied problems involving sales tax and percent.

b Solve applied problems involving commission and percent.

c Solve applied problems involving discount and percent.

a Sales Tax

Sales tax computations represent a special type of percent of increase problem. The sales tax rate in Maryland is 5%. This means that the tax is 5% of the purchase price. Suppose the purchase price on a coat is $124.95. The sales tax is then 5% of $124.95, or 0.05 × 124.95, or 6.2475, or about $6.25.

$124.95 + 5% sales tax

Baltimore

Annapolis

BILL:		
Purchase price	=	$124.95
Sales tax (5% of $124.95)	=	+ 6.25
Total price		$131.20

The total that you pay is the price plus the sales tax:

$124.95 + $6.25,   or $131.20.

SALES TAX

Sales tax = Sales tax rate × Purchase price

Total price = Purchase price + Sales tax

EXAMPLE 1 *Florida Sales Tax.* The sales tax rate in Florida is 6%. How much tax is charged on the purchase of 4 inflatable rafts at $89.99 each? What is the total price?

a) We first find the cost of the rafts. It is

4 × $89.99 = $359.96.

b) The sales tax on items costing $359.96 is

$$\underbrace{\text{Sales tax rate}}_{6\%} \times \underbrace{\text{Purchase price}}_{\$359.96}$$

or 0.06 × 359.96, or 21.5976. Thus the tax is $21.60 (rounded to the nearest cent).

c) The total price is given by the purchase price plus the sales tax:

$359.96 + $21.60,   or $381.56.

To check, note that the total price is the purchase price plus 6% of the purchase price. Thus the total price is 106% of the purchase price. Since 1.06 × 359.96 ≈ 381.56, we have a check. The sales tax is $21.60 and the total price is $381.56.

Do Exercises 1 and 2.

$89⁹⁹ plus 6% each

1. California Sales Tax. The sales tax rate in California is 7.25%. How much tax is charged on the purchase of a refrigerator that sells for $668.95? What is the total price?

2. Louisiana Sales Tax. Sam buys 5 hardcover copies of Dean Koontz's novel *From the Corner of His Eye* for $26.95 each. The sales tax rate in Louisiana is 4%. How much sales tax will be charged? What is the total price?

Answers on page A-14

3. The sales tax is $50.94 on the purchase of a night table that costs $849. What is the sales tax rate?

4. The sales tax on a portable navigation system is $59.94 and the sales tax rate is 6%. Find the purchase price (the price before taxes are added).

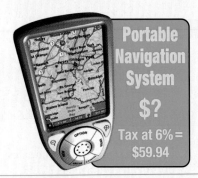

Portable Navigation System

$?

Tax at 6% = $59.94

EXAMPLE 2 The sales tax is $43.96 on the purchase of this wooden play center, which costs $1099. What is the sales tax rate?

Wooden Play Center
27 sq ft play deck
with slide and
swing set

$1099

+ $43.96 sales tax at ?% sales tax rate

Rephrase: Sales tax   is   what percent   of   purchase price?

Translate: $43.96   = r × 1099

To solve the equation, we divide by 1099 on both sides:

$$\frac{43.96}{1099} = \frac{r \times 1099}{1099}$$

$$\frac{43.96}{1099} = r$$

$$0.04 = r$$

$$4\% = r.$$

The sales tax rate is 4%.

Do Exercise 3.

EXAMPLE 3 The sales tax on a Tiffany torchiere lamp is $8.93 and the sales tax rate is 5%. Find the purchase price (the price before taxes are added).

Rephrase: Sales tax   is   5%   of   what?

Translate: $8.93   =   5%   × b,   or $8.93 = 0.05 \times b$.

To solve, we divide by 0.05 on both sides:

$$\frac{8.93}{0.05} = \frac{0.05 \times b}{0.05}$$

$$\frac{8.93}{0.05} = b$$

$$\$178.60 = b.$$

The purchase price is $178.60.

Do Exercise 4.

Answers on page A-14

b   Commission

5. Raul's commission rate is 30%. What is the commission from the sale of $18,760 worth of air conditioners?

When you work for a **salary,** you receive the same amount of money each week or month. When you work for a **commission,** you are paid a percentage of the total sales for which you are responsible.

COMMISSION	
Commission = Commission rate × Sales	

EXAMPLE 4   *Exercise Equipment Sales.*   A salesperson's commission rate is 16%. What is the commission from the sale of $9700 worth of exercise equipment?

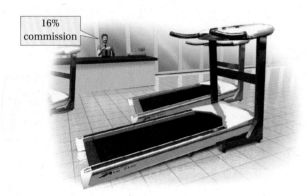

Commission	=	*Commission rate*	×	*Sales*
C	=	16%	×	9700
C	=	0.16	×	9700
C	=	1552		

The commission is $1552.

Do Exercise 5.

EXAMPLE 5   *Farm Machinery Sales.*   Dawn earns a commission of $30,000 selling $600,000 worth of farm machinery. What is the commission rate?

Commission	=	*Commission rate*	×	*Sales*
30,000	=	*r*	×	600,000

Answer on page A-14

6. Liz earns a commission of $3000 selling $24,000 worth of *NSYNC concert tickets. What is the commission rate?

To solve this equation, we divide by 600,000 on both sides:

$$\frac{30{,}000}{600{,}000} = \frac{r \times 600{,}000}{600{,}000}$$

$$\frac{1}{20} = r$$

$$0.05 = r$$

$$5\% = r.$$

The commission rate is 5%.

Do Exercise 6.

EXAMPLE 6 *Motorcycle Sales.* Joyce's commission rate is 12%. She receives a commission of $936 on the sale of a motorcycle. How much did the motorcycle cost?

Motorcycle Shop
Sales Commission
Contract

12%

The Salesperson, known as
_____, will receive a
commission of 12% of the final
price on each motorcycle he/she
sells. This contract shall be legal
for the extent of the employment
of the salesperson.

Employee _____
Date _____

7. Ben's commission rate is 16%. He receives a commission of $268 from sales of clothing. How many dollars worth of clothing were sold?

$$\begin{array}{ccccc} Commission & = & Commission\ rate & \times & Sales \\ 936 & = & 12\% & \times & S, \quad \text{or } 936 = 0.12 \times S \end{array}$$

To solve this equation, we divide by 0.12 on both sides:

$$\frac{936}{0.12} = \frac{0.12 \times S}{0.12}$$

$$\frac{936}{0.12} = S$$

$$7800 = S.$$

The motorcycle cost $7800.

Do Exercise 7.

C Discount

Suppose that the regular price of a rug is $60, and the rug is on sale at 25% off. Since 25% of $60 is $15, the sale price is $60 − $15, or $45. We call $60 the **original,** or **marked price,** 25% the **rate of discount,** $15 the **discount,** and $45 the **sale price.** Note that discount problems are a type of percent of decrease problem.

DISCOUNT AND SALE PRICE
Discount = Rate of discount × Original price
Sale price = Original price − Discount

EXAMPLE 7 A masonite door marked $1389 is on sale at $33\frac{1}{3}\%$ off. What is the discount? the sale price?

a) *Discount* = *Rate of discount* × *Original price*

$$D = 33\frac{1}{3}\% \times 1389$$

$$D = \frac{1}{3} \times 1389$$

$$D = \frac{1389}{3} = 463$$

b) *Sale price* = *Original price* − *Discount*

$$S = 1389 - 463$$

$$S = 926$$

The discount is $463 and the sale price is $926.

Do Exercise 8.

EXAMPLE 8 *Antique Pricing.* An antique table is marked down from $620 to $527. What is the rate of discount?

We first find the discount by subtracting the sale price from the original price:

$$620 - 527 = 93.$$

The discount is $93.

Next, we use the equation for discount:

Discount = *Rate of discount* × *Original price*

$$93 = r \times 620.$$

To solve, we divide by 620 on both sides:

$$\frac{93}{620} = \frac{r \times 620}{620}$$

$$\frac{93}{620} = r$$

$$0.15 = r$$

$$15\% = r.$$

The discount rate is 15%.

> To check, note that a 15% discount rate means that 85% of the original price is paid:
>
> $$0.85 \times 620 = 527.$$

Do Exercise 9.

8. A suit marked $540 is on sale at $33\frac{1}{3}\%$ off. What is the discount? the sale price?

9. A pair of hiking boots is reduced from $75 to $60. Find the rate of discount.

Reduced to
$60
Original price
$75

Answers on page A-14

6.6
EXERCISE SET

For Extra Help

MathXL   MyMathLab   InterAct   Math Tutor   Digital Video   Student's
                        Math   Center   Tutor CD 3   Solutions
                                                 Videotape 6   Manual

a   Solve.

1. *Tennessee Sales Tax.*   The sales tax rate in Tennessee is 7%. How much sales tax would be charged on a lawn mower that costs $279?

2. *Arizona Sales Tax.*   The sales tax rate in Arizona is 5.6%. How much sales tax would be charged on a lawn mower that costs $279?

3. *Kansas Sales Tax.*   The sales tax rate in Kansas is 5.3%. How much sales tax would be charged on a video game, Quest of the Planets, which sells for $49.99?

4. *New Jersey Sales Tax.*   The sales tax rate in New Jersey is 6%. How much sales tax would be charged on a copy of John Grisham's novel *A Painted House,* which sells for $27.95?

Source: Borders Bookstore; Andrea Sutcliffe, *Numbers*

5. *Utah Sales Tax.*   The sales tax rate in Utah is 4.75%. How much tax is charged on a purchase of 5 telephones at $69 apiece? What is the total price?

6. *New York Sales Tax.*   The sales tax rate in New York is 4.25%. How much tax is charged on a purchase of 5 teapots at $37.99 apiece? What is the total price?

7. The sales tax is $48 on the purchase of a dining room set that sells for $960. What is the sales tax rate?

8. The sales tax is $15 on the purchase of a diamond ring that sells for $500. What is the sales tax rate?

9. The sales tax is $35.80 on the purchase of a refrigerator–freezer that sells for $895. What is the sales tax rate?

10. The sales tax is $9.12 on the purchase of a patio set that sells for $456. What is the sales tax rate?

11. The sales tax on a used car is $100 and the sales tax rate is 5%. Find the purchase price (the price before taxes are added).

12. The sales tax on the purchase of a new boat is $112 and the sales tax rate is 2%. Find the purchase price.

13. The sales tax on a dining room set is $28 and the sales tax rate is 3.5%. Find the purchase price.

14. The sales tax on a portable DVD player is $24.75 and the sales tax rate is 5.5%. Find the purchase price.

15. The sales tax rate in Austin is 2% for the city and county and 6.25% for the state. Find the total amount paid for 2 shower units at $332.50 apiece.

16. The sales tax rate in Omaha is 1.5% for the city and 5% for the state. Find the total amount paid for 3 air conditioners at $260 apiece.

17. The sales tax is $1030.40 on an automobile purchase of $18,400. What is the sales tax rate?

18. The sales tax is $979.60 on an automobile purchase of $15,800. What is the sales tax rate?

b Solve.

19. Katrina's commission rate is 6%. What is the commission from the sale of $45,000 worth of furnaces?

20. Jose's commission rate is 32%. What is the commission from the sale of $12,500 worth of sailboards?

21. Mitchell earns $120 selling $2400 worth of television sets in a consignment shop. What is the commission rate?

22. Donna earns $408 selling $3400 worth of shoes. What is the commission rate?

23. An art gallery's commission rate is 40%. They receive a commission of $392. How many dollars worth of artwork were sold?

24. A real estate agent's commission rate is 7%. She receives a commission of $5600 on the sale of a home. How much did the home sell for?

25. A real estate commission is 6%. What is the commission on the sale of a $98,000 home?

26. A real estate commission is 8%. What is the commission on the sale of a piece of land for $68,000?

27. Bonnie earns $280.80 selling $2340 worth of tee shirts. What is the commission rate?

28. Chuck earns $1147.50 selling $7650 worth of ski passes. What is the commission rate?

29. Miguel's commission is increased according to how much he sells. He receives a commission of 5% for the first $2000 and 8% on the amount over $2000. What is the total commission on sales of $6000?

30. Lucinda earns a salary of $500 a month, plus a 2% commission on sales. One month, she sold $990 worth of encyclopedias. What were her wages that month?

C Find what is missing.

	MARKED PRICE	RATE OF DISCOUNT	DISCOUNT	SALE PRICE
31.	$300	10%		
32.	$2000	40%		
33.	$17	15%		
34.	$20	25%		
35.		10%	$12.50	
36.		15%	$65.70	
37.	$600		$240	
38.	$12,800		$1920	

39. Find the discount and the rate of discount for the car seat in this ad.

Sale
Car Seat
$149.99
Was $179.99

40. Find the discount and the rate of discount for the wicker chair in this ad.

Best price of the season!
Now only
$90
Was $125

41. Find the marked price and the rate of discount for the stacked tool storage units in this ad.

CLOSEOUT
$349
buys both
SAVE
$200

42. Find the marked price and the rate of discount for the basketball system in this ad.

SAVE $400
Basketball System
Now
$599⁹⁹

CHAPTER 6: Percent Notation

43. D_W Is the following ad mathematically correct? Why or why not?

44. D_W An item that is no longer on sale at "25% off" receives a price tag that is $33\frac{1}{3}\%$ more than the sale price. Has the item price been restored to its original price? Why or why not?

45. D_W Which is better, a discount of 40% or a discount of 20% followed by another of 20%? Explain.

46. D_W You take 40% of 50% of a number. What percent of the number could you take to obtain the same result making only one multiplication? Explain your answer.

SKILL MAINTENANCE

Solve.   [5.3b]

47. $\dfrac{x}{12} = \dfrac{24}{16}$

48. $\dfrac{7}{2} = \dfrac{11}{x}$

Solve.   [4.4b]

49. $0.64 \cdot x = 170$

50. $28.5 = 25.6 \times y$

Find decimal notation.   [4.5a]

51. $\dfrac{5}{9}$

52. $\dfrac{23}{11}$

53. $\dfrac{11}{12}$

54. $\dfrac{13}{7}$

55. $\dfrac{15}{7}$

56. $\dfrac{19}{12}$

Convert to standard notation.   [4.3b]

57. $4.03 trillion

58. 5.8 million

59. 42.7 million

60. 6.09 trillion

SYNTHESIS

61. 🖩 *Magazine Subscriptions.* In a recent subscription drive, *People* offered a subscription of 52 weekly issues for a price of $1.89 per issue. They advertised that this was a savings of 29.7% off the newsstand price. What was the newsstand price?

Source: *People Magazine*

62. 🖩 Gordon receives a 10% commission on the first $5000 in sales and 15% on all sales beyond $5000. If Gordon receives a commission of $2405, how much did he sell? Use a calculator and trial and error if you wish.

63. Herb collects baseball memorabilia. He bought two autographed plaques, but became short of funds and had to sell them quickly for $200 each. On one, he made a 20% profit and on the other, he lost 20%. Did he make or lose money on the sale?

64. Tee shirts are being sold at the mall for $5 each, or 3 for $10. If you buy three tee shirts, what is the rate of discount?

Objectives

a Solve applied problems involving simple interest.

b Solve applied problems involving compound interest.

1. What is the simple interest on $4300 invested at an interest rate of 7% for 1 year?

a Simple Interest

Suppose you put $1000 into an investment for 1 year. The $1000 is called the **principal.** If the **interest rate** is 8%, in addition to the principal, you get back 8% of the principal, which is

$$8\% \text{ of } \$1000, \quad \text{or} \quad 0.08 \times 1000, \quad \text{or} \quad \$80.00.$$

The $80.00 is called the **simple interest.** It is, in effect, the price that a financial institution pays for the use of the money over time.

SIMPLE INTEREST FORMULA

The **simple interest** I on principal P, invested for t years at interest rate r, is given by

$$I = P \cdot r \cdot t.$$

EXAMPLE 1 What is the simple interest on $2500 invested at an interest rate of 6% for 1 year?

We use the formula $I = P \cdot r \cdot t$:

$$
\begin{aligned}
I = P \cdot r \cdot t &= \$2500 \times 6\% \times 1 \\
&= \$2500 \times 0.06 \\
&= \$150.
\end{aligned}
$$

The simple interest for 1 year is $150.

Do Exercise 1.

2. What is the simple interest on a principal of $4300 invested at an interest rate of 7% for $\frac{3}{4}$ year?

EXAMPLE 2 What is the simple interest on a principal of $2500 invested at an interest rate of 6% for $\frac{1}{4}$ year?

We use the formula $I = P \cdot r \cdot t$:

$$
\begin{aligned}
I = P \cdot r \cdot t &= \$2500 \times 6\% \times \frac{1}{4} \\
&= \frac{\$2500 \times 0.06}{4} \\
&= \$37.50.
\end{aligned}
$$

> We could instead have found $\frac{1}{4}$ of 6% and then multiplied by 2500.

The simple interest for $\frac{1}{4}$ year is $37.50.

Do Exercise 2.

When time is given in days, we generally divide it by 365 to express the time as a fractional part of a year.

EXAMPLE 3 To pay for a shipment of tee shirts, New Wave Designs borrows $8000 at $9\frac{3}{4}\%$ for 60 days. Find (a) the amount of simple interest that is due and (b) the total amount that must be paid after 60 days.

a) We express 60 days as a fractional part of a year:

$$I = P \cdot r \cdot t = \$8000 \times 9\frac{3}{4}\% \times \frac{60}{365}$$

$$= \$8000 \times 0.0975 \times \frac{60}{365}$$

$$\approx \$128.22.$$

The interest due for 60 days is $128.22.

b) The total amount to be paid after 60 days is the principal plus the interest:

$$\$8000 + \$128.22 = \$8128.22.$$

The total amount due is $8128.22.

Do Exercise 3.

3. The Glass Nook borrows $4800 at $8\frac{1}{2}\%$ for 30 days. Find (a) the amount of simple interest due and (b) the total amount that must be paid after 30 days.

b Compound Interest

When interest is paid *on interest*, we call it **compound interest.** This is the type of interest usually paid on investments. Suppose you have $5000 in a savings account at 6%. In 1 year, the account will contain the original $5000 plus 6% of $5000. Thus the total in the account after 1 year will be

106% of $5000,   or   1.06 × $5000,   or $5300.

Now suppose that the total of $5300 remains in the account for another year. At the end of this second year, the account will contain the $5300 plus 6% of $5300. The total in the account would thus be

106% of $5300,   or   1.06 × $5300,   or $5618.

Note that in the second year, interest is earned on the first year's interest. When this happens, we say that interest is **compounded annually.**

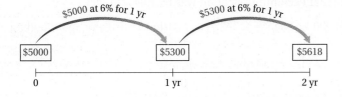

Answer on page A-15

4. Find the amount in an account if $2000 is invested at 9%, compounded annually, for 2 years.

EXAMPLE 4 Find the amount in an account if $2000 is invested at 8%, compounded annually, for 2 years.

a) After 1 year, the account will contain 108% of $2000:

$$1.08 \times \$2000 = \$2160.$$

b) At the end of the second year, the account will contain 108% of $2160:

$$1.08 \times \$2160 = \$2332.80.$$

The amount in the account after 2 years is $2332.80.

Do Exercise 4.

Suppose that the interest in Example 4 were **compounded semiannually**—that is, every half year. Interest would then be calculated twice a year at a rate of 8% ÷ 2, or 4% each time. The approach used in Example 4 can then be adapted, as follows.

After the first $\frac{1}{2}$ year, the account will contain 104% of $2000:

$$1.04 \times \$2000 = \$2080.$$

After a second $\frac{1}{2}$ year (1 full year), the account will contain 104% of $2080:

$$1.04 \times \$2080 = \$2163.20.$$

After a third $\frac{1}{2}$ year $\left(1\frac{1}{2} \text{ full years}\right)$, the account will contain 104% of $2163.20:

$$1.04 \times \$2163.20 = \$2249.728$$
$$\approx \$2249.73. \qquad \text{Rounding to the nearest cent}$$

Finally, after a fourth $\frac{1}{2}$ year (2 full years), the account will contain 104% of $2249.73:

$$1.04 \times \$2249.73 = \$2339.7192$$
$$\approx \$2339.72. \qquad \text{Rounding to the nearest cent}$$

Let's summarize our results and look at them another way:

End of 1st $\frac{1}{2}$ year $\;\rightarrow\; 1.04 \times 2000 = 2000 \times (1.04)^1$;

End of 2nd $\frac{1}{2}$ year $\;\rightarrow\; 1.04 \times (1.04 \times 2000) = 2000 \times (1.04)^2$;

End of 3rd $\frac{1}{2}$ year $\;\rightarrow\; 1.04 \times (1.04 \times 1.04 \times 2000) = 2000 \times (1.04)^3$;

End of 4th $\frac{1}{2}$ year $\;\rightarrow\; 1.04 \times (1.04 \times 1.04 \times 1.04 \times 2000) = 2000 \times (1.04)^4$.

Note that each multiplication was by 1.04 and that

$$\$2000 \times 1.04^4 \approx \$2339.72. \qquad \text{Using a calculator and rounding to the nearest cent}$$

We have illustrated the following result.

COMPOUND INTEREST FORMULA
If a principal P has been invested at interest rate r, compounded n times a year, in t years it will grow to an amount A given by $$A = P \cdot \left(1 + \frac{r}{n}\right)^{n \cdot t}.$$

Answer on page A-15

Let's apply this formula to confirm our preceding discussion, where the amount invested is $P = \$2000$, the number of years is $t = 2$, and the number of compounding periods each year is $n = 2$. Substituting into the compound interest formula, we have

$$A = P \cdot \left(1 + \frac{r}{n}\right)^{n \cdot t} = 2000 \cdot \left(1 + \frac{8\%}{2}\right)^{2 \cdot 2}$$

$$= 2000 \cdot \left(1 + \frac{0.08}{2}\right)^{4} = 2000(1.04)^4$$

$$= 2000 \times 1.16985856 \approx \$2339.72.$$

If you are using a calculator, you could perform this computation in one step.

EXAMPLE 5 The Ibsens invest \$4000 in an account paying $5\frac{5}{8}\%$, compounded quarterly. Find the amount in the account after $2\frac{1}{2}$ years.

The compounding is quarterly, so n is 4. We substitute \$4000 for P, $5\frac{5}{8}\%$, or 0.05625, for r, 4 for n, and $2\frac{1}{2}$, or $\frac{5}{2}$, for t and compute A:

$$A = P \cdot \left(1 + \frac{r}{n}\right)^{n \cdot t} = \$4000 \cdot \left(1 + \frac{5\frac{5}{8}\%}{4}\right)^{4 \cdot 5/2}$$

$$= \$4000 \cdot \left(1 + \frac{0.05625}{4}\right)^{10}$$

$$= \$4000(1.0140625)^{10}$$

$$\approx \$4599.46.$$

The amount in the account after $2\frac{1}{2}$ years is \$4599.46.

Do Exercise 5.

Answer on page A-15

CALCULATOR CORNER

Compound Interest   A calculator is useful in computing compound interest. Not only does it do computations quickly but it also eliminates the need to round until the computation is completed. This minimizes "round-off errors" that occur when rounding is done at each stage of the computation. We must keep order of operations in mind when computing compound interest.

To find the amount due on a \$20,000 loan made for 25 days at 11% interest, compounded daily, we would compute $20{,}000\left(1 + \frac{0.11}{365}\right)^{25}$. To do this on a calculator, we press $\boxed{2}\boxed{0}\boxed{0}\boxed{0}\boxed{0} \times \boxed{(}\boxed{(}\boxed{1} + \boxed{.}\boxed{1}\boxed{1} \div$

$\boxed{3}\boxed{6}\boxed{5}\boxed{)}\boxed{y^x}$ (or $\boxed{x^y}$) $\boxed{2}\boxed{5}\boxed{=}$. Without parentheses, we would first find $1 + \frac{0.11}{365}$, raise this result to the

25th power, and then multiply by 20,000. To do this, we press $\boxed{1}\boxed{+}\boxed{.}\boxed{1}\boxed{1}\boxed{\div}\boxed{3}\boxed{6}\boxed{5}\boxed{=}\boxed{y^x}$ (or $\boxed{x^y}$)

$\boxed{2}\boxed{5}\boxed{=}\boxed{\times}\boxed{2}\boxed{0}\boxed{0}\boxed{0}\boxed{0}$. In either case, the result is 20,151.23, rounded to the nearest cent.
Some calculators have business keys that allow such computations to be done more quickly.

Exercises:

1. Find the amount due on a \$16,000 loan made for 62 days at 13% interest, compounded daily.

2. An investment of \$12,500 is made for 90 days at 8.5% interest, compounded daily. How much is the investment worth after 90 days?

5. A couple invests \$7000 in an account paying $6\frac{3}{8}\%$, compounded semiannually. Find the amount in the account after $1\frac{1}{2}$ years.

a   Find the simple interest.

	PRINCIPAL	RATE OF INTEREST	TIME	SIMPLE INTEREST
1.	$200	4%	1 year	
2.	$450	2%	1 year	
3.	$2000	8.4%	$\frac{1}{2}$ year	
4.	$200	7.7%	$\frac{1}{2}$ year	
5.	$4300	10.56%	$\frac{1}{4}$ year	
6.	$8000	9.42%	$\frac{1}{6}$ year	
7.	$20,000	$4\frac{5}{8}\%$	1 year	
8.	$100,000	$3\frac{7}{8}\%$	1 year	
9.	$50,000	$5\frac{3}{8}\%$	$\frac{1}{4}$ year	
10.	$80,000	$6\frac{3}{4}\%$	$\frac{1}{12}$ year	

Solve. Assume that simple interest is being calculated in each case.

11. CopiPix, Inc. borrows $10,000 at 9% for 60 days. Find (a) the amount of interest due and (b) the total amount that must be paid after 60 days.

12. Sal's Laundry borrows $8000 at 10% for 90 days. Find (a) the amount of interest due and (b) the total amount that must be paid after 90 days.

13. Animal Instinct, a pet supply shop, borrows $6500 at 5% for 90 days. Find (a) the amount of interest due and (b) the total amount that must be paid after 90 days.

14. Andante's Cafe borrows $4500 at 12% for 60 days. Find (a) the amount of interest due and (b) the total amount that must be paid after 60 days.

15. Jean's Garage borrows $5600 at 10% for 30 days. Find (a) the amount of interest due and (b) the total amount that must be paid after 30 days.

16. Shear Delights, a hair salon, borrows $3600 at 4% for 30 days. Find (a) the amount of interest due and (b) the total amount that must be paid after 30 days.

b Interest is compounded annually. Find the amount in the account after the given length of time. Round to the nearest cent.

	PRINCIPAL	RATE OF INTEREST	TIME	AMOUNT IN THE ACCOUNT
17.	$400	5%	2 years	
18.	$450	4%	2 years	
19.	$2000	8.8%	4 years	
20.	$4000	7.7%	4 years	
21.	$4300	10.56%	6 years	
22.	$8000	9.42%	6 years	
23.	$20,000	$6\frac{5}{8}$%	25 years	
24.	$100,000	$5\frac{7}{8}$%	30 years	

Interest is compounded semiannually. Find the amount in the account after the given length of time. Round to the nearest cent.

	PRINCIPAL	RATE OF INTEREST	TIME	AMOUNT IN THE ACCOUNT
25.	$4000	6%	1 year	
26.	$1000	5%	1 year	
27.	$20,000	8.8%	4 years	
28.	$40,000	7.7%	4 years	
29.	$5000	10.56%	6 years	
30.	$8000	9.42%	8 years	
31.	$20,000	$7\frac{5}{8}$%	25 years	
32.	$100,000	$4\frac{7}{8}$%	30 years	

Solve.

33. A family invests $4000 in an account paying 6%, compounded monthly. How much is in the account after 5 months?

34. A couple invests $2500 in an account paying 3%, compounded monthly. How much is in the account after 6 months?

35. A couple invests $1200 in an account paying 10%, compounded quarterly. How much is in the account after 1 year?

36. The O'Hares invest $6000 in an account paying 8%, compounded quarterly. How much is in the account after 18 months?

37. D_W Which is a better investment and why: $1000 invested at $7\frac{3}{4}$% simple interest for 1 year, or $1000 invested at 7% compounded monthly for 1 year?

38. D_W A firm must choose between borrowing $5000 at 10% for 30 days and borrowing $10,000 at 8% for 60 days. Give arguments in favor of and against each option.

SKILL MAINTENANCE

VOCABULARY REINFORCEMENT

In each of Exercises 39–46, fill in the blank with the correct term from the given list. Some of the choices may not be used.

39. If the product of two numbers is 1, they are _____ of each other.   [2.7a]

40. A number is _____ if its ones digit is even and the sum of its digits is divisible by 3.   [2.2a]

41. The number 0 is the _____ identity.   [1.2a]

42. A(n) _____ is the ratio of price to the number of units.   [5.2b]

43. The distance around an object is its _____ .   [1.2b]

44. A number is _____ if the sum of its digits is divisible by 3.   [2.2a]

45. A natural number that has exactly two different factors, only itself and 1, is called a _____ number.   [2.1c]

46. When two pairs of numbers have the same ratio, they are _____ .   [5.3a]

divisible by 3

divisible by 4

divisible by 6

divisible by 9

perimeter

area

unit rate

reciprocals

proportional

composite

prime

additive

multiplicative

SYNTHESIS

Effective Yield.   The *effective yield* is the yearly rate of simple interest that corresponds to a rate for which interest is compounded two or more times a year. For example, if P is invested at 12%, compounded quarterly, we would multiply P by $(1 + 0.12/4)^4$, or 1.03^4. Since $1.03^4 \approx 1.126$, the 12% compounded quarterly corresponds to an effective yield of approximately 12.6%. In Exercises 47 and 48, find the effective yield for the indicated account.

47. The account pays 9% compounded monthly.

48. The account pays 10% compounded daily.

6.8 INTEREST RATES ON CREDIT CARDS AND LOANS

Objective

a Solve applied problems involving interest rates on credit cards and loans.

a Credit Cards and Loans

Look at the following graphs. They offer good reason for a study of the real-world applications of percent, interest, loans, and credit cards.

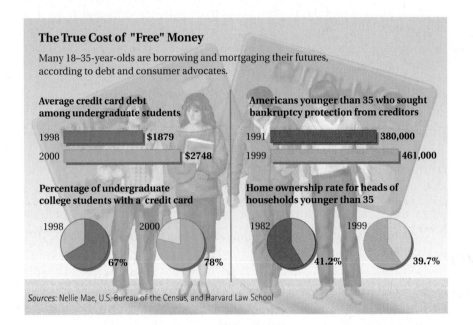

The True Cost of "Free" Money

Many 18–35-year-olds are borrowing and mortgaging their futures, according to debt and consumer advocates.

Average credit card debt among undergraduate students

1998	$1879
2000	$2748

Americans younger than 35 who sought bankruptcy protection from creditors

1991	380,000
1999	461,000

Percentage of undergraduate college students with a credit card

1998 — 67%   2000 — 78%

Home ownership rate for heads of households younger than 35

1982 — 41.2%   1999 — 39.7%

Sources: Nellie Mae, U.S. Bureau of the Census, and Harvard Law School

Comparing interest rates is essential if one is to become financially responsible. A small change in an interest rate can make a *large* difference in the cost of a loan. When you make a payment on a loan, do you know how much of that payment is interest and how much is applied to reducing the principal?

We begin with an example involving credit cards. A balance carried on a credit card is a type of loan. In a recent year in the United States, 100,000 young adults declared bankruptcy because of excessive credit card debt. The money you obtain through the use of a credit card is not "free" money. There is a price (interest) to be paid for the privilege.

EXAMPLE 1 *Credit Cards.* After the holidays, Sarah has a balance of $3216.28 on a credit card with an annual percentage rate (APR) of 19.7%. She decides not to make additional purchases with this card until she has paid off the balance.

a) Many credit cards require a minimum monthly payment of 2% of the balance. What is Sarah's minimum payment on a balance of $3216.28? Round the answer to the nearest dollar.

b) Find the amount of interest and the amount applied to reduce the principal in the minimum payment found in part (a).

c) If Sarah had transferred her balance to a card with an APR of 12.5%, how much of her first payment would be interest and how much would be applied to reduce the principal?

d) Compare the amounts for 12.5% from part (c) with the amounts for 19.7% from part (b).

1. Credit Cards. After the holidays, Jamal has a balance of $4867.59 on a credit card with an annual percentage rate (APR) of 21.3%. He decides not to make additional purchases with this card until he has paid off the balance.

a) Many credit cards require a minimum monthly payment of 2% of the balance. What is Jamal's minimum payment on a balance of $4867.59? Round the answer to the nearest dollar.

We solve as follows.

a) We multiply the balance of $3216.28 by 2%:

$$0.02 \times \$3216.28 = \$64.3256.$$

Sarah's minimum payment, rounded to the nearest dollar, is $64.

b) The amount of interest on $3216.28 at 19.7% for one month* is given by

$$I = P \cdot r \cdot t = \$3216.28 \times 0.197 \times \frac{1}{12} \approx \$52.80.$$

We subtract to find the amount applied to reduce the principal in the first payment:

$$\text{Amount applied to reduce the principal} = \text{Minimum payment} - \text{Interest for the month}$$

$$= \$64 - \$52.80$$

$$= \$11.20.$$

b) Find the amount of interest and the amount applied to reduce the principal in the minimum payment found in part (a).

Thus the principal of $3216.28 is decreased by only $11.20 with the first payment. (Sarah still owes $3205.08.)

c) The amount of interest on $3216.28 at 12.5% for one month is

$$I = P \cdot r \cdot t = \$3216.28 \times 0.125 \times \frac{1}{12} \approx \$33.50.$$

We subtract to find the amount applied to reduce the principal in the first payment:

c) If Jamal had transferred his balance to a card with an APR of 13.6%, how much of his first payment would be interest and how much would be applied to reduce the principal?

$$\text{Amount applied to reduce the principal} = \text{Minimum payment} - \text{Interest for the month}$$

$$= \$64 - \$33.50$$

$$= \$30.50.$$

Thus the principal of $3216.28 is decreased by $30.50 with the first payment. (Sarah still owes $3185.78.)

d) Let's organize the information for both rates in the following table.

BALANCE BEFORE FIRST PAYMENT	FIRST MONTH'S PAYMENT	% APR	AMOUNT OF INTEREST	AMOUNT APPLIED TO PRINCIPAL	BALANCE AFTER FIRST PAYMENT
$3216.28	$64	19.7%	$52.80	$11.20	$3205.08
3216.28	64	12.5	33.50	30.50	3185.78

Difference in balance after first payment → $19.30

d) Compare the amounts for 13.6% from part (c) with the amounts for 21.3% from part (b).

At 19.7%, the interest is $52.80 and the principal is decreased by $11.20. At 12.5%, the interest is $33.50 and the principal is decreased by $30.50. Thus the principal is decreased by $30.50 − $11.20, or $19.30 more with the 12.5% rate than with the 19.7% rate. Thus the interest at 19.7% is $19.30 greater than the interest at 12.5%.

---

*Actually, the interest on a credit card is computed daily with a rate called a daily percentage rate (DPR). The DPR for Example 1 would be 19.7%/365 ≈ 0.054%. When no payments or additional purchases are made during the month, the difference in total interest for the month is minimal and we will not deal with it here.

Answers on page A-15

Do Exercise 1 on the preceding page.

Even though the mathematics of the information in the chart below is beyond the scope of this text, it is interesting to compare how long it takes to pay off the balance of Example 1 if Sarah continues to pay $64 for each payment with how long it takes if she pays double that amount, $128, for each payment. Financial consultants frequently tell clients that if they want to take control of their debt, they should pay double the minimum payment.

RATE	PAYMENT PER MONTH	NUMBER OF PAYMENTS TO PAY OFF DEBT	TOTAL PAID BACK	ADDITIONAL COST OF PURCHASES
19.7%	$64	107, or 8 yr 11 mo	$6848	$3631.72
19.7	128	33, or 2 yr 9 mo	4224	1007.72
12.5	64	72, or 6 yr	4608	1391.72
12.5	128	29, or 2 yr 5 mo	3712	495.72

As with most loans, if you pay an extra amount toward the principal with each payment, the length of the loan can be greatly reduced. Note that at the rate of 19.7%, it will take Sarah almost 9 yr to pay off her debt if she pays only $64 per month and does not make additional purchases. If she transfers her balance to a card with a 12.5% rate and pays $128 per month, she could eliminate her debt in approximately $2\frac{1}{2}$ yr. You can see how debt can get out of control if you continue to make purchases and pay only the minimum payment. The debt will never be eliminated.

The Federal Stafford Loan program provides educational loans to students at interest rates that are much lower than those on credit cards. Payments on a loan do not begin until 6 months after graduation. At that time, the student has 10 years, or 120 monthly payments, to pay off the loan.

EXAMPLE 2 *Federal Stafford Loans.* After graduation, the balance on Taylor's Stafford loan is $28,650. If the rate on his loan is 3.37%, he will make 120 payments of approximately $282 each to pay off the loan.

a) Find the amount of interest and the amount of principal in the first payment.

b) If the interest rate were 5.25%, he would make 120 monthly payments of approximately $307 each. How much more of the first payment is interest if the loan is 5.25% rather than 3.37%?

c) Compare the total amount of interest on the loan at 3.37% with the amount on the loan at 5.25%. How much more would Taylor pay in interest on the 5.25% loan than on the 3.37% loan?

We solve as follows.

a) We use the formula $I = P \cdot r \cdot t$, substituting $28,650 for P, 0.0337 for r, and 1/12 for t:

$$I = \$28{,}650 \times 0.0337 \times \frac{1}{12}$$

$$\approx \$80.46.$$

The amount of interest in the first payment is $80.46. The payment is $282. We subtract to determine the amount applied to the principal:

$$\$282 - \$80.46 = \$201.54.$$

With the first payment, the principal will be reduced by $201.54.

5. Refinancing a Home Loan.

Consider Example 4 for a 15-yr loan. The new monthly payment is $1250.14.

a) How much of the first payment is interest and how much is applied to reduce the principal?

b) If the Sawyers pay the entire 180 payments, how much interest will be paid on this loan?

c) Compare the amount of interest to pay off the 15-yr loan at $5\frac{1}{2}$% with the amount of interest to pay off the 15-yr loan at $6\frac{5}{8}$% in Margin Exercise 4.

Answers on page A-15

EXAMPLE 4 *Refinancing a Home Loan.* Refer to Example 3. Ten months after the Sawyers buy their home financed at a rate of $6\frac{5}{8}$%, the rates drop to $5\frac{1}{2}$%. After much consideration, they decide to refinance even though the new loan will cost them $1200 in refinance charges. They have reduced the principal a small amount in the 10 payments they have made, but they decide to again borrow $153,000 for 30 years at the new rate. Their new monthly payment is $868.72.

a) How much of the first payment is interest and how much is applied to the principal?

b) Compare the amounts at $5\frac{1}{2}$% found in part (a) with the amounts at $6\frac{5}{8}$% found in Example 3(a).

c) With the lower house payment, how long will it take the Sawyers to recoup the refinance charge of $1200?

d) If the Sawyers pay the entire 360 payments, how much interest will be paid on this loan? How much less is the total interest at $5\frac{1}{2}$% than at $6\frac{5}{8}$%?

We solve as follows.

a) To find the interest paid in the first payment, we use the formula $I = P \cdot r \cdot t$:

$$I = P \cdot r \cdot t = \$153{,}000 \times 0.055 \times \frac{1}{12} = \$701.25.$$

The amount applied to the principal is

$868.72 − $701.25, or $167.47.

b) We compare the amounts found in part (a) with the amounts found in Example 3(a):

Rate	Monthly payment	Interest in first payment	Amount applied to principal
$6\frac{5}{8}$%	$979.68	$844.69	$134.99
$5\frac{1}{2}$%	$868.72	$701.25	$167.47

At $5\frac{1}{2}$%, the amount of interest in the first payment is $844.69 − $701.25, or $143.44, less than at $6\frac{5}{8}$%. The amount applied to the principal is $167.47 − $134.99, or $32.48, more.

c) The monthly payment at $5\frac{1}{2}$% is $979.68 − $868.72, or $110.96, less than the payment at $6\frac{5}{8}$%. The total savings each month is approximately $111. We can divide the cost of the refinancing by this monthly savings to determine the number of months it will take to recoup the $1200 refinancing charge: $1200 ÷ $111 ≈ 11. It will take the Sawyers approximately 11 months to break even.

d) Over the 30-year period, the total paid will be

360 × $868.72, or $312,739.20.

The total amount of interest paid over the lifetime of the loan is

$312,739.20 − $153,000, or $159,739.20.

The total interest paid at $5\frac{1}{2}$% is

$199,684.80 (see Example 3) − $159,739.20, or $39,945.60,

less than the total interest paid at $6\frac{5}{8}$%. Thus the $5\frac{1}{2}$% loan saves the Sawyers approximately $40,000 in interest charges over the 30 years.

Do Exercise 5.

6.8

EXERCISE SET   For Extra Help

MathXL · MyMathLab · InterAct Math · Math Tutor Center · Digital Video Tutor CD 3 Videotape 6 · Student's Solutions Manual

a   Solve.

1. *Credit Cards.*   At the end of his freshman year of college, Antonio has a balance of $4876.54 on a credit card with an annual percentage rate (APR) of 21.3%. He decides not to make additional purchases with his card until he has paid off the balance.

a) Many credit cards require a minimum monthly payment of 2% of the balance. What is Antonio's minimum payment on a balance of $4876.54? Round the answer to the nearest dollar.

b) Find the amount of interest and the amount applied to reduce the principal in the minimum payment found in part (a).

c) If Antonio had transferred his balance to a card with an APR of 12.6%, how much of his first payment would be interest and how much would be applied to reduce the principal?

d) Compare the amounts for 12.6% from part (c) with the amounts for 21.3% from part (b).

2. *Credit Cards.*   At the end of her junior year of college, Becky had a balance of $5328.88 on a credit card with an annual percentage rate (APR) of 18.7%. She decides not to make additional purchases with this card until she has paid off the balance.

a) Many credit cards require a minimum monthly payment of 2% of the balance. What is Becky's minimum payment on a balance of $5328.88? Round the answer to the nearest dollar.

b) Find the amount of interest and the amount applied to reduce the principal in the minimum payment found in part (a).

c) If Becky had transferred her balance to a card with an APR of 13.2%, how much of her first payment would be interest and how much would be applied to reduce the principal?

d) Compare the amounts for 13.2% from part (c) with the amounts for 18.7% from part (b).

3. *Federal Stafford Loans.*   After graduation, the balance on Grace's Stafford loan is $44,560. To pay off the loan at 3.37%, she will make 120 payments of approximately $437.93 each.

a) Find the amount of interest and the amount applied to reduce the principal in the first payment.

b) If the interest rate were 4.75%, she would make 120 monthly payments of approximately $467.20 each. How much more of the first payment is interest if the loan is 4.75% rather than 3.37%?

c) Compare the total amount of interest on a loan at 3.37% with the amount on the loan at 4.75%. How much more would Grace pay on the 4.75% loan than on the 3.37% loan?

4. *Federal Stafford Loans.*   After graduation, the balance on Ricky's Stafford loan is $38,970. To pay off the loan at 3.37%, he will make 120 payments of approximately $382.99 each.

a) Find the amount of interest and the amount applied to reduce the principal in the first payment.

b) If the interest rate were 5.4%, he would make 120 monthly payments of approximately $421 each. How much more of the first payment is interest if the loan is 5.4% rather than 3.37%?

c) Compare the total amount of interest on the loan at 3.37% with the amount on the loan at 5.4%. How much more would Ricky pay on the 5.4% loan than on the 3.37% loan?

5. *Home Loan.*   The Martinez family recently purchased a home. They borrowed $164,000 at $6\frac{1}{4}$% for 30 years (360 payments). Their monthly payment (excluding insurance and taxes) is $1009.78.

a) How much of the first payment is interest and how much is applied to reduce the principal?

b) If this family pays the entire 360 payments, how much interest will be paid on the loan?

c) Determine the new principal after the first payment. Use that new principal to determine how much of the second payment is interest and how much is applied to reduce the principal.

6. *Home Loan.*   The Kaufmans recently purchased a home. They borrowed $136,000 at 5.75% for 30 years (360 payments). Their monthly payment (excluding insurance and taxes) is $793.66.

a) How much of the first payment is interest and how much is applied to reduce the principal?

b) If the Kaufmans pay the entire 360 payments, how much interest will be paid on the loan?

c) Determine the new principal after the first payment. Use that new principal to determine how much of the second payment is interest and how much is applied to reduce the principal.

7. *Refinancing a Home Loan.* Refer to Exercise 5. The Martinez family decides to change the period of their home loan to 15 years. Their monthly payment increases to $1406.17.

a) How much of the first payment is interest and how much is applied to reduce the principal?

b) If the Martinez family pays the entire 180 payments, how much interest will be paid on the loan?

c) Compare the amount of interest to pay off the 15-yr loan with the amount of interest to pay off the 30-yr loan.

8. *Refinancing a Home Loan.* Refer to Exercise 6. The Kaufmans decide to change the period of their home loan to 15 years. Their monthly payment increased to $1129.36.

a) How much of the first payment is interest and how much is applied to reduce the principal?

b) If the Kaufmans pay the entire 180 payments, how much interest will be paid on the loan?

c) Compare the amount of interest to pay off the 15-yr loan with the amount of interest to pay off the 30-yr loan.

Complete the following table, assuming monthly payments as given.

	INTEREST RATE	HOME MORTGAGE	TIME OF LOAN	MONTHLY PAYMENT	PRINCIPAL AFTER FIRST PAYMENT	PRINCIPAL AFTER SECOND PAYMENT
9.	6.98%	$100,000	360 mos	$663.96		
10.	6.98%	$100,000	180 mos	$897.71		
11.	8.04%	$100,000	180 mos	$957.96		
12.	8.04%	$100,000	360 mos	$736.55		
13.	7.24%	$150,000	360 mos	$1022.25		
14.	7.24%	$75,000	180 mos	$684.22		
15.	7.24%	$200,000	180 mos	$1824.60		
16.	7.24%	$180,000	360 mos	$1226.70		

17. *Dealership's Car Loan Offer.* For a trip to Colorado, Michael and Rebecca buy a 2005 Toyota Sienna van whose selling price is $23,950. For financing, they accept the promotion from the manufacturer that offers a 48-month loan at 2.9% with 10% down. Their monthly payment is $454.06.

a) What is the down payment? the amount borrowed?

b) How much of the first payment is interest and how much is applied to reduce the principal?

c) What is the total interest cost of the loan if they pay all of the 48 payments?

18. *New-Car Loan.* After working at her first job for 2 years, Janice buys a new Saturn for $16,385. She makes a down payment of $1385 and finances $15,000 for 4 years at a new-car loan rate of 8.99%. Her monthly payment is $373.20.

a) How much of her first payment is interest and how much is applied to reduce the principal?

b) Find the principal balance at the beginning of the second month and determine how much less interest she will pay in the second payment than in the first.

c) What is the total interest cost of the loan if she pays all of the 48 payments?

19. *Used-Car Loan.* Twin brothers, Jerry and Terry, each take a job at the college cafeteria in order to have the money to make payments on the purchase of a 2002 Chrysler PT Cruiser for $11,900. They make a down payment of 5% and finance the remainder at 9.3% for 3 years. (Used-car loan rates are generally higher than new-car loan rates.) Their monthly payment is $361.08.

a) What is the down payment? the amount borrowed?
b) How much of the first payment is interest and how much is applied to reduce the principal?
c) If they pay all 36 payments, how much interest will they pay for the loan?

20. *Used-Car Loan.* For his construction job, Clint buys a 2003 Dodge Ram 1500 truck for $13,800. He makes a down payment of $1380 and finances the remainder for 4 years at 8.8%. The monthly payment is $307.89.

a) How much is financed?
b) How much of the first payment is interest and how much is applied to reduce the principal?
c) If he pays all 48 payments, how much interest will he pay for the loan?

21. D_W Based on the skills of mathematics you have obtained in this section, discuss the significant new ideas you now have about interest rates and credit cards that you didn't have before.

22. D_W Examine the information in the graphs at the beginning of the section. Discuss how a knowledge of this section might have been of help to some of these students.

23. D_W Compare the following two purchases and describe a situation in which each purchase is the best choice.

Purchase A: A new car for $15,145. The loan is for $14,500 at 6.9% for 4 years. The monthly payment is $346.55.

Purchase B: A used car for $10,600. The loan is for $9300 at 12.5% for 3 years. The monthly payment is $311.12.

24. D_W Look over the examples and exercises in this section. What seems to happen to the monthly payment on a loan if the time of payment changes from 30 years to 15 years, assuming the interest rate stays the same? Discuss the pros and cons of both time periods.

SKILL MAINTENANCE

Solve. Round the answer to the nearest hundredth where appropriate. [5.3b]

25. $\dfrac{5}{8} = \dfrac{x}{28}$

26. $\dfrac{5}{8} = \dfrac{17.5}{y}$

27. $\dfrac{13}{16} = \dfrac{81.25}{N}$

28. $\dfrac{9}{16} = \dfrac{p}{100}$

29. $\dfrac{1284}{t} = \dfrac{3456}{5000}$

30. $\dfrac{12.8}{32.5} = \dfrac{x}{2000}$

31. $\dfrac{56.3}{78.4} = \dfrac{t}{100}$

32. $\dfrac{28}{x} = \dfrac{8}{5}$

33. $\dfrac{16}{9} = \dfrac{100}{p}$

34. $\dfrac{t}{1284} = \dfrac{5000}{3456}$

The review that follows is meant to prepare you for a chapter exam. It consists of three parts. The first part, Concept Reinforcement, is designed to increase understanding through true/false exercises. The second part is a list of important properties and formulas. The third part is the Review Exercises. These provide practice exercises for the exam, together with references to section objectives so you can go back and review. Before beginning, stop and look back over the skills you have obtained. What skills in mathematics do you have now that you did not have before studying this chapter?

CONCEPT REINFORCEMENT

Determine whether the statement is true or false. Answers are given at the back of the book.

_____ 1. A fixed principal invested for four years will earn more interest when interest is compounded quarterly than when interest is compounded semi-annually.

_____ 2. Of the numbers 0.5%, $\frac{5}{1000}\%$, $\frac{1}{2}\%$, $\frac{1}{5}$, and $0.\overline{1}$, the largest number is $0.\overline{1}$.

_____ 3. If principal A equals principal B and principal A is invested for 2 years at 4% compounded quarterly while principal B is invested for 4 years at 2% compounded semi-annually, the interest earned from each investment is the same.

_____ 4. The symbol % is equivalent to $\times \frac{1}{10}$.

IMPORTANT PROPERTIES AND FORMULAS

Commission = Commission rate × Sales

Discount = Rate of discount × Original price

Sale price = Original price − Discount

Simple Interest: $I = P \cdot r \cdot t$

Compound Interest: $A = P \cdot \left(1 + \frac{r}{n}\right)^{n \cdot t}$

Review Exercises

Find percent notation for the decimal notation in the sentence in Exercises 1 and 2. [6.1b]

1. Of all the snacks eaten on Super Bowl Sunday, 0.56 of them are chips and salsa.

   Source: Korbel Research and Pace Foods

2. Of all the vehicles in Mexico City, 0.017 of them are taxis.

   Source: The Handy Geography Answer Book

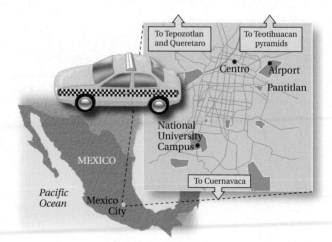

Find percent notation.   [6.2a]

3. $\dfrac{3}{8}$

4. $\dfrac{1}{3}$

Find decimal notation.   [6.1b]

5. 73.5%

6. $6\dfrac{1}{2}\%$

Find fraction notation.   [6.2b]

7. 24%

8. 6.3%

Translate to a percent equation. Then solve.   [6.3a, b]

9. 30.6 is what percent of 90?

10. 63 is 84 percent of what?

11. What is $38\dfrac{1}{2}\%$ of 168?

Translate to a proportion. Then solve.   [6.4a, b]

12. 24 percent of what is 16.8?

13. 42 is what percent of 30?

14. What is 10.5% of 84?

Solve.   [6.5a, b]

15. *Favorite Ice Creams.*   According to a recent survey, 8.9% of those interviewed chose chocolate as their favorite ice cream flavor and 4.2% chose butter pecan. Of the 2500 students in a freshman class, how many would choose chocolate as their favorite ice cream? butter pecan?

Source: International Ice Cream Association

16. *Prescriptions.*   Of the 295 million people in the United States, 123.64 million take at least one kind of prescription drug per day. What percent take at least one kind of prescription drug per day?

Source: American Society of Health-System Pharmacies

17. *Water Output.*   The average person expels 200 mL of water per day by sweating. This is 8% of the total output of water from the body. How much is the total output of water?

Source: Elaine N. Marieb, *Essentials of Human Anatomy and Physiology,* 6th ed. Boston: Addison Wesley Longman, Inc., 2000

18. *Test Scores.*   Jason got a 75 on a math test. He was allowed to go to the math lab and take a retest. He increased his score to 84. What was the percent of increase?

19. *Test Scores.*   Jenny got an 81 on a math test. By taking a retest in the math lab, she increased her score by 15%. What was her new score?

Solve.   [6.6a, b, c]

20. A state charges a meals tax of $4\dfrac{1}{2}\%$. What is the meals tax charged on a dinner party costing $320?

21. In a certain state, a sales tax of $378 is collected on the purchase of a used car for $7560. What is the sales tax rate?

22. Kim earns $753.50 selling $6850 worth of televisions. What is the commission rate?

23. An air conditioner has a marked price of $350. It is placed on sale at 12% off. What are the discount and the sale price?

24. A fax machine priced at $305 is discounted at the rate of 14%. What are the discount and the sale price?

25. An insurance salesperson receives a 7% commission. If $42,000 worth of life insurance is sold, what is the commission?

26. Find the rate of discount.

Our lowest price of the season!

18-ft metal frame

$399⁶⁹

Reg. 489.99

Family-size metal-frame pool

Solve. [6.7a, b]

27. What is the simple interest on $1800 at 6% for $\frac{1}{3}$ year?

28. The Dress Shack borrows $24,000 at 10% simple interest for 60 days. Find (a) the amount of interest due and (b) the total amount that must be paid after 60 days.

29. What is the simple interest on $2200 principal at the interest rate of 5.5% for 1 year?

30. The Kleins invest $7500 in an investment account paying an annual interest rate of 12%, compounded monthly. How much is in the account after 3 months?

31. Find the amount in an investment account if $8000 is invested at 9%, compounded annually, for 2 years.

Solve. [6.8a]

32. *Credit Cards.* At the end of her junior year of college, Judy has a balance of $6428.74 on a credit card with an annual percentage rate (APR) of 18.7%. She decides not to make additional purchases with this card until she has paid off the balance.

a) Many credit cards require a minimum payment of 2% of the balance. What is Judy's minimum payment on a balance of $6428.74? Round the answer to the nearest dollar.

b) Find the amount of interest and the amount applied to reduce the principal in the minimum payment found in part (a).

c) If Judy had transferred her balance to a card with an APR of 13.2%, how much of her first payment would be interest and how much would be applied to reduce the principal?

d) Compare the amounts for 13.2% from part (c) with the amounts for 18.7% from part (b).

33. **D**_W Ollie buys a microwave oven during a 10%-off sale. The sale price that Ollie paid was $162. To find the original price, Ollie calculates 10% of $162 and adds that to $162. Is this correct? Why or why not? [6.6c]

34. **D**_W Which is the better deal for a consumer and why: a discount of 40% or a discount of 20% followed by another of 22%? [6.6c]

SYNTHESIS

35. 🖩 *Land Area of the United States.* After Hawaii and Alaska became states, the total land area of the United States increased from 2,963,681 mi² to 3,540,939 mi². What was the percent of increase? [6.5b]

36. Rhonda's Dress Shop reduces the price of a dress by 40% during a sale. By what percent must the store increase the sale price, after the sale, to get back to the original price? [6.6c]

37. A $200 coat is marked up 20%. After 30 days, it is marked down 30% and sold. What was the final selling price of the coat? [6.6c]

1. *Bookmobiles.* Since 1991, the number of bookmobiles has decreased by approximately 6.4%. Find decimal notation for 6.4%.
   Source: American Library Association

2. *Gravity.* The gravity of Mars is 0.38 as strong as Earth's. Find percent notation for 0.38.
   Source: www.marsinstitute.info/epo/mermarsfacts.html

3. Find percent notation for $\frac{11}{8}$.

4. Find fraction notation for 65%.

5. Translate to a percent equation. Then solve.
   What is 40% of 55?

6. Translate to a proportion. Then solve.
   What percent of 80 is 65?

Solve.

7. *Cruise Ship Passengers.* Of the passengers on a typical cruise ship, 16% are in the 25–34 age group and 23% are in the 35–44 age group. A cruise ship has 2500 passengers. How many are in the 25–34 age group? the 35–44 age group?
   Source: Polk

8. *Batting Averages.* Luis Castillo, second baseman for the Florida Marlins, got 180 hits during the 2000 baseball season. This was about 33.4% of his at-bats. How many at-bats did he have?
   Source: Major League Baseball

9. *Airline Profits.* Profits of the entire U. S. Airline industry decreased from $5.5 billion in 1999 to $2.7 billion in 2000. Find the percent of decrease.
   Source: Air Transport Association

10. There are 6.6 billion people living in the world today. It is estimated that the total number who have ever lived is about 120 billion. What percent of people who have ever lived are alive today?
    Source: *The Handy Geography Answer Book*

11. *Maine Sales Tax.* The sales tax rate in Maine is 5%. How much tax is charged on a purchase of $324? What is the total price?

12. Gwen's commission rate is 15%. What is the commission from the sale of $4200 worth of merchandise?

13. The marked price of a DVD player is $200 and the item is on sale at 20% off. What are the discount and the sale price?

14. What is the simple interest on a principal of $120 at the interest rate of 7.1% for 1 year?

15. The Burnham Parents–Teachers Association invests $5200 at 6% simple interest. How much is in the account after $\frac{1}{2}$ year?

16. Find the amount in an account if $1000 is invested at $5\frac{3}{8}$%, compounded annually, for 2 years.

17. The Suarez family invests $10,000 at an annual interest rate of 4.9%, compounded monthly. How much is in the account after 3 years?

18. *Job Opportunities.* The table below lists job opportunities, in millions, in 2002 and projected increases to 2012. Find the missing numbers.

OCCUPATION	NUMBER OF JOBS IN 2002 (in millions)	NUMBER OF JOBS IN 2012 (in millions)	CHANGE	PERCENT OF INCREASE
Retail salespersons	4.1	4.8	0.7	17.1%
Registered nurses	2.3		0.6	
Post-secondary teachers	1.6	2.2		
Food preparation and service workers		2.4	0.4	
Restaurant servers		2.5		19.0%

Source: Department of Labor

19. Find the discount and the discount rate of the washer-dryer duet in this ad.

SHORT TIME ONLY

$1675

Was $1950

No interest for 18 months

20. *Home Loan.* Complete the following table, assuming the monthly payment as given.

Interest Rate	7.4%
Mortgage	$120,000
Time of Loan	360 mos
Monthly Payment	$830.86
Principal after First Payment	
Principal after Second Payment	

21. By selling a home without using a realtor, Juan and Marie can avoid paying a 7.5% commission. They receive an offer of $180,000 from a potential buyer. In order to give a comparable offer, for what price would a realtor need to sell the house? Round to the nearest hundred.

22. Karen's commission rate is 16%. She invests her commission from the sale of $15,000 worth of merchandise at the interest rate of 12%, compounded quarterly. How much is Karen's investment worth after 6 months?

Data, Graphs, and Statistics

Real-World Application

The rhinoceros is considered one of the world's most endangered animals. The worldwide total number of rhinoceroses is approximately 17,800. Using the pictograph shown in Example 3 on page 429, determine how many more black rhinos there are than Indian/Nepalese rhinos.

This problem appears as Example 3 in Section 7.2.

Use the pictograph in Example 4 to answer Margin Exercises 16–18.

16. Determine the approximate coffee consumption per capita of France.

17. Determine the approximate coffee consumption per capita of Italy.

18. The approximate coffee consumption of Finland is about the same as the combined coffee consumptions of Switzerland and the United States. What is the approximate coffee consumption of Finland?

Answers on page A-16

EXAMPLE 4 *Coffee Consumption.* For selected countries, the following pictograph shows approximately how many cups of coffee each person (per capita) drinks annually.

Coffee Consumption

Germany	
United States	
Switzerland	
France	
Italy	

= 100 cups

Source: Beverage Marketing Corporation

a) Determine the approximate annual coffee consumption per capita of Germany.

b) Which two countries have the greatest difference in coffee consumption? Estimate that difference.

We use the data from the pictograph as follows.

a) Germany's consumption is represented by 11 whole symbols (1100 cups) and, though it is visually debatable, about $\frac{1}{8}$ of another symbol (about 13 cups), for a total of 1113 cups.

b) Visually, we see that Switzerland has the most consumption and that the United States has the least consumption. Switzerland's annual coffee consumption per capita is represented by 12 whole symbols (1200 cups) and about $\frac{1}{5}$ of another symbol (20 cups), for a total of 1220 cups. U.S. consumption is represented by 6 whole symbols (600 cups) and about $\frac{1}{10}$ of another symbol (10 cups), for a total of 610 cups. The difference between these amounts is $1220 - 610$, or 610 cups.

One advantage of pictographs is that the appropriate choice of a symbol will tell you, at a glance, the kind of measurement being made. Another advantage is that the comparison of amounts represented in the graph can be expressed more easily by just counting symbols. For instance, in Example 3, the ratio of Indian/Nepalese rhinoceroses to black rhinoceroses is 8:12.

There are at least three disadvantages of pictographs:

1. To make a pictograph easy to read, the amounts must be rounded significantly to the unit that a symbol represents. This makes it difficult to accurately represent an amount.

2. It is difficult to determine very accurately how much a partial symbol represents.

3. Some mathematics is required to finally compute the amount represented, since there is usually no explicit statement of the amount.

Do Exercises 16–18.

a *Planets.* Use the following table, which lists information about the planets, for Exercises 1–10.

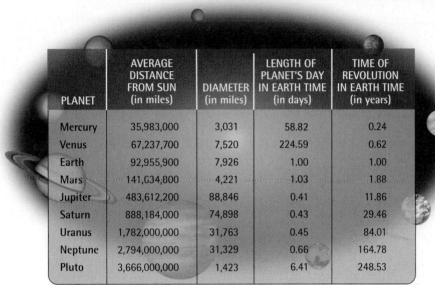

PLANET	AVERAGE DISTANCE FROM SUN (in miles)	DIAMETER (in miles)	LENGTH OF PLANET'S DAY IN EARTH TIME (in days)	TIME OF REVOLUTION IN EARTH TIME (in years)
Mercury	35,983,000	3,031	58.82	0.24
Venus	67,237,700	7,520	224.59	0.62
Earth	92,955,900	7,926	1.00	1.00
Mars	141,634,800	4,221	1.03	1.88
Jupiter	483,612,200	88,846	0.41	11.86
Saturn	888,184,000	74,898	0.43	29.46
Uranus	1,782,000,000	31,763	0.45	84.01
Neptune	2,794,000,000	31,329	0.66	164.78
Pluto	3,666,000,000	1,423	6.41	248.53

Source: *The Handy Science Answer Book*, Gale Research, Inc.

1. Find the average distance from the sun to Jupiter.

2. How long is a day on Venus?

3. Which planet has a time of revolution of 164.78 yr?

4. Which planet has a diameter of 4221 mi?

5. Which planets have an average distance from the sun that is greater than 1,000,000 mi?

6. Which planets have a diameter that is less than 100,000 mi?

7. About how many Earth diameters would it take to equal one Jupiter diameter?

8. How much longer is the longest time of revolution than the shortest?

9. What are the average, the median, and the mode of the diameters of the planets?

10. What are the average, the median, and the mode of the average distances from the sun of the planets?

Heat Index.   In warm weather, a person can feel hotter due to reduced heat loss from the skin caused by higher humidity. The **temperature–humidity index,** or **apparent temperature,** is what the temperature would have to be with no humidity in order to give the same heat effect. The following table lists the apparent temperatures for various actual temperatures and relative humidities. Use this table for Exercises 11–22.

ACTUAL TEMPERATURE (°F)	RELATIVE HUMIDITY									
	10%	20%	30%	40%	50%	60%	70%	80%	90%	100%
	APPARENT TEMPERATURE (°F)									
75°	75	77	79	80	82	84	86	88	90	92
80°	80	82	85	87	90	92	94	97	99	102
85°	85	88	91	94	97	100	103	106	108	111
90°	90	93	97	100	104	107	111	114	118	121
95°	95	99	103	107	111	115	119	123	127	131
100°	100	105	109	114	118	123	127	132	137	141
105°	105	110	115	120	125	131	136	141	146	151

In Exercises 11–14, find the apparent temperature for the given actual temperature and humidity combinations.

11. 80°, 60%

12. 90°, 70%

13. 85°, 90%

14. 95°, 80%

15. How many listed temperature–humidity combinations give an apparent temperature of 100°?

16. How many listed temperature–humidity combinations given an apparent temperature of 111°?

17. At a relative humidity of 50%, what actual temperatures give an apparent temperature above 100°?

18. At a relative humidity of 90%, what actual temperatures give an apparent temperature above 100°?

19. At an actual temperature of 95°, what relative humidities give an apparent temperature above 100°?

20. At an actual temperature of 85°, what relative humidities give an apparent temperature above 100°?

21. At an actual temperature of 85°, by how much would the humidity have to increase in order to raise the apparent temperature from 94° to 108°?

22. At an actual temperature of 80°, by how much would the humidity have to increase in order to raise the apparent temperature from 87° to 102°?

Cigarette Consumption.   The May 2004 U.S. Surgeon General's report, *The Health Consequences of Smoking,* reports that smoking causes many diseases and reduces the health of smokers. The per capita cigarette consumption in the United States for specific years from 1920 to 2003 is listed in the table below. Use this data for Exercises 23–26.

U.S. Cigarette Consumption (1920 – 2003) (Per capita among persons 18 and older)

YEAR	1920	1930	1940	1950	1960	1970	1980	1990	2000	2003
Cigarette Consumption	665	1485	1976	3552	4171	3985	3849	2817	2092	1903

Sources: U.S. Department of Health and Human Services, Centers for Disease Control and Prevention; USDA, Economic Research Service

23. Find the cigarette consumption in 1940 and 1980. What was the percent of increase in the consumption from 1940 to 1980?

24. Find the cigarette consumption in 1960 and 2000. What was the percent of decrease in the consumption from 1960 to 2000?

25. Find the average of the cigarette consumption for the years 1920 to 1950. Find the average of the cigarette consumption for the years 1970 to 2000. By how many cigarettes per capita does the latter average exceed the former?

26. Find the average of the cigarette consumption for the years 2000 and 2003. Find the average of the cigarette consumption for the years 1920 to 2000. By how many cigarettes per capita does the average for 1920 to 2000 exceed the average of the years 2000 and 2003?

b *World Population Growth.*   The following pictograph shows world population in various years. Use the pictograph for Exercises 27–34.

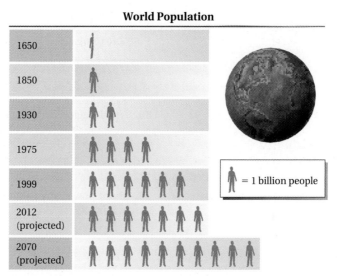

World Population

Source: U.S. Bureau of the Census, International Data Base

27. What was the world population in 1850?

28. What was the world population in 1975?

29. In which year will the population be the greatest?

30. In which year was the population the least?

31. Between which two years was the amount of growth the least?

32. Between which two years was the amount of growth the greatest?

33. How much greater will the world population in 2012 be than in 1975? What is the percent of increase?

34. How much greater was the world population in 1999 than in 1930? What is the percent of increase?

Water Consumption. The following pictograph shows water consumption, per person, in different regions of the world in a recent year. Use the pictograph for Exercises 35–40.

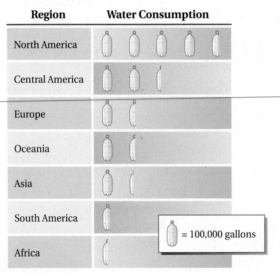

Sources: World Resources Institute; U.S. Energy Information Administration

35. What region consumes the least water?

36. Which region consumes the most water?

37. About how many gallons are consumed per person in North America?

38. About how many gallons are consumed per person in Europe?

39. Approximately how many more gallons are consumed per person in North America than in Asia?

40. Approximately how many more gallons are consumed per person in Central America than in Africa?

41. $\mathbf{D_W}$ Loreena is drawing a pictograph in which dollar bills are used as symbols to represent the tuition at various private colleges. Should each dollar bill represent $10,000, $1000, or $100? Why?

42. $\mathbf{D_W}$ What advantage(s) does a table have over a pictograph?

SKILL MAINTENANCE

Solve. [6.5a]

43. *Kitchen Costs.* The average cost of a kitchen is $26,888. Some of the cost percentages are as follows.

Cabinets: 50%

Countertops: 15%

Appliances: 8%

Fixtures: 3%

Find the costs for each part of a kitchen.

Source: National Kitchen and Bath Association

44. *Bathroom Costs.* The average cost of a bathroom is $11,605. Some of the cost percentages are as follows.

Cabinets: 31%

Countertops: 11%

Labor: 25%

Flooring: 6%

Find the costs for each part of a bathroom.

Source: National Kitchen and Bath Association

Convert to fraction notation and simplify.   [6.2b]

45. 24%

46. 45%

47. 4.8%

48. 6.4%

49. 53.1%

50. 87.3%

51. 100%

52. 2%

SYNTHESIS

53. Redraw the pictograph appearing in Example 4 as one in which each symbol represents 150 cups of coffee.

Objectives

a Extract and interpret data from bar graphs.

b Draw bar graphs.

c Extract and interpret data from line graphs.

d Draw line graphs.

Use the bar graph in Example 1 to answer Margin Exercises 1–3.

1. About how many fans does the NHL (National Hockey League) have?

2. Which sport has the fewest number of fans?

3. Which sports have 100 million or more fans?

CHAPTER 7: Data, Graphs, and Statistics

A **bar graph** is convenient for showing comparisons because you can tell at a glance which amount represents the largest or smallest quantity. Of course, since a bar graph is a more abstract form of pictograph, this is true of pictographs as well. However, with bar graphs, a *second scale* is usually included so that a more accurate determination of the amount can be made.

a Reading and Interpreting Bar Graphs

EXAMPLE 1 *Major League Sports Fans.* As NASCAR racing increases in popularity, its fan base is growing rapidly. The following horizontal bar graph shows the number of fans of various major league sports.

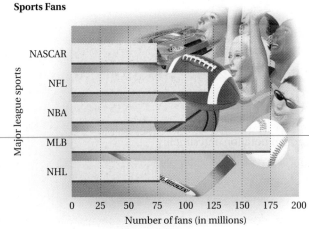

Sports Fans

Sources: NASCAR; the individual leagues; ESPN

a) Which of the major league sports shown in the graph above has the greatest number of fans?

b) About how many fans does the NFL (National Football League) have?

c) Which of the major league sports has about 100 million fans?

We look at the graph to answer the questions.

a) The longest bar is for MLB (Major League Baseball). Thus, that sport has the greatest number of fans.

b) We move to the right along the bar representing the NFL. We can read, fairly accurately, that this sport has approximately 120 million fans.

c) We locate the line representing 100 million and then go up until we reach a bar that ends at 100 million. We then go to the left and read the name of the sport, NBA (National Basketball Association).

Do Exercises 1–3.

Bar graphs are often drawn vertically and sometimes a double bar graph is used to make comparisons.

EXAMPLE 2 *Breast Cancer.* The following graph indicates the incidence and mortality rates of breast cancer for women of various age groups.

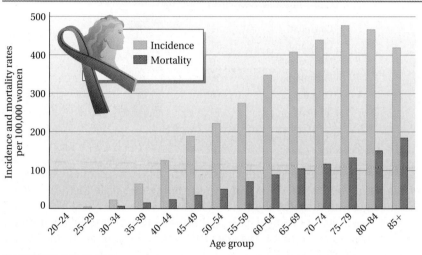

When Breast Cancer Strikes

Source: National Cancer Institute

a) Approximately how many women, per 100,000, develop breast cancer between the ages of 40 and 44?

b) In what age range is the mortality rate for breast cancer approximately 100 for every 100,000 women?

c) In what age range is the incidence of breast cancer the highest?

d) Does the incidence of breast cancer seem to increase from the youngest to the oldest age group?

We look at the graph to answer the questions.

a) We go to the right, across the bottom, to the green bar above the age group 40–44. Next, we go up to the top of that bar and, from there, back to the left to read approximately 130 on the vertical scale. About 130 out of every 100,000 women develop breast cancer between the ages of 40 and 44.

b) We read up the vertical scale to the number 100. From there we move to the right until we come to the top of a red bar. Moving down that bar, we find that in the 65–69 age group, about 100 out of every 100,000 women die of breast cancer.

c) We look for the tallest green bar and read the age range below it. The incidence of breast cancer is highest for women in the 75–79 age group.

d) Looking at the heights of the bars, we see that the incidence of breast cancer increases to a high point in the 75–79 age group and then decreases.

Do Exercises 4–7.

Use the bar graph in Example 2 to answer Margin Exercises 4–7.

4. Approximately how many women, per 100,000, develop breast cancer between the ages of 35 and 39?

5. In what age group is the mortality rate the highest?

6. In what age group do about 350 out of every 100,000 women develop breast cancer?

7. Does the breast cancer mortality rate seem to increase from the youngest to the oldest age group?

Answers on page A-16

8. Planetary Moons. Make a horizontal bar graph to show the number of moons orbiting the various planets.

PLANET	MOONS
Earth	1
Mars	2
Jupiter	17
Saturn	28
Uranus	21
Neptune	8
Pluto	1

Source: National Aeronautics and Space Administration

b Drawing Bar Graphs

EXAMPLE 3 *Police Officers.* Listed below are the numbers of police officers per 10,000 people in various cities. Make a vertical graph of the data.

CITY	POLICE OFFICERS, PER 10,000 PEOPLE
Cincinnati	31
Cleveland	37
Minneapolis	26
Pittsburgh	30
Columbus	26
St. Louis	44

Sources: U.S. Bureau of the Census; FBI Uniform Crime Reports

First, we indicate the different names of the cities in six equally spaced intervals on the horizontal scale and give the horizontal scale the title "Cities." (See the figure on the left below.)

Next, we scale the vertical axis. To do so, we look over the data and note that it ranges from 26 to 44. We start the vertical scaling at 0, labeling the marks by 5's from 0 to 50. We give the vertical scale the title "Number of Officers (per 10,000 people)."

Finally, we draw vertical bars to show the various numbers, as shown in the figure at the right. We give the graph an overall title, "Police Officers."

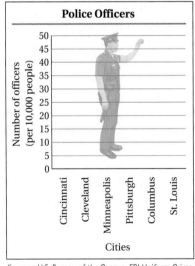

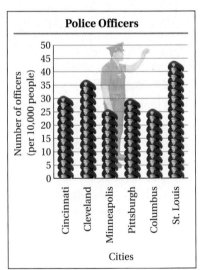

Sources: U.S. Bureau of the Census; FBI Uniform Crime Reports

Do Exercise 8.

c Reading and Interpreting Line Graphs

Line graphs are often used to show a change over time as well as to indicate patterns or trends.

EXAMPLE 4 *New Home Sales.* The following line graph shows the number of new home sales, in thousands, over a twelve-month period. The jagged

Answer on page A-16

line at the base of the vertical scale indicates an unnecessary portion of the scale. Note that the vertical scale differs from the horizontal scale so that the data can be shown reasonably.

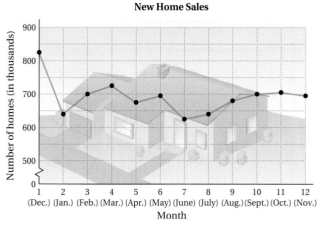

New Home Sales

Source: U.S. Department of Commerce

Use the line graph in Example 4 to answer Margin Exercises 9–11.

9. For which month were new home sales lowest?

a) For which month were new home sales the greatest?

b) Between which months did new home sales increase?

c) For which months were new home sales about 700 thousand?

We look at the graph to answer the questions.

a) The greatest number of new home sales was about 825 thousand in month 1, December.

b) Reading the graph from left to right, we see that new home sales increased from month 2 to month 3, from month 3 to month 4, from month 5 to month 6, from month 7 to month 8, from month 8 to month 9, from month 9 to month 10, and from month 10 to month 11.

c) We look from left to right along the line at 700.

10. Between which months did new home sales decrease?

New Home Sales

11. For which months were new home sales about 650 thousand?

We see that points are close to 700 thousand at months 3, 6, 10, 11, and 12.

Do Exercises 9–11.

EXAMPLE 5 *Monthly Loan Payment.* Suppose that you borrow $110,000 at an interest rate of 9% to buy a home. The following graph shows the monthly payment required to pay off the loan, depending on the length of

Answers on page A-16

Use the line graph in Example 5 to answer Margin Exercises 12–14.

12. Estimate the monthly payment for a loan of 25 yr.

13. What time period corresponds to a monthly payment of about $850?

14. By how much does the monthly payment decrease when the loan period is increased from 5 yr to 20 yr?

the loan. (*Caution:* A low monthly payment means that you will pay more interest over the duration of the loan.)

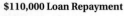

$110,000 Loan Repayment

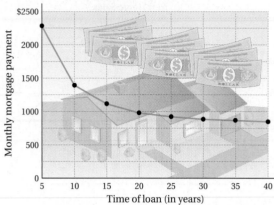

a) Estimate the monthly payment for a loan of 15 yr.

b) What time period corresponds to a monthly payment of about $1400?

c) By how much does the monthly payment decrease when the loan period is increased from 10 yr to 20 yr?

We look at the graph to answer the questions.

a) We find the time period labeled "15" on the bottom scale and move up from that point to the line. We then go straight across to the left and find that the monthly payment is about $1100.

b) We locate $1400 on the vertical axis. Then we move to the right until we hit the line. The point $1400 is on the line at the 10-yr time period.

c) The graph shows that the monthly payment for 10 yr is about $1400; for 20 yr, it is about $990. Thus the monthly payment is decreased by $1400 − $990, or $410. (It should be noted that you will pay back $990 · 20 · 12 − $1400 · 10 · 12, or $69,600, more in interest for a 20-yr loan.)

Do Exercises 12–14.

d Drawing Line Graphs

EXAMPLE 6 *Cell Phones with Internet Access.* Listed below are projections on the use of cell phones with access to the Internet. Make a line graph of the data.

YEAR	CELL PHONES WITH WEB ACCESS (in millions)
2001	29.4
2002	69.6
2003	120.1
2004	152.4
2005	171.1

Source: Forrester Research

First, we indicate the different years on the horizontal scale and give the horizontal scale the title "Year." (See the figure on the left below.) Next, we scale the vertical axis by 25's to show the number of phones, in millions, and give the vertical scale the title "Number of cell phones (in millions)". We also give the graph the overall title "Cell Phones with Web Access."

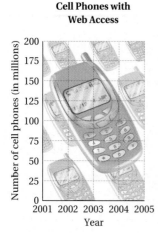

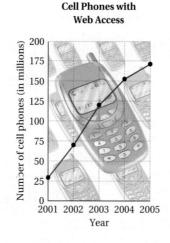

Next, we mark the number of phones at the appropriate level above each year. Then we draw line segments connecting the points. The dramatic change over time can now be observed easily from the graph.

Do Exercise 15.

15. Cell Phones. Listed below are projections on the use of cell phones with or without access to the Internet. Make a line graph of the data.

YEAR	NUMBER OF CELL PHONES (in millions)
2001	119.8
2002	135.3
2003	150.2
2004	163.8
2005	176.9

Source: Forrester Research

Answer on page A-16

MathXL MyMathLab InterAct Math Math Tutor Center Digital Video Tutor CD 4 Videotape 7 Student's Solutions Manual

a *Chocolate Desserts.* The following horizontal bar graph shows the average caloric content of various kinds of chocolate desserts. Use the bar graph for Exercises 1–12.

Chocolate Desserts

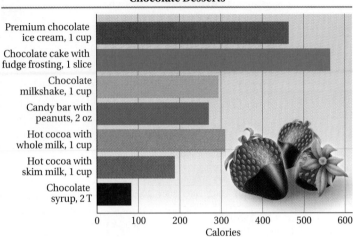

Premium chocolate ice cream, 1 cup
Chocolate cake with fudge frosting, 1 slice
Chocolate milkshake, 1 cup
Candy bar with peanuts, 2 oz
Hot cocoa with whole milk, 1 cup
Hot cocoa with skim milk, 1 cup
Chocolate syrup, 2 T

0   100   200   300   400   500   600
Calories

Source: Better Homes and Gardens, December 1996

1. Estimate how many calories there are in 1 cup of hot cocoa with skim milk.

2. Estimate how many calories there are in 1 cup of premium chocolate ice cream.

3. Which dessert has the highest caloric content?

4. Which dessert has the lowest caloric content?

5. Which dessert contains about 460 calories?

6. Which desserts contain about 300 calories?

7. How many more calories are there in 1 cup of hot cocoa made with whole milk than in 1 cup of hot cocoa made with skim milk?

8. Fred generally drinks a 4-cup chocolate milkshake. How many calories does he consume?

9. Kristin likes to eat 2 cups of premium chocolate ice cream at bedtime. How many calories does she consume?

10. Barney likes to eat a 6-oz chocolate bar with peanuts for lunch. How many calories does he consume?

11. Paul adds a 2-oz chocolate bar with peanuts to his diet each day for 1 yr (365 days) and makes no other changes in his eating or exercise habits. Consumption of 3500 extra calories will add about 1 lb to his body weight. How many pounds will he gain?

12. Tricia adds one slice of chocolate cake with fudge frosting to her diet each day for one year (365 days) and makes no other changes in her eating or exercise habits. The consumption of 3500 extra calories will add about 1 lb to her body weight. How many pounds will she have gained at the end of the year?

Education and Earnings. Side-by-side bar graphs allow for comparisons. The one shown at right provides data on the effect of education on earning power for men and women from 1970 to 2002. Use the bar graph in Exercises 13–20.

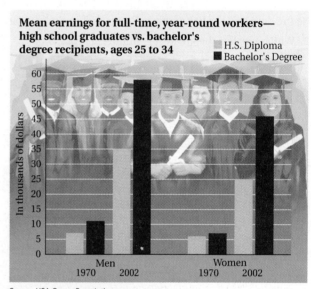

Mean earnings for full-time, year-round workers—high school graduates vs. bachelor's degree recipients, ages 25 to 34

H.S. Diploma
Bachelor's Degree

Source: USA Group Foundation

13. How much were the mean earnings for men with bachelor's degrees in 1970? in 2002? How much had they increased? What was the percent of increase?

14. How much were the mean earnings for women with bachelor's degrees in 1970? in 2002? How much had they increased? What was the percent of increase?

15. How much were the mean earnings for women who had ended their education at high school graduation in 1970? in 2002? How much had they increased? What was the percent of increase?

16. How much were the mean earnings for men who had ended their education at high school graduation in 1970? in 2002? How much had they increased? What was the percent of increase?

17. In 1970, how much more did men with bachelor's degrees earn than men who ended their education at high school graduation?

18. In 2002, how much more did men with bachelor's degrees earn than men who ended their education at high school graduation?

19. In 2002, how much more did women with bachelor's degrees earn than men who ended their education at high school graduation?

20. In 1970, how much more did men with bachelor's degrees earn than women who ended their education at high school graduation?

b

21. *Commuting Time.* The following table lists the average commuting time in six metropolitan areas with more than 1 million people. Make a vertical bar graph to illustrate the data.

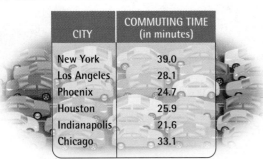

CITY	COMMUTING TIME (in minutes)
New York	39.0
Los Angeles	28.1
Phoenix	24.7
Houston	25.9
Indianapolis	21.6
Chicago	33.1

Source: U.S. Bureau of the Census

Use the data and the bar graph in Exercise 21 to do Exercises 22–25.

22. Which city has the greatest commuting time?

23. Which city has the least commuting time?

24. What was the median commuting time for all six cities?

25. What was the average commuting time for the six cities?

26. *Airline Net Profits.* The net profits (the amount remaining after all deductions like expenses have been made) of U.S. airlines in various years are listed in the table below. Make a horizontal bar graph illustrating the data.

YEAR	NET PROFIT (in billions)
1995	$2.3
1996	2.8
1997	5.2
1998	4.9
1999	5.5
2000	2.7

Source: Air Transportation Association

Use the data and the bar graph in Exercise 26 to do Exercises 27–32.

27. Between which pairs of years was there an increase in profit?

28. Between which pairs of years was there a decrease in profit?

29. What was the percent of decrease between 1999 and 2000?

30. What was the percent of increase between 1996 and 1997?

31. What was the average net profit for all 6 yr?

32. What was the median net profit for all 6 yr?

444

b Drawing Circle Graphs

To draw a circle graph, or pie chart, like the one in Example 1, think of a pie cut into 100 equally sized pieces. We would then shade in a wedge equal in size to 36 of these pieces to represent 36% for food. We shade a wedge equal in size to 5 of these pieces to represent 5% for toys, and so on.

EXAMPLE 2 *Fruit Juice Sales.* The percents of various kinds of fruit juice sold are given in the list at right. Use this information to draw a circle graph.

Source: Beverage Marketing Corporation

Apple:	14%
Orange:	56%
Blends:	6%
Grape:	5%
Grapefruit:	4%
Prune:	1%
Other:	14%

Using a circle with 100 equally spaced tick marks, we start with the 14% given for apple juice. We draw a line from the center to any tick mark. Then we count off 14 ticks and draw another line. We shade the wedge with a color—in this case, red—and label the wedge as shown in the figure on the left below.

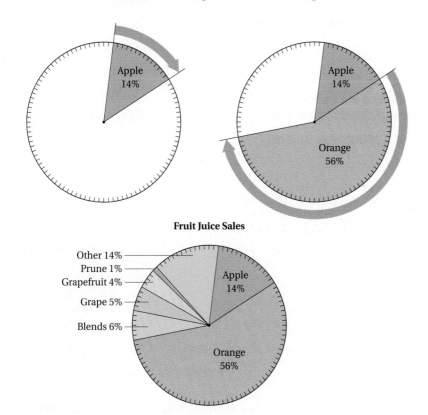

Fruit Juice Sales

To shade a wedge for orange juice, at 56%, we start at one side of the apple wedge, count off 56 ticks, and draw another line. We shade the wedge with a different color—in this case, orange—and label the wedge as shown in the figure on the right above. Continuing in this manner and choosing different colors, we obtain the graph shown above. Finally, we give the graph the overall title "Fruit Juice Sales."

Do Exercise 5.

5. **Lengths of Engagement of Married Couples.** The data below relate the percent of married couples who were engaged for a certain time period before marriage. Use this information to draw a circle graph.

ENGAGEMENT PERIOD	PERCENT
Less than 1 year	24
1–2 years	21
More than 2 years	35
Never engaged	20

Source: Bruskin Goldring Research

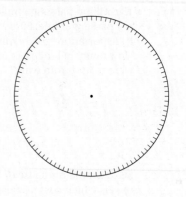

Answer on page A-17

Study Tips

TUNE OUT DISTRACTIONS

Are the places you generally study noisy? If there is constant noise in your home, dorm, or sorority/fraternity house, consider finding a quiet place in the library—maybe a place where the flow of people is minimized and you are not distracted by people-watching!

Translating for Success

1. *Vacation Miles.* The Saenz family drove their new van 13,640.8 mi in the first year. Of this total, 2018.2 miles were driven while on vacation. How many nonvacation miles did they drive?

2. *Rail Miles.* Of the recent $15\frac{1}{2}$ million passenger miles on a rail passenger line, 80% were transportation-to-work miles. How many rail miles, in millions, were to and from work?

3. *Sales Tax Rate.* The sales tax is $8.42 on the purchase of 10 bath towels which cost $129.50. What is the sales tax rate?

4. *Water Level.* During heavy rains in early spring, the water level in a pond rose 0.5 in. every 35 minutes. How much did the water rise in 90 minutes?

5. *Marathon Training.* When training for a marathon, Vebjoern ran $15\frac{1}{2}$ miles per day six days a week. This distance is 80% of the distance Yuriy ran per day. How far did Yuriy run each day?

The goal of these matching questions is to practice step (2), *Translate,* of the five-step problem-solving process. Translate each word problem to an equation and select a correct translation from equations A–O.

A. $8.42 \cdot x = 129.50$

B. $x = 80\% \cdot 15\frac{1}{2}$

C. $x = \dfrac{84 - 68}{84}$

D. $2018.2 + x = 13{,}640.8$

E. $\dfrac{5}{100} = \dfrac{x}{3875}$

F. $2018.2 = x \cdot 13{,}640.8$

G. $4\frac{1}{6} \cdot 73 = x$

H. $\dfrac{x}{5} = \dfrac{100}{3875}$

I. $15\frac{1}{2} = 80\% \cdot x$

J. $8.42 = x \cdot 129.50$

K. $\dfrac{0.5}{35} = \dfrac{x}{90}$

L. $x \cdot 4\frac{1}{6} = 73$

M. $x = \dfrac{84 - 68}{68}$

N. $x = 8.42\% \cdot 129.50$

O. $0.5 \times 35 = 90 \cdot x$

Answers on page A-17

---

6. *Vacation Miles.* The Ning family drove 2018.2 miles on their summer vacation. If they put a total of 13,640.8 miles on their new van during that year, what percent were vacation miles?

7. *Sales Tax.* The sales tax rate is 8.42%. Salena purchased 10 pillows at $12.95 each. How much tax is charged on this purchase?

8. *Charity Donations.* Rachel donated $5 to her favorite charity for each $100 she earned. One month, she earned $3875. How much did she donate that month?

9. *Tuxedos.* Emil Tailoring Company purchased 73 yards of fabric for a new line of tuxedos. How many tuxedos can be produced if it takes $4\frac{1}{6}$ yd of fabric for each tuxedo?

10. *Percent of Increase.* In a calculus-based physics course, Mime got 68% on the first exam and 84% on the second. What was the percent of increase in her score?

5. Is there any difference in price between sending a 5-oz package FedEx Priority Overnight and sending an 8-oz package in the same way?

6. An author has a 4-lb manuscript to send by FedEx Standard Overnight delivery to her publisher. She calls and the package is picked up. Later that day she completes work on another part of her manuscript that weighs 5 lb. She calls and sends it by FedEx Standard Overnight delivery to the same address. How much could she have saved if she had waited and sent both packages as one?

U.S. Police Forces.   This pictograph shows the number of officers in the largest U.S. police forces. Use the graph for Exercises 7–10.

America's Largest Police Forces

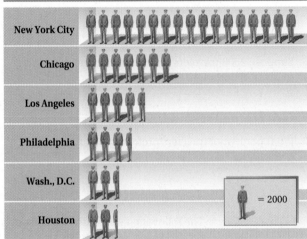

Source: International Association of Chiefs of Police

7. About how many officers are in the Chicago police force?   [7.2b]

8. Which city has about 9000 officers on its force?   [7.2b]

9. Of the cities listed, which has the smallest police force?   [7.2b]

10. Estimate the average size of these six police forces. [7.1a], [7.2b]

Find the mode.   [7.1c]

11. 26, 34, 43, 26, 51

12. 17, 7, 11, 11, 14, 17, 18

13. 0.2, 0.2, 1.7, 1.9, 2.4, 0.2

14. 700, 700, 800, 2700, 800

15. $14, $17, $21, $29, $17, $2

16. 20, 20, 20, 20, 20, 500

17. One summer, a student earned the following amounts over a four-week period: $102, $112, $130, and $98. What was the average amount earned per week? the median?   [7.1a, b]

18. *Gas Mileage.*   A 2001 Ford Focus gets 520 miles of highway driving on 16 gallons of gasoline. What is the gas mileage?   [7.1a]
Source: Ford Motor Company

19. To get an A in math, a student must score an average of 90 on four tests. Scores on the first three tests were 94, 78, and 92. What is the lowest score that the student can make on the last test and still get an A?   [7.1a]

Calorie Content in Fast Foods.   Wendy's Hamburgers is a national food franchise. The following bar graph shows the caloric content of various sandwiches sold by Wendy's. Use the graph for Exercises 20–27.   [7.3a]

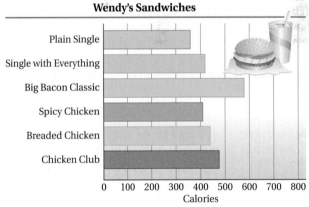

Wendy's Sandwiches

Source: Wendy's International

20. How many calories are in a Single with Everything?

21. How many calories are in a Breaded Chicken sandwich?

22. Which sandwich has the highest caloric content?

23. Which sandwich has the lowest caloric content?

24. Which sandwich contains about 360 calories?

25. Which sandwich contains about 470 calories?

26. How many more calories are in a Chicken Club than in a Single with Everything?

27. How many more calories are in a Big Bacon Classic than in a Plain Single?

Accidents by Driver Age. The following line graph shows the number of accidents per 100 drivers, by age. Use the graph for Exercises 28–33.   [7.3c]

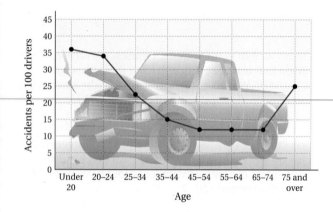

28. Which age group has the most accidents per 100 drivers?

29. What is the fewest number of accidents per 100 in any age group?

30. How many more accidents do people over 75 yr of age have than those in the age range of 65–74?

31. Between what ages does the number of accidents stay basically the same?

32. How many fewer accidents do people 25–34 yr of age have than those 20–24 yr of age?

33. Which age group has accidents right around three times as often as people 55–64 yr of age?

Hotel Preferences. This circle graph shows hotel preferences for travelers. Use the graph for Exercises 34–37. [7.4a]

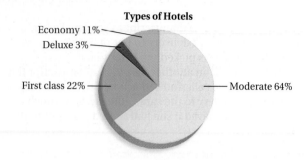

34. What percent of travelers prefer a first-class hotel?

35. What percent of travelers prefer an economy hotel?

36. Suppose 2500 travelers arrive in a city one day. How many of them might seek a moderate room?

37. What percent of travelers prefer either a first-class or a deluxe hotel?

First-Class Postage. The following table shows the cost of first-class postage in various years. Use the table for Exercises 38 and 39.

YEAR	FIRST-CLASS POSTAGE
1983	20¢
1989	25¢
1991	29¢
1995	32¢
1999	33¢
2001	34¢
2002	37¢

Source: U.S. Postal Service

38. Make a vertical bar graph of the data.   [7.3b]

39. Make a line graph of the data.   [7.3d]

CHAPTER 7: Data, Graphs, and Statistics

40. *Battery Testing.* An experiment is performed to compare battery quality. Two kinds of battery were tested to see how long, in hours, they kept a hand radio running. On the basis of this test, which battery is better? [7.1d]

BATTERY A: TIMES (in hours)			BATTERY B: TIMES (in hours)		
38.9	39.3	40.4	39.3	38.6	38.8
53.1	41.7	38.0	37.4	47.6	37.9
36.8	47.7	48.1	46.9	37.8	38.1
38.2	46.9	47.4	47.9	50.1	38.2

Find the average. [7.1a]

41. 26, 34, 43, 51

42. 11, 14, 17, 18, 7

43. 0.2, 1.7, 1.9, 2.4

44. 700, 2700, 3000, 900, 1900

45. $2, $14, $17, $17, $21, $29

46. 20, 190, 280, 470, 470, 500

Find the median. [7.1b]

47. 26, 34, 43, 51

48. 7, 11, 14, 17, 18

49. 0.2, 1.7, 1.9, 2.4

50. 700, 900, 1900, 2700, 3000

51. $2, $17, $21, $29, $14, $17

52. 470, 20, 190, 280, 470, 500

53. *Grade Point Average.* Find the grade point average for one semester given the following grades. Assume the grade point values are 4.0 for A, 3.0 for B, and so on. Round to the nearest tenth. [7.1a]

COURSE	GRADE	NUMBER OF CREDIT HOURS IN COURSE
Basic math	A	5
English	B	3
Computer applications	C	4
Russian	B	3
College skills	B	1

54. D_W Compare and contrast averages, medians, and modes. Discuss why you might use one over the others to analyze a set of data. [7.1a, b, c]

55. D_W Find a real-world situation that fits this equation: [7.1a]

$$T = \frac{(20{,}500 + 22{,}800 + 23{,}400 + 26{,}000)}{4}.$$

SYNTHESIS

56. The ordered set of data 298, 301, 305, *a*, 323, *b*, 390 has a median of 316 and an average of 326. Find *a* and *b*. [7.1a, b]

Desirable Body Weights. The following tables list the desirable body weights for men and women over age 25. Use the tables for Exercises 1–4.

DESIRABLE WEIGHT OF MEN			
HEIGHT	SMALL FRAME (in pounds)	MEDIUM FRAME (in pounds)	LARGE FRAME (in pounds)
5 ft, 7 in.	138	152	166
5 ft, 9 in.	146	160	174
5 ft, 11 in.	154	169	184
6 ft, 1 in.	163	179	194
6 ft, 3 in.	172	188	204

DESIRABLE WEIGHT OF WOMEN			
HEIGHT	SMALL FRAME (in pounds)	MEDIUM FRAME (in pounds)	LARGE FRAME (in pounds)
5 ft, 1 in.	105	113	122
5 ft, 3 in.	111	120	130
5 ft, 5 in.	118	128	139
5 ft, 7 in.	126	137	147
5 ft, 9 in.	134	144	155

Source: U.S. Department of Agriculture

1. What is the desirable weight for a 6 ft, 1 in. man with a medium frame?

2. What is the desirable weight for a 5 ft, 3 in. woman with a small frame?

3. What size woman has a desirable weight of 120 lb?

4. What size man has a desirable weight of 169 lb?

Waste Generated. The number of pounds of waste generated per person per year varies greatly among countries around the world. In the pictograph at right, each symbol represents approximately 100 pounds of waste. Use the pictograph for Exercises 5–8.

5. In which country does each person generate 600 pounds of waste per year?

6. In which country does each person generate 1000 pounds of waste per year?

7. How many pounds of waste per person per year are generated in France?

8. How many pounds of waste per person per year are generated in Finland?

Amount of Waste Generated 2000
(per person per year)

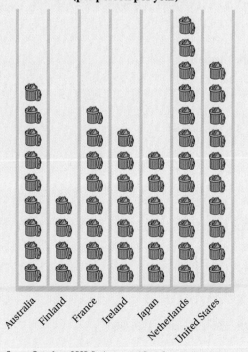

Source: Data from OECD Environmental Data Compendium: 2002

Find the average.

9. 45, 49, 52, 52

10. 1, 1, 3, 5, 3

11. 3, 17, 17, 18, 18, 20

Find the median and the mode.

12. 45, 49, 52, 52

13. 1, 1, 3, 5, 3

14. 3, 17, 17, 18, 18, 20

15. *Gas Mileage.* A 2006 Mitsubishi Eclipse GT V-6 gets 432 miles of highway driving on 16 gallons of gasoline. What is the gas mileage?

Source: Mitsubishi Motors

16. *Grades.* To get a C in chemistry, a student must score an average of 70 on four tests. Scores on the first three tests were 68, 71, and 65. What is the lowest score that the student can make on the last test and still get a C?

Food Dollars Spent Away from Home. The line graph below shows the percentage of food dollars spent away from home for various years, and projected to 2010. Use the graph for Exercises 17–20.

Food dollars spent away from home

Sources: U.S. Bureau of Labor Statistics; National Restaurant Association

17. What percent of meals will be eaten away from home in 2010?

18. What percent of meals were eaten away from home in 1985?

19. In what year was the percent of meals eaten away from home about 30%?

20. In what year will the percent of meals eaten away from home be about 50%?

21. *Animal Speeds.* The following table lists maximum speeds of movement for various animals, in miles per hour, compared to the speed of the fastest human. Make a vertical bar graph of the data.

ANIMAL	SPEED (in miles per hour)
Antelope	61
Peregrine falcon	225
Cheetah	70
Fastest human	28
Greyhound	42
Golden eagle	150
Grant's gazelle	47

Source: Barbara Ann Kipfer, *The Order of Things.*
New York: Random House, 1998.

Refer to the table and the graph in Exercise 21 for Exercises 22–25.

22. By how much does the fastest speed exceed the slowest speed?

23. Does a human have a chance of outrunning a greyhound? Explain.

24. Find the average of all the speeds.

25. Find the median of all the speeds.

26. *Shoplifting and Employee Theft.* The following table lists ways in which American retailers lost money recently. Construct a circle graph representing these data.

TYPE OF LOSS	PERCENT
Employee theft	44
Shoplifting	32.7
Administrative error	17.5
Vendor fraud	5.1
Other	0.7

Source: University of Florida, Department of
Sociology for Sensormatic Electronics
Corporation

27. In reference to Exercise 26, it is known that retailers lost $23 billion. Using the percents from the table and the circle graph, find the amount of money lost from each type of loss.

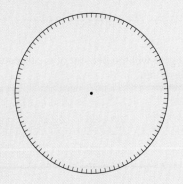

Porsche Sales.   The table below lists the number of Porsche sales in the United States for various years. Use the table for Exercises 28 and 29.

YEAR	PORSCHE U.S. SALES
1996	7,152
1997	12,980
1998	17,239
1999	20,877
2000	23,000

Sources: Autodata, Bridge Information Systems

28. Make a bar graph of the data.

29. Make a line graph of the data.

30. *Chocolate Bars.*   An experiment is performed to compare the quality of new Swiss chocolate bars being introduced in the United States. People were asked to taste the candies and rate them on a scale of 1 to 10. On the basis of this test, which chocolate bar is better?

BAR A: SWISS PECAN			BAR B: SWISS HAZELNUT		
9	10	8	10	6	8
10	9	7	9	10	10
6	9	10	8	7	6
7	8	8	9	10	8

31. *Grade Point Average.*   Find the grade point average for one semester given the following grades. Assume the grade point values are 4.0 for A, 3.0 for B, and so on. Round to the nearest tenth.

COURSE	GRADE	NUMBER OF CREDIT HOURS IN COURSE
Introductory algebra	B	3
English	A	3
Business	C	4
Spanish	B	3
Typing	B	2

SYNTHESIS

32. The ordered set of data 69, 71, 73, *a*, 78, 98, *b* has a median of 74 and a mean of 82. Find *a* and *b*.

Cumulative Review

1. *Net Worth.* In 2004, Bill Gates, of Microsoft fame, was worth $46.6 billion. Write standard notation for $46.6 billion.

Source: Forbes

2. *Gas Mileage.* A 2005 Subaru Impreza WRX gets 324 miles of highway driving on 12 gallons of gasoline. What is the gas mileage?

Source: EPA; *Car and Driver,* September 2005

3. In 402,513, what does the digit 5 mean?

4. Evaluate: $3 + 5^3$.

5. Find all the factors of 60.

6. Round 52.045 to the nearest tenth.

7. Convert to fraction notation: $3\frac{3}{10}$.

8. Convert from cents to dollars: 210¢.

9. Convert to standard notation: $3.25 trillion.

10. Determine whether 11, 30 and 4, 12 are proportional.

Compute and simplify.

11. $2\frac{2}{5} + 4\frac{3}{10}$

12. $41.063 + 3.5721$

13. $\frac{14}{15} - \frac{3}{5}$

14. $350 - 24.57$

15. $3\frac{3}{7} \cdot 4\frac{3}{8}$

16. $12,456 \times 220$

17. $\frac{13}{15} \div \frac{26}{27}$

18. $104,676 \div 24$

Solve.

19. $\frac{5}{8} = \frac{6}{x}$

20. $\frac{2}{5} \cdot y = \frac{3}{10}$

21. $21.5 \cdot y = 146.2$

22. $x = 398,112 \div 26$

Solve.

23. Tortilla chips cost $2.99 for 14.5 oz. Find the unit price rounded to the nearest tenth of a cent, in cents per ounce.

24. A college has a student body of 6000 students. Of these, 55.4% own a car. How many students own a car?

25. A piece of fabric $1\frac{3}{4}$ yd long is cut into 7 equal strips. What is the length of each strip?

26. A recipe calls for $\frac{3}{4}$ cup of sugar. How much sugar should be used for $\frac{1}{2}$ of the recipe?

27. *Peanut Products.* In any given year, the average American eats 2.7 lb of peanut butter, 1.5 lb of salted peanuts, 1.2 lb of peanut candy, 0.7 lb of in-shell peanuts, and 0.1 lb of peanuts in other forms. How many pounds of peanuts and products containing peanuts does the average American eat in one year?

28. *Energy Consumption.* In a recent year, American utility companies generated 1464 billion kilowatt-hours of electricity using coal, 455 billion using nuclear power, 273 billion using natural gas, 250 billion using hydroelectric plants, 118 billion using petroleum, and 12 billion using geothermal technology and other methods. How many kilowatt-hours of electricity were produced that year?

29. *Heart Disease.* Of the 295 million people in the United States, about 7.4 million have coronary heart disease and about 500,000 die of heart attacks each year. What percent have coronary heart disease? What percent die of heart attacks? Round your answers to the nearest tenth of a percent.

Source: U.S. Centers for Disease Control

30. *Billionaires.* In 2003, the mean net worth of U.S. billionaires was $3.18 billion. By 2004, this figure had increased to $3.31 billion. What was the percent of increase?

Source: Forbes

31. *Football Fields.* The Arena Football League (AFL) is a professional league playing indoors, mostly on converted basketball and/or hockey rinks. The figure shows the AFL field compared with the larger field of the National Football League (NFL).

a) Find the area of an AFL field. Include the end zones in your calculation.
b) Find the area of an NFL field. Include the end zones in your calculation.
c) How much larger is an NFL field than an AFL field?

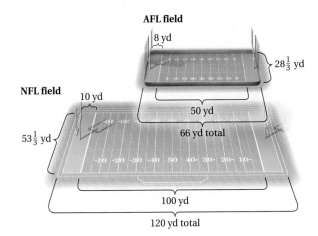

AFL field

8 yd

$28\frac{1}{3}$ yd

NFL field

10 yd

50 yd

66 yd total

$53\frac{1}{3}$ yd

-10 -20 -30 -40 50 40- 30- 20- 10-

100 yd

120 yd total

FedEx. The following table lists the cost of delivering a package by FedEx Priority Overnight shipping in Zone 4. Use the table for Questions 32–34.

WEIGHT (in pounds)	COST
1	$24.25
2	27.25
3	30.25
4	33.00
5	35.75
6	38.25
7	41.00
8	43.25
9	46.50
10	49.25
11	52.00

Source: Federal Express Corporation

32. Find the average and the median of these costs.

33. Make a vertical bar graph of the data.

34. Make a line graph of the data.

35. A business is owned by four people. One owns $\frac{1}{3}$, the second owns $\frac{1}{4}$, and the third owns $\frac{1}{6}$. How much does the fourth person own?

36. In manufacturing valves for engines, a factory was discovered to have made 4 defective valves in a lot of 18 valves. At this rate, how many defective valves can be expected in a lot of 5049 valves?

37. A landscaper bought 22 evergreen trees for $210. What was the cost of each tree? Round to the nearest cent.

38. A salesperson earns $182 selling $2600 worth of electronic equipment. What is the commission rate?

Teen Spending. Teenagers are big spenders. More and more retailers are catering to the 13–19 year-old crowd. Those in this group who shop regularly spend an average of $381 per month. Use the table to answer Exercises 39–42.

Whose Money Do They Spend?

Two-thirds of the money teens spend is their own, whether they earn it or receive it as an allowance or gift.

$\frac{1}{3}$

$\frac{2}{3}$

Parents provide the rest.

How Money Spent by Teens Today Compares to the Past:

2000: $129.6 billion

1995: $74.9 billion

ITEM	PERCENT
Clothing	34
Entertainment	22
Food	22
Other	22

Source: Rand Youth Poll, eMarketer

39. How is their monthly spending allocated?

40. How much of their monthly spending, whether they earn it or receive it as an allowance or gift, is their own? The rest of their spending money comes from their parents. How much of the monthly spending money comes from their parents?

41. In 2000, teenagers spent $129.6 billion. How was it allocated?

42. By what percent has teenage spending increased from 1995 to 2000?

43. A photography club meets four times a month. In September, the attendance figures were 28, 23, 26, and 23. In October, the attendance figures were 26, 20, 14, and 28. What was the percent of increase or decrease in average attendance from September to October?

Real Numbers

10

Real-World Application

Surface temperatures on Mars vary from −128°C during polar night to 27°C at the equator during midday at the closest point in orbit to the sun. Find the difference between the highest value and the lowest value in this temperature range.

Source: Mars Institute

This problem appears as Example 13 in Section 10.3.

Objectives

a State the integer that corresponds to a real-world situation.

b Graph rational numbers on a number line.

c Convert from fraction notation for a rational number to decimal notation.

d Determine which of two real numbers is greater and indicate which, using < or >.

e Find the absolute value of a real number.

In this section, we introduce the *real numbers*. We begin with numbers called *integers* and build up to the real numbers. To describe integers, we start with the whole numbers, 0, 1, 2, 3, and so on. For each number 1, 2, 3, and so on, we obtain a new number to the left of zero on the number line:

For the number 1, there will be an *opposite* number -1 (negative 1).

For the number 2, there will be an *opposite* number -2 (negative 2).

For the number 3, there will be an *opposite* number -3 (negative 3), and so on.

The **integers** consist of the whole numbers and these new numbers. We picture them on a number line as follows.

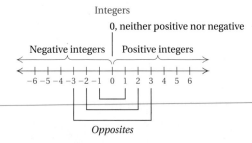

Opposites

We call the numbers to the left of zero on the number line **negative integers.** The natural numbers are called **positive integers.** Zero is neither positive nor negative. We call -1 and 1 **opposites** of each other. Similarly, -2 and 2 are opposites, -3 and 3 are opposites, -100 and 100 are opposites, and 0 is its own opposite. Opposite pairs of numbers like -3 and 3 are the same distance from 0. The integers extend infinitely on the number line to the left and right of zero.

INTEGERS

The **integers:** $\ldots, -5, -4, -3, -2, -1, 0, 1, 2, 3, 4, 5, \ldots$

---

a Integers and the Real World

Integers correspond to many real-world problems and situations. The following examples will help you get ready to translate problem situations that involve integers to mathematical language.

EXAMPLE 1 Tell which integer corresponds to this situation: The temperature is 4 degrees below zero.

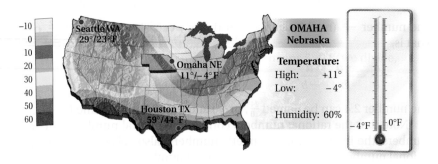

The integer −4 corresponds to the situation. The temperature is −4°.

EXAMPLE 2 *Elevation.* Tell which integer corresponds to this situation: The shores of California's largest lake, the Salton Sea, are 227 ft below sea level.

Source: *National Geographic,* February 2005, p. 88. "Salton Sea," by Joel K. Bourne, Jr., Senior Writer

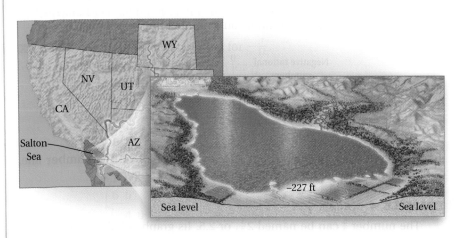

The integer −227 corresponds to the situation. The elevation is −227 ft.

EXAMPLE 3 *Stock Price Change.* Tell which integers correspond to the situation: The stock price of Pearson Education decreased from $27 per share to $11 per share over a recent time period. The price of Safeway stock increased from $20 per share to $22 per share over a recent time period.

Source: The New York Stock Exchange

The integer −16 corresponds to the decrease in the value of the stock. The integer 2 represents the increase in the value of the stock.

Do Exercises 1–5.

b The Rational Numbers

Fractions such as $\frac{1}{2}$ are not integers. A larger system called the **rational numbers** contains integers and fractions. The rational numbers consist of quotients of integers with nonzero divisors.

Tell which integers correspond to the situation.

1. The halfback gained 8 yd on first down. The quarterback was sacked for a 5-yd loss on second down.

2. **Temperature High and Low.** The highest recorded temperature in Nevada is 125°F on June 29, 1994, in Laughlin. The lowest recorded temperature in Nevada is 50°F below zero on June 8, 1937, in San Jacinto.

   Source: National Climatic Data Center, Asheville, NC, and Storm Phillips, STORMFAX, INC.

3. **Stock Decrease.** The stock of Wendy's decreased from $41 per share to $38 per share over a recent period.

   Source: The New York Stock Exchange

4. At 10 sec before liftoff, ignition occurs. At 148 sec after liftoff, the first stage is detached from the rocket.

5. A submarine dove 120 ft, rose 50 ft, and then dove 80 ft.

Answers on page A-23

a Tell which integers correspond to the situation.

1. *Pollution Fine.* In 2003, The Colonial Pipeline Company was fined a record $34 million for pollution.
Source: Green Consumer Guide.com

2. *Lake Powell.* The water level of Lake Powell, a desert reservoir behind Glen Canyon Dam in northern Arizona and southeastern Utah, has dropped 130 ft since 2000.

3. On Wednesday, the temperature was 24° above zero. On Thursday, it was 2° below zero.

4. A student deposited her tax refund of $750 in a savings account. Two weeks later, she withdrew $125 to pay sorority fees.

5. *Highest and Lowest Temperatures* The highest temperature ever created on earth was 950,000,000°F. The lowest temperature ever created was approximately 460°F below zero.
Source: *The Guinness Book of Records,* 2004

6. *Extreme Climate.* Verkhoyansk, a river port in northeast Siberia, has the most extreme climate on the planet. Its average monthly winter temperature is 58.5°F below zero, and its average monthly summer temperature is 56.5°F.
Source: *The Guinness Book of Records,* 2004

7. In bowling, after the game, team A is 34 pins behind team B, and team B is 15 pins ahead of team C.

8. During a video game, Sara intercepted a missile worth 20 points, lost a starship worth 150 points, and captured a base worth 300 points.

b Graph the number on the number line.

9. $\dfrac{10}{3}$

10. $-\dfrac{17}{4}$

11. -5.2

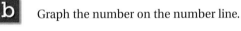

12. 4.78

c Convert to decimal notation.

13. $-\dfrac{7}{8}$

14. $-\dfrac{1}{8}$

15. $\dfrac{5}{6}$

16. $\dfrac{5}{3}$

17. $\dfrac{7}{6}$

18. $\dfrac{5}{12}$

19. $\dfrac{2}{3}$

20. $\dfrac{1}{4}$

21. $-\dfrac{1}{2}$

22. $-\dfrac{5}{8}$

23. $-8\dfrac{7}{25}$

24. $-9\dfrac{5}{16}$

d Use either < or > for ☐ to write a true sentence.

25. 8 ☐ 0

26. 3 ☐ 0

27. −8 ☐ 3

28. 6 ☐ −6

29. −8 ☐ 8

30. 0 ☐ −9

31. −8 ☐ −5

32. −4 ☐ −3

33. −5 ☐ −11

34. −3 ☐ −4

35. −6 ☐ −5

36. −10 ☐ −14

37. 2.14 ☐ 1.24

38. −3.3 ☐ −2.2

39. −14.5 ☐ 0.011

40. 17.2 ☐ −1.67

41. $-12\frac{5}{8}$ ☐ $-6\frac{3}{8}$

42. $-7\frac{5}{16}$ ☐ $-3\frac{11}{16}$

43. $\frac{5}{12}$ ☐ $\frac{11}{25}$

44. $-\frac{13}{16}$ ☐ $-\frac{5}{9}$

e Find the absolute value.

45. $|-3|$

46. $|-7|$

47. $|18|$

48. $|0|$

49. $|325|$

50. $|-4|$

51. $|-3.625|$

52. $\left|-7\frac{4}{5}\right|$

53. $\left|-\frac{2}{3}\right|$

54. $\left|-\frac{10}{7}\right|$

55. $\left|\frac{0}{4}\right|$

56. $|14.8|$

57. **D**w Give three examples of rational numbers that are not integers. Explain.

58. **D**w Give three examples of irrational numbers. Explain the difference between an irrational number and a rational number.

SKILL MAINTENANCE

Find the prime factorization. [2.1d]

59. 54

60. 192

61. 102

62. 260

63. 864

64. 468

Find the LCM. [3.1a]

65. 6, 18

66. 18, 24

67. 6, 24, 32

68. 12, 24, 36

69. 48, 56, 64

70. 12, 36, 84

SYNTHESIS

Use either <, >, or = for ☐ to write a true sentence.

71. $|-5|$ ☐ $|-2|$

72. $|4|$ ☐ $|-7|$

73. $|-8|$ ☐ $|8|$

List in order from the least to the greatest.

74. $-\frac{2}{3}, \frac{1}{2}, -\frac{3}{4}, -\frac{5}{6}, \frac{3}{8}, \frac{1}{6}$

75. $-8\frac{7}{8}, 7, -5, |-6|, 4, |3|, -8\frac{5}{8}, -100, 0, 1^7, \frac{14}{4}, -\frac{67}{8}$

Objectives

a Add real numbers without using a number line.

b Find the opposite, or additive inverse, of a real number.

Add using a number line.

1. $0 + (-3)$

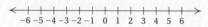

2. $1 + (-4)$

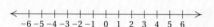

3. $-3 + (-2)$

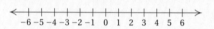

4. $-3 + 7$

5. $-2.4 + 2.4$

6. $-\dfrac{5}{2} + \dfrac{1}{2}$

Answers on page A-23

10.2 ADDITION OF REAL NUMBERS

We now consider addition of real numbers. First, to gain an understanding, we add using a number line. Then we consider rules for addition.

ADDITION ON A NUMBER LINE

Addition of numbers can be illustrated on a number line. To do the addition $a + b$, we start at 0. Then move to a and then move according to b.

a) If b is positive, we move from a to the right.

b) If b is negative, we move from a to the left.

c) If b is 0, we stay at a.

EXAMPLE 1 Add: $3 + (-5)$.

We start at 0 and move to 3. Then we move 5 units left since -5 is negative.

$3 + (-5) = -2$

EXAMPLE 2 Add: $-4 + (-3)$.

We start at 0 and move to -4. Then we move 3 units left since -3 is negative.

$-4 + (-3) = -7$

EXAMPLE 3 Add: $-4 + 9$.

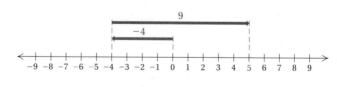

$-4 + 9 = 5$

EXAMPLE 4 Add: $-5.2 + 0$.

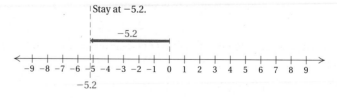

$-5.2 + 0 = -5.2$

a Addition Without a Number Line

You may have noticed some patterns in the preceding examples. These lead us to rules for adding without using a number line that are more efficient for adding larger or more complicated numbers.

RULES FOR ADDITION OF REAL NUMBERS

1. *Positive numbers*: Add the same as arithmetic numbers. The answer is positive.
2. *Negative numbers*: Add absolute values. The answer is negative.
3. *A positive and a negative number*: Subtract the smaller absolute value from the larger. Then:

   a) If the positive number has the greater absolute value, the answer is positive.
   b) If the negative number has the greater absolute value, the answer is negative.
   c) If the numbers have the same absolute value, the answer is 0.

4. *One number is zero*: The sum is the other number.

Rule 4 is known as the **identity property of 0.** It says that for any real number a, $a + 0 = a$.

EXAMPLES   Add without using a number line.

5. $-12 + (-7) = -19$ Add the absolute values, 12 and 7, getting 19. Make the answer *negative*, -19.

6. $-1.4 + 8.5 = 7.1$ The absolute values are 1.4 and 8.5. The difference is 7.1. The positive number has the larger absolute value, so the answer is *positive*, 7.1.

7. $-36 + 21 = -15$ The absolute values are 36 and 21. The difference is 15. The negative number has the larger absolute value, so the answer is *negative*, -15.

8. $1.5 + (-1.5) = 0$ The numbers have the same absolute value. The sum is 0.

9. $-\dfrac{7}{8} + 0 = -\dfrac{7}{8}$ One number is zero. The sum is $-\dfrac{7}{8}$.

10. $-9.2 + 3.1 = -6.1$

11. $-\dfrac{3}{2} + \dfrac{9}{2} = \dfrac{6}{2} = 3$

12. $-\dfrac{2}{3} + \dfrac{5}{8} = -\dfrac{16}{24} + \dfrac{15}{24} = -\dfrac{1}{24}$

Do Exercises 7–20.

Suppose we wish to add several numbers, some positive and some negative, as follows. How can we proceed?

$$15 + (-2) + 7 + 14 + (-5) + (-12)$$

Add without using a number line.

7. $-5 + (-6)$

8. $-9 + (-3)$

9. $-4 + 6$

10. $-7 + 3$

11. $5 + (-7)$

12. $-20 + 20$

13. $-11 + (-11)$

14. $10 + (-7)$

15. $-0.17 + 0.7$

16. $-6.4 + 8.7$

17. $-4.5 + (-3.2)$

18. $-8.6 + 2.4$

19. $\dfrac{5}{9} + \left(-\dfrac{7}{9}\right)$

20. $-\dfrac{1}{5} + \left(-\dfrac{3}{4}\right)$

Answers on page A-23

Add.

21. $(-15) + (-37) + 25 + 42 + (-59) + (-14)$

22. $42 + (-81) + (-28) + 24 + 18 + (-31)$

23. $-2.5 + (-10) + 6 + (-7.5)$

24. $-35 + 17 + 14 + (-27) + 31 + (-12)$

Find the opposite, or additive inverse, of each of the following.

25. -4

26. 8.7

27. -7.74

28. $-\dfrac{8}{9}$

29. 0

30. 12

Answers on page A-23

The commutative and associative laws hold for real numbers. Thus we can change grouping and order as we please when adding. For instance, we can group the positive numbers together and the negative numbers together and add them separately. Then we add the two results.

EXAMPLE 13   Add: $15 + (-2) + 7 + 14 + (-5) + (-12)$.

a) $15 + 7 + 14 = 36$ Adding the positive numbers

b) $-2 + (-5) + (-12) = -19$ Adding the negative numbers

c) $36 + (-19) = 17$ Adding the results of (a) and (b)

We can also add the numbers in any other order we wish, say, from left to right as follows:

$$
\begin{aligned}
15 + (-2) + 7 + 14 + (-5) + (-12) &= 13 + 7 + 14 + (-5) + (-12) \\
&= 20 + 14 + (-5) + (-12) \\
&= 34 + (-5) + (-12) \\
&= 29 + (-12) \\
&= 17
\end{aligned}
$$

Do Exercises 21–24.

b Opposites, or Additive Inverses

Suppose we add two numbers that are **opposites,** such as 6 and -6. The result is 0. When opposites are added, the result is always 0. Such numbers are also called **additive inverses.** Every real number has an opposite, or additive inverse.

OPPOSITES, OR ADDITIVE INVERSES

Two numbers whose sum is 0 are called **opposites,** or **additive inverses,** of each other.

EXAMPLES   Find the opposite, or additive inverse, of each number.

14. 34 The opposite of 34 is -34 because $34 + (-34) = 0$.

15. -8 The opposite of -8 is 8 because $-8 + 8 = 0$.

16. 0 The opposite of 0 is 0 because $0 + 0 = 0$.

17. $-\dfrac{7}{8}$ The opposite of $-\dfrac{7}{8}$ is $\dfrac{7}{8}$ because $-\dfrac{7}{8} + \dfrac{7}{8} = 0$.

Do Exercises 25–30.

To name the opposite, we use the symbol $-$, as follows.

SYMBOLIZING OPPOSITES

The opposite, or additive inverse, of a number a can be named $-a$ (read "the opposite of a," or "the additive inverse of a").

Note that if we take a number, say 8, and find its opposite, -8, and then find the opposite of the result, we will have the original number, 8, again.

THE OPPOSITE OF THE OPPOSITE

The opposite of the opposite of a number is the number itself. (The additive inverse of the additive inverse of a number is the number itself.) That is, for any number a,

$$-(-a) = a.$$

EXAMPLE 18 Evaluate $-x$ and $-(-x)$ when $x = 16$.

We replace x in each case with 16.

a) If $x = 16$, then $-x = -16 = -16$.   The opposite of 16 is -16.

b) If $x = 16$, then $-(-x) = -(-16) = 16$.   The opposite of the opposite of 16 is 16.

EXAMPLE 19 Evaluate $-x$ and $-(-x)$ when $x = -3$.

We replace x in each case with -3.

a) If $x = -3$, then $-x = -(-3) = 3$.

b) If $x = -3$, then $-(-x) = -(-(-3)) = -(3) = -3$.

Note that in Example 19 we used an extra set of parentheses to show that we are substituting the negative number -3 for x. Symbolism like $--x$ is not considered meaningful.

Do Exercises 31–36.

A symbol such as -8 is usually read "negative 8." It could be read "the additive inverse of 8," because the additive inverse of 8 is negative 8. It could also be read "the opposite of 8," because the opposite of 8 is -8. Thus a symbol like -8 can be read in more than one way. A symbol like $-x$, which has a variable, should be read "the opposite of x" or "the additive inverse of x" and *not* "negative x," because we do not know whether x represents a positive number, a negative number, or 0.

We can use the symbolism $-a$ to restate the definition of opposite, or additive inverse.

THE SUM OF OPPOSITES

For any real number a, the opposite, or additive inverse, of a, expressed as $-a$, is such that

$$a + (-a) = (-a) + a = 0.$$

SIGNS OF NUMBERS

A negative number is sometimes said to have a "negative sign." A positive number is said to have a "positive sign." When we replace a number with its opposite, we can say that we have "changed its sign."

EXAMPLES Change the sign. (Find the opposite.)

20. -3 $-(-3) = 3$

21. $-\dfrac{2}{13}$ $-\left(-\dfrac{2}{13}\right) = \dfrac{2}{13}$

22. 0 $-(0) = 0$

23. 14 $-(14) = -14$

Do Exercises 37–40.

Evaluate $-x$ and $-(-x)$ when:

31. $x = 14$.

32. $x = 1$.

33. $x = -19$.

34. $x = -1.6$.

35. $x = \dfrac{2}{3}$.

36. $x = -\dfrac{9}{8}$.

Find the opposite. (Change the sign.)

37. -4

38. -13.4

39. 0

40. $\dfrac{1}{4}$

Answers on page A-23

CALCULATOR CORNER

Entering Negative Numbers On many calculators, we can enter negative numbers using the $\boxed{+/-}$ key. This allows us to perform calculations with real numbers. To enter -8, for example, we press $\boxed{8}$ $\boxed{+/-}$. To find the sum $-14 + (-9)$, we press $\boxed{1}$ $\boxed{4}$ $\boxed{+/-}$ $\boxed{+}$ $\boxed{9}$ $\boxed{+/-}$ $\boxed{=}$. The result is -23. Note that it is not necessary to use parentheses when entering this expression.

Exercises: Add.

1. $-5 + 7$

2. $-4 + 17$

3. $-6 + (-9)$

4. $3 + (-11)$

5. $1.5 + (-4.8)$

6. $-2.8 + (-10.6)$

593

MathXL MyMathLab InterAct Math Math Tutor Center Digital Video Tutor CD 5 Videotape 10 Student's Solutions Manual

a   Add. Do not use a number line except as a check.

1. $-9 + 2$

2. $-5 + 2$

3. $-10 + 6$

4. $4 + (-3)$

5. $-8 + 8$

6. $4 + (-4)$

7. $-3 + (-5)$

8. $-6 + (-8)$

9. $-7 + 0$

10. $-10 + 0$

11. $0 + (-27)$

12. $0 + (-36)$

13. $17 + (-17)$

14. $-20 + 20$

15. $-17 + (-25)$

16. $-23 + (-14)$

17. $18 + (-18)$

18. $-13 + 13$

19. $-18 + 18$

20. $11 + (-11)$

21. $8 + (-5)$

22. $-7 + 8$

23. $-4 + (-5)$

24. $10 + (-12)$

25. $13 + (-6)$

26. $-3 + 14$

27. $-25 + 25$

28. $40 + (-40)$

29. $63 + (-18)$

30. $85 + (-65)$

31. $-6.5 + 4.7$

32. $-3.6 + 1.9$

33. $-2.8 + (-5.3)$

34. $-7.9 + (-6.5)$

35. $-\dfrac{3}{5} + \dfrac{2}{5}$

36. $-\dfrac{4}{3} + \dfrac{2}{3}$

37. $-\dfrac{3}{7} + \left(-\dfrac{5}{7}\right)$

38. $-\dfrac{4}{9} + \left(-\dfrac{6}{9}\right)$

39. $-\dfrac{5}{8} + \dfrac{1}{4}$

40. $-\dfrac{5}{6} + \dfrac{2}{3}$

41. $-\dfrac{3}{7} + \left(-\dfrac{2}{5}\right)$

42. $-\dfrac{5}{8} + \left(-\dfrac{1}{3}\right)$

43. $-\dfrac{3}{5} + \left(-\dfrac{2}{15}\right)$

44. $-\dfrac{5}{9} + \left(-\dfrac{5}{18}\right)$

45. $-5.7 + (-7.2) + 6.6$

46. $-10.3 + (-7.5) + 3.1$

47. $-\dfrac{7}{16} + \dfrac{7}{8}$

48. $-\dfrac{3}{24} + \dfrac{7}{36}$

49. $75 + (-14) + (-17) + (-5)$

50. $28 + (-44) + 17 + 31 + (-94)$

51. $-44 + \left(-\dfrac{3}{8}\right) + 95 + \left(-\dfrac{5}{8}\right)$

52. $24 + 3.1 + (-44) + (-8.2) + 63$

53. $98 + (-54) + 113 + (-998) + 44 + (-612) + (-18) + 334$

54. $-455 + (-123) + 1026 + (-919) + 213 + 111 + (-874)$

b   Find the opposite, or additive inverse.

55. 24   **56.** -84 **57.** -26.9 **58.** 27.4

Find $-x$ when:

59. $x = 9.$ **60.** $x = -26.$ **61.** $x = -\dfrac{14}{3}.$ **62.** $x = \dfrac{1}{526}.$

Find $-(-x)$ when:

63. $x = -65.$ **64.** $x = 31.$ **65.** $x = \dfrac{5}{3}.$ **66.** $x = -7.8.$

Change the sign. (Find the opposite.)

67. -14 **68.** -18.3 **69.** 10   **70.** $-\dfrac{5}{8}$

71. **D_W** Explain in your own words why the sum of two negative numbers is always negative.

72. **D_W** A student states that -93 is "bigger than" -47. What mistake is the student making?

Find the area.

73. [9.2a]

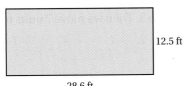

12.5 ft

28.6 ft

74. [9.2b]

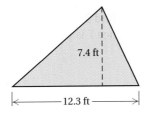

7.4 ft

12.3 ft

75. [9.2a]

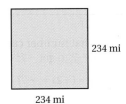

234 mi

234 mi

76. [9.2b]

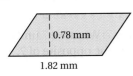

0.78 mm

1.82 mm

77. [9.2b]

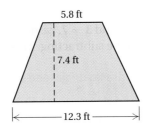

5.8 ft

7.4 ft

12.3 ft

78. [9.3c]

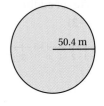

50.4 m

79. For what numbers x is $-x$ negative?

80. For what numbers x is $-x$ positive?

Add.

81. ▦ $-345,882 + (-295,097)$

82. ▦ $2706.835 + (-0.005684)$

Tell whether the sum is positive, negative, or zero.

83. If n is positive and m is negative, then $-n + m$ is _____ .

84. If $n = m$ and n is negative, then $-n + (-m)$ is _____ .

595

Read each of the following. Then subtract by adding the opposite of the number being subtracted.

17. $3 - 11$

18. $12 - 5$

19. $-12 - (-9)$

20. $-12.4 - 10.9$

21. $-\dfrac{4}{5} - \left(-\dfrac{4}{5}\right)$

Simplify.

22. $-6 - (-2) - (-4) - 12 + 3$

23. $\dfrac{2}{3} - \dfrac{4}{5} - \left(-\dfrac{11}{15}\right) + \dfrac{7}{10} - \dfrac{5}{2}$

24. $-9.6 + 7.4 - (-3.9) - (-11)$

25. Temperature Extremes.
The highest temperature ever recorded in the United States was 134°F in Greenland Ranch, California, on July 10, 1913. The lowest temperature ever recorded was −80°F in Prospect Creek, Alaska, on January 23, 1971. How much higher was the temperature in Greenland Ranch than the temperature in Prospect Creek?

Source: National Oceanographic and Atmospheric Administration

Answers on page A-23

When several additions and subtractions occur together, we can make them all additions.

EXAMPLES *Simplify.*

10. $8 - (-4) - 2 - (-4) + 2 = 8 + 4 + (-2) + 4 + 2$ Adding the opposite
$$= 16$$

11. $8.2 - (-6.1) + 2.3 - (-4) = 8.2 + 6.1 + 2.3 + 4 = 20.6$

12. $\dfrac{3}{4} - \left(-\dfrac{1}{12}\right) - \dfrac{5}{6} - \dfrac{2}{3} = \dfrac{9}{12} + \dfrac{1}{12} + \left(-\dfrac{10}{12}\right) + \left(-\dfrac{8}{12}\right)$

$$= \dfrac{9 + 1 + (-10) + (-8)}{12}$$

$$= \dfrac{-8}{12} = -\dfrac{8}{12} = -\dfrac{2}{3}$$

Do Exercises 22–24.

b   Applications and Problem Solving

Let's now see how we can use addition and subtraction of real numbers to solve applied problems.

EXAMPLE 13 *Surface Temperatures on Mars.* Surface temperatures on Mars vary from −128°C during polar night to 27°C at the equator during midday at the closest point in orbit to the Sun. Find the difference between the highest value and the lowest value in this temperature range.

Source: Mars Institute

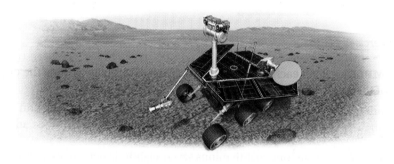

We let D = the difference in the temperatures. Then the problem translates to the following subtraction:

Difference in temperature	is	Highest temperature	minus	Lowest temperature.
↓	↓	↓	↓	↓
D	$=$	27	$-$	(-128)

We then solve the equation: $D = 27 - (-128) = 27 + 128 = 155.$

The difference in the temperatures is 155°C.

Do Exercise 25.

10.3

EXERCISE SET

For Extra Help

MathXL | MyMathLab | InterAct Math | Math Tutor Center | Digital Video Tutor CD 5 Videotape 10 | Student's Solutions Manual

a   Subtract.

1. $3 - 7$

2. $5 - 10$

3. $0 - 7$

4. $0 - 8$

5. $-8 - (-2)$

6. $-6 - (-8)$

7. $-10 - (-10)$

8. $-8 - (-8)$

9. $12 - 16$

10. $14 - 19$

11. $20 - 27$

12. $26 - 7$

13. $-9 - (-3)$

14. $-6 - (-9)$

15. $-11 - (-11)$

16. $-14 - (-14)$

17. $8 - (-3)$

18. $-7 - 4$

19. $-6 - 8$

20. $6 - (-10)$

21. $-4 - (-9)$

22. $-14 - 2$

23. $2 - 9$

24. $2 - 8$

25. $0 - 5$

26. $0 - 10$

27. $-5 - (-2)$

28. $-3 - (-1)$

29. $2 - 25$

30. $18 - 63$

31. $-42 - 26$

32. $-18 - 63$

33. $-71 - 2$

34. $-49 - 3$

35. $24 - (-92)$

36. $48 - (-73)$

37. $-2.8 - 0$

38. $6.04 - 1.1$

39. $\dfrac{3}{8} - \dfrac{5}{8}$

40. $\dfrac{3}{9} - \dfrac{9}{9}$

41. $\dfrac{3}{4} - \dfrac{2}{3}$

42. $\dfrac{5}{8} - \dfrac{3}{4}$

43. $-\dfrac{3}{4} - \dfrac{2}{3}$

44. $-\dfrac{5}{8} - \dfrac{3}{4}$

45. $-\dfrac{5}{8} - \left(-\dfrac{3}{4}\right)$

46. $-\dfrac{3}{4} - \left(-\dfrac{2}{3}\right)$

47. $6.1 - (-13.8)$

48. $1.5 - (-3.5)$

49. $-3.2 - 5.8$

50. $-2.7 - 5.9$

51. $0.99 - 1$

52. $0.87 - 1$

53. $3 - 5.7$

54. $5.1 - 3.02$

55. $7 - 10.53$

56. $8 - (-9.3)$

57. $\dfrac{1}{6} - \dfrac{2}{3}$

58. $-\dfrac{3}{8} - \left(-\dfrac{1}{2}\right)$

59. $-\dfrac{4}{7} - \left(-\dfrac{10}{7}\right)$

60. $\dfrac{12}{5} - \dfrac{12}{5}$

61. $-\dfrac{7}{10} - \dfrac{10}{15}$

62. $-\dfrac{4}{18} - \left(-\dfrac{2}{9}\right)$

63. $\dfrac{1}{13} - \dfrac{1}{12}$

64. $-\dfrac{1}{7} - \left(-\dfrac{1}{6}\right)$

Simplify.

65. $18 - (-15) - 3 - (-5) + 2$

66. $22 - (-18) + 7 + (-42) - 27$

67. $-31 + (-28) - (-14) - 17$

68. $-43 - (-19) - (-21) + 25$

69. $-93 - (-84) - 41 - (-56)$

70. $84 + (-99) + 44 - (-18) - 43$

71. $-5 - (-30) + 30 + 40 - (-12)$

72. $14 - (-50) + 20 - (-32)$

73. $132 - (-21) + 45 - (-21)$

74. $81 - (-20) - 14 - (-50) + 53$

b Solve.

75. *Lake Level.* In the course of one four-month period, the water level of Lake Champlain went down 2 ft, up 1 ft, down 5 ft, and up 3 ft. How much had the lake level changed at the end of the four months?

76. *Credit Card Bills.* On August 1, Lyle's credit card bill shows that he owes $470. During August, he sends a check to the credit card company for $45, charges another $160 in merchandise, and then pays off another $500 of his bill. What is the new balance of Lyle's account at the end of August (excluding interest for August)?

77. *Temperature Changes.* One day the temperature in Lawrence, Kansas, is 32° at 6:00 A.M. It rises 15° by noon, but falls 50° by midnight when a cold front moves in. What is the final temperature?

78. *Stock Price Changes.* On a recent day, the price of a stock opened at a value of $61.38. It rose $4.75, dropped $7.38, and rose $5.13. Find the value of the stock at the end of the day.

79. *Changes in Elevation.* The lowest elevation in North America, Death Valley, California, is 282 ft below sea level. The highest elevation in North America, Mt. McKinley, Alaska, is 20,320 ft. Find the difference in elevation between the highest point and the lowest.

Source: National Geographic Society

80. *Tallest Mountain.* The tallest mountain in the world, when measured from base to peak, is Mauna Kea (White Mountain) in Hawaii. From its base 19,684 ft below sea level in the Hawaiian Trough, it rises 33,480 ft. What is the elevation of the peak?

Source: *The Guinness Book of Records*

81. *Account Balance.* Leah has $460 in her checking account. She writes a check for $530, makes a deposit of $75, and then writes a check for $90. What is the balance in the account?

82. *Cell Phone Bill.* Erika's cell phone bill for July was $82. She made a payment of $50 and then made $37 worth of calls in August. How much did she then owe on her cell phone bill?

83. *Temperature Records.* The greatest recorded temperature change in one 24-hr period occurred between January 23 and January 24, 1916, in Browning, Montana, where the temperature fell from 44°F to −56°F. How much did the temperature drop that day?

Source: *The Guinness Book of Records, 2004*

84. *Low Points on Continents.* The lowest point in Africa is Lake Assal, which is 512 ft below sea level. The lowest point in South America is the Valdes Peninsula, which is 131 ft below sea level. How much lower is Lake Assal than the Valdes Peninsula?

Source: National Geographic Society

85. $\mathbf{D_W}$ If a negative number is subtracted from a positive number, will the result always be positive? Why or why not?

86. $\mathbf{D_W}$ Write a problem for a classmate to solve. Design the problem so that the solution is "The temperature dropped to −9°."

> **SKILL MAINTENANCE**

87. Find the area of a rectangle that is 8.4 cm by 11.5 cm. [9.2a]

88. Find the prime factorization of 750. [2.1d]

89. Find the LCM of 36 and 54. [3.1a]

90. Find the area of a square whose sides are of length 11.2 km. [9.2a]

Evaluate. [1.9b]

91. 4^3

92. 5^3

Solve. [1.8a]

93. How many 12-oz cans of soda can be filled with 96 oz of soda?

94. A case of soda contains 24 bottles. If each bottle contains 12 oz, how many ounces of soda are in the case?

> **SYNTHESIS**

Tell whether the statement is true or false for all integers m and n. If false, give an example to show why.

95. $-n = 0 - n$

96. $n - 0 = 0 - n$

97. If $m \neq n$, then $m - n \neq 0$.

98. If $m = -n$, then $m + n = 0$.

99. If $m + n = 0$, then m and n are opposites.

100. If $m - n = 0$, then $m = -n$.

101. $m = -n$ if m and n are opposites.

102. If $m = -m$, then $m = 0$.

601

Objective

a Multiply real numbers.

1. Complete, as in the example.

$$4 \cdot 10 = 40$$
$$3 \cdot 10 = 30$$
$$2 \cdot 10 =$$
$$1 \cdot 10 =$$
$$0 \cdot 10 =$$
$$-1 \cdot 10 =$$
$$-2 \cdot 10 =$$
$$-3 \cdot 10 =$$

Multiply.

2. $-3 \cdot 6$

3. $20 \cdot (-5)$

4. $4 \cdot (-20)$

5. $-\dfrac{2}{3} \cdot \dfrac{5}{6}$

6. $-4.23(7.1)$

7. $\dfrac{7}{8}\left(-\dfrac{4}{5}\right)$

8. Complete, as in the example.

$$3 \cdot (-10) = -30$$
$$2 \cdot (-10) = -20$$
$$1 \cdot (-10) =$$
$$0 \cdot (-10) =$$
$$-1 \cdot (-10) =$$
$$-2 \cdot (-10) =$$
$$-3 \cdot (-10) =$$

Answers on page A-23

a Multiplication

Multiplication of real numbers is very much like multiplication of arithmetic numbers. The only difference is that we must determine whether the answer is positive or negative.

MULTIPLICATION OF A POSITIVE NUMBER AND A NEGATIVE NUMBER

To see how to multiply a positive number and a negative number, consider the pattern of the following.

This number decreases by 1 each time.

$$4 \cdot 5 = 20$$
$$3 \cdot 5 = 15$$
$$2 \cdot 5 = 10$$
$$1 \cdot 5 = 5$$
$$0 \cdot 5 = 0$$
$$-1 \cdot 5 = -5$$
$$-2 \cdot 5 = -10$$
$$-3 \cdot 5 = -15$$

This number decreases by 5 each time.

Do Exercise 1.

According to this pattern, it looks as though the product of a negative number and a positive number is negative. That is the case, and we have the first part of the rule for multiplying real numbers.

> **THE PRODUCT OF A POSITIVE NUMBER AND A NEGATIVE NUMBER**
>
> To multiply a positive number and a negative number, multiply their absolute values. The answer is negative.

EXAMPLES Multiply.

1. $8(-5) = -40$　　**2.** $-\dfrac{1}{3} \cdot \dfrac{5}{7} = -\dfrac{5}{21}$　　**3.** $(-7.2)5 = -36$

Do Exercises 2–7.

MULTIPLICATION OF TWO NEGATIVE NUMBERS

How do we multiply two negative numbers? Again we look for a pattern.

This number decreases by 1 each time.

$$4 \cdot (-5) = -20$$
$$3 \cdot (-5) = -15$$
$$2 \cdot (-5) = -10$$
$$1 \cdot (-5) = -5$$
$$0 \cdot (-5) = 0$$
$$-1 \cdot (-5) = 5$$
$$-2 \cdot (-5) = 10$$
$$-3 \cdot (-5) = 15$$

This number increases by 5 each time.

Do Exercise 8.

49. $4 \cdot (-4) \cdot (-5) \cdot (-12)$

50. $-2 \cdot (-3) \cdot (-4) \cdot (-5)$

51. $0.07 \cdot (-7) \cdot 6 \cdot (-6)$

52. $80 \cdot (-0.8) \cdot (-90) \cdot (-0.09)$

53. $\left(-\dfrac{5}{6}\right)\left(\dfrac{1}{8}\right)\left(-\dfrac{3}{7}\right)\left(-\dfrac{1}{7}\right)$

54. $\left(\dfrac{4}{5}\right)\left(-\dfrac{2}{3}\right)\left(-\dfrac{15}{7}\right)\left(\dfrac{1}{2}\right)$

55. $(-14) \cdot (-27) \cdot (-2)$

56. $7 \cdot (-6) \cdot 5 \cdot (-4) \cdot 3 \cdot (-2) \cdot 1 \cdot (-1)$

57. $(-8)(-9)(-10)$

58. $(-7)(-8)(-9)(-10)$

59. $(-6)(-7)(-8)(-9)(-10)$

60. $(-5)(-6)(-7)(-8)(-9)(-10)$

61. $\mathbf{D_W}$ What rule have we developed that would tell you the sign of $(-7)^8$ and $(-7)^{11}$ without doing the computations? Explain.

62. $\mathbf{D_W}$ Which number is larger, $(-3)^{79}$ or $(-5)^{79}$? Why?

VOCABULARY REINFORCEMENT

In each of Exercises 63–70, fill in the blank with the correct term from the given list. Some of the choices may not be used.

63. A(n) _____ triangle is a triangle in which two or more sides are the same length.   [9.5d]

64. A(n) _____ angle is an angle whose measure is greater than 0° and less than 90°.   [9.5b]

65. Two angles are _____ if the sum of their measures is 90°.   [9.5c]

66. The _____ interest I on principal P, invested for t years at interest rate r, is given by $I = Prt$.   [6.7a]

67. A(n) _____ price is the ratio of price to the number of units.   [5.2b]

68. The _____ of a set of data is the number or numbers that occur most often.   [7.1c]

69. A(n) _____ is a figure with four sides and four 90° angles.   [9.2a]

70. If a number is a product of two identical factors, then either factor is called a _____ of the number.   [9.6a]

parallelogram

rectangle

complementary

supplementary

scalene

isosceles

square root

unit

median

mode

obtuse

acute

simple

compound

71. What must be true of a and b if $-ab$ is to be (a) positive? (b) zero? (c) negative?

Objectives

a Divide integers.

b Find the reciprocal of a real number.

c Divide real numbers.

d Solve applied problems involving multiplication and division of real numbers.

e Simplify expressions using rules for order of operations.

Divide.

1. $6 \div (-3)$

Think: What number multiplied by -3 gives 6?

2. $\dfrac{-15}{-3}$

Think: What number multiplied by -3 gives -15?

3. $-24 \div 8$

Think: What number multiplied by 8 gives -24?

4. $\dfrac{-72}{-8}$

5. $\dfrac{30}{-5}$

6. $\dfrac{30}{-7}$

Answers on page A-24

10.5 DIVISION OF REAL NUMBERS AND ORDER OF OPERATIONS

We now consider division of real numbers. The definition of division results in rules for division that are the same as those for multiplication.

a Division of Integers

> **DIVISION**
>
> The quotient $a \div b$, or $\dfrac{a}{b}$, where $b \neq 0$, is that unique real number c for which $a = b \cdot c$.

EXAMPLES Divide, if possible. Check your answer.

1. $14 \div (-7) = -2$ *Think*: What number multiplied by -7 gives 14? That number is -2. *Check*: $(-2)(-7) = 14$.

2. $\dfrac{-32}{-4} = 8$ *Think*: What number multiplied by -4 gives -32? That number is 8. *Check*: $8(-4) = -32$.

3. $\dfrac{-10}{7} = -\dfrac{10}{7}$ *Think*: What number multiplied by 7 gives -10? That number is $-\frac{10}{7}$. *Check*: $-\frac{10}{7} \cdot 7 = -10$.

4. $\dfrac{-17}{0}$ is **not defined.**   *Think*: What number multiplied by 0 gives -17? There is no such number because the product of 0 and *any* number is 0.

Do Exercises 1–3.

The rules for division are the same as those for multiplication.

> To multiply or divide two real numbers (where the divisor is nonzero):
>
> **a)** Multiply or divide the absolute values.
> **b)** If the signs are the same, the answer is positive.
> **c)** If the signs are different, the answer is negative.

Do Exercises 4–6.

EXCLUDING DIVISION BY ZERO

Example 4 shows why we cannot divide -17 by 0. We can use the same argument to show why we cannot divide any nonzero number b by 0. Consider $b \div 0$. We look for a number that when multiplied by 0 gives b. There is no such number because the product of 0 and any number is 0. Thus we cannot divide a nonzero number b by 0.

On the other hand, if we divide 0 by 0, we look for a number c such that $0 \cdot c = 0$. But $0 \cdot c = 0$ for any number c. Thus it appears that $0 \div 0$ could be any number we choose. Getting any answer we want when we divide 0 by 0 would be very confusing. Thus we agree that division by zero is not defined.

EXCLUDING DIVISION BY 0

Division by 0 is not defined:

$a \div 0$, or $\dfrac{a}{0}$, is not defined for all real numbers a.

DIVIDING 0 BY OTHER NUMBERS

Note that $0 \div 8 = 0$ because $0 = 0 \cdot 8$.

DIVIDENDS OF 0

Zero divided by any nonzero real number is 0:

$$\frac{0}{a} = 0, \qquad a \neq 0.$$

EXAMPLES Divide.

5. $0 \div (-6) = 0$ **6.** $\dfrac{0}{12} = 0$ **7.** $\dfrac{-3}{0}$ is not defined.

Do Exercises 7 and 8.

b   Reciprocals

When two numbers like $\frac{7}{8}$ and $\frac{8}{7}$ are multiplied, the result is 1. Such numbers are called **reciprocals** of each other. Every nonzero real number has a reciprocal, also called a **multiplicative inverse.**

RECIPROCALS

Two numbers whose product is 1 are called **reciprocals** of each other.

EXAMPLES Find the reciprocal.

8. -5 The reciprocal of -5 is $-\frac{1}{5}$ because $-5\left(-\frac{1}{5}\right) = 1$.
9. $-\frac{1}{2}$ The reciprocal of $-\frac{1}{2}$ is -2 because $\left(-\frac{1}{2}\right)(-2) = 1$.
10. $-\frac{2}{3}$ The reciprocal of $-\frac{2}{3}$ is $-\frac{3}{2}$ because $\left(-\frac{2}{3}\right)\left(-\frac{3}{2}\right) = 1$.

PROPERTIES OF RECIPROCALS

For $a \neq 0$, the reciprocal of a can be named $\dfrac{1}{a}$ and the reciprocal of $\dfrac{1}{a}$ is a.

The reciprocal of a nonzero number $\dfrac{a}{b}$ can be named $\dfrac{b}{a}$.

The number 0 has no reciprocal.

Do Exercises 9–14.

Divide, if possible.

7. $\dfrac{-5}{0}$

8. $\dfrac{0}{-3}$

Find the reciprocal.

9. $\dfrac{2}{3}$

10. $-\dfrac{5}{4}$

11. -3

12. $-\dfrac{1}{5}$

13. 5.78

14. $-\dfrac{2}{7}$

Answers on page A-24

15. Complete the following table.

NUMBER	OPPOSITE	RECIPROCAL
$\dfrac{2}{3}$		
$-\dfrac{5}{4}$		
0		
1		
-4.5		

The reciprocal of a positive number is also a positive number, because their product must be the positive number 1. The reciprocal of a negative number is also a negative number, because their product must be the positive number 1.

THE SIGN OF A RECIPROCAL

The reciprocal of a number has the same sign as the number itself.

It is important not to confuse *opposite* with *reciprocal*. Keep in mind that the opposite, or additive inverse, of a number is what we add to the number to get 0. A reciprocal, or multiplicative inverse, is what we multiply the number by to get 1. Compare the following.

Rewrite the division as a multiplication.

16. $\dfrac{4}{7} \div \left(-\dfrac{3}{5}\right)$

NUMBER	OPPOSITE (Change the sign.)	RECIPROCAL (Invert but do not change the sign.)
$-\dfrac{3}{8}$	$\dfrac{3}{8}$	$-\dfrac{8}{3}$
19	-19	$\dfrac{1}{19}$
$\dfrac{18}{7}$	$-\dfrac{18}{7}$	$\dfrac{7}{18}$
-7.9	7.9	$-\dfrac{1}{7.9}$ or $-\dfrac{10}{79}$
0	0	Undefined

$\left(-\dfrac{3}{8}\right)\left(-\dfrac{8}{3}\right) = 1$

$-\dfrac{3}{8} + \dfrac{3}{8} = 0$

17. $\dfrac{5}{-8}$

Do Exercise 15.

18. $\dfrac{-10}{7}$

C Division of Real Numbers

We know that we can subtract by adding an opposite. Similarly, we can divide by multiplying by a reciprocal.

RECIPROCALS AND DIVISION

For any real numbers a and b, $b \neq 0$,

$$a \div b = \frac{a}{b} = a \cdot \frac{1}{b}.$$

(To divide, multiply by the reciprocal of the divisor.)

---

19. $-\dfrac{2}{3} \div \dfrac{4}{7}$

20. $-5 \div 7$

EXAMPLES Rewrite the division as a multiplication.

11. $-4 \div 3$ $-4 \div 3$ is the same as $-4 \cdot \dfrac{1}{3}$

12. $\dfrac{6}{-7}$ $\dfrac{6}{-7} = 6\left(-\dfrac{1}{7}\right)$

13. $\dfrac{3}{5} \div \left(-\dfrac{9}{7}\right)$ $\dfrac{3}{5} \div \left(-\dfrac{9}{7}\right) = \dfrac{3}{5}\left(-\dfrac{7}{9}\right)$

Answers on page A-24

Do Exercises 16–20 on the preceding page.

When actually doing division calculations, we sometimes multiply by a reciprocal and we sometimes divide directly. With fraction notation, it is generally better to multiply by a reciprocal. With decimal notation, it is generally better to divide directly.

EXAMPLES Divide by multiplying by the reciprocal of the divisor.

14. $\dfrac{2}{3} \div \left(-\dfrac{5}{4}\right) = \dfrac{2}{3} \cdot \left(-\dfrac{4}{5}\right) = -\dfrac{8}{15}$

15. $-\dfrac{5}{6} \div \left(-\dfrac{3}{4}\right) = -\dfrac{5}{6} \cdot \left(-\dfrac{4}{3}\right) = \dfrac{20}{18} = \dfrac{10 \cdot 2}{9 \cdot 2} = \dfrac{10}{9} \cdot \dfrac{2}{2} = \dfrac{10}{9}$

> **Caution!**
>
> Be careful not to change the sign when taking a reciprocal!

16. $-\dfrac{3}{4} \div \dfrac{3}{10} = -\dfrac{3}{4} \cdot \left(\dfrac{10}{3}\right) = -\dfrac{30}{12} = -\dfrac{5}{2} \cdot \dfrac{6}{6} = -\dfrac{5}{2}$

With decimal notation, it is easier to carry out long division than to multiply by the reciprocal.

EXAMPLES Divide.

17. $-27.9 \div (-3) = \dfrac{-27.9}{-3} = 9.3$ Do the long division $3\overline{)27.9}$ (9.3)
The answer is positive.

18. $-6.3 \div 2.1 = -3$ Do the long division $2.1\overline{)6.3{\scriptstyle\wedge}0}$ (3.0)
The answer is negative.

Do Exercises 21–24.

d   Applications and Problem Solving

We can use multiplication and division to solve applied problems.

EXAMPLE 19 *Chemical Reaction.* During a chemical reaction, the temperature in the beaker decreased every minute by the same number of degrees. The temperature was 56°F at 10:10 A.M. By 10:42 A.M., the temperature had dropped to −12°F. By how many degrees did it change each minute?

Divide by multiplying by the reciprocal of the divisor.

21. $\dfrac{4}{7} \div \left(-\dfrac{3}{5}\right)$

22. $-\dfrac{8}{5} \div \dfrac{2}{3}$

23. $-\dfrac{12}{7} \div \left(-\dfrac{3}{4}\right)$

24. Divide: $21.7 \div (-3.1)$.

Answers on page A-24

25. Chemical Reaction. During a chemical reaction, the temperature in the beaker decreased every minute by the same number of degrees. The temperature was 71°F at 2:12 P.M. By 2:37 P.M., the temperature had changed to −14°F. By how many degrees did it change each minute?

We first determine by how many degrees d the temperature changed altogether. We subtract −12 from 56:

$$d = 56 - (-12) = 56 + 12 = 68.$$

The temperature changed a total of 68°. We can express this as −68° since the temperature dropped.

The amount of time t that passed was 42 − 10, or 32 min. Thus the number of degrees T that the temperature dropped each minute is given by

$$T = \frac{d}{t} = \frac{-68}{32} = -2.125.$$

The change was −2.125°F per minute.

Do Exercise 25.

e Order of Operations

When several operations are to be done in a calculation or a problem, we apply the same rules that we did in Sections 1.9, 3.7, and 4.4. We repeat them here for review. If you did not study those sections before, you should do so before continuing.

> **RULES FOR ORDER OF OPERATIONS**
>
> 1. Do all calculations within grouping symbols before operations outside.
> 2. Evaluate all exponential expressions.
> 3. Do all multiplications and divisions in order from left to right.
> 4. Do all additions and subtractions in order from left to right.

EXAMPLE 20 Simplify: $-34 \cdot 56 - 17$.

There are no parentheses or powers so we start with the third step.

$-34 \cdot 56 - 17 = -1904 - 17$ Carrying out all multiplications and divisions in order from left to right

$\qquad\qquad\qquad = -1921$ Carrying out all additions and subtractions in order from left to right

EXAMPLE 21 Simplify: $2^4 + 51 \cdot 4 - (37 + 23 \cdot 2)$.

$2^4 + 51 \cdot 4 - (37 + 23 \cdot 2)$

$= 2^4 + 51 \cdot 4 - (37 + 46)$ Carrying out all operations inside parentheses first, multiplying 23 by 2, following the rules for order of operations within the parentheses

$= 2^4 + 51 \cdot 4 - 83$ Completing the addition inside parentheses

$= 16 + 51 \cdot 4 - 83$ Evaluating exponential expressions

$= 16 + 204 - 83$ Doing all multiplications

$= 220 - 83$ Doing all additions and subtractions in order from left to right

$= 137$

Answer on page A-24

A fraction bar can play the role of a grouping symbol.

EXAMPLE 22 Simplify: $\dfrac{-64 \div (-16) \div (-2)}{2^3 - 3^2}$.

An equivalent expression with brackets as grouping symbols is

$$[-64 \div (-16) \div (-2)] \div [2^3 - 3^2].$$

This shows, in effect, that we can do the calculations in the numerator and then in the denominator, and divide the results:

$$\frac{-64 \div (-16) \div (-2)}{2^3 - 3^2} = \frac{4 \div (-2)}{8 - 9} = \frac{-2}{-1} = 2.$$

Do Exercises 26–29.

Simplify.

26. $23 - 42 \cdot 30$

27. $32 \div 8 \cdot 2$

28. $52 \cdot 5 + 5^3 - (4^2 - 48 \div 4)$

29. $\dfrac{5 - 10 - 5 \cdot 23}{2^3 + 3^2 - 7}$

Answers on page A-24

Study Tips

BEGINNING TO STUDY FOR THE FINAL EXAM (PART 2)

The best scenario for preparing for a final exam is to do so over a period of at least two weeks. Work in a diligent, disciplined manner, doing some final-exam preparation each day. Here is a detailed plan that many find useful.

1. Begin by browsing through each chapter, reviewing the highlighted or boxed information regarding important formulas in both the text and the Summary and Review. There may be some formulas that you will need to memorize.

2. Retake each chapter test that you took in class, assuming your instructor has returned it. Otherwise, use the chapter test in the book. Restudy the objectives in the text that correspond to each question you missed.

3. Then work the Cumulative Review that covers all chapters up to that point. Be careful to avoid any questions corresponding to objectives not covered. Again, restudy the objectives in the text that correspond to each question you missed.

4. If you are still missing questions, use the supplements for extra review. For example, you might check out the videotapes or audio recordings, the *Student's Solutions Manual*, the InterAct Math Tutorial Web site, or MathXL.

5. For remaining difficulties, see your instructor, go to a tutoring session, or participate in a study group.

6. Check for former final exams that may be on file in the math department or a study center, or with students who have already taken the course. Use them for practice, being alert to trouble spots.

7. Take the Final Examination in the text during the last couple of days before the final. Set aside the same amount of time that you will have for the final. See how much of the final exam you can complete under test-like conditions.

"Without some goal and effort to reach it, no man can live."

Fyodor Dostoyevsky, nineteenth-century Russian novelist

611

Translating
for Success

1. *Gas Mileage.* After driving his sports car for 761.4 miles on the first day of a recent trip, Nathan noticed that it took 23.5 gal of gasoline to fill the tank. How many miles per gallon did the sports car get?

The goal of these matching questions is to practice step (2), *Translate,* of the five-step problem-solving process. Translate each word problem to an equation and select a correct translation from equations A–O.

2. *Apartment Rent.* Cecilia needs $4500 for tuition. This is 2.5 times as much as she needs for apartment rent. How much does she need for the rent?

A. $7\dfrac{3}{4} \cdot x = 589$

B. $52 + x = 73.10$

C. $2.5 \cdot x = 4500$

D. $x = 4500 \cdot 5\% \cdot \dfrac{1}{2}$

3. *Sales Tax.* The sales tax on an office copier is $73.10 and the tax rate is 5%. Find the purchase price.

E. $23.5(761.4) = x$

F. $73.10 = 5\% \cdot x$

G. $\dfrac{1}{2} \cdot 4500 = 5\% \cdot x$

H. $x = 5\% \cdot 4500$

4. *Change in Elevation.* The lowest elevation in Australia, Lake Eyre, is 52 ft below sea level. The highest elevation in Australia, Mt. Kosciusko, is 7310 ft. Find the difference in elevation between the highest point and the lowest point.

I. $23.5 \cdot x = 761.4$

J. $7\dfrac{3}{4} \div 589 = x$

K. $x = 23.5 + 761.4$

L. $x = 7310 - (-52)$

M. $x = 589 \cdot 7\dfrac{3}{4}$

5. *Cell Phone Bill.* Jeff's cell phone bill for September was $73.10. He made a payment of $52. How much did he then owe on his phone bill?

N. $2.5(4500) = x$

O. $52 \cdot x = 7310$

Answers on page A-24

6. *Camp Sponsorships.* Donations of $52 per camper are needed for camp sponsorships at Lazy Day Summer Camp. Two weeks prior to camp, the sponsorship fund had only $7310. How many campers can be enrolled?

7. *Drain Pipe.* A construction engineer has 589 ft of flexible drain pipe. How many $7\frac{3}{4}$-ft lengths can be cut from the total pipe available?

8. *Simple Interest.* What is the simple interest on a principal of $4500 invested at an interest rate of 5% for $\frac{1}{2}$ year?

9. *Donation to Orphanage.* Matt plans to donate 5% of his winnings to the building-repair fund for a Russian orphanage. If he wins $4500, how much will he donate?

10. *Drain Pipe.* An irrigation subcontractor needs 589 pieces of pipe for a large development project. If each piece must be $7\frac{3}{4}$ ft long, how many feet need to be purchased?

a   Divide, if possible. Check each answer.

1. $36 \div (-6)$

2. $\dfrac{42}{-7}$

3. $\dfrac{26}{-2}$

4. $24 \div (-12)$

5. $\dfrac{-16}{8}$

6. $-18 \div (-2)$

7. $\dfrac{-48}{-12}$

8. $-72 \div (-9)$

9. $\dfrac{-72}{9}$

10. $\dfrac{-50}{25}$

11. $-100 \div (-50)$

12. $\dfrac{-200}{8}$

13. $-108 \div 9$

14. $\dfrac{-64}{-7}$

15. $\dfrac{200}{-25}$

16. $-300 \div (-13)$

17. $\dfrac{75}{0}$

18. $\dfrac{0}{-5}$

19. $\dfrac{81}{-9}$

20. $\dfrac{-145}{-5}$

b   Find the reciprocal.

21. $-\dfrac{15}{7}$

22. $-\dfrac{5}{8}$

23. 13

24. -8

c   Divide.

25. $\dfrac{3}{4} \div \left(-\dfrac{2}{3}\right)$

26. $\dfrac{7}{8} \div \left(-\dfrac{1}{2}\right)$

27. $-\dfrac{5}{4} \div \left(-\dfrac{3}{4}\right)$

28. $-\dfrac{5}{9} \div \left(-\dfrac{5}{6}\right)$

29. $-\dfrac{2}{7} \div \left(-\dfrac{4}{9}\right)$

30. $-\dfrac{3}{5} \div \left(-\dfrac{5}{8}\right)$

31. $-\dfrac{3}{8} \div \left(-\dfrac{8}{3}\right)$

32. $-\dfrac{5}{8} \div \left(-\dfrac{6}{5}\right)$

33. $-6.6 \div 3.3$

34. $-44.1 \div (-6.3)$

35. $\dfrac{-11}{-13}$

36. $\dfrac{-1.7}{20}$

37. $\dfrac{48.6}{-3}$

38. $\dfrac{-17.8}{3.2}$

39. $\dfrac{-9}{17 - 17}$

40. $\dfrac{-8}{-5 + 5}$

d   Solve.

41. *Chemical Reaction.*   The temperature of a chemical compound was at 0°C at 11:00 A.M. During a reaction, it dropped 3°C per minute until 11:18 A.M. What was the temperature at 11:18 A.M.?

42. *Chemical Reaction.*   The temperature in a chemical compound was −5°C at 3:20 P.M. During a reaction, it increased 2°C per minute until 3:52 P.M. What was the temperature at 3:52 P.M.?

43. *Stock Price.* The price of ePDQ.com began the day at $23.75 per share and dropped $1.38 per hour for 8 hr. What was the price of the stock after 8 hr?

44. *Population Decrease.* The population of a rural town was 12,500. It decreased 380 each year for 4 yr. What was the population of the town after 4 yr?

45. *Diver's Position.* After diving 95 m below sea level, a diver rises at a rate of 7 meters per minute for 9 min. Where is the diver in relation to the surface?

46. *Debit Card Balance.* Karen had $234 in her checking account. After using her debit card to make seven purchases at $39 each, what was the balance in her checking account?

Percent of Increase or Decrease in Employment. A percent of increase is usually considered positive and a percent of decrease is considered negative. The following table lists estimates of the number of job opportunities for various occupations in 2002 and 2012. In Exercises 47–50, find the missing numbers.

	OCCUPATION	NUMBER OF JOBS IN 2002 (in thousands)	NUMBER OF JOBS IN 2012 (in thousands)	CHANGE	PERCENT OF INCREASE OR DECREASE
	Electrician	659	814	155	23.5%
	Travel agent	118	102	−16	−13.6%
47.	Fitness trainer/ aerobics instructor	183	264	81	
48.	Child-care worker	1211	1353	142	
49.	Telemarketer	428	406	−22	
50.	Aerospace engineer	78	74	−4	

Source: Handbook of U.S. Labor Statistics

e Simplify.

51. $8 - 2 \cdot 3 - 9$

52. $8 - (2 \cdot 3 - 9)$

53. $(8 - 2 \cdot 3) - 9$

54. $(8 - 2)(3 - 9)$

55. $16 \cdot (-24) + 50$

56. $10 \cdot 20 - 15 \cdot 24$

57. $2^4 + 2^3 - 10$

58. $40 - 3^2 - 2^3$

59. $5^3 + 26 \cdot 71 - (16 + 25 \cdot 3)$

60. $4^3 + 10 \cdot 20 + 8^2 - 23$

61. $4 \cdot 5 - 2 \cdot 6 + 4$

62. $4 \cdot (6 + 8)/(4 + 3)$

63. $4^3/8$

64. $5^3 - 7^2$

65. $8(-7) + 6(-5)$

66. $10(-5) + 1(-1)$

67. $19 - 5(-3) + 3$

68. $14 - 2(-6) + 7$

69. $9 \div (-3) + 16 \div 8$

70. $-32 - 8 \div 4 - (-2)$

71. $-4^2 + 6$

72. $-5^2 + 7$

73. $-8^2 - 3$

74. $-9^2 - 11$

75. $12 - 20^3$

76. $20 + 4^3 \div (-8)$

77. $2 \times 10^3 - 5000$

78. $-7(3^4) + 18$

79. $6[9 - (3 - 4)]$

80. $8[(6 - 13) - 11]$

81. $-1000 \div (-100) \div 10$

82. $256 \div (-32) \div (-4)$

83. $8 - (7 - 9)$

84. $(8 - 7) - 9$

85. $\dfrac{10 - 6^2}{9^2 + 3^2}$

86. $\dfrac{5^2 - 4^3 - 3}{9^2 - 2^2 - 1^5}$

87. $\dfrac{20(8 - 3) - 4(10 - 3)}{10(2 - 6) - 2(5 + 2)}$

88. $\dfrac{(3 - 5)^2 - (7 - 13)}{(12 - 9)^2 + (11 - 14)^2}$

89. ▦ **D**$_W$ Jake keys 18/2 · 3 into his calculator and expects the result to be 3. What mistake is he making?

90. **D**$_W$ Explain how multiplication can be used to justify why the quotient of two negative integers is positive.

SKILL MAINTENANCE

Find the prime factorization. [2.1d]

91. 960

92. 1025

Find the LCM. [3.1a]

93. 5, 19, 35

94. 20, 40, 64

Solve. [6.3b], [6.4b]

95. What is 45% of 3800?

96. 344 is what percent of 8600?

97. *Sound Levels.* Use the information in the following table to make a horizontal bar graph illustrating the loudness of various sounds. (A decibel is a measure of the loudness of sound.) [7.3b]

SOUND	LOUDNESS (in decibels)
Light whisper	10
Normal conversation	30
Noisy office	60
Thunder	90
Moving car	80
Chain saw	100
Jet takeoff	140

Source: Barbara Ann Kipfer, *The Order of Things.*
New York: Random House, 1998

SYNTHESIS

Simplify.

98. ▦ $\dfrac{19 - 17^2}{13^2 - 34}$

99. ▦ $\dfrac{195 + (-15)^3}{195 - 7 \cdot 5^2}$

Determine the sign of the expression if m is negative and n is positive.

100. $\dfrac{-n}{m}$

101. $\dfrac{-n}{-m}$

102. $-\left(\dfrac{-n}{m}\right)$

103. $-\left(\dfrac{n}{-m}\right)$

104. $-\left(\dfrac{-n}{-m}\right)$

615

The review that follows is meant to prepare you for a chapter exam. It consists of two parts. The first part, Concept Reinforcement, is designed to increase understanding of the concepts through true/false exercises. The second part is the Review Exercises. These provide practice exercises for the exam, together with references to section objectives so you can go back and review. Before beginning, stop and look back over the skills you have obtained. What skills in mathematics do you have now that you did not have before studying this chapter?

CONCEPT REINFORCEMENT

Determine whether the statement is true or false. Answers are given at the back of the book.

_____ **1.** The rational numbers consist of all numbers that can be named in terminating or repeating decimal notation.

_____ **2.** The product of a number and its reciprocal is -1.

_____ **3.** The absolute value of a number is always nonnegative.

_____ **4.** The product of an even number of negative numbers is positive.

_____ **5.** The opposite of the opposite of a number is the reciprocal of the number.

_____ **6.** The set of natural numbers is the same as the set of positive integers.

Review Exercises

1. State the integers that correspond to this situation: [10.1a]

> David has a debt of $45 and Joe has $72 in his savings account.

Find the absolute value. [10.1e]

2. $|-38|$

3. $|7.3|$

4. $\left|\dfrac{5}{2}\right|$

5. $-|-0.2|$

Find decimal notation. [10.1c]

6. $-\dfrac{5}{4}$

7. $-\dfrac{5}{6}$

8. $-\dfrac{5}{12}$

9. $-\dfrac{3}{11}$

Graph the number on a number line. [10.1b]

10. -2.5

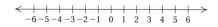

11. $\dfrac{8}{9}$

Use either $<$ or $>$ for ☐ to write a true sentence. [10.1d]

12. -3 ☐ 10

13. -1 ☐ -6

14. 0.126 ☐ -12.6

15. $-\dfrac{2}{3}$ ☐ $-\dfrac{1}{10}$

Find the opposite, or additive inverse, of the number. [10.2b]

16. 3.8

17. $-\dfrac{3}{4}$

18. Evaluate $-x$ when x is -34. [10.2b]

19. Evaluate $-(-x)$ when x is 5. [10.2b]

Find the reciprocal. [10.5b]

20. $\dfrac{3}{8}$ **21.** -7

22. $-\dfrac{1}{10}$

Compute and simplify.

23. $4 + (-7)$ [10.2a]

24. $-\dfrac{2}{3} + \dfrac{1}{12}$ [10.2a]

25. $6 + (-9) + (-8) + 7$ [10.2a]

26. $-3.8 + 5.1 + (-12) + (-4.3) + 10$ [10.2a]

27. $-3 - (-7)$ [10.3a]

28. $-\dfrac{9}{10} - \dfrac{1}{2}$ [10.3a]

29. $-3.8 - 4.1$ [10.3a]

30. $-9 \cdot (-6)$ [10.4a]

31. $-2.7(3.4)$ [10.4a]

32. $\dfrac{2}{3} \cdot \left(-\dfrac{3}{7}\right)$ [10.4a]

33. $3 \cdot (-7) \cdot (-2) \cdot (-5)$ [10.4a]

34. $35 \div (-5)$ [10.5a]

35. $-5.1 \div 1.7$ [10.5c]

36. $-\dfrac{3}{11} \div \left(-\dfrac{4}{11}\right)$ [10.5c]

37. $(-3.4 - 12.2) - 8(-7)$ [10.5e]

Simplify. [10.5e]

38. $[-12(-3) - 2^3] - (-9)(-10)$

39. $625 \div (-25) \div 5$

40. $-16 \div 4 - 30 \div (-5)$

41. $9[(7 - 14) - 13]$

Solve.

42. On the first, second, and third downs, a football team had these gains and losses: 5-yd gain, 12-yd loss, and 15-yd gain, respectively. Find the total gain (or loss). [10.3b]

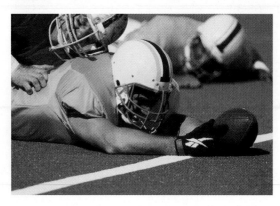

43. Kaleb's total assets are $170. He borrows $300. What are his total assets now? [10.3b]

44. *Stock Price.* The price of a stock opened at a value of $17.68 per share and dropped by $1.63 per hour for 8 hr. What was the price of the stock after 8 hr? [10.5d]

45. *Checking Account Balance.* Yuri had $68 in his checking account. After writing checks to make seven purchases of DVDs at the same price for each, the balance in his account was −$64.65. What was the price of each DVD? [10.5d]

46. $\mathbf{D_W}$ Is it possible for a number to be its own reciprocal? Explain. [10.5b]

47. $\mathbf{D_W}$ Write as many arguments as you can to convince a fellow classmate that $-(-a) = a$ for all real numbers a. [10.2b]

48. The sum of two numbers is 800. The difference is 6. Find the numbers. [10.3b]

49. The sum of two numbers is 5. The product is −84. Find the numbers. [10.3b], [10.5d]

50. The following are examples of consecutive integers: 4, 5, 6, 7, 8: and −13, −12, −11, −10. [10.3b], [10.5d]

a) Express the number 8 as the sum of 16 consecutive integers.
b) Find the product of the 16 consecutive integers in part (a).

51. Describe how you might find the following product quickly: [10.4a]

$$\left(-\tfrac{1}{11}\right)\left(-\tfrac{1}{9}\right)\left(-\tfrac{1}{7}\right)\left(-\tfrac{1}{5}\right)\left(-\tfrac{1}{3}\right)(-1)(-3)(-5)(-7)(-9)(-11).$$

52. Simplify: $-\left|\dfrac{7}{8} - \left(-\dfrac{1}{2}\right) - \dfrac{3}{4}\right|.$ [10.1e], [10.3a]

53. Simplify: $\left(|2.7 - 3| + 3^2 - |-3|\right) \div (-3).$ [10.1e], [10.5e]

Use either < or > for ☐ to write a true sentence.

1. −4 ☐ 0

2. −3 ☐ −8

3. −0.78 ☐ −0.87

4. −$\frac{1}{8}$ ☐ $\frac{1}{2}$

Find decimal notation.

5. −$\frac{1}{8}$

6. −$\frac{4}{9}$

7. −$\frac{2}{11}$

Find the absolute value.

8. $|-7|$

9. $\left|\frac{9}{4}\right|$

10. $-|-2.7|$

Find the opposite, or additive inverse.

11. $\frac{2}{3}$

12. −1.4

13. Evaluate $-x$ when x is −8.

14. Graph −0.2 on a number line.

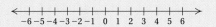

Find the reciprocal.

15. −2

16. $\frac{4}{7}$

Compute and simplify.

17. $3.1 - (-4.7)$

18. $-8 + 4 + (-7) + 3$

19. $-\frac{1}{5} + \frac{3}{8}$

20. $2 - (-8)$

21. $3.2 - 5.7$

22. $\frac{1}{8} - \left(-\frac{3}{4}\right)$

23. $4 \cdot (-12)$

24. $-\dfrac{1}{2} \cdot \left(-\dfrac{3}{8}\right)$

25. $-45 \div 5$

26. $-\dfrac{3}{5} \div \left(-\dfrac{4}{5}\right)$

27. $4.864 \div (-0.5)$

28. $-2(16) - [2(-8) - 5^3]$

29. *Antarctica Highs and Lows.* The continent of Antarctica, which lies in the southern hemisphere, experiences winter in July. The average high temperature is $-67°F$ and the average low temperature is $-81°F$. How much higher is the average high than the average low?

Source: National Climatic Data Center

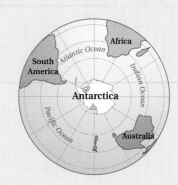

30. Maureen is a stockbroker. She kept track of the changes in the stock market over a period of 5 weeks. By how many points had the market risen or fallen over this time?

WEEK 1	WEEK 2	WEEK 3	WEEK 4	WEEK 5
Down 13 pts	Down 16 pts	Up 36 pts	Down 11 pts	Up 19 pts

31. *Population Decrease.* The population of a city was 18,600. It decreased by 420 each year for 6 yr. What was the population of the city after 6 yr?

32. *Chemical Reaction.* During a chemical reaction, the temperature in the beaker decreased every minute by the same number of degrees. The temperature was $16°C$ at 11:08 A.M. By 11:43 A.M., the temperature had dropped to $-17°C$. By how many degrees did it drop each minute?

SYNTHESIS

33. Simplify: $|-27 - 3(4)| - |-36| + |-12|$.

34. The deepest point in the Pacific Ocean is the Marianas Trench with a depth of 11,033 m. The deepest point in the Atlantic Ocean is the Puerto Rico Trench with a depth of 8648 m. How much higher is the Puerto Rico Trench than the Marianas Trench?

Source: Defense Mapping Agency, Hydrographic/Topographic Center

35. Find the next three numbers in each sequence.

a) $6, 5, 3, 0, \_\_\_, \_\_\_, \_\_\_$
b) $14, 10, 6, 2, \_\_\_, \_\_\_, \_\_\_$
c) $-4, -6, -9, -13, \_\_\_, \_\_\_, \_\_\_$
d) $8, -4, 2, -1, 0.5, \_\_\_, \_\_\_, \_\_\_$

Algebra: Solving Equations and Problems

Real-World Application

The average top speed of the three fastest roller coasters in the world is 109 mph. The third-fastest roller coaster, Superman the Escape (located at Six Flags Magic Mountain, Los Angeles, California), reaches a top speed of 20 mph less than the fastest roller coaster, Top Thrill Dragster (located in Cedar Point, Sandusky, Ohio). The second-fastest roller coaster, Dodonpa (located in Fujikyu Highlands, Japan), has a top speed of 107 mph. What is the top speed of the fastest roller coaster?

Source: Fortune Small Business, June 2004, p. 48

This problem appears as Example 10 in Section 11.5.

Objectives

a Evaluate an algebraic expression by substitution.

b Use the distributive laws to multiply expressions like 8 and $x - y$.

c Use the distributive laws to factor expressions like $4x - 12 + 24y$.

d Collect like terms.

Many types of problems require the use of equations in order to be solved efficiently. The study of algebra involves the use of equations to solve problems. Equations are constructed from algebraic expressions.

a Evaluating Algebraic Expressions

In arithmetic, you have worked with expressions such as

$$37 + 86, \quad 7 \times 8, \quad 19 - 7, \quad \text{and} \quad \frac{3}{8}.$$

In algebra, we use letters for numbers and work with *algebraic expressions* such as

$$x + 86, \quad 7 \times t, \quad 19 - y, \quad \text{and} \quad \frac{a}{b}.$$

Expressions like these should be familiar from the equation and problem solving that we have already done.

Sometimes a letter can stand for various numbers. In that case, we call the letter a **variable.** Let a = your age. Then a is a variable since a changes from year to year. Sometimes a letter can stand for just one number. In that case, we call the letter a **constant.** Let b = your date of birth. Then b is a constant.

An **algebraic expression** consists of variables, constants, numerals, and operation signs. When we replace a variable with a number, we say that we are **substituting** for the variable. This process is called **evaluating the expression.**

1. Evaluate $a + b$ when $a = 38$ and $b = 26$.

EXAMPLE 1 Evaluate $x + y$ for $x = 37$ and $y = 29$.

We substitute 37 for x and 29 for y and carry out the addition:

$$x + y = 37 + 29 = 66.$$

The number 66 is called the **value** of the expression.

Do Exercises 1 and 2.

2. Evaluate $x - y$ when $x = 57$ and $y = 29$.

Algebraic expressions involving multiplication can be written in several ways. For example, "8 times a" can be written as

$$8 \times a, \quad 8 \cdot a, \quad 8(a), \quad \text{or} \quad \text{simply } 8a.$$

Two letters written together without an operation sign, such as ab, also indicates a multiplication.

EXAMPLE 2 Evaluate $3y$ for $y = 14$.

$$3y = 3(14) = 42$$

Answers on page A-25

EXAMPLE 3 *Area of a Rectangle.* The area A of a rectangle of length l and width w is given by the formula $A = lw$. Find the area when l is 24.5 in. and w is 16 in.

We substitute 24.5 in. for l and 16 in. for w and carry out the multiplication:

$$A = lw = (24.5 \text{ in.})(16 \text{ in.})$$
$$= (24.5)(16)(\text{in.})(\text{in.})$$
$$= 392 \text{ in}^2, \text{ or } 392 \text{ square inches.}$$

Do Exercises 3 and 4.

Algebraic expressions involving division can also be written in several ways. For example, "8 divided by t" can be written as

$$8 \div t, \quad \frac{8}{t}, \quad 8/t, \quad \text{or} \quad 8 \cdot \frac{1}{t},$$

where the fraction bar is a division symbol.

EXAMPLE 4 Evaluate $\frac{a}{b}$ for $a = 63$ and $b = 9$.

We substitute 63 for a and 9 for b and carry out the division:

$$\frac{a}{b} = \frac{63}{9} = 7.$$

3. Evaluate $4t$ when $t = 15$ and when $t = -6.8$.

4. Find the area of a rectangle when l is 24 ft and w is 8 ft.

Answers on page A-25

CALCULATOR CORNER

Evaluating Algebraic Expressions We can use a calculator to evaluate algebraic expressions. To evaluate $x - y$ when $x = 48$ and $y = 19$, for example, we press $\boxed{4}\,\boxed{8}\,\boxed{-}\,\boxed{1}\,\boxed{9}\,\boxed{=}$. The calculator displays the result, 29. To evaluate $3x$ when $x = -27$, we press $\boxed{3}\,\boxed{\times}\,\boxed{2}\,\boxed{7}\,\boxed{+/-}\,\boxed{=}$. The result is -81. When we evaluate an expression like $\frac{x + y}{4}$, we must enclose the numerator in parentheses. To evaluate this expression when $x = 29$ and $y = 15$, we press $\boxed{(}\,\boxed{2}\,\boxed{9}\,\boxed{+}\,\boxed{1}\,\boxed{5}\,\boxed{)}\,\boxed{\div}\,\boxed{4}\,\boxed{=}$. The calculator displays the result, 11.

A calculator can also be used to demonstrate the distributive laws. We can evaluate $5(x + y)$ and $5x + 5y$ when $x = 3$ and $y = 9$, for example, and see that the results are the same. To evaluate $5(x + y)$ when $x = 3$ and $y = 9$, we press $\boxed{5}\,\boxed{\times}\,\boxed{(}\,\boxed{3}\,\boxed{+}\,\boxed{9}\,\boxed{)}\,\boxed{=}$. The calculator displays the result, 60. Next, we evaluate $5x + 5y$ when $x = 3$ and $y = 9$. We press $\boxed{5}\,\boxed{\times}\,\boxed{3}\,\boxed{+}\,\boxed{5}\,\boxed{\times}\,\boxed{9}\,\boxed{=}$. Again the calculator displays 60. This verifies that $5(3 + 9) = 5 \cdot 3 + 5 \cdot 9$.

Exercises: Evaluate.

1. $x + y$, when $x = 35$ and $y = 16$

2. $7t$, when $t = 14$

3. $\frac{a}{b}$, when $a = 54$ and $b = -9$

4. $\frac{2m}{n}$, when $m = 38$ and $n = -4$

5. $\frac{x - y}{7}$, when $x = 94$ and $y = 31$

6. $\frac{p + q}{12}$, when $p = 47$ and $q = 97$

7. $4(x + y)$ and $4x + 4y$, when $x = 6$ and $y = 7$

8. $3(x + y)$ and $3x + 3y$, when $x = 34$ and $y = 18$

9. $6(a - b)$ and $6a - 6b$, when $a = 67$ and $b = 29$

10. $7(a - b)$ and $7a - 7b$, when $a = 18$ and $b = 6$

5. Evaluate $\dfrac{a}{b}$ when $a = -200$ and $b = 8$.

6. Evaluate $\dfrac{10p}{q}$ when $p = 40$ and $q = 25$.

Complete the table by evaluating each expression for the given values.

7.

VALUE OF x	$1 \cdot x$	x
$x = 3$		
$x = -6$		
$x = 4.8$		

8.

VALUE OF x	$2x$	$5x$
$x = 2$		
$x = -6$		
$x = 4.8$		

Answers on page A-25

EXAMPLE 5 Evaluate $\dfrac{12m}{n}$ for $m = 8$ and $n = 16$.

$$\frac{12m}{n} = \frac{12 \cdot 8}{16} = \frac{96}{16} = 6$$

Do Exercises 5 and 6.

b Equivalent Expressions and the Distributive Laws

In solving and doing other kinds of work in algebra, we manipulate expressions in various ways. To see how to do this, we consider some examples in which we evaluate expressions.

EXAMPLE 6 Evaluate $1 \cdot x$ when $x = 5$ and $x = -8$ and compare the results to x.

We substitute 5 for x:

$$1 \cdot x = 1 \cdot 5 = 5.$$

Then we substitute -8 for x:

$$1 \cdot x = 1 \cdot (-8) = -8.$$

We see that $1 \cdot x$ and x represent the same number.

Do Exercises 7 and 8.

We see in Example 6 and Margin Exercise 7 that the expressions represent the same number for any allowable replacement of x. In that sense, the expressions $1 \cdot x$ and x are **equivalent.**

> **EQUIVALENT EXPRESSIONS**
>
> Two expressions that have the same value for all allowable replacements are called **equivalent.**

In the expression $3/x$, the number 0 is not allowable because $3/0$ is not defined. Even so, the expressions $6/2x$ and $3/x$ are *equivalent* because they represent the same number for any allowable (not 0) replacement of x. For example, when $x = 5$,

$$\frac{6}{2x} = \frac{6}{2 \cdot 5} = \frac{6}{10} = \frac{3}{5} \quad \text{and} \quad \frac{3}{x} = \frac{3}{5}.$$

We see in Margin Exercise 8 that the expressions $2x$ and $5x$ are *not* equivalent.

The fact that $1 \cdot x$ and x are equivalent is a law of real numbers. It is called the **identity property of 1.** We often refer to the use of the identity property of 1 as "multiplying by 1." We have used multiplying by 1 for understanding many times in this text.

> **THE IDENTITY PROPERTY OF 1 (MULTIPLICATIVE IDENTITY)**
>
> For any real number a,
>
> $$a \cdot 1 = 1 \cdot a = a.$$

We now consider two other laws of real numbers called the **distributive laws.** They are the basis of many procedures in both arithmetic and algebra and are probably the most important laws that we use to manipulate algebraic expressions. The first distributive law involves two operations: addition and multiplication.

Let's begin by considering a multiplication problem from arithmetic:

$$
\begin{array}{r}
4\ 5 \\
\times \quad 7 \\
\hline
3\ 5 \leftarrow \\
2\ 8\ 0 \leftarrow \\
3\ 1\ 5 \leftarrow
\end{array}
$$

3 5 ← This is $7 \cdot 5$.
2 8 0 ← This is $7 \cdot 40$.
3 1 5 ← This is the sum $7 \cdot 40 + 7 \cdot 5$.

To carry out the multiplication, we actually added two products. That is,

$$7 \cdot 45 = 7(40 + 5) = 7 \cdot 40 + 7 \cdot 5.$$

Let's examine this further. If we wish to multiply a sum of several numbers by a factor, we can either add and then multiply or multiply and then add.

EXAMPLE 7   Evaluate $5(x + y)$ and $5x + 5y$ when $x = 2$ and $y = 8$ and compare the results.

We substitute 2 for x and 8 for y in each expression. Then we use the rules for order of operations to calculate.

a) $5(x + y) = 5(2 + 8)$

$\qquad = 5(10)$ \qquad Adding within parentheses first, and then multiplying

$\qquad = 50$

b) $5x + 5y = 5 \cdot 2 + 5 \cdot 8$

$\qquad = 10 + 40$ \qquad Multiplying first and then adding

$\qquad = 50$

The results of (a) and (b) are the same.

Do Exercises 9–11.

The expressions $5(x + y)$ and $5x + 5y$, in Example 7 and Margin Exercise 9, are equivalent. They illustrate the distributive law of multiplication over addition.

THE DISTRIBUTIVE LAW OF MULTIPLICATION OVER ADDITION

For any numbers a, b, and c,

$$a(b + c) = ab + ac.$$

Margin Exercises 10 and 11 also illustrate the distributive law.

In the statement of the distributive law, we know that in an expression such as $ab + ac$, the multiplications are to be done first according to the rules for order of operations. So, instead of writing $(4 \cdot 5) + (4 \cdot 7)$, we can write $4 \cdot 5 + 4 \cdot 7$. However, in $a(b + c)$, we cannot omit the parentheses. If we did, we would have $ab + c$, which means $(ab) + c$. For example, $3(4 + 2) = 18$, but $3 \cdot 4 + 2 = 14$.

9. Complete this table.

VALUES OF x AND y	$5(x + y)$	$5x + 5y$
$x = 6, y = 7$		
$x = -3, y = 4$		
$x = -10, y = 5$		

10. Evaluate $6x + 6y$ and $6(x + y)$ when $x = 10$ and $y = 5$.

11. Evaluate $4(x + y)$ and $4x + 4y$ when $x = 11$ and $y = 5$.

12. Evaluate $7(x - y)$ and $7x - 7y$ when $x = 9$ and $y = 7$.

13. Evaluate $6x - 6y$ and $6(x - y)$ when $x = 10$ and $y = 5$.

14. Evaluate $2(x - y)$ and $2x - 2y$ when $x = 11$ and $y = 5$.

Answers on page A-25

What are the terms of the expression?

15. $5x - 4y + 3$

16. $-4y - 2x + 3z$

Multiply.

17. $3(x - 5)$

18. $5(x + 1)$

19. $\dfrac{5}{4}(x - y + 4)$

20. $-2(x - 3)$

21. $-5(x - 2y + 4z)$

The second distributive law relates multiplication and subtraction. This law says that to multiply by a difference, we can either subtract and then multiply or multiply and then subtract.

> **THE DISTRIBUTIVE LAW OF MULTIPLICATION OVER SUBTRACTION**
>
> For any numbers a, b, and c,
> $$a(b - c) = ab - ac.$$

We often refer to "*the* distributive law" when we mean *either or both* of these laws.

Do Exercises 12–14 on the preceding page.

What do we mean by the *terms* of an expression? **Terms** are separated by addition signs. If there are subtraction signs, we can find an equivalent expression that uses addition signs.

EXAMPLE 8 What are the terms of $3x - 4y + 2z$?

$$3x - 4y + 2z = 3x + (-4y) + 2z \qquad \text{Separating parts with + signs}$$

The terms are $3x$, $-4y$, and $2z$.

Do Exercises 15 and 16.

The distributive laws are the basis for a procedure in algebra called **multiplying.** In an expression such as $8(a + 2b - 7)$, we multiply each term inside the parentheses by 8:

$$8(a + 2b - 7) = 8 \cdot a + 8 \cdot 2b - 8 \cdot 7 = 8a + 16b - 56.$$

EXAMPLES Multiply.

9. $9(x - 5) = 9x - 9(5)$ Using the distributive law of multiplication over subtraction

$$= 9x - 45$$

10. $\dfrac{2}{3}(w + 1) = \dfrac{2}{3} \cdot w + \dfrac{2}{3} \cdot 1$ Using the distributive law of multiplication over addition

$$= \dfrac{2}{3}w + \dfrac{2}{3}$$

Answers on page A-25

EXAMPLE 11 Multiply: $-4(x - 2y + 3z)$.

$$-4(x - 2y + 3z) = -4 \cdot x - (-4)(2y) + (-4)(3z) \quad \text{Using both distributive laws}$$

$$= -4x - (-8y) + (-12z) \quad \text{Multiplying}$$

$$= -4x + 8y - 12z.$$

We can also do this problem by first finding an equivalent expression with all plus signs and then multiplying:

$$-4(x - 2y + 3z) = -4[x + (-2y) + 3z]$$

$$= -4 \cdot x + (-4)(-2y) + (-4)(3z) = -4x + 8y - 12z.$$

Do Exercises 17–21 on the preceding page.

C | Factoring

Factoring is the reverse of multiplying. To factor, we can use the distributive laws in reverse:

$$ab + ac = a(b + c) \quad \text{and} \quad ab - ac = a(b - c).$$

> **FACTOR**
>
> To **factor** an expression is to find an equivalent expression that is a product.

Look at Example 9. To *factor* $9x - 45$, we find an equivalent expression that is a product, $9(x - 5)$. When all the terms of an expression have a factor in common, we can "factor it out" using the distributive laws. Note the following.

$9x$ has the factors $9, -9, 3, -3, 1, -1, x, -x, 3x, -3x, 9x, -9x$;

-45 has the factors $1, -1, 3, -3, 5, -5, 9, -9, 15, -15, 45, -45$.

We remove the greatest common factor. In this case, that factor is 9. Thus,

$$9x - 45 = 9 \cdot x - 9 \cdot 5 = 9(x - 5).$$

Remember that an expression is factored when we find an equivalent expression that is a product.

EXAMPLES Factor.

12. $5x - 10 = 5 \cdot x - 5 \cdot 2 \quad$ Try to do this step mentally.

$$= 5(x - 2) \longleftarrow \text{You can check by multiplying.}$$

13. $9x + 27y - 9 = 9 \cdot x + 9 \cdot 3y - 9 \cdot 1 = 9(x + 3y - 1)$

> **Caution!**
>
> Note that although $3(3x + 9y - 3)$ is also equivalent to $9x + 27y - 9$, it is *not* the desired form. However, we can complete the process by factoring out another factor of 3:
>
> $$9x + 27y - 9 = 3(3x + 9y - 3) = 3 \cdot 3(x + 3y - 1) = 9(x + 3y - 1).$$
>
> Remember to factor out the *greatest common factor*.

Factor.

22. $6z - 12$

23. $3x - 6y + 9$

24. $16a - 36b + 42$

25. $-12x + 32y - 16z$

Answers on page A-25

Collect like terms.

26. $6x - 3x$

27. $7x - x$

28. $x - 9x$

29. $x - 0.41x$

30. $5x + 4y - 2x - y$

31. $3x - 7x - 11 + 8y + 4 - 13y$

32. $-\dfrac{2}{3} - \dfrac{3}{5}x + y + \dfrac{7}{10}x - \dfrac{2}{9}y$

EXAMPLES Factor. Try to write just the answer, if you can.

14. $5x - 5y = 5(x - y)$

15. $-3x + 6y - 9z = -3 \cdot x - 3(-2y) - 3(3z) = -3(x - 2y + 3z)$

We usually factor out a negative factor when the first term is negative. The way we factor can depend on the situation in which we are working. We might also factor the expression in Example 15 as follows:

$$-3x + 6y - 9z = 3(-x + 2y - 3z).$$

16. $18z - 12x - 24 = 6(3z - 2x - 4)$

Remember that you can always check such factoring by multiplying. Keep in mind that an expression is factored when it is written as a product.

Do Exercises 22–25 on the preceding page.

d Collecting Like Terms

Terms such as $5x$ and $-4x$, whose variable factors are exactly the same, are called **like terms.** Similarly, numbers, such as -7 and 13, are like terms. Also, $3y^2$ and $9y^2$ are like terms because the variables are raised to the same power. Terms such as $4y$ and $5y^2$ are not like terms, and $7x$ and $2y$ are not like terms.

The process of **collecting like terms** is based on the distributive laws. We can also apply the distributive law when a factor is on the right.

EXAMPLES Collect like terms. Try to write just the answer, if you can.

17. $4x + 2x = (4 + 2)x = 6x$ Factoring out the x using a distributive law

18. $2x + 3y - 5x - 2y = 2x - 5x + 3y - 2y$

$$= (2 - 5)x + (3 - 2)y = -3x + y$$

19. $3x - x = 3x - 1x = (3 - 1)x = 2x$

20. $x - 0.24x = 1 \cdot x - 0.24x = (1 - 0.24)x = 0.76x$

21. $x - 6x = 1 \cdot x - 6 \cdot x = (1 - 6)x = -5x$

22. $4x - 7y + 9x - 5 + 3y - 8 = 13x - 4y - 13$

23. $\dfrac{2}{3}a - b + \dfrac{4}{5}a + \dfrac{1}{4}b - 10 = \dfrac{2}{3}a - 1 \cdot b + \dfrac{4}{5}a + \dfrac{1}{4}b - 10$

$$= \left(\dfrac{2}{3} + \dfrac{4}{5}\right)a + \left(-1 + \dfrac{1}{4}\right)b - 10$$

$$= \left(\dfrac{10}{15} + \dfrac{12}{15}\right)a + \left(-\dfrac{4}{4} + \dfrac{1}{4}\right)b - 10$$

$$= \dfrac{22}{15}a - \dfrac{3}{4}b - 10$$

Do Exercises 26–32.

Answers on page A-25

a   Evaluate.

1. $6x$, when $x = 7$

2. $9t$, when $t = 8$

3. $\dfrac{x}{y}$, when $x = 9$ and $y = 3$

4. $\dfrac{m}{n}$, when $m = 18$ and $n = 3$

5. $\dfrac{3p}{q}$, when $p = -2$ and $q = 6$

6. $\dfrac{5y}{z}$, when $y = -15$ and $z = -25$

7. $\dfrac{x + y}{5}$, when $x = 10$ and $y = 20$

8. $\dfrac{p - q}{2}$, when $p = 17$ and $q = 3$

9. ab, when $a = -5$ and $b = 4$

10. ba, when $a = -5$ and $b = 4$

b   Evaluate.

11. $10(x + y)$ and $10x + 10y$, when $x = 20$ and $y = 4$

12. $5(a + b)$ and $5a + 5b$, when $a = 16$ and $b = 6$

13. $10(x - y)$ and $10x - 10y$, when $x = 20$ and $y = 4$

14. $5(a - b)$ and $5a - 5b$, when $a = 16$ and $b = 6$

Multiply.

15. $2(b + 5)$

16. $4(x + 3)$

17. $7(1 - t)$

18. $4(1 - y)$

19. $6(5x + 2)$

20. $9(6m + 7)$

21. $7(x + 4 + 6y)$

22. $4(5x + 8 + 3p)$

23. $-7(y - 2)$

24. $-9(y - 7)$

25. $-9(-5x - 6y + 8)$

26. $-7(-2x - 5y + 9)$

27. $\dfrac{3}{4}(x - 3y - 2z)$

28. $\dfrac{2}{5}(2x - 5y - 8z)$

29. $3.1(-1.2x + 3.2y - 1.1)$

30. $-2.1(-4.2x - 4.3y - 2.2)$

c   Factor. Check by multiplying.

31. $2x + 4$

32. $5y + 20$

33. $30 + 5y$

34. $7x + 28$

35. $14x + 21y$

36. $18a + 24b$

37. $5x + 10 + 15y$

38. $9a + 27b + 81$

39. $8x - 24$

40. $10x - 50$

41. $32 - 4y$

42. $24 - 6m$

43. $8x + 10y - 22$ **44.** $9a + 6b - 15$ **45.** $-18x - 12y + 6$ **46.** $-14x + 21y + 7$

d Collect like terms.

47. $9a + 10a$

48. $14x + 3x$

49. $10a - a$

50. $-10x + x$

51. $2x + 9z + 6x$

52. $3a - 5b + 4a$

53. $41a + 90 - 60a - 2$

54. $42x - 6 - 4x + 20$

55. $23 + 5t + 7y - t - y - 27$

56. $95 - 90d - 87 - 9d + 3 + 7d$

57. $11x - 3x$

58. $9t - 13t$

59. $6n - n$

60. $10t - t$

61. $y - 17y$

62. $5m - 8m + 4$

63. $-8 + 11a - 5b + 6a - 7b + 7$

64. $8x - 5x + 6 + 3y - 2y - 4$

65. $9x + 2y - 5x$

66. $8y - 3z + 4y$

67. $\dfrac{11}{4}x + \dfrac{2}{3}y - \dfrac{4}{5}x - \dfrac{1}{6}y + 12$

68. $\dfrac{13}{2}a + \dfrac{9}{5}b - \dfrac{2}{3}a - \dfrac{3}{10}b - 42$

69. $2.7x + 2.3y - 1.9x - 1.8y$

70. $6.7a + 4.3b - 4.1a - 2.9b$

71. $\mathbf{D_W}$ Determine whether $(a + b)^2$ and $a^2 + b^2$ are equivalent for all real numbers. Explain.

72. $\mathbf{D_W}$ The distributive law is introduced before the material on collecting like terms. Why do you think this is?

SKILL MAINTENANCE

For a circle with the given radius, find the diameter, the circumference, and the area. Use 3.14 for π. [9.3a, b, c]

73. $r = 15$ yd **74.** $r = 8.2$ m **75.** $r = 9\frac{1}{2}$ mi **76.** $r = 2400$ cm

For a circle with the given diameter, find the radius, the circumference, and the area. Use 3.14 for π. [9.3a, b, c]

77. $d = 20$ mm **78.** $d = 264$ km **79.** $d = 4.6$ ft **80.** $d = 10.3$ m

---

SYNTHESIS

Collect like terms, if possible, and factor the result.

81. $q + qr + qrs + qrst$

82. $21x + 44xy + 15y - 16x - 8y - 38xy + 2y + xy$

630

11.2 SOLVING EQUATIONS: THE ADDITION PRINCIPLE

Objective

a | Solve equations using the addition principle.

a | Using the Addition Principle

Consider the equation $x = 7$. We can easily "see" that the solution of this equation is 7. If we replace x with 7, we get $7 = 7$, which is true. Now consider the equation $x + 6 = 13$. The solution of this equation is also 7, but the fact that 7 is the solution is not as obvious. We now begin to consider principles that allow us to start with an equation like $x + 6 = 13$ and end up with an equation like $x = 7$, in which the variable is alone on one side and for which the solution is easier to find. The equations $x + 6 = 13$ and $x = 7$ are **equivalent.**

1. Solve $x + 2 = 11$ using the addition principle.

   a) First, complete this sentence:

      $2 + \square = 0.$

   b) Then solve the equation.

> **EQUIVALENT EQUATIONS**
>
> Equations with the same solutions are called **equivalent equations.**

One principle that we use to solve equations involves the addition principle, which we have used throughout this text.

> **THE ADDITION PRINCIPLE**
>
> For any real numbers a, b, and c,
>
> $a = b$ is equivalent to $a + c = b + c.$

Let's solve $x + 6 = 13$ using the addition principle. We want to get x alone on one side. To do so, we use the addition principle, choosing to add -6 on both sides because $6 + (-6) = 0$:

$$x + 6 = 13$$
$$x + 6 + (-6) = 13 + (-6) \qquad \text{Using the addition principle; adding } -6 \text{ on both sides}$$
$$x + 0 = 7 \qquad \text{Simplifying}$$
$$x = 7. \qquad \text{Identity property of 0}$$

The solution of $x + 6 = 13$ is 7.

Do Exercise 1.

To visualize the addition principle, think of a jeweler's balance. When both sides of the balance hold equal amounts of weight, the balance is level. If weight is added or removed, equally, on both sides, the balance remains level.

Answers on page A-25

2. Solve using the addition principle:

$$x + 7 = 2.$$

When we use the addition principle, we sometimes say that we "add the same number on both sides of the equation." This is also true for subtraction, since we can express every subtraction as an addition. That is, since

$$a - c = b - c \quad \text{is equivalent to} \quad a + (-c) = b + (-c),$$

the addition principle tells us that we can "subtract the same number on both sides of an equation."

EXAMPLE 1 Solve: $x + 5 = -7$.

We have

$$
\begin{aligned}
x + 5 &= -7 \\
x + 5 - 5 &= -7 - 5 && \text{Using the addition principle: adding } -5 \text{ on} \\
& && \text{both sides or subtracting 5 on both sides} \\
x + 0 &= -12 && \text{Simplifying} \\
x &= -12. && \text{Identity property of 0}
\end{aligned}
$$

To check the answer, we substitute -12 in the original equation.

Check:
$$
\begin{array}{c}
x + 5 = -7 \\
\hline
-12 + 5 \ ? \ -7 \\
-7 \ | \qquad \text{TRUE}
\end{array}
$$

The solution of the original equation is -12.

In Example 1, to get x alone, we used the addition principle and subtracted 5 on both sides. This eliminated the 5 on the left. We started with $x + 5 = -7$, and using the addition principle we found a simpler equation $x = -12$, for which it was easier to "*see*" the solution. The equations $x + 5 = -7$ and $x = -12$ are *equivalent*.

Do Exercise 2.

Now we solve an equation that involves a subtraction by using the addition principle.

EXAMPLE 2 Solve: $-6.5 = y - 8.4$.

We have

$$
\begin{aligned}
-6.5 &= y - 8.4 \\
-6.5 + 8.4 &= y - 8.4 + 8.4 && \text{Using the addition principle: adding 8.4} \\
& && \text{to eliminate } -8.4 \text{ on the right} \\
1.9 &= y.
\end{aligned}
$$

Check:
$$
\begin{array}{c}
-6.5 = y - 8.4 \\
\hline
-6.5 \ ? \ 1.9 - 8.4 \\
| \ -6.5 \qquad \text{TRUE}
\end{array}
$$

The solution is 1.9.

Note that equations are reversible. That is, if $a = b$ is true, then $b = a$ is true. Thus, when we solve $-6.5 = y - 8.4$, we can reverse it and solve $y - 8.4 = -6.5$ if we wish.

Do Exercises 3 and 4.

Solve.

3. $8.7 = n - 4.5$

4. $y + 17.4 = 10.9$

Answers on page A-25

CHAPTER 11: Algebra: Solving Equations
and Problems

11.2 EXERCISE SET

For Extra Help

a Solve using the addition principle. Don't forget to check!

1. $x + 2 = 6$

Check: $x + 2 = 6$
$\overset{?}{\rule{3cm}{0.4pt}}$

2. $y + 4 = 11$

Check: $y + 4 = 11$
$\overset{?}{\rule{3cm}{0.4pt}}$

3. $x + 15 = -5$

Check: $x + 15 = -5$
$\overset{?}{\rule{3cm}{0.4pt}}$

4. $t + 10 = 44$

Check: $t + 10 = 44$
$\overset{?}{\rule{3cm}{0.4pt}}$

5. $x + 6 = -8$

6. $y + 8 = 37$

7. $x + 5 = 12$

8. $x + 3 = 7$

9. $-22 = t + 4$

10. $t + 8 = -14$

11. $x + 16 = -2$

12. $y + 34 = -8$

13. $x - 9 = 6$

14. $x - 9 = 2$

15. $x - 7 = -21$

16. $x - 5 = -16$

17. $5 + t = 7$

18. $6 + y = 22$

19. $-7 + y = 13$

20. $-8 + z = 16$

21. $-3 + t = -9$

22. $-8 + y = -23$

23. $r + \dfrac{1}{3} = \dfrac{8}{3}$

24. $t + \dfrac{3}{8} = \dfrac{5}{8}$

25. $m + \dfrac{5}{6} = -\dfrac{11}{12}$

26. $x + \dfrac{2}{3} = -\dfrac{5}{6}$

27. $x - \dfrac{5}{6} = \dfrac{7}{8}$

28. $y - \dfrac{3}{4} = \dfrac{5}{6}$

29. $-\dfrac{1}{5} + z = -\dfrac{1}{4}$

30. $-\dfrac{1}{8} + y = -\dfrac{3}{4}$

31. $7.4 = x + 2.3$

32. $9.3 = 4.6 + x$

633

33. $7.6 = x - 4.8$

34. $9.5 = y - 8.3$

35. $-9.7 = -4.7 + y$

36. $-7.8 = 2.8 + x$

37. $5\frac{1}{6} + x = 7$

38. $5\frac{1}{4} = 4\frac{2}{3} + x$

39. $q + \frac{1}{3} = -\frac{1}{7}$

40. $47\frac{1}{8} = -76 + z$

41. $\mathbf{D_W}$ Explain the following mistake made by a fellow student.

$$x + \frac{1}{3} = -\frac{5}{3}$$
$$x = -\frac{4}{3}$$

42. $\mathbf{D_W}$ Explain the role of the opposite of a number when using the addition principle.

SKILL MAINTENANCE

Add. [10.2a]

43. $-3 + (-8)$

44. $-\frac{2}{3} + \frac{5}{8}$

45. $-14.3 + (-19.8)$

46. $3.2 + (-4.9)$

Subtract. [10.3a]

47. $-3 - (-8)$

48. $-\frac{2}{3} - \frac{5}{8}$

49. $-14.3 - (-19.8)$

50. $3.2 - (-4.9)$

Multiply. [10.4a]

51. $-3(-8)$

52. $-\frac{2}{3} \cdot \frac{5}{8}$

53. $-14.3 \times (-19.8)$

54. $3.2(-4.9)$

Divide. [10.5c]

55. $\frac{-24}{-3}$

56. $-\frac{2}{3} \div \frac{5}{8}$

57. $\frac{283.14}{-19.8}$

58. $\frac{-15.68}{3.2}$

SYNTHESIS

Solve.

59. ▦ $-356.788 = -699.034 + t$

60. $-\frac{4}{5} + \frac{7}{10} = x - \frac{3}{4}$

61. $x + \frac{4}{5} = -\frac{2}{3} - \frac{4}{15}$

62. $8 - 25 = 8 + x - 21$

63. $16 + x - 22 = -16$

64. $x + x = x$

65. $-\frac{3}{2} + x = -\frac{5}{17} - \frac{3}{2}$

66. $|x| = 5$

11.3 SOLVING EQUATIONS: THE MULTIPLICATION PRINCIPLE

Objective

a Solve equations using the multiplication principle.

a Using the Multiplication Principle

Suppose that $a = b$ is true, and we multiply a by some number c. We get the same answer if we multiply b by c, because a and b are the same number.

THE MULTIPLICATION PRINCIPLE

For any real numbers a, b, and c, $c \neq 0$,

$$a = b \quad \text{is equivalent to} \quad a \cdot c = b \cdot c.$$

When using the multiplication principle, we sometimes say that we "multiply on both sides of the equation by the same number."

EXAMPLE 1 Solve: $5x = 70$.

To get x alone, we multiply by the *multiplicative inverse*, or *reciprocal*, of 5. Then we get the *multiplicative identity* 1 times x, or $1 \cdot x$, which simplifies to x. This allows us to eliminate 5 on the left.

$$5x = 70 \qquad \text{The reciprocal of 5 is } \tfrac{1}{5}.$$

$$\frac{1}{5} \cdot 5x = \frac{1}{5} \cdot 70 \qquad \begin{array}{l}\text{Multiplying by } \tfrac{1}{5} \text{ to get } 1 \cdot x \text{ and} \\ \text{eliminate 5 on the left}\end{array}$$

$$1 \cdot x = 14 \qquad \text{Simplifying}$$

$$x = 14 \qquad \text{Identity property of 1: } 1 \cdot x = x$$

Check:
$$\begin{array}{c} 5x = 70 \\ \hline 5 \cdot 14 \ ? \ 70 \\ 70 \ \big| \qquad \text{TRUE} \end{array}$$

The solution is 14.

1. Solve. Multiply on both sides.

$$6x = 90$$

The multiplication principle also tells us that we can "divide on both sides of the equation by a nonzero number." This is because division is the same as multiplying by a reciprocal. That is,

$$\frac{a}{c} = \frac{b}{c} \quad \text{is equivalent to} \quad a \cdot \frac{1}{c} = b \cdot \frac{1}{c}, \quad \text{when } c \neq 0.$$

In an expression like $5x$ in Example 1, the number 5 is called the **coefficient**. Example 1 could be done as follows, dividing on both sides by 5, the coefficient of x.

2. Solve. Divide on both sides.

$$4x = -7$$

EXAMPLE 2 Solve: $5x = 70$.

$$5x = 70$$

$$\frac{5x}{5} = \frac{70}{5} \qquad \text{Dividing by 5 on both sides}$$

$$1 \cdot x = 14 \qquad \text{Simplifying}$$

$$x = 14 \qquad \text{Identity property of 1}$$

Answers on page A-25

Do Exercises 1 and 2.

3. Solve: $-6x = 108$.

EXAMPLE 3 Solve: $-4x = 92$.

We have

$$-4x = 92$$

$$\frac{-4x}{-4} = \frac{92}{-4} \qquad \text{Using the multiplication principle. Dividing by } -4 \text{ on both sides is the same as multiplying by } -\frac{1}{4}.$$

$$1 \cdot x = -23 \qquad \text{Simplifying}$$

$$x = -23. \qquad \text{Identity property of 1}$$

Check:
$$\frac{-4x = 92}{-4(-23) \; \overset{?}{\vert} \; 92}$$
$$92 \;\vert \qquad \text{TRUE}$$

The solution is -23.

Do Exercise 3.

EXAMPLE 4 Solve: $-x = 9$.

$$-x = 9$$

$$-1(-x) = -1 \cdot 9 \qquad \text{Multiplying by } -1 \text{ on both sides}$$

$$-1 \cdot (-1) \cdot x = -9 \qquad\qquad -x = (-1) \cdot x$$

$$1 \cdot x = -9$$

$$x = -9.$$

4. Solve: $-x = -10$.

Check:
$$\frac{-x = 9}{-(-9) \; \overset{?}{\vert} \; 9}$$
$$9 \;\vert \qquad \text{TRUE}$$

The solution is -9.

Do Exercise 4.

In practice, it is generally more convenient to "divide" on both sides of the equation if the coefficient of the variable is in decimal notation or is an integer. If the coefficient is in fraction notation, it is more convenient to "multiply" by a reciprocal.

EXAMPLE 5 Solve: $\dfrac{3}{8} = -\dfrac{5}{4}x$.

$$\frac{3}{8} = -\frac{5}{4}x$$

$$\text{The reciprocal of } -\tfrac{5}{4} \text{ is } -\tfrac{4}{5}. \text{ There is no sign change.}$$

$$-\frac{4}{5} \cdot \frac{3}{8} = -\frac{4}{5} \cdot \left(-\frac{5}{4}x\right) \qquad \text{Multiplying by } -\tfrac{4}{5} \text{ to get } 1 \cdot x \text{ and eliminate } -\tfrac{5}{4} \text{ on the right}$$

$$-\frac{12}{40} = 1 \cdot x$$

$$-\frac{3}{10} = 1 \cdot x \qquad \text{Simplifying}$$

$$-\frac{3}{10} = x \qquad \text{Identity property of 1}$$

Answers on page A-25

Check:
$$\frac{3}{8} = -\frac{5}{4}x$$

$$\frac{3}{8} \;?\; -\frac{5}{4}\left(-\frac{3}{10}\right)$$

$$\frac{3}{8} \qquad \text{TRUE}$$

The solution is $-\dfrac{3}{10}$.

If $a = b$ is true, then $b = a$ is true. Thus when we solve $\frac{3}{8} = -\frac{5}{4}x$, we can reverse it and solve $-\frac{5}{4}x = \frac{3}{8}$ if we wish.

Do Exercise 5.

EXAMPLE 6 Solve: $1.16y = 9744$.

$$\frac{1.16y}{1.16} = \frac{9744}{1.16} \qquad \text{Dividing by 1.16 on both sides}$$

$$y = \frac{9744}{1.16}$$

$$y = 8400 \qquad \text{Using a calculator to divide}$$

Check:
$$1.16y = 9744$$

$$1.16(8400) \;?\; 9744$$

$$9744 \qquad \text{TRUE}$$

The solution is 8400.

Do Exercises 6 and 7.

Now we use the multiplication principle to solve an equation that involves division.

EXAMPLE 7 Solve: $\dfrac{-y}{9} = 14$.

$$9 \cdot \frac{-y}{9} = 9 \cdot 14 \qquad \text{Multiplying by 9 on both sides}$$

$$-y = 126$$

$$-1 \cdot (-y) = -1 \cdot 126 \qquad \text{Multiplying by } -1 \text{ on both sides}$$

$$y = -126$$

Check:
$$\frac{-y}{9} = 14$$

$$\frac{-(-126)}{9} \;?\; 14$$

$$\frac{126}{9}$$

$$14 \qquad \text{TRUE}$$

The solution is -126.

Do Exercise 8.

5. Solve: $\dfrac{2}{3} = -\dfrac{5}{6}y$.

Solve.

6. $1.12x = 8736$

7. $6.3 = -2.1y$

8. Solve: $-14 = \dfrac{-y}{2}$.

Answers on page A-25

Objectives

1. Solve: $9x + 6 = 51$.

Solve.

2. $8x - 4 = 28$

3. $-\dfrac{1}{2}x + 3 = 1$

11.4 USING THE PRINCIPLES TOGETHER

a Applying Both Principles

Consider the equation $3x + 4 = 13$. It is more complicated than those in the preceding two sections. In order to solve such an equation, we first isolate the x-term, $3x$, using the addition principle. Then we apply the multiplication principle to get x by itself.

EXAMPLE 1 Solve: $3x + 4 = 13$.

$$3x + 4 = 13$$

$$3x + 4 - 4 = 13 - 4 \qquad \text{Using the addition principle: adding } -4 \text{ or subtracting 4 on both sides}$$

$$3x = 9 \qquad \text{Simplifying}$$

$$\frac{3x}{3} = \frac{9}{3} \qquad \text{Using the multiplication principle: multiplying by } \frac{1}{3} \text{ or dividing by 3 on both sides}$$

$$x = 3 \qquad \text{Simplifying}$$

Check:
$$\begin{array}{c|c} 3x + 4 = 13 \\ \hline 3 \cdot 3 + 4 \; ? \; 13 \\ 9 + 4 \\ 13 & \text{TRUE} \end{array}$$

The solution is 3.

Do Exercise 1.

EXAMPLE 2 Solve: $-5x - 6 = 16$.

$$-5x - 6 = 16$$

$$-5x - 6 + 6 = 16 + 6 \qquad \text{Adding 6 on both sides}$$

$$-5x = 22$$

$$\frac{-5x}{-5} = \frac{22}{-5} \qquad \text{Dividing by } -5 \text{ on both sides}$$

$$x = -\frac{22}{5}, \text{ or } -4\frac{2}{5} \qquad \text{Simplifying}$$

Check:
$$\begin{array}{c|c} -5x - 6 = 16 \\ \hline -5\left(-\dfrac{22}{5}\right) - 6 \; ? \; 16 \\ 22 - 6 \\ 16 & \text{TRUE} \end{array}$$

The solution is $-\dfrac{22}{5}$.

Do Exercises 2 and 3.

EXAMPLE 3 Solve: $45 - x = 13$.

$$45 - x = 13$$
$$-45 + 45 - x = -45 + 13 \quad \text{Adding } -45 \text{ on both sides}$$
$$-x = -32$$
$$-1 \cdot (-x) = -1 \cdot (-32) \quad \text{Multiplying by } -1 \text{ on both sides}$$
$$-1 \cdot (-1) \cdot x = 32$$
$$x = 32$$

Check:
$$\frac{45 - x = 13}{45 - 32 \stackrel{?}{} 13}$$
$$13 \mid \quad \text{TRUE}$$

The solution is 32.

Do Exercise 4.

EXAMPLE 4 Solve: $16.3 - 7.2y = -8.18$.

$$16.3 - 7.2y = -8.18$$
$$-16.3 + 16.3 - 7.2y = -16.3 + (-8.18) \quad \text{Adding } -16.3 \text{ on both sides}$$
$$-7.2y = -24.48$$
$$\frac{-7.2y}{-7.2} = \frac{-24.48}{-7.2} \quad \text{Dividing by } -7.2 \text{ on both sides}$$
$$y = 3.4$$

Check:
$$\frac{16.3 - 7.2y = -8.18}{16.3 - 7.2(3.4) \stackrel{?}{} -8.18}$$
$$16.3 - 24.48 \mid$$
$$-8.18 \mid \quad \text{TRUE}$$

The solution is 3.4.

Do Exercises 5 and 6.

b   Collecting Like Terms

If there are like terms on one side of the equation, we collect them before using the addition or multiplication principle.

EXAMPLE 5 Solve: $3x + 4x = -14$.

$$3x + 4x = -14$$
$$7x = -14 \quad \text{Collecting like terms}$$
$$\frac{7x}{7} = \frac{-14}{7} \quad \text{Dividing by 7 on both sides}$$
$$x = -2.$$

The number -2 checks, so the solution is -2.

Do Exercises 7 and 8.

4. Solve: $-18 - x = -57$.

Solve.

5. $-4 - 8x = 8$

6. $41.68 = 4.7 - 8.6y$

Solve.

7. $4x + 3x = -21$

8. $x - 0.09x = 728$

Answers on page A-25

Solve.

9. $7y + 5 = 2y + 10$

10. $5 - 2y = 3y - 5$

Solve.

11. $7x - 17 + 2x = 2 - 8x + 15$

12. $3x - 15 = 5x + 2 - 4x$

If there are like terms on opposite sides of the equation, we get them on the same side by using the addition principle. Then we collect them. In other words, we get all terms with a variable on one side and all numbers on the other.

EXAMPLE 6 Solve: $2x - 2 = -3x + 3$.

$$2x - 2 = -3x + 3$$
$$2x - 2 + 2 = -3x + 3 + 2 \qquad \text{Adding 2}$$
$$2x = -3x + 5 \qquad \text{Collecting like terms}$$
$$2x + 3x = -3x + 5 + 3x \qquad \text{Adding } 3x$$
$$5x = 5 \qquad \text{Simplifying}$$
$$\frac{5x}{5} = \frac{5}{5} \qquad \text{Dividing by 5}$$
$$x = 1 \qquad \text{Simplifying}$$

Check:

$$\begin{array}{c|c}
\multicolumn{2}{c}{2x - 2 = -3x + 3} \\
\hline
2 \cdot 1 - 2 \ ? \ -3 \cdot 1 + 3 & \text{Substituting in the original equation} \\
2 - 2 \ \big| \ -3 + 3 & \\
0 \ \big| \ 0 & \text{TRUE}
\end{array}$$

The solution is 1.

Do Exercises 9 and 10.

In Example 6, we used the addition principle to get all terms with a variable on one side and all numbers on the other side. Then we collected like terms and proceeded as before. If there are like terms on one side at the outset, they should be collected first.

EXAMPLE 7 Solve: $6x + 5 - 7x = 10 - 4x + 3$.

$$6x + 5 - 7x = 10 - 4x + 3$$
$$-x + 5 = 13 - 4x \qquad \text{Collecting like terms}$$
$$4x - x + 5 = 13 - 4x + 4x \qquad \text{Adding } 4x$$
$$3x + 5 = 13 \qquad \text{Simplifying}$$
$$3x + 5 - 5 = 13 - 5 \qquad \text{Subtracting 5}$$
$$3x = 8 \qquad \text{Simplifying}$$
$$\frac{3x}{3} = \frac{8}{3} \qquad \text{Dividing by 3}$$
$$x = \frac{8}{3} \qquad \text{Simplifying}$$

The number $\frac{8}{3}$ checks, so $\frac{8}{3}$ is the solution.

Do Exercises 11 and 12.

Answers on page A-25

CHAPTER 11: Algebra: Solving Equations
and Problems

CLEARING FRACTIONS AND DECIMALS

For the equations considered thus far, we generally use the addition principle first. There are, however, some situations in which it is to our advantage to use the multiplication principle first. Consider, for example,

$$\frac{1}{2}x = \frac{3}{4}.$$

The LCM of the denominators is 4. If we multiply by 4 on both sides, we get $2x = 3$, which has no fractions. We have "cleared fractions." Now consider

$$2.3x = 4.78.$$

If we multiply by 100 on both sides, we get $230x = 478$, which has no decimal points. We have "cleared decimals." The equations are then easier to solve. It is your choice whether to clear fractions or decimals, but doing so often eases computations.

In what follows, we use the multiplication principle first to "clear," or "eliminate," fractions or decimals. For fractions, the number by which we multiply is the **least common multiple of all the denominators.**

EXAMPLE 8   Solve:

$$\frac{2}{3}x - \frac{1}{6} + \frac{1}{2}x = \frac{7}{6} + 2x.$$

The number 6 is the least common multiple of all the denominators. We multiply by 6 on both sides:

$$6\left(\frac{2}{3}x - \frac{1}{6} + \frac{1}{2}x\right) = 6\left(\frac{7}{6} + 2x\right) \quad \text{Multiplying by 6 on both sides}$$

$$6 \cdot \frac{2}{3}x - 6 \cdot \frac{1}{6} + 6 \cdot \frac{1}{2}x = 6 \cdot \frac{7}{6} + 6 \cdot 2x \quad \text{Using the distributive laws. (Caution! Be sure to multiply all terms by 6.)}$$

$$4x - 1 + 3x = 7 + 12x \quad \text{Simplifying. Note that the fractions are cleared.}$$

$$7x - 1 = 7 + 12x \quad \text{Collecting like terms}$$

$$7x - 1 - 12x = 7 + 12x - 12x \quad \text{Subtracting } 12x$$

$$-5x - 1 = 7 \quad \text{Simplifying}$$

$$-5x - 1 + 1 = 7 + 1 \quad \text{Adding 1}$$

$$-5x = 8 \quad \text{Collecting like terms}$$

$$\frac{-5x}{-5} = \frac{8}{-5} \quad \text{Dividing by } -5$$

$$x = -\frac{8}{5}.$$

Study Tips

BEGINNING TO STUDY FOR THE FINAL EXAM (PART 3): THREE DAYS TO TWO WEEKS OF STUDY TIME

1. Begin by browsing through each chapter, reviewing the highlighted or boxed information regarding important formulas in both the text and the Summary and Review. There may be some formulas that you will need to memorize.

2. Retake each chapter test that you took in class, assuming your instructor has returned it. Otherwise, use the chapter test in the book. Restudy the objectives in the text that correspond to each question you missed.

3. Work the Cumulative Review/Final Examination during the last couple of days before the final. Set aside the same amount of time that you will have for the final. See how much of the final exam you can complete under test-like conditions. Be careful to avoid any questions corresponding to objectives not covered. Again, restudy the objectives in the text that correspond to each question you missed.

4. For remaining difficulties, see your instructor, go to a tutoring session, or participate in a study group.

"It is a great piece of skill to know how to guide your luck, even while waiting for it."

Baltasar Gracian, seventeenth-century Spanish philosopher and writer

643

13. Solve: $\dfrac{7}{8}x - \dfrac{1}{4} + \dfrac{1}{2}x = \dfrac{3}{4} + x.$

Check:

$$\dfrac{2}{3}x - \dfrac{1}{6} + \dfrac{1}{2}x = \dfrac{7}{6} + 2x$$

$$\dfrac{2}{3}\left(-\dfrac{8}{5}\right) - \dfrac{1}{6} + \dfrac{1}{2}\left(-\dfrac{8}{5}\right) \;?\; \dfrac{7}{6} + 2\left(-\dfrac{8}{5}\right)$$

$$-\dfrac{16}{15} - \dfrac{1}{6} - \dfrac{8}{10} \;\bigg|\; \dfrac{7}{6} - \dfrac{16}{5}$$

$$-\dfrac{32}{30} - \dfrac{5}{30} - \dfrac{24}{30} \;\bigg|\; \dfrac{35}{30} - \dfrac{96}{30}$$

$$\dfrac{-32 - 5 - 24}{30} \;\bigg|\; -\dfrac{61}{30}$$

$$-\dfrac{61}{30} \qquad\qquad\qquad \text{TRUE}$$

The solution is $-\dfrac{8}{5}$.

Do Exercise 13.

To illustrate clearing decimals, we repeat Example 4, but this time we clear the decimals first.

EXAMPLE 9 Solve: $16.3 - 7.2y = -8.18$.

The greatest number of decimal places in any one number is *two*. Multiplying by 100, which has *two* 0's, will clear the decimals.

$$100(16.3 - 7.2y) = 100(-8.18) \qquad \text{Multiplying by 100 on both sides}$$

$$100(16.3) - 100(7.2y) = 100(-8.18) \qquad \text{Using a distributive law}$$

$$1630 - 720y = -818 \qquad \text{Simplifying}$$

$$1630 - 720y - 1630 = -818 - 1630 \qquad \text{Subtracting 1630 on both sides}$$

$$-720y = -2448 \qquad \text{Collecting like terms}$$

$$\dfrac{-720y}{-720} = \dfrac{-2448}{-720} \qquad \text{Dividing by } -720 \text{ on both sides}$$

$$y = \dfrac{17}{5}, \text{ or } 3.4$$

The number $\dfrac{17}{5}$, or 3.4, checks, as shown in Example 4, so it is the solution.

Do Exercise 14.

14. Solve: $41.68 = 4.7 - 8.6y$.

Answers on page A-25

c Equations Containing Parentheses

To solve certain kinds of equations that contain parentheses, we first use the distributive laws to remove the parentheses. Then we proceed as before.

EXAMPLE 10 Solve: $8x = 2(12 - 2x)$.

$$8x = 2(12 - 2x)$$
$$8x = 24 - 4x \qquad \text{Using the distributive law to multiply and remove parentheses}$$
$$8x + 4x = 24 - 4x + 4x \qquad \text{Adding } 4x \text{ to get all } x\text{-terms on one side}$$
$$12x = 24 \qquad \text{Collecting like terms}$$
$$\frac{12x}{12} = \frac{24}{12} \qquad \text{Dividing by 12}$$
$$x = 2$$

Check:
$$\begin{array}{c|c} \multicolumn{2}{c}{8x = 2(12 - 2x)} \\ \hline 8 \cdot 2 \; ? \; 2(12 - 2 \cdot 2) & \\ 16 & 2(12 - 4) \\ & 2 \cdot 8 \\ & 16 \quad \text{TRUE} \end{array}$$

We use the rules for order of operations to carry out the calculations on each side of the equation.

The solution is 2.

Do Exercises 15 and 16.

Here is a procedure for solving the types of equations discussed in this section.

> **AN EQUATION-SOLVING PROCEDURE**
>
> 1. Multiply on both sides to clear the equation of fractions or decimals. (This is optional, but it can ease computations.)
> 2. If parentheses occur, multiply using the *distributive laws* to remove them.
> 3. Collect like terms on each side, if necessary.
> 4. Get all terms with variables on one side and all constant terms on the other side, using the *addition principle*.
> 5. Collect like terms again, if necessary.
> 6. Multiply or divide to solve for the variable, using the *multiplication principle*.
> 7. Check all possible solutions in the original equation.

Solve.

15. $2(2y + 3) = 14$

16. $5(3x - 2) = 35$

Answers on page A-25

Solve.

17. $3(7 + 2x) = 30 + 7(x - 1)$

EXAMPLE 11 Solve: $2 - 5(x + 5) = 3(x - 2) - 1$.

$$2 - 5(x + 5) = 3(x - 2) - 1$$

$2 - 5x - 25 = 3x - 6 - 1$	Using the distributive laws to multiply and remove parentheses
$-5x - 23 = 3x - 7$	Collecting like terms
$-5x - 23 + 5x = 3x - 7 + 5x$	Adding $5x$
$-23 = 8x - 7$	Collecting like terms
$-23 + 7 = 8x - 7 + 7$	Adding 7
$-16 = 8x$	Collecting like terms
$\dfrac{-16}{8} = \dfrac{8x}{8}$	Dividing by 8
$-2 = x$	

18. $4(3 + 5x) - 4 = 3 + 2(x - 2)$

Check:
$$2 - 5(x + 5) = 3(x - 2) - 1$$
$$\begin{array}{c|c} 2 - 5(-2 + 5) & 3(-2 - 2) - 1 \\ 2 - 5(3) & 3(-4) - 1 \\ 2 - 15 & -12 - 1 \\ -13 & -13 \end{array}$$ TRUE

The solution is -2.

Note that the solution of $-2 = x$ is -2, which is also the solution of $x = -2$.

Do Exercises 17 and 18.

Answers on page A-25

CALCULATOR CORNER

Checking Solutions of Equations We can use a calculator to check solutions of equations by substituting the possible solution for each occurrence of the variable on the left side of the equation and then on the right side of the equation. If both sides have the same value, then the number that was substituted for the variable is the solution of the equation. In Example 5, for instance, to check if -2 is the solution of the equation $3x + 4x = -14$, we substitute -2 for x on the left side of the equation. To do this, we press $\boxed{3}\ \boxed{\times}\ \boxed{2}\ \boxed{+/-}\ \boxed{+}\ \boxed{4}\ \boxed{\times}\ \boxed{2}\ \boxed{+/-}\ \boxed{=}$. The result is -14. Note that the right side of the equation does not contain a variable. It is -14, the value that was obtained when -2 was substituted for x on the left side. Thus, the number -2 is the solution of the equation.

In Example 6, we can check if 1 is the solution of the equation $2x - 2 = -3x + 3$. First, we substitute 1 for x on the left side of the equation by pressing $\boxed{2}\ \boxed{\times}\ \boxed{1}\ \boxed{-}\ \boxed{2}\ \boxed{=}$. We get 0. Next, we substitute 1 for x on the right side of the equation by pressing $\boxed{3}\ \boxed{+/-}\ \boxed{\times}\ \boxed{1}\ \boxed{+}\ \boxed{3}\ \boxed{=}$. We get 0 again. Since the same value was obtained on both sides of the equation, the number 1 is the solution.

Exercises:

1. Use a calculator to check the solutions of the equations in Examples 1–4 and 7–11.

2. Use a calculator to check the solutions of the equations in Margin Exercises 1–18.

CHAPTER 11: Algebra: Solving Equations
and Problems

a   Solve. Don't forget to check!

1. $5x + 6 = 31$ **2.** $8x + 6 = 30$ **3.** $8x + 4 = 68$ **4.** $8z + 7 = 79$

5. $4x - 6 = 34$ **6.** $4x - 11 = 21$ **7.** $3x - 9 = 33$ **8.** $6x - 9 = 57$

9. $7x + 2 = -54$ **10.** $5x + 4 = -41$ **11.** $-45 = 3 + 6y$ **12.** $-91 = 9t + 8$

13. $-4x + 7 = 35$ **14.** $-5x - 7 = 108$ **15.** $-7x - 24 = -129$ **16.** $-6z - 18 = -132$

b   Solve.

17. $5x + 7x = 72$ **18.** $4x + 5x = 45$ **19.** $8x + 7x = 60$

20. $3x + 9x = 96$ **21.** $4x + 3x = 42$ **22.** $6x + 19x = 100$

23. $-6y - 3y = 27$ **24.** $-4y - 8y = 48$ **25.** $-7y - 8y = -15$

26. $-10y - 3y = -39$ **27.** $10.2y - 7.3y = -58$ **28.** $6.8y - 2.4y = -88$

29. $x + \frac{1}{3}x = 8$

30. $x + \frac{1}{4}x = 10$

31. $8y - 35 = 3y$

32. $4x - 6 = 6x$

33. $8x - 1 = 23 - 4x$

34. $5y - 2 = 28 - y$

35. $2x - 1 = 4 + x$

36. $5x - 2 = 6 + x$

37. $6x + 3 = 2x + 11$

38. $5y + 3 = 2y + 15$

39. $5 - 2x = 3x - 7x + 25$

40. $10 - 3x = 2x - 8x + 40$

41. $4 + 3x - 6 = 3x + 2 - x$

42. $5 + 4x - 7 = 4x - 2 - x$

43. $4y - 4 + y + 24 = 6y + 20 - 4y$

44. $5y - 7 + y = 7y + 21 - 5y$

Solve. Clear fractions or decimals first.

45. $\frac{7}{2}x + \frac{1}{2}x = 3x + \frac{3}{2} + \frac{5}{2}x$

46. $\frac{7}{8}x - \frac{1}{4} + \frac{3}{4}x = \frac{1}{16} + x$

47. $\frac{2}{3} + \frac{1}{4}t = \frac{1}{3}$

48. $-\frac{3}{2} + x = -\frac{5}{6} - \frac{4}{3}$

49. $\frac{2}{3} + 3y = 5y - \frac{2}{15}$

50. $\frac{1}{2} + 4m = 3m - \frac{5}{2}$

51. $\frac{5}{3} + \frac{2}{3}x = \frac{25}{12} + \frac{5}{4}x + \frac{3}{4}$

52. $1 - \frac{2}{3}y = \frac{9}{5} - \frac{y}{5} + \frac{3}{5}$

53. $2.1x + 45.2 = 3.2 - 8.4x$

54. $0.96y - 0.79 = 0.21y + 0.46$

55. $1.03 - 0.62x = 0.71 - 0.22x$

56. $1.7t + 8 - 1.62t = 0.4t - 0.32 + 8$

57. $\dfrac{2}{7}x - \dfrac{1}{2}x = \dfrac{3}{4}x + 1$

58. $\dfrac{5}{16}y + \dfrac{3}{8}y = 2 + \dfrac{1}{4}y$

C   Solve.

59. $3(2y - 3) = 27$

60. $4(2y - 3) = 28$

61. $40 = 5(3x + 2)$

62. $9 = 3(5x - 2)$

63. $2(3 + 4m) - 9 = 45$

64. $3(5 + 3m) - 8 = 88$

65. $5r - (2r + 8) = 16$

66. $6b - (3b + 8) = 16$

67. $6 - 2(3x - 1) = 2$

68. $10 - 3(2x - 1) = 1$

69. $5(d + 4) = 7(d - 2)$

70. $3(t - 2) = 9(t + 2)$

71. $8(2t + 1) = 4(7t + 7)$

72. $7(5x - 2) = 6(6x - 1)$

73. $3(r - 6) + 2 = 4(r + 2) - 21$

74. $5(t + 3) + 9 = 3(t - 2) + 6$

75. $19 - (2x + 3) = 2(x + 3) + x$

76. $13 - (2c + 2) = 2(c + 2) + 3c$

77. $0.7(3x + 6) = 1.1 - (x + 2)$

78. $0.9(2x + 8) = 20 - (x + 5)$

79. $a + (a - 3) = (a + 2) - (a + 1)$

80. $0.8 - 4(b - 1) = 0.2 + 3(4 - b)$

81. $\mathbf{D_W}$ A student begins solving the equation $\frac{2}{3}x + 1 = \frac{5}{6}$ by multiplying by 6 on both sides. Is this a wise thing to do? Why or why not?

82. $\mathbf{D_W}$ Describe a procedure that a classmate could use to solve the equation $ax + b = c$ for x.

SKILL MAINTENANCE

✎ VOCABULARY REINFORCEMENT

In each of Exercises 83–90, fill in the blank with the correct term from the given list. Some of the choices may not be used.

is greater than	absolute value
is less than	opposite
acute	equilateral
obtuse	scalene
negative	meter
one	gram
zero	rational
factor	irrational
multiply	

83. The _____ numbers consist of all numbers that can be named in the form $\frac{a}{b}$, where a and b are integers and b is not _____ . [10.1b]

84. The symbol $>$ means _____ . [1.4c]

85. Two numbers whose product is _____ are called reciprocals of each other. [2.7a]

86. The _____ of a number is its distance from zero on a number line. [10.1e]

87. A(n) _____ angle is an angle whose measure is greater than 90° and less than 180°. [9.5b]

88. A(n) _____ triangle is a triangle in which all sides are the same length. [9.5d]

89. The basic unit of length in the metric system is the _____ . [8.2a]

90. To _____ an expression is to find an equivalent expression that is a product. [11.1c]

SYNTHESIS

Solve.

91. $\dfrac{y - 2}{3} = \dfrac{2 - y}{5}$

92. $3x = 4x$

93. $\dfrac{5 + 2y}{3} = \dfrac{25}{12} + \dfrac{5y + 3}{4}$

94. ▦ $0.05y - 1.82 = 0.708y - 0.504$

95. $\dfrac{2}{3}(2x - 1) = 10$

96. $\dfrac{2}{3}\left(\dfrac{7}{8} - 4x\right) - \dfrac{5}{8} = \dfrac{3}{8}$

97. The perimeter of the figure shown is 15 cm. Solve for x.

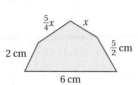

CHAPTER 11: Algebra: Solving Equations
and Problems

11.5 APPLICATIONS AND PROBLEM SOLVING

Objectives

a Translate phrases to algebraic expressions.

b Solve applied problems by translating to equations.

a Translating to Algebraic Expressions

In algebra, we translate problems to equations. The different parts of an equation are translations of word phrases to algebraic expressions. To translate, it helps to learn which words translate to certain operation symbols.

KEY WORDS

ADDITION (+)	SUBTRACTION (−)	MULTIPLICATION (·)	DIVISION (÷)
add	subtract	multiply	divide
added to	subtracted from	multiplied by	quotient
sum	difference	product	divided by
total	minus	times	
plus	less than	of	
more than	decreased by		
increased by	take away		

EXAMPLE 1 Translate to an algebraic expression:

   Twice (or two times) some number.

   Think of some number—say, 8. We can write 2 times 8 as 2×8, or $2 \cdot 8$. We multiplied by 2. Do the same thing using a variable. We can use any variable we wish, such as x, y, m, or n. Let's use y to stand for some number. If we multiply by 2, we get an expression

   $$y \times 2, \quad 2 \times y, \quad 2 \cdot y, \quad \text{or} \quad 2y.$$

In algebra, $2y$ is the expression used most often.

EXAMPLE 2 Translate to an algebraic expression:

   Seven less than some number.

   We let

   $x =$ the number.

   If the number were 23, then 7 less than 23 is 16, $(23 - 7)$ not $(7 - 23)$. If we knew the number to be 345, then the translation would be $345 - 7$. Thus if the number is x, then the translation is

   $x - 7$.

Caution!

Note that $7 - x$ is *not* a correct translation of the expression in Example 2. The expression $7 - x$ is a translation of "seven minus some number" or "some number less than seven."

Translate to an algebraic expression.

1. Twelve less than some number

2. Twelve more than some number

3. Four less than some number

4. Half of some number

5. Six more than eight times some number

6. The difference of two numbers

7. Fifty-nine percent of some number

8. Two hundred less than the product of two numbers

9. The sum of two numbers

EXAMPLE 3 Translate to an algebraic expression:

Eighteen more than a number.

We let

t = the number.

Now if the number were 26, then the translation would be 18 + 26, or 26 + 18. If we knew the number to be 174, then the translation would be 18 + 174, or 174 + 18. The translation is

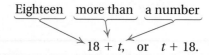

Eighteen   more than   a number

18 + t,   or t + 18.

EXAMPLE 4 Translate to an algebraic expression:

A number divided by 5.

We let

m = the number.

If the number were 76, then the translation would be 76 ÷ 5, or 76/5, or $\frac{76}{5}$. If the number were 213, then the translation would be 213 ÷ 5, or 213/5, or $\frac{213}{5}$. The translation is found as follows:

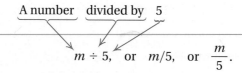

A number   divided by   5

m ÷ 5,   or m/5,   or $\dfrac{m}{5}$.

EXAMPLE 5 Translate to an algebraic expression.

PHRASE	ALGEBRAIC EXPRESSION
Five more than some number	5 + n, or n + 5
Half of a number	$\frac{1}{2}t$, or $\frac{t}{2}$
Five more than three times some number	5 + 3p, or 3p + 5
The difference of two numbers	$x - y$
Six less than the product of two numbers	$mn - 6$
Seventy-six percent of some number	76%z, or 0.76z

Do Exercises 1–9.

b Five Steps for Solving Problems

We have studied many new equation-solving tools in this chapter. We now apply them to problem solving. We have purposely used the following strategy throughout this text in order to introduce you to algebra.

> **FIVE STEPS FOR PROBLEM SOLVING IN ALGEBRA**
>
> 1. *Familiarize* yourself with the problem situation.
> 2. *Translate* to an equation.
> 3. *Solve* the equation.
> 4. *Check* your possible answer in the original problem.
> 5. *State* the answer clearly.

Of the five steps, the most important is probably the first one: becoming familiar with the problem situation. The table below lists some hints for familiarization.

To familiarize yourself with a problem:

- If a problem is given in words, read it carefully. Reread the problem, perhaps aloud. Try to verbalize the problem as if you were explaining it to someone else.

- Choose a variable (or variables) to represent the unknown and clearly state what the variable represents. Be descriptive! For example, let L = the length, d = the distance, and so on.

- Make a drawing and label it with known information, using specific units if given. Also, indicate unknown information.

- Find further information. Look up formulas or definitions with which you are not familiar. (Geometric formulas appear on the inside back cover of this text.) Consult a reference librarian or an expert in the field.

- Create a table that lists all the information you have available. Look for patterns that may help in the translation to an equation.

- Think of a possible answer and check the guess. Observe the manner in which the guess is checked.

EXAMPLE 6 *Hiking.* In 1998, at age 79, Earl Shaffer became the oldest person to thru-hike all 2100 miles of the Appalachian Trail—from Springer Mountain, Georgia, to Mount Katahdin, Maine. Shaffer thru-hiked the trail three times, in 1948 (Georgia to Maine), in 1965 (Maine to Georgia), and in 1998 (Georgia to Maine) near the 50th anniversary of his first hike. At one point in 1998, Shaffer stood atop Big Walker Mountain, Virginia, which is three times as far from the northern end as from the southern end. How far was Shaffer from each end of the trail?

Source: Appalachian Trail Conference; Earl Shaffer Foundation

10. Running. In 1997, Yiannis Kouros of Australia set the record for the greatest distance run in 24 hr by running 188 mi. After 8 hr, he was approximately twice as far from the finish line as he was from the start. How far had he run?

Source: *Guinness World Records 2004 Millennium Edition*

1. Familiarize. Let's consider a drawing.

To become familiar with the problem, let's guess a possible distance that Shaffer stood from Springer Mountain—say, 600 mi. Three times 600 mi is 1800 mi. Since 600 mi + 1800 mi = 2400 mi and 2400 mi is greater than 2100 mi, we see that our guess is too large. Rather than guess again, let's use the skills we have obtained in the ability to solve equations. We let

d = the distance, in miles, to the southern end, and

$3d$ = the distance, in miles, to the northern end.

(We could also let x = the distance to the northern end and $\frac{1}{3}x$ = the distance to the southern end.)

2. Translate. From the drawing, we see that the lengths of the two parts of the trail must add up to 2100 mi. This leads to our translation.

$$
\underbrace{\text{Distance to southern end}}_{d} \quad \underset{+}{\text{plus}} \quad \underbrace{\text{Distance to northern end}}_{3d} \quad \underset{=}{\text{is}} \quad \underset{2100}{\text{2100 mi}}
$$

3. Solve. We solve the equation:

$$d + 3d = 2100$$

$$4d = 2100 \qquad \text{Collecting like terms}$$

$$\frac{4d}{4} = \frac{2100}{4} \qquad \text{Dividing by 4 on both sides}$$

$$d = 525.$$

4. Check. As expected, d is less than 600 mi. If $d = 525$ mi, then $3d = 1575$ mi. Since 525 mi + 1575 mi = 2100 mi, we have a check.

5. State. Atop Big Walker Mountain, Shaffer stood 525 mi from Springer Mountain and 1575 mi from Mount Katahdin.

Answer on page A-26

Do Exercise 10.

CHAPTER 11: Algebra: Solving Equations and Problems

EXAMPLE 7 *Rocket Sections.* A rocket is divided into three sections: the payload and navigation section at the top, the fuel section in the middle, and the rocket engine section at the bottom. The top section is one-sixth the length of the bottom section. The middle section is one-half the length of the bottom section. The total length of the rocket is 240 ft. Find the length of each section.

1. **Familiarize.** We first make a drawing. Noting that the lengths of the top and middle sections are expressed in terms of the bottom section, we let

x = the length of the bottom section.

Then $\frac{1}{2}x$ = the length of the middle section

and $\frac{1}{6}x$ = the length of the top section.

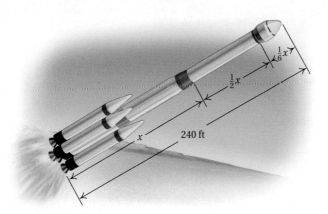

2. **Translate.** From the statement of the problem and the drawing, we see that the lengths add up to 240 ft. This gives us our translation.

Length of top	plus	Length of middle	plus	Length of bottom	is	Total length
$\frac{1}{6}x$	+	$\frac{1}{2}x$	+	x	=	240

3. **Solve.** We solve the equation by clearing fractions, as follows:

$$\frac{1}{6}x + \frac{1}{2}x + x = 240 \qquad \text{The LCM of all the denominators is 6.}$$

$$6 \cdot \left(\frac{1}{6}x + \frac{1}{2}x + x\right) = 6 \cdot 240 \qquad \text{Multiplying by the LCM, 6}$$

$$6 \cdot \frac{1}{6}x + 6 \cdot \frac{1}{2}x + 6 \cdot x = 6 \cdot 240 \qquad \text{Using the distributive law}$$

$$x + 3x + 6x = 1440 \qquad \text{Simplifying}$$

$$10x = 1440 \qquad \text{Adding}$$

$$\frac{10x}{10} = \frac{1440}{10} \qquad \text{Dividing by 10}$$

$$x = 144.$$

4. **Check.** Do we have an answer *to the problem*? If the rocket engine (bottom section) is 144 ft, then the middle section is $\frac{1}{2} \cdot 144$, or 72 ft, and the top section is $\frac{1}{6} \cdot 144$, or 24 ft. Since these lengths total 240 ft, our answer checks.

5. **State.** The top section is 24 ft, the middle 72 ft, and the bottom 144 ft.

Do Exercise 11.

11. Gourmet Sandwiches. A gourmet sandwich shop located near a college campus specializes in sandwiches prepared in buns of length 18 in. Suppose Jenny, Emma, and Sarah buy one of these sandwiches and take it back to their apartment. Since they have different appetites, Jenny cuts the sandwich in such a way that Emma gets half of what Jenny gets and Sarah gets three-fourths of what Jenny gets. Find the length of each person's sandwich.

Answer on page A-26

12. Van Rental. Truck-Rite also rents vans at a daily rate of $64.95 plus 57 cents per mile. What mileage will allow a salesperson to stay within a daily budget of $400?

Answer on page A-26

EXAMPLE 8 *Truck Rental.* Truck-Rite Rentals rents trucks at a daily rate of $59.95 plus 49¢ per mile. Concert Productions has budgeted $400 per day for renting a truck to haul equipment to an upcoming concert. How many miles can a rental truck be driven on a $400 daily budget?

1. **Familiarize.** Suppose that Concert Productions drives 75 mi. Then the cost is

Daily charge	plus		Mileage charge	
($59.95)	plus	(Cost per mile)	times	(Number of miles driven)
$59.95	+	$0.49	·	75,

which is $59.95 + $36.75, or $96.70. This familiarizes us with the way in which a calculation is made. Note that we convert 49 cents to $0.49 so that we are using the same units, dollars, throughout the problem.

Let m = the number of miles that can be driven for $400.

2. **Translate.** We reword the problem and translate as follows.

Daily rate	plus	Cost per mile	times	Number of miles driven	is	Total cost
$59.95	+	$0.49	·	m	=	$400

3. **Solve.** We solve the equation:

$$59.95 + 0.49m = 400$$
$$100(59.95 + 0.49m) = 100(400) \quad \text{Multiplying by 100 on both sides to clear decimals}$$
$$100(59.95) + 100(0.49m) = 40{,}000 \quad \text{Using the distributive law}$$
$$5995 + 49m = 40{,}000$$
$$49m = 34{,}005 \quad \text{Subtracting 5995}$$
$$\frac{49m}{49} = \frac{34{,}005}{49} \quad \text{Dividing by 49}$$
$$m \approx 694.0. \quad \text{Rounding to the nearest tenth}$$

4. **Check.** We check in the original problem. We multiply 694 by $0.49, getting $340.06. Then we add $340.06 to $59.95 and get $400.01, which is just about the $400 allotted.

5. **State.** The truck can be driven about 694 mi on the rental allotment of $400.

Do Exercise 12.

EXAMPLE 9 *Angles of a Triangle.* The second angle of a triangle is twice as large as the first. The measure of the third angle is 20° greater than that of the first angle. How large are the angles?

1. **Familiarize.** We first make a drawing, letting

   the measure of the first angle $= x$.

   Then   the measure of the second angle $= 2x$

   and   the measure of the third angle $= x + 20$.

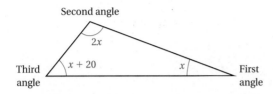

2. **Translate.** To translate, we recall from Section 9.5 that the measures of the angles of any triangle add up to 180°.

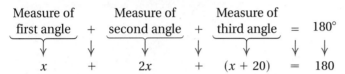

3. **Solve.** We solve the equation:

$$x + 2x + (x + 20) = 180$$
$$4x + 20 = 180$$
$$4x + 20 - 20 = 180 - 20$$
$$4x = 160$$
$$\frac{4x}{4} = \frac{160}{4}$$
$$x = 40.$$

Possible measures for the angles are as follows:

First angle: $x = 40°$;
Second angle: $2x = 2(40) = 80°$;
Third angle: $x + 20 = 40 + 20 = 60°$.

4. **Check.** Consider 40°, 80°, and 60°. The second is twice the first, and the third is 20° greater than the first. The sum is 180°. These numbers check.

5. **State.** The measures of the angles are 40°, 80°, and 60°.

Caution!

Units are important in answers. Remember to include them, where appropriate.

Do Exercise 13.

13. Angles of a Triangle. The second angle of a triangle is three times as large as the first. The third angle measures 30° more than the first angle. Find the measures of the angles.

Answer on page A-26

EXAMPLE 10 *Top Speeds of Roller Coasters.* The average top speed of the three fastest roller coasters in the world is 109 mph. The third-fastest roller coaster, Superman the Escape (located at Six Flags Magic Mountain, Los Angeles, California), reaches a top speed of 20 mph less than the fastest roller coaster, Top Thrill Dragster (located in Cedar Point, Sandusky, Ohio). The second-fastest roller coaster, Dodonpa (located in Fujikyu Highlands, Japan), has a top speed of 107 mph. What is the top speed of the fastest roller coaster?

Source: *Fortune Small Business*, June 2004, p. 48

1. **Familiarize.** The **average** of a set of numbers is the sum of the numbers divided by the number of addends.

   We are given that the second-fastest speed is 107 mph. Suppose the three top speeds are 90, 107, and 112. The average is then

   $$\frac{90 + 107 + 112}{3} = \frac{309}{3} = 103,$$

   which is too low. Instead of continuing to guess, let's use the equation-solving skills we have learned in this chapter. We let x represent the top speed of the fastest roller coaster. Then $x - 20$ is the top speed of the third-fastest roller coaster.

2. **Translate.** We reword the problem and translate as follows.

$$\frac{\text{Speed of fastest coaster} + \text{Speed of second-fastest coaster} + \text{Speed of third-fastest coaster}}{\text{Number of roller coasters}} = \frac{\text{Average speed of three fastest roller coasters}}{}$$

$$\frac{x + 107 + (x - 20)}{3} = 109$$

3. **Solve.** We solve as follows.

$$\frac{x + 107 + (x - 20)}{3} = 109$$

$$3 \cdot \frac{x + 107 + (x - 20)}{3} = 3 \cdot 109 \qquad \text{Multiplying on both sides by 3 to clear the fraction}$$

$$x + 107 + (x - 20) = 327$$

$$2x + 87 = 327 \qquad \text{Collecting like terms}$$

$$2x = 240 \qquad \text{Subtracting 87}$$

$$x = 120 \qquad \text{Dividing by 2}$$

4. Check. If the top speed of the fastest roller coaster is 120 mph, then the top speed of the third-fastest is $120 - 20$, or 100 mph. The average of the top speeds of the three fastest is $(120 + 107 + 100) \div 3 = 327 \div 3$, or 109 mph. The answer checks.

5. State. The top speed of the fastest roller coaster in the world is 120 mph.

Do Exercise 14.

EXAMPLE 11 *Savings Investment.* An investment is made at 6% simple interest for 1 year. It grows to $768.50. How much was originally invested (the principal)?

1. Familiarize. Suppose that $100 was invested. Recalling the formula for simple interest, $I = Prt$, we know that the interest for 1 year on $100 at 6% simple interest is given by $I = \$100 \cdot 0.06 \cdot 1 = \$6$. Then, at the end of the year, the amount in the account is found by adding the principal and the interest:

Principal $+$ Interest $=$ Amount
$\downarrow$ $\downarrow$ $\downarrow$ $\downarrow$ $\downarrow$ $\downarrow$
$\$100$ $+$ $\$6$ $=$ $\$106.$

In this problem, we are working backward. We are trying to find the principal, which is the original investment. We let $x =$ the principal. Then the interest earned is 6%x.

2. Translate. We reword the problem and then translate.

Principal $+$ Interest $=$ Amount
$\downarrow$ $\downarrow$ $\downarrow$ $\downarrow$ $\downarrow$
x $+$ $6\%x$ $=$ 768.50 Interest is 6% of the principal.

3. Solve. We solve the equation:

$x + 6\%x = 768.50$

$x + 0.06x = 768.50$ Converting to decimal notation

$1x + 0.06x = 768.50$ Identity property of 1

$1.06x = 768.50$ Collecting like terms

$\dfrac{1.06x}{1.06} = \dfrac{768.50}{1.06}$ Dividing by 1.06

$x = 725.$

4. Check. We check by taking 6% of $725 and adding it to $725:

$6\% \times \$725 = 0.06 \times 725 = \$43.50.$

Then $\$725 + \$43.50 = \$768.50$, so $725 checks.

5. State. The original investment was $725.

Do Exercise 15.

---

14. Average Test Score. Sam's average score on his first three math tests is 77. He scored 62 on the first test. On the third test, he scored nine points more than he scored on his second test. What did he score on the second and third tests?

15. Savings Investment. An investment is made at 7% simple interest for 1 year. It grows to $8988. How much was originally invested (the principal)?

Answers on page A-26

Study Tips

FINAL STUDY TIP

You are arriving at the end of your course in Basic Mathematics. If you have not begun to prepare for the final examination, be sure to read the comments in the Study Tips on pp. 545, 611, 643, and 656.

"We make a living by what we get, but we make a life by what we give."

Winston Churchill

Translating for Success

1. *Angle Measures.* The measure of the second angle of a triangle is 51° more than that of the first angle. The measure of the third angle is 3° less than twice the first angle. Find the measures of the angles.

2. *Sales Tax.* Tina paid $3976 for a used car. This amount included 5% for sales tax. How much did the car cost before tax?

3. *Perimeter.* The perimeter of a rectangle is 2347 ft. The length is 28 ft greater than the width. Find the length and the width.

4. *Fraternity or Sorority Membership.* At Arches Tech University, 3976 students belong to a fraternity or a sorority. This is 35% of the total enrollment. What is the total enrollment at Arches Tech?

5. *Fraternity or Sorority Membership.* At Moab Tech University, 35% of the students belong to a fraternity or a sorority. The total enrollment of the university is 11,360 students. How many students belong to either a fraternity or a sorority?

The goal of these matching questions is to practice step (2), *Translate,* of the five-step problem-solving process. Translate each word problem to an equation and select a correct translation from equations A–O.

A. $x + (x - 3) + \dfrac{4}{5}x = 384$

B. $x + (x + 51) + (2x - 3) = 180$

C. $x + (x + 96{,}000) = 180{,}000$

D. $2 \cdot 96 + 2x = 3976$

E. $x + (x + 1) + (x + 2) = 384$

F. $3976 = x \cdot 11{,}360$

G. $2x + 2(x + 28) = 2347$

H. $3976 = x + 5\%x$

I. $x + (x + 28) = 2347$

J. $x = 35\% \cdot 11{,}360$

K. $x + 96 = 3976$

L. $x + (x + 3) + \dfrac{4}{5}x = 384$

M. $x + (x + 2) + (x + 4) = 384$

N. $35\% \cdot x = 3976$

O. $x + (x + 28) = 2347$

Answers on page A-26

6. *Island Population.* There are 180,000 people living on a small Caribbean island. The women outnumber the men by 96,000. How many men live on the island?

7. *Wire Cutting.* A 384-m wire is cut into three pieces. The second piece is 3 m longer than the first. The third is four-fifths as long as the first. How long is each piece?

8. *Locker Numbers.* The numbers on three adjoining lockers are consecutive integers whose sum is 384. Find the integers.

9. *Fraternity or Sorority Membership.* The total enrollment at Canyonlands Tech University is 11,360 students. Of these, 3976 students belong to a fraternity or a sorority. What percent of the students belong to a fraternity or a sorority?

10. *Width of a Rectangle.* The length of a rectangle is 96 ft. The perimeter of the rectangle is 3976 ft. Find the width.

a   Translate to an algebraic expression.

1. Three less than twice a number

2. Three times a number divided by *a*

3. The product of 97% and some number

4. 43% of some number

5. Four more than five times some number

6. Seventy-five less than eight times a number

7. *Pipe Cutting.*   A 240-in. pipe is cut into two pieces. One piece is three times the length of the other. Let *x* = the length of the longer piece. Write an expression for the length of the shorter piece.

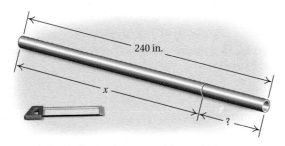

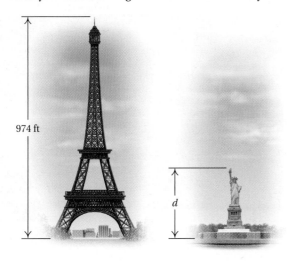

8. The price of a book is decreased by 30% during a sale. Let *b* = the price of the book before the reduction. Write an expression for the sale price.

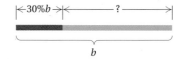

b   Solve.

9. What number added to 85 is 117?

10. Eight times what number is 2552?

11. *Statue of Liberty.*   The height of the Eiffel Tower is 974 ft, which is about 669 ft higher than the Statue of Liberty. What is the height of the Statue of Liberty?

12. *Area of Lake Ontario.*   The area of Lake Superior is about four times the area of Lake Ontario. The area of Lake Superior is 30,172 mi². What is the area of Lake Ontario?

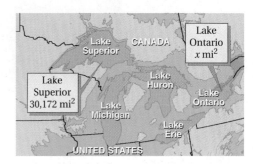

13. *Cinnamon Life* Recently, the cost of four 21-oz boxes of Cinnamon Life cereal was $17.16. What was the cost of one box?

Source: General Mills

14. *Women's Dresses.* In a recent year, the total amount spent on women's blouses was $6.5 billion. This was $0.2 billion more than what was spent on women's dresses. How much was spent on women's dresses?

15. When 17 is subtracted from four times a certain number, the result is 211. What is the number?

16. When 36 is subtracted from five times a certain number, the result is 374. What is the number?

17. If you double a number and then add 16, you get $\frac{2}{3}$ of the original number. What is the original number?

18. If you double a number and then add 85, you get $\frac{3}{4}$ of the original number. What is the original number?

19. *Iditarod Race.* The Iditarod sled dog race extends for 1049 mi from Anchorage to Nome. If a musher is twice as far from Anchorage as from Nome, how many miles has the musher traveled?

Source: Iditarod Trail Commission

20. *Home Remodeling.* In a recent year, Americans spent a total of approximately $32.8 billion to remodel bathrooms and kitchens. Twice as much was spent on kitchens as on bathrooms. How much was spent on each?

Source: *Remodeling Magazine*

21. *Pipe Cutting.*   A 480-m pipe is cut into three pieces. The second piece is three times as long as the first. The third piece is four times as long as the second. How long is each piece?

22. *Rope Cutting.*   A 180-ft rope is cut into three pieces. The second piece is twice as long as the first. The third piece is three times as long as the second. How long is each piece of rope?

23. *Perimeter of NBA Court.*   The perimeter of an NBA basketball court is 288 ft. The length is 44 ft longer than the width. Find the dimensions of the court.

Source: National Basketball Association

24. *Perimeter of High School Court.*   The perimeter of a standard high school basketball court is 268 ft. The length is 34 ft longer than the width. Find the dimensions of the court.

Source: Indiana High School Athletic Association

25. *Hancock Building Dimensions.*   The ground floor of the John Hancock Building in Chicago is in the shape of a rectangle whose length is 100 ft more than the width. The perimeter is 860 ft. Find the length, the width, and the area of the ground floor.

26. *Hancock Building Dimensions.*   The top floor of the John Hancock Building in Chicago is in the shape of a rectangle whose length is 60 ft more than the width. The perimeter is 520 ft. Find the length, the width, and the area of the top floor.

27. *Car Rental.*   Value Rent-A-Car rents a family-sized car at a daily rate of $74.95 plus 40 cents per mile. Rick Moneycutt is allotted a daily budget of $240. How many miles can he drive per day and stay within his budget?

28. *Van Rental.*   Value Rent-A-Car rents a van at a daily rate of $84.95 plus 60 cents per mile. Molly Rickert rents a van to deliver electrical parts to her customers. She is allotted a daily budget of $320. How many miles can she drive per day and stay within her budget?

29. *Angles of a Triangle.* The second angle of a triangular parking lot is four times as large as the first. The third angle is 45° less than the sum of the other two angles. How large are the angles?

30. *Angles of a Triangle.* The second angle of a triangular field is three times as large as the first. The third angle is 40° greater than the first. How large are the angles?

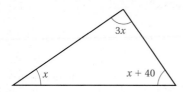

31. *Stock Prices.* Sarah's investment in AOL/Time Warner stock grew 28% to $448. How much did she invest?

32. *Savings Interest.* Sharon invested money in a savings account at a rate of 6% simple interest. After 1 yr, she has $6996 in the account. How much did Sharon originally invest?

33. *Credit Cards.* The balance in Will's Mastercard® account grew 2%, to $870, in one month. What was his balance at the beginning of the month?

34. *Loan Interest.* Alvin borrowed money from a cousin at a rate of 10% simple interest. After 1 yr, $7194 paid off the loan. How much did Alvin borrow?

35. *Taxi Fares.* In Beniford, taxis charge $3 plus 75¢ per mile for an airport pickup. How far from the airport can Courtney travel for $12?

36. *Taxi Fares.* In Cranston, taxis charge $4 plus 90¢ per mile for an airport pickup. How far from the airport can Ralph travel for $17.50?

37. *Tipping.* Leon left a 15% tip for a meal. The total cost of the meal, including the tip, was $41.40. What was the cost of the meal before the tip was added?

38. *Tipping.* Selena left an 18% tip for a meal. The total cost of the meal, including the tip, was $40.71. What was the cost of the meal before the tip was added?

39. *Standard Billboard Sign.* A standard rectangular highway billboard sign has a perimeter of 124 ft. The length is 6 ft more than three times the width. Find the dimensions.

40. *Two-by-Four.* The perimeter of a cross section of a "two-by-four" piece of lumber is 10 in. The length is 2 in. more than the width. Find the actual dimensions of the cross section of a two-by-four.

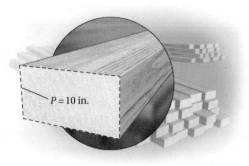

41. **D**w A fellow student claims to be able to solve most of the problems in this section by guessing. Is there anything wrong with this approach? Why or why not?

42. **D**w Write a problem for a classmate to solve so that it can be translated to the equation

$$\tfrac{2}{3}x + (x + 5) + x = 375.$$

Calculate.

43. $-\dfrac{4}{5} - \left(\dfrac{3}{8}\right)$ [10.3a]

44. $-\dfrac{4}{5} + \dfrac{3}{8}$ [10.2a]

45. $-\dfrac{4}{5} \cdot \dfrac{3}{8}$ [10.4a]

46. $-\dfrac{4}{5} \div \left(\dfrac{3}{8}\right)$ [10.5c]

47. $-25.6 \div (-16)$ [10.5c]

48. $-25.6(-16)$ [10.4a]

49. $-25.6 - (-16)$ [10.3a]

50. $-25.6 + (-16)$ [10.2a]

---

51. Abraham Lincoln's 1863 Gettysburg Address refers to the year 1776 as "Four *score* and seven years ago." Write an equation to find out what a score is.

52. *Test Questions.* A student scored 78 on a test that had 4 seven-point fill-ins and 24 three-point multiple-choice questions. The student had 1 fill-in wrong. How many multiple-choice questions did the student get right?

53. The width of a rectangle is $\tfrac{3}{4}$ of the length. The perimeter of the rectangle becomes 50 cm when the length and the width are each increased by 2 cm. Find the length and the width.

54. Cookies are set out on a tray for six people to take home. One-third, one-fourth, one-eighth, and one-fifth are given to four people, respectively. The fifth person eats ten cookies on the spot, with one cookie remaining for the sixth person. Find the original number of cookies on the tray.

55. A storekeeper goes to the bank to get $10 worth of change. She requests twice as many quarters as half dollars, twice as many dimes as quarters, three times as many nickels as dimes, and no pennies or dollars. How many of each coin did the storekeeper receive?

56. A student has an average score of 82 on three tests. His average score on the first two tests is 85. What was the score on the third test?

Summary and Review

The review that follows is meant to prepare you for a chapter exam. It consists of three parts. The first part, Concept Reinforcement, is designed to increase understanding of the concepts through true/false exercises. The second part is a list of important properties and formulas. The third part is the Review Exercises. These provide practice exercises for the exam, together with references to section objectives so you can go back and review. Before beginning, stop and look back over the skills you have obtained. What skills in mathematics do you have now that you did not have before studying this chapter?

✎ CONCEPT REINFORCEMENT

Determine whether the statement is true or false. Answers are given at the back of the book.

_____ **1.** The expression $2(x + 3)$ is equivalent to the expression $2 \cdot x + 3$.

_____ **2.** The expression $x - 7$ is not equivalent to the expression $7 - x$.

_____ **3.** To factor an expression is to find an equivalent expression that is a product.

_____ **4.** $3 - x = 4x$ and $5x = -3$ are equivalent equations.

_____ **5.** Collecting like terms is based on the distributive laws.

IMPORTANT PROPERTIES AND FORMULAS

The Addition Principle: For any real numbers a, b, and c, $a = b$ is equivalent to $a + c = b + c$.
The Multiplication Principle: For any real numbers a, b, and c, $c \neq 0$, $a = b$ is equivalent to $a \cdot c = b \cdot c$.
The Distributive Laws: $a(b + c) = ab + ac$, $a(b - c) = ab - ac$

Review Exercises

1. Evaluate $\dfrac{x - y}{3}$ when $x = 17$ and $y = 5$.   [11.1a]

Multiply.   [11.1b]

2. $5(3x - 7)$

3. $-2(4x - 5)$

4. $10(0.4x + 1.5)$

5. $-8(3 - 6x)$

Factor.   [11.1c]

6. $2x - 14$

7. $6x - 6$

8. $5x + 10$

9. $12 - 3x$

Collect like terms.   [11.1d]

10. $11a + 2b - 4a - 5b$

11. $7x - 3y - 9x + 8y$

12. $6x + 3y - x - 4y$

13. $-3a + 9b + 2a - b$

Solve. [11.2a], [11.3a]

14. $x + 5 = -17$

15. $-8x = -56$

16. $-\dfrac{x}{4} = 48$

17. $n - 7 = -6$

18. $15x = -35$

19. $x - 11 = 14$

20. $-\dfrac{2}{3} + x = -\dfrac{1}{6}$

21. $\dfrac{4}{5}y = -\dfrac{3}{16}$

22. $y - 0.9 = 9.09$

23. $5 - x = 13$

Solve. [11.4a, b, c]
24. $5t + 9 = 3t - 1$

25. $7x - 6 = 25x$

26. $\dfrac{1}{4}x - \dfrac{5}{8} = \dfrac{3}{8}$

27. $14y = 23y - 17 - 10$

28. $0.22y - 0.6 = 0.12y + 3 - 0.8y$

29. $\dfrac{1}{4}x - \dfrac{1}{8}x = 3 - \dfrac{1}{16}x$

30. $4(x + 3) = 36$

31. $3(5x - 7) = -66$

32. $8(x - 2) - 5(x + 4) = 20x + x$

33. $-5x + 3(x + 8) = 16$

34. Translate to an algebraic expression: [11.5a]
Nineteen percent of some number.

Solve. [11.5b]

35. *Dimensions of Wyoming.* The state of Wyoming is roughly in the shape of a rectangle whose perimeter is 1280 mi. The length is 90 mi more than the width. Find the dimensions.

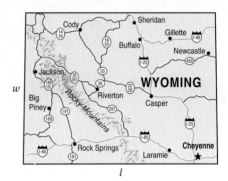

36. An entertainment center sold for $2449 in June. This was $332 more than the cost in February. Find the cost in February.

37. Ty is paid a commission of $8 for each appliance he sells. One week, he received $216 in commissions. How many appliances did he sell?

38. The measure of the second angle of a triangle is 50° more than that of the first angle. The measure of the third angle is 10° less than twice the first angle. Find the measures of the angles.

39. After a 30% reduction, a bread maker is on sale for $154. What was the marked price (the price before the reduction)?

40. A hotel manager's salary is $90,000, which is a 20% increase over the previous year's salary. What was the previous salary?

41. A tax-exempt charity received a bill of $145.90 for a sump pump. The bill incorrectly included sales tax of 5%. How much does the charity actually owe?

42. *Nile and Amazon Rivers.* The total length of the Nile and Amazon Rivers is 13,108 km. If the Amazon were 234 km longer, it would be as long as the Nile. Find the length of each river.

Source: *The Handy Geography Answer Book*

43. *HDTV Costs.* An HDTV television sold for $829 in May. This was $38 more than the cost in January. Find the cost in January.

44. *Writing Pad.* The perimeter of a rectangular writing pad is 56 cm. The width is 6 cm less than the length. Find the width and the length.

45. $\mathbf{D_W}$ Explain at least three uses of the distributive laws considered in this chapter. [11.1b, c, d]

46. $\mathbf{D_W}$ Explain all the errors in each of the following. [11.4a, c]

a) $4 - 3x = 9$
$3x = 9$
$x = 3$

b) $2(x - 5) = 7$
$2x - 5 = 7$
$2x = 12$
$x = 6$

SYNTHESIS

Solve.   [10.1e], [11.4a, b]

47. $2|n| + 4 = 50$

48. $|3n| = 60$

1. Evaluate $\dfrac{3x}{y}$ when $x = 10$ and $y = 5$.

Multiply.

2. $3(6 - x)$

3. $-5(y - 1)$

Factor.

4. $12 - 22x$

5. $7x + 21 + 14y$

Collect like terms.

6. $9x - 2y - 14x + y$

7. $-a + 6b + 5a - b$

Solve.

8. $x + 7 = 15$

9. $t - 9 = 17$

10. $3x = -18$

11. $-\dfrac{4}{7}x = -28$

12. $3t + 7 = 2t - 5$

13. $\dfrac{1}{2}x - \dfrac{3}{5} = \dfrac{2}{5}$

14. $8 - y = 16$

15. $-\dfrac{2}{5} + x = -\dfrac{3}{4}$

16. $0.4p + 0.2 = 4.2p - 7.8 - 0.6p$

17. $3(x + 2) = 27$

18. $-3x - 6(x - 4) = 9$

19. Translate to an algebraic expression:
    Nine less than some number.

Solve.

20. *Perimeter of a Photograph.*   The perimeter of a rectangular photograph is 36 cm. The length is 4 cm greater than the width. Find the width and the length.

21. *Charitable Contributions.*   About 35.9% of all charitable contributions are made to religious organizations. In 2003, about $86.4 billion was given to religious organizations. How much was given to charities in general?

Source: AAFRC Trust for Philanthropy/Giving USA 2004

22. *Board Cutting.*   An 8-m board is cut into two pieces. One piece is 2 m longer than the other. How long are the pieces?

23. *Savings Account.*   Money is invested in a savings account at 5% simple interest. After 1 year, there is $924 in the account. How much was originally invested?

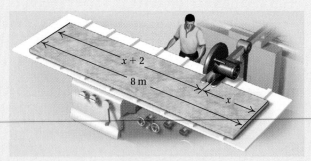

24. If you triple a number and then subtract 14, you get $\frac{2}{3}$ of the original number. What is the original number?

25. The second angle of a triangle is three times as large as the first. The third angle is 25° less than the sum of the other two angles. Find the measure of the first angle.

SYNTHESIS

26. Solve: $3|w| - 8 = 37$.

27. A movie theater had a certain number of tickets to give away. Five people got the tickets. The first got $\frac{1}{3}$ of the tickets, the second got $\frac{1}{4}$ of the tickets, and the third got $\frac{1}{5}$ of the tickets. The fourth person got 8 tickets, and there were 5 tickets left for the fifth person. Find the total number of tickets given away.

CHAPTER 11: Algebra: Solving Equations and Problems

Cumulative Review/ Final Examination

This cumulative review also serves as a final examination for the entire book. A question that may occur at this point is what notation to use for a particular problem or exercise. Although there is no particular rule, especially as you use mathematics outside the classroom, here is the guideline that we follow: Use the notation given in the problem. That is, if the problem is given using mixed numerals, give the answer in mixed numerals. If the problem is given in decimal notation, give the answer in decimal notation.

1. *Pears.* Find the unit price of each brand. Then determine which package has the lower unit price.

BRAND	PACKAGE	PRICE	UNIT PRICE
A	$8\frac{1}{2}$ oz	$0.65	
B	15 oz	$1.07	
C	$15\frac{1}{4}$ oz	$1.07	
D	29 oz	$1.69	
E	29 oz	$1.32	

2. Write a word name for 7.463.

3. *Pluto.* The planet Pluto has a diameter of 1400 mi. Use $\frac{22}{7}$ for π.

a) Find the circumference of Pluto.

b) Find the volume of Pluto.

Kitchen Costs. The average cost of a remodeled kitchen is $26,888, according to the National Kitchen and Bath Association. Complete the table below, which relates percents and costs of certain items.

	ITEM	PERCENT OF COST	COST
4.	Cabinets	50%	
5.	Countertops		$4033.20
6.	Appliances	8%	
7.	Fixtures		$8066.40
8.	Flooring	2%	

Source: National Kitchen and Bath Association

9. In 47,201, what digit tells the number of thousands?

10. Write expanded notation for 7405.

Add and simplify, if appropriate.

11.
```
  7 4 1
+ 2 7 1
```

12.
```
  4 9 0 3
  5 2 7 8
  6 3 9 1
+ 4 5 1 3
```

13. $\dfrac{2}{13} + \dfrac{1}{26}$

14.
$$2\frac{4}{9}$$
$$+\ 3\frac{1}{3}$$

15.
```
      2.0 4 8
     6 3.9 1 4
   + 4 2 8.0 0 9
```

16. $34.56 + 2.783 + 0.433 + 765.1$

Subtract and simplify, if possible.

17.
```
  6 7 4
− 5 2 2
```

18.
```
  9 4 6 5
− 8 7 9 1
```

19. $\dfrac{7}{8} - \dfrac{2}{3}$

20.
$$4\dfrac{1}{3}$$
$$- 1\dfrac{5}{8}$$

21.
```
  2 0.0
−    0.0 0 2 7
```

22. $40.03 - 5.789$

Multiply and simplify, if possible.

23.
```
  2 9 7
×   1 6
```

24.
```
  3 4 9
× 7 6 3
```

25. $1\dfrac{3}{4} \cdot 2\dfrac{1}{3}$

26. $\dfrac{9}{7} \cdot \dfrac{14}{15}$

27. $12 \cdot \dfrac{5}{6}$

28.
```
  3 4.0 9
×     7.6
```

Divide and simplify. State the answer using a whole-number quotient and remainder.

29. $6\overline{)3\,4\,3\,8}$

30. $3\,4\overline{)1\,9\,1\,4}$

31. Give a mixed numeral for the quotient in Question 30.

Divide and simplify, if possible.

32. $\dfrac{4}{5} \div \dfrac{8}{15}$

33. $2\dfrac{1}{3} \div 30$

34. $2.7\overline{)1\,0\,5.3}$

35. Round 68,489 to the nearest thousand.

36. Round 0.4275 to the nearest thousandth.

37. Round $21.\overline{83}$ to the nearest hundredth.

38. Determine whether 1368 is divisible by 8.

39. Find all the factors of 15.

40. Find the LCM of 16, 25, and 32.

Simplify.

41. $\dfrac{21}{30}$

42. $\dfrac{275}{5}$

43. Convert to a mixed numeral: $\dfrac{18}{5}$.

44. Use = or ≠ for ☐ to write a true sentence:
$$\dfrac{4}{7} \;\square\; \dfrac{3}{5}.$$

45. Use < or > for ☐ to write a true sentence:
$$\dfrac{4}{7} \;\square\; \dfrac{3}{5}.$$

46. Which number is greater, 1.001 or 0.9976?

CHAPTER 11: Algebra: Solving Equations
and Problems

47. Use < or > for ☐ to write a true sentence: 987 ☐ 879.

48. What part is shaded?

Convert to decimal notation.

49. $\dfrac{37}{1000}$

50. $\dfrac{13}{25}$

51. $\dfrac{8}{9}$

52. 7%

Convert to fraction notation.

53. 4.63

54. $7\dfrac{1}{4}$

55. 40%

Convert to percent notation.

56. $\dfrac{17}{20}$

57. 1.5

Solve.

58. $234 + y = 789$

59. $3.9 \times y = 249.6$

60. $\dfrac{2}{3} \cdot t = \dfrac{5}{6}$

61. $\dfrac{8}{17} = \dfrac{36}{x}$

Golf Rounds. The data in the following table show the percent of golfers who play a certain number of rounds of golf per year.

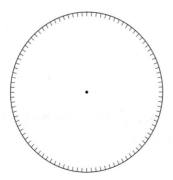

NUMBER OF ROUNDS PER YEAR	PERCENT
1–7	2.2
8–24	14.9
25–49	25.3
50–99	39.0
100 or more	18.6

Source: U.S. Golf Foundation

62. Make a circle graph of the data.

63. Make a bar graph of the data.

64. Find the missing angle measure.

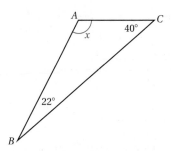

65. Classify the triangle in Exercise 64 as right, obtuse, or acute.

Solve.

66. *Donations.* Lorenzo makes donations of $627 and $48. What was the total donation?

67. *Candy Bars.* A machine wraps 134 candy bars per minute. How long does it take this machine to wrap 8710 bars?

68. *Stock Prices.* A share of stock bought for $29.63 dropped $3.88 before it was resold. What was the price when it was resold?

69. *Length of Trip.* At the start of a trip, a car's odometer read 27,428.6 mi, and at the end of the trip, the reading was 27,914.5 mi. How long was the trip?

70. *Taxes.* From an income of $12,000, amounts of $2300 and $1600 are paid for federal and state taxes. How much remains after these taxes have been paid?

71. *Teacher Salary.* A substitute teacher is paid $87 a day for 9 days. How much was received altogether?

72. *Walking Distance.* A person walks $\frac{3}{5}$ km per hour. At this rate, how far would the person walk in $\frac{1}{2}$ hr?

73. *Sweater Costs.* Eight identical sweaters cost a total of $679.68. What is the cost of each sweater?

74. *Paint Needs.* Eight gallons of exterior paint covers 400 ft². How much paint is needed to cover 650 ft²?

75. *Simple Interest.* What is the simple interest on $4000 principal at 5% for $\frac{3}{4}$ year?

76. *Commission Rate.* A real estate agent received $5880 commission on the sale of an $84,000 home. What was the rate of commission?

77. *Population Growth.* The population of a city is 29,000 this year and is increasing at 4% per year. What will the population be next year?

78. *Student Ages.* The ages of students in a math class at a community college are as follows:

18, 21, 26, 31, 32, 18, 50.

Find the average, the median, and the mode of their ages.

Evaluate.

79. 18^2

80. 20^2

Simplify.

81. $\sqrt{9}$

82. $\sqrt{121}$

83. Approximate to three decimal places: $\sqrt{20}$.

Complete.

84. $\frac{1}{3}$ yd = _____ in.

85. 4280 mm = _____ cm

86. 3 days = _____ hr

87. 20,000 g = _____ kg

88. 5 lb = _____ oz

89. 0.008 cg = _____ mg

90. 8190 mL = _____ L

91. 20 qt = _____ gal

92. Find the length of the third side of this right triangle. Give an exact answer and an approximation to three decimal places.

93. Find the perimeter and the area.

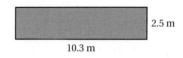

Find the area.

94.

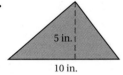

95.

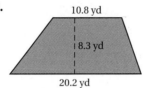

96.

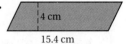

97. Find the diameter, the circumference, and the area of this circle. Use 3.14 for π.

98. Find the volume.

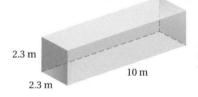

Find the volume. Use 3.14 for π.

99.

100.

Compute and simplify.

101. $12 \times 20 - 10 \div 5$

102. $4^3 - 5^2 + (16 \cdot 4 + 23 \cdot 3)$

103. $|(-1) \cdot 3|$

104. $17 + (-3)$

105. $\left(-\frac{1}{3}\right) - \left(-\frac{2}{3}\right)$

106. $(-6) \cdot (-5)$

107. $-\frac{5}{7} \cdot \frac{14}{35}$

108. $\frac{48}{-6}$

Solve.

109. $7 - x = 12$

110. $-4.3x = -17.2$

111. $5x + 7 = 3x - 9$

112. $5(x - 2) - 8(x - 4) = 20$

Translate to an algebraic expression.

113. 17 more than some number

114. 38 percent of some number

Solve.

115. *Rollerblade Costs.*   Melinda and Susan purchased rollerblades for a total of $107. Melinda paid $17 more for her rollerblades than Susan did. What did Susan pay?

116. *Savings Investment.*   Money is invested in a savings account at 8% simple interest. After 1 year, there is $1134 in the account. How much was originally invested?

117. *Wire Cutting.*   A 143-m wire is cut into three pieces. The second piece is 3 m longer than the first. The third is four-fifths as long as the first. How long is each piece?

Solve.

118. $\dfrac{2}{3}x + \dfrac{1}{6} - \dfrac{1}{2}x = \dfrac{1}{6} - 3x$

119. $29.966 - 8.673y = -8.18 + 10.4y$

For each of Questions 120–123, choose the correct answer from the selection given.

120. Collect like terms: $\dfrac{1}{4}x - \dfrac{3}{4}y + \dfrac{1}{4}x - \dfrac{3}{4}y$.

a) 0   **b)** $-\dfrac{2}{3}y$ **c)** $\dfrac{1}{2}x - \dfrac{3}{2}y$

d) $\dfrac{1}{2}x$ **e)** None

121. Factor: $8x + 4y - 12z$.

a) $2x + y - 3z$ **b)** $4x + 2y - 6z$ **c)** $2x - 3z$
d) $2x + 4y - 3z$ **e)** None

122. Divide: $-\dfrac{13}{25} \div \left(-\dfrac{13}{5}\right)$.

a) $\dfrac{169}{125}$ **b)** 5   **c)** $\dfrac{125}{169}$

d) $\dfrac{1}{5}$ **e)** None

123. Add: $-27 + (-11)$.

a) -38 **b)** -16 **c)** 16
d) 38   **e)** None

Answers

CHAPTER 1

Margin Exercises, Section 1.1, pp. 2–5

1. 2 ten thousands **2.** 2 hundred thousands
3. 2 millions **4.** 2 ten millions
5. 2 tens **6.** 2 hundreds
7. 2 hundred thousands; 8 ten thousands; 0 thousands; 2 hundreds; 1 ten; 9 ones
8. 1 thousand + 8 hundreds + 9 tens + 5 ones
9. 2 ten thousands + 3 thousands + 4 hundreds + 1 ten + 6 ones
10. 3 thousands + 0 hundreds + 3 tens + 1 one, or 3 thousands + 3 tens + 1 one
11. 4 thousands + 1 hundred + 8 tens + 0 ones, or 4 thousands + 1 hundred + 8 tens
12. 1 hundred thousand + 5 ten thousands + 4 thousands + 6 hundreds + 1 ten + 6 ones
13. Forty-nine **14.** Sixteen **15.** Thirty-eight
16. Two hundred four
17. Forty-four thousand, one hundred fifty-five
18. One million, eight hundred seventy-nine thousand, two hundred four **19.** Six billion, four hundred forty-nine million **20.** 213,105,329

Exercise Set 1.1, p. 6

1. 5 thousands **3.** 5 hundreds **5.** 2 **7.** 1
9. 5 thousands + 7 hundreds + 0 tens + 2 ones, or 5 thousands + 7 hundreds + 2 ones
11. 9 ten thousands + 3 thousands + 9 hundreds + 8 tens + 6 ones
13. 2 thousands + 0 hundreds + 5 tens + 8 ones, or 2 thousands + 5 tens + 8 ones
15. 1 thousand + 2 hundreds + 6 tens + 8 ones
17. 4 hundred thousands + 0 ten thousands + 5 thousands + 6 hundreds + 9 tens + 8 ones, or 4 hundred thousands + 5 thousands + 6 hundreds + 9 tens + 8 ones
19. 2 hundred thousands + 7 ten thousands + 2 thousands + 1 hundred + 6 tens + 1 one
21. 1 million + 1 hundred thousand + 8 ten thousands + 0 thousands + 2 hundreds + 1 ten + 2 ones, or 1 million + 1 hundred thousand + 8 ten thousands + 2 hundreds + 1 ten + 2 ones **23.** Eighty-five

25. Eighty-eight thousand **27.** One hundred twenty-three thousand, seven hundred sixty-five **29.** Seven billion, seven hundred fifty-four million, two hundred eleven thousand, five hundred seventy-seven
31. 2,233,812 **33.** 8,000,000,000 **35.** Five hundred sixty-six thousand, two hundred eighty **37.** seventy-six million, eighty-six thousand, seven hundred ninety-two
39. 9,460,000,000,000 **41.** 64,186,000 **43.** D_W
45. 138

Margin Exercises, Section 1.2, pp. 10–11

1. 13,465 **2.** 9745 **3.** 16,182 **4.** 27,474 **5.** 29 in.
6. 62 ft **7.** 16 in.; 26 in.

Calculator Corner, p. 12

1. 55 **2.** 121 **3.** 1602 **4.** 734 **5.** 1932 **6.** 864

Exercise Set 1.2, p. 13

1. 387 **3.** 5198 **5.** 164 **7.** 100 **9.** 8503 **11.** 5266
13. 4466 **15.** 6608 **17.** 34,432 **19.** 101,310
21. 230 **23.** 18,424 **25.** 31,685 **27.** 114 mi
29. 570 ft **31.** D_W **33.** 8 ten thousands
34. Five billion, two hundred ninety-four million, two hundred forty-seven thousand
35. $1 + 99 = 100, 2 + 98 = 100, \ldots, 49 + 51 = 100$. Then $49 \cdot 100 = 4900$ and $4900 + 50 + 100 = 5050$.

Margin Exercises, Section 1.3, pp. 16–19

1. $7 = 2 + 5$, or $7 = 5 + 2$ **2.** $17 = 9 + 8$, or $17 = 8 + 9$
3. $5 = 13 - 8; 8 = 13 - 5$ **4.** $11 = 14 - 3; 3 = 14 - 11$
5. 3801 **6.** 6328 **7.** 4747 **8.** 56 **9.** 205
10. 658 **11.** 2851 **12.** 1546

Calculator Corner, p. 18

1. 28 **2.** 47 **3.** 67 **4.** 119 **5.** 2128 **6.** 2593

Exercise Set 1.3, p. 20

1. $7 = 3 + 4$, or $7 = 4 + 3$ **3.** $13 = 5 + 8$, or $13 = 8 + 5$
5. $23 = 14 + 9$, or $23 = 9 + 14$ **7.** $43 = 27 + 16$, or
$43 = 16 + 27$ **9.** $6 = 15 - 9$; $9 = 15 - 6$
11. $8 = 15 - 7$; $7 = 15 - 8$ **13.** $17 = 23 - 6$; $6 = 23 - 17$
15. $23 = 32 - 9$; $9 = 32 - 23$ **17.** 44   **19.** 533
21. 39   **23.** 234   **25.** 5382   **27.** 3831   **29.** 7748
31. 43,028   **33.** 56   **35.** 454   **37.** 3749   **39.** 2191
41. 95,974   **43.** 9989   **45.** 4206   **47.** 10,305   **49.** **D**_W
51. 1024   **52.** 12,732   **53.** 90,283   **54.** 29,364
55. 1345   **56.** 924   **57.** 22,692   **58.** 10,920
59. Six million, three hundred seventy-five thousand, six
hundred two   **60.** 7 ten thousands   **61.** 3; 4

Margin Exercises, Section 1.4, pp. 22–26

1. 40   **2.** 50   **3.** 70   **4.** 100   **5.** 40   **6.** 80   **7.** 90
8. 140   **9.** 470   **10.** 240   **11.** 290   **12.** 600   **13.** 800
14. 800   **15.** 9300   **16.** 8000   **17.** 8000   **18.** 19,000
19. 69,000   **20.** 48,970; 49,000; 49,000   **21.** 269,580;
269,600; 270,000   **22.** Eliminate the power sunroof and
the power package. Answers may vary.   **23.** **(a)** $18,300;
(b) yes   **24.** $70 + 20 + 40 + 70 = 200$
25. $700 + 700 + 200 + 200 = 1800$
26. $9300 - 6700 = 2600$ **27.** $23,000 - 12,000 = 11,000$
28. <   **29.** >   **30.** >   **31.** <   **32.** <   **33.** >

Exercise Set 1.4, p. 27

1. 50   **3.** 470   **5.** 730   **7.** 900   **9.** 100   **11.** 1000
13. 9100   **15.** 32,900   **17.** 6000   **19.** 8000
21. 45,000   **23.** 373,000   **25.** 180   **27.** 5720
29. 220; incorrect   **31.** 890; incorrect   **33.** 16,500
35. 5200   **37.** $11,200   **39.** $18,900; no   **41.** Answers
will vary depending on the options chosen.   **43.** 1600
45. 1500   **47.** 31,000   **49.** 69,000   **51.** <   **53.** >
55. <   **57.** >   **59.** >   **61.** >
63. $1,800,607 < 2,136,068$, or $2,136,068 > 1,800,607$
65. $6482 > 4827$, or $4827 < 6482$ **67.** **D**_W
69. 7 thousands + 9 hundreds + 9 tens + 2 ones
70. 2 ten millions + 3 millions   **71.** Two hundred forty-
six billion, six hundred five million, four thousand, thirty-
two   **72.** One million, five thousand, one hundred
73. 86,754   **74.** 13,589   **75.** 48,824   **76.** 4415
77. Left to the student   **79.** Left to the student

Margin Exercises, Section 1.5, pp. 32–36

1. 116   **2.** 148   **3.** 4938   **4.** 6740   **5.** 1035   **6.** 3024
7. 46,252   **8.** 205,065   **9.** 144,432   **10.** 287,232
11. 14,075,720   **12.** 391,760   **13.** 17,345,600
14. 56,200   **15.** 562,000   **16.** **(a)** 1081; **(b)** 1081; **(c)** same
17. 40   **18.** 15   **19.** $15,300   **20.** $840 \times 250 = 210,000$;
$800 \times 200 = 160,000$ **21.** 45 sq ft

Calculator Corner, p. 35

1. 448   **2.** 21,970   **3.** 6380   **4.** 39,564   **5.** 180,480
6. 2,363,754

Exercise Set 1.5, p. 37

1. 870   **3.** 2,340,000   **5.** 520   **7.** 564   **9.** 1527
11. 64,603   **13.** 4770   **15.** 3995   **17.** 46,080
19. 14,652   **21.** 207,672   **23.** 798,408   **25.** 20,723,872
27. 362,128   **29.** 20,064,048   **31.** 25,236,000
33. 302,220   **35.** 49,101,136   **37.** $50 \cdot 70 = 3500$
39. $30 \cdot 30 = 900$ **41.** $900 \cdot 300 = 270,000$
43. $400 \cdot 200 = 80,000$ **45.** **(a)** $2,840,000; **(b)** $2,850,000
47. 529,984 sq mi   **49.** 8100 sq ft   **51.** **D**_W   **53.** 12,685
54. 10,834   **55.** 427,477   **56.** 111,110   **57.** 1241
58. 8889   **59.** 254,119   **60.** 66,444   **61.** 6,376,000
62. 6,375,600   **63.** 247,464 sq ft

Margin Exercises, Section 1.6, pp. 40–46

1. $\frac{54}{6} = 9$; $6\overline{)54}$ with quotient 9 **2.** $15 = 5 \cdot 3$, or $15 = 3 \cdot 5$
3. $72 = 9 \cdot 8$, or $72 = 8 \cdot 9$ **4.** $6 = 12 \div 2$; $2 = 12 \div 6$
5. $6 = 42 \div 7$; $7 = 42 \div 6$ **6.** 6; $6 \cdot 9 = 54$ **7.** 6 R 7;
$6 \cdot 9 = 54$, $54 + 7 = 61$ **8.** 4 R 5; $4 \cdot 12 = 48$, $48 + 5 = 53$
9. 6 R 13; $6 \cdot 24 = 144$, $144 + 13 = 157$ **10.** 59 R 3
11. 1475 R 5   **12.** 1015   **13.** 134   **14.** 63 R 12
15. 807 R 4   **16.** 1088   **17.** 360 R 4   **18.** 800 R 47

Calculator Corner, p. 47

1. 3 R 11   **2.** 28   **3.** 124 R 2   **4.** 131 R 18   **5.** 283 R 57
6. 843 R 187

Exercise Set 1.6, p. 48

1. $18 = 3 \cdot 6$, or $18 = 6 \cdot 3$ **3.** $22 = 22 \cdot 1$, or $22 = 1 \cdot 22$
5. $54 = 6 \cdot 9$, or $54 = 9 \cdot 6$ **7.** $37 = 1 \cdot 37$, or $37 = 37 \cdot 1$
9. $9 = 45 \div 5$; $5 = 45 \div 9$ **11.** $37 = 37 \div 1$; $1 = 37 \div 37$
13. $8 = 64 \div 8$ **15.** $11 = 66 \div 6$; $6 = 66 \div 11$ **17.** 12
19. 1   **21.** 22   **23.** Not defined   **25.** 55 R 2   **27.** 108
29. 307   **31.** 753 R 3   **33.** 74 R 1   **35.** 92 R 2
37. 1703   **39.** 987 R 5   **41.** 12,700   **43.** 127
45. 52 R 52   **47.** 29 R 5   **49.** 40 R 12   **51.** 90 R 22
53. 29   **55.** 105 R 3   **57.** 1609 R 2   **59.** 1007 R 1
61. 23   **63.** 107 R 1   **65.** 370   **67.** 609 R 15   **69.** 304
71. 3508 R 219   **73.** 8070   **75.** **D**_W   **77.** perimeter
78. equation, inequality   **79.** digits, periods
80. additive   **81.** dividend   **82.** factors, product
83. minuend   **84.** associative   **85.** 54, 122; 33, 2772;
4, 8   **87.** 30 buses

Margin Exercises, Section 1.7, pp. 52–55

1. 7   **2.** 5   **3.** No   **4.** Yes   **5.** 5   **6.** 10   **7.** 5
8. 22   **9.** 22,490   **10.** 9022   **11.** 570   **12.** 3661
13. 8   **14.** 45   **15.** 77   **16.** 3311   **17.** 6114   **18.** 8
19. 16   **20.** 644   **21.** 96   **22.** 94

Exercise Set 1.7, p. 56

1. 14   **3.** 0   **5.** 29   **7.** 0   **9.** 8   **11.** 14   **13.** 1035
15. 25   **17.** 450   **19.** 90,900   **21.** 32   **23.** 143
25. 79   **27.** 45   **29.** 324   **31.** 743   **33.** 37   **35.** 66

37. 15 **39.** 48 **41.** 175 **43.** 335 **45.** 104 **47.** 45
49. 4056 **51.** 17,603 **53.** 18,252 **55.** 205 **57.** $\mathbf{D_W}$
59. $7 = 15 - 8; 8 = 15 - 7$ **60.** $6 = 48 \div 8; 8 = 48 \div 6$
61. < **62.** > **63.** > **64.** < **65.** 142 R 5
66. 142 **67.** 334 **68.** 334 R 11 **69.** 347

Margin Exercises, Section 1.8, pp. 59–66

1. 11,277 adoptions **2.** 8441 adoptions
3. 19,089 adoptions **4.** $1874 **5.** $171 **6.** $5572
7. 9180 sq in. **8.** 378 cartons with 1 can left over
9. 79 gal **10.** 181 seats

Translating for Success, p. 67

1. E **2.** M **3.** D **4.** G **5.** A **6.** O **7.** F **8.** K
9. J **10.** H

Exercise Set 1.8, p. 68

1. 33,042 performances **3.** 704 performances
5. 2054 miles **7.** 18 rows **9.** 792,316 degrees;
1,291,900 degrees **11.** 192,268 degrees **13.** $69,277
15. 240 mi **17.** 168 hr **19.** 225 squares **21.** $24,456
23. 35 weeks; 2 episodes left over **25.** 236 gal
27. 3616 mi **29.** 12,804 gal **31.** $14,445 **33.** $247
35. (a) 4200 sq ft; **(b)** 268 ft **37.** $29,105,000,000
39. 151,500 **41.** 563 packages; 7 bars left over
43. 384 mi; 27 in. **45.** 21 columns **47.** 56 full cartons;
11 books left over. If 1355 books are shipped, it will take
57 cartons. **49.** 32 $10 bills **51.** $400
53. 280 min; or 4 hr 40 min **55.** 525 min, or 8 hr 45 min
57. 106 bones **59.** 3000 sq in. **61.** $\mathbf{D_W}$ **63.** 234,600
64. 234,560 **65.** 235,000 **66.** 22,000 **67.** 16,000
68. 8000 **69.** 4000 **70.** 320,000 **71.** 720,000
72. 46,800,000 **73.** 792,000 mi; 1,386,000 mi

Margin Exercises, Section 1.9, pp. 75–80

1. 5^4 **2.** 5^5 **3.** 10^2 **4.** 10^4 **5.** 10,000 **6.** 100
7. 512 **8.** 32 **9.** 51 **10.** 30 **11.** 584 **12.** 84
13. 4; 1 **14.** 52; 52 **15.** 29 **16.** 1880 **17.** 253
18. 93 **19.** 1880 **20.** 305 **21.** 75 **22.** 4
23. 1496 ft **24.** 46 **25.** 4

Calculator Corner, p. 76

1. 243 **2.** 15,625 **3.** 20,736 **4.** 2048

Calculator Corner, p. 78

1. 49 **2.** 85 **3.** 36 **4.** 0 **5.** 73 **6.** 49

Exercise Set 1.9, p. 81

1. 3^4 **3.** 5^2 **5.** 7^5 **7.** 10^3 **9.** 49 **11.** 729
13. 20,736 **15.** 121 **17.** 22 **19.** 20 **21.** 100
23. 1 **25.** 49 **27.** 5 **29.** 434 **31.** 41 **33.** 88

35. 4 **37.** 303 **39.** 20 **41.** 70 **43.** 295 **45.** 32
47. 906 **49.** 62 **51.** 102 **53.** 32 **55.** $94
57. 401 **59.** 110 **61.** 7 **63.** 544 **65.** 708 **67.** 27
69. $\mathbf{D_W}$ **71.** 452 **72.** 835 **73.** 13 **74.** 37
75. 2342 **76.** 4898 **77.** 25 **78.** 100
79. 104,286 mi^2 **80.** 98 gal **81.** 24; $1 + 5 \cdot (4 + 3) = 36$
83. 7; $12 \div (4 + 2) \cdot 3 - 2 = 4$

Concept Reinforcement, p. 84

1. False **2.** True **3.** True **4.** True **5.** False
6. False

Summary and Review: Chapter 1, p. 84

1. 8 thousands **2.** 3
3. 2 thousands + 7 hundreds + 9 tens + 3 ones
4. 5 ten thousands + 6 thousands + 0 hundreds +
7 tens + 8 ones, or 5 ten thousands + 6 thousands +
7 tens + 8 ones **5.** 4 millions + 0 hundred thousands +
0 ten thousands + 7 thousands + 1 hundred + 0 tens +
1 one, or 4 millions + 7 thousands + 1 hundred + 1 one
6. Sixty-seven thousand, eight hundred nineteen
7. Two million, seven hundred eighty-one thousand,
four hundred twenty-seven **8.** 1 billion, sixty-five million,
seventy thousand, six hundred seven **9.** 476,588
10. 2,000,400,000 **11.** 14,272 **12.** 66,024 **13.** 21,788
14. 98,921 **15.** $10 = 6 + 4$, or $10 = 4 + 6$
16. $8 = 11 - 3; 3 = 11 - 8$ **17.** 5148 **18.** 1689
19. 2274 **20.** 17,757 **21.** 345,800 **22.** 345,760
23. 346,000 **24.** 300,000 **25.** $41,300 + 19,700 = 61,000$
26. $38,700 - 24,500 = 14,200$ **27.** $400 \cdot 700 = 280,000$
28. > **29.** < **30.** 5,100,000 **31.** 6,276,800
32. 506,748 **33.** 27,589 **34.** 5,331,810
35. $56 = 8 \cdot 7$, or $56 = 7 \cdot 8$ **36.** $4 = 52 \div 13; 13 = 52 \div 4$
37. 12 R 3 **38.** 5 **39.** 913 R 3 **40.** 384 R 1
41. 4 R 46 **42.** 54 **43.** 452 **44.** 5008
45. 4389 **46.** 8 **47.** 45 **48.** 58 **49.** 0 **50.** 4^3
51. 10,000 **52.** 36 **53.** 65 **54.** 233 **55.** 56
56. 32 **57.** 260 **58.** 165 **59.** $502 **60.** $484
61. 1982 **62.** 19 cartons **63.** 14 beehives
64. $13,585 **65.** $27,598 **66.** 137 beakers filled; 13 mL
left over **67.** 98 ft^2; 42 ft **68.** $\mathbf{D_W}$ A vat contains
1152 oz of hot sauce. If 144 bottles are to be filled equally,
how much will each bottle contain? Answers may vary.
69. $\mathbf{D_W}$ No; if subtraction were associative, then
$a - (b - c) = (a - b) - c$ for any $a, b,$ and c. But, for
example,
$$12 - (8 - 4) = 12 - 4 = 8,$$
whereas
$$(12 - 8) - 4 = 4 - 4 = 0.$$
Since $8 \neq 0$, this example shows that subtraction is not
associative. **70.** $d = 8$ **71.** $a = 8, b = 4$ **72.** 6 days

Test: Chapter 1, p. 87

1. [1.1a] 5 **2.** [1.1b] 8 thousands + 8 hundreds +
4 tens + 3 ones **3.** [1.1c] Thirty-eight million, four
hundred three thousand, two hundred seventy-seven

4. [1.2a] 9989   5. [1.2a] 63,791   6. [1.2a] 34
7. [1.2a] 10,515   8. [1.3b] 3630   9. [1.3b] 1039
10. [1.3b] 6848   11. [1.3b] 5175   12. [1.5a] 41,112
13. [1.5a] 5,325,600   14. [1.5a] 2405
15. [1.5a] 534,264   16. [1.6b] 3 R 3   17. [1.6b] 70
18. [1.6b] 97   19. [1.6b] 805 R 8
20. [1.8a] 1852 12-packs; 7 cakes left over
21. [1.8a] 1,256,615 mi^2 22. (a) [1.2b], [1.5c] 300 in., 5000 in^2; 264 in., 3872 in^2; 228 in., 2888 in^2; (b) [1.8a] 2112 in^2 23. [1.8a] 206,330 voters
24. [1.8a] 1808 lb   25. [1.8a] 20 staplers   26. [1.7b] 46
27. [1.7b] 13   28. [1.7b] 14   29. [1.7b] 381
30. [1.4a] 35,000   31. [1.4a] 34,580   32. [1.4a] 34,600
33. [1.4b] $23,600 + 54,700 = 78,300$
34. [1.4b] $54,800 - 23,600 = 31,200$
35. [1.5b] $800 \cdot 500 = 400,000$ 36. [1.4c] >
37. [1.4c] <   38. [1.9a] 12^4 39. [1.9b] 343
40. [1.9b] 100,000   41. [1.9b] 625   42. [1.9c] 31
43. [1.9c] 98   44. [1.9c] 2   45. [1.9d] 216
46. [1.9c] 18   47. [1.9c] 92   48. [1.5c], [1.8a] 336 in^2
49. [1.9c] 9   50. [1.8a] 80 payments

CHAPTER 2

Margin Exercises, Section 2.1, pp. 91–95

1. Yes   2. No   3. 1, 2, 5, 10   4. 1, 3, 5, 9, 15, 45
5. 1, 2, 31, 62   6. 1, 2, 3, 4, 6, 8, 12, 24   7. $5 = 1 \cdot 5$; $45 = 9 \cdot 5$; $100 = 20 \cdot 5$ 8. $10 = 1 \cdot 10$; $60 = 6 \cdot 10$; $110 = 11 \cdot 10$ 9. 5, 10, 15, 20, 25, 30, 35, 40, 45, 50
10. Yes   11. Yes   12. No   13. 2, 13, 19, 41, 73 are prime; 6, 12, 65, 99 are composite; 1 is neither   14. $2 \cdot 3$
15. $2 \cdot 2 \cdot 3$ 16. $3 \cdot 3 \cdot 5$ 17. $2 \cdot 7 \cdot 7$
18. $2 \cdot 3 \cdot 3 \cdot 7$ 19. $2 \cdot 2 \cdot 2 \cdot 2 \cdot 3 \cdot 3$
20. $2 \cdot 2 \cdot 2 \cdot 5 \cdot 7 \cdot 7$ 21. $5 \cdot 5 \cdot 7 \cdot 11$

Calculator Corner, p. 92

1. Yes   2. No   3. No   4. Yes   5. No   6. Yes
7. Yes   8. No   9. Yes   10. No

Exercise Set 2.1, p. 96

1. No   3. Yes   5. 1, 2, 3, 6, 9, 18
7. 1, 2, 3, 6, 9, 18, 27, 54   9. 1, 2, 4   11. 1
13. 1, 2, 7, 14, 49, 98   15. 1, 3, 5, 15, 17, 51, 85, 255
17. 4, 8, 12, 16, 20, 24, 28, 32, 36, 40
19. 20, 40, 60, 80, 100, 120, 140, 160, 180, 200
21. 3, 6, 9, 12, 15, 18, 21, 24, 27, 30
23. 12, 24, 36, 48, 60, 72, 84, 96, 108, 120
25. 10, 20, 30, 40, 50, 60, 70, 80, 90, 100
27. 9, 18, 27, 36, 45, 54, 63, 72, 81, 90   29. No   31. Yes
33. Yes   35. No   37. No   39. Neither
41. Composite   43. Prime   45. Prime   47. $2 \cdot 2 \cdot 2$
49. $2 \cdot 7$ 51. $2 \cdot 3 \cdot 7$ 53. $5 \cdot 5$ 55. $2 \cdot 5 \cdot 5$
57. $13 \cdot 13$ 59. $2 \cdot 2 \cdot 5 \cdot 5$ 61. $5 \cdot 7$
63. $2 \cdot 2 \cdot 2 \cdot 3 \cdot 3$ 65. $7 \cdot 11$ 67. $2 \cdot 2 \cdot 7 \cdot 103$
69. $3 \cdot 17$ 71. $2 \cdot 2 \cdot 2 \cdot 2 \cdot 3 \cdot 5 \cdot 5$ 73. $3 \cdot 7 \cdot 13$

75. $2 \cdot 3 \cdot 11 \cdot 17$ 77. D$_W$ 79. 26   80. 256
81. 425   82. 4200   83. 0   84. 22   85. 1   86. 3
87. $612   88. 201 min, or 3 hr 21 min   89. Row 1: 48, 90, 432, 63; row 2: 7, 2, 2, 10, 8, 6, 21, 10; row 3: 9, 18, 36, 14, 12, 11, 21; row 4: 29, 19, 42

Margin Exercises, Section 2.2, pp. 98–101

1. Yes   2. No   3. Yes   4. No   5. Yes   6. No
7. Yes   8. No   9. Yes   10. No   11. No   12. Yes
13. No   14. Yes   15. No   16. Yes   17. No   18. Yes
19. No   20. Yes   21. Yes   22. No   23. No   24. Yes
25. Yes   26. No   27. No   28. Yes   29. No   30. Yes
31. Yes   32. No

Exercise Set 2.2, p. 102

1. 46, 224, 300, 36, 45,270, 4444, 256, 8064, 21,568
3. 224, 300, 36, 4444, 256, 8064, 21,568
5. 300, 36, 45,270, 8064   7. 36, 45,270, 711, 8064
9. 324, 42, 501, 3009, 75, 2001, 402, 111,111, 1005
11. 55,555, 200, 75, 2345, 35, 1005   13. 324   15. 200
17. 313,332, 7624, 111,126, 876, 1110, 5128, 64,000, 9990
19. 313,332, 111,126, 876, 1110, 9990
21. 9990   23. 1110, 64,000, 9990   25. D$_W$ 27. 138
28. 139   29. 874   30. 56   31. 26   32. 13   33. 234
34. 4003   35. 45 gal   36. 4320 min
37. $2 \cdot 2 \cdot 2 \cdot 3 \cdot 5 \cdot 5 \cdot 13$ 39. $2 \cdot 2 \cdot 3 \cdot 3 \cdot 7 \cdot 11$
41. 95,238

Margin Exercises, Section 2.3, pp. 104–109

1. Numerator: 83; denominator: 100
2. Numerator: 27; denominator: 50
3. Numerator: 11; denominator: 25
4. Numerator: 21; denominator: 1000
5. $\frac{1}{2}$ 6. $\frac{1}{3}$ 7. $\frac{1}{3}$ 8. $\frac{2}{3}$ 9. $\frac{3}{4}$ 10. $\frac{15}{16}$ 11. $\frac{15}{15}$ 12. $\frac{5}{4}$
13. $\frac{7}{4}$ 14. Clocks: $\frac{3}{5}$; thermometers: $\frac{2}{5}$ 15. $\frac{98}{64}, \frac{98}{162}, \frac{61}{162}$
16. 1   17. 1   18. 1   19. 1   20. 1   21. 1   22. 0
23. 0   24. 0   25. 0   26. Not defined
27. Not defined   28. 8   29. 10   30. 346   31. 23

Exercise Set 2.3, p. 110

1. Numerator: 3; denominator: 4
3. Numerator: 11; denominator: 2
5. Numerator: 0; denominator: 7
7. $\frac{2}{4}$ 9. $\frac{1}{8}$ 11. $\frac{4}{3}$ 13. $\frac{12}{16}$ 15. $\frac{38}{16}$ 17. $\frac{3}{4}$ 19. $\frac{12}{12}$
21. $\frac{4}{8}$ 23. $\frac{6}{12}$ 25. $\frac{5}{8}$ 27. $\frac{4}{7}$ 29. (a) $\frac{2}{8}$; (b) $\frac{6}{8}$
31. (a) $\frac{3}{8}$; (b) $\frac{5}{8}$ 33. (a) $\frac{3}{7}$; (b) $\frac{3}{4}$; (c) $\frac{4}{7}$; (d) $\frac{4}{3}$
35. (a) $\frac{35}{10,000}$; (b) $\frac{50}{10,000}$; (c) $\frac{44}{10,000}$; (d) $\frac{63}{10,000}$; (e) $\frac{43}{10,000}$; (f) $\frac{21}{10,000}$
37. (a) $\frac{390}{13}$; (b) $\frac{13}{390}$ 39. $\frac{850}{1000}$ 41. 0   43. 7   45. 1
47. 1   49. 0   51. 1   53. 1   55. 1   57. 1   59. 18
61. Not defined   63. Not defined   65. D$_W$
67. 34,560   68. 34,600   69. 35,000   70. 30,000
71. $15,691   72. 96 gal   73. 2203

74. 848 **75.** 37,239 **76.** 11,851 **77.** $\frac{1}{6}$ **79.** $\frac{2}{16}$, or $\frac{1}{8}$
81. ⬡⬡⬢⬢⬡ **83.**

Margin Exercises, Section 2.4, pp. 115–119

1. $\frac{2}{3}$ **2.** $\frac{5}{8}$ **3.** $\frac{10}{3}$ **4.** $\frac{33}{8}$ **5.** $\frac{46}{5}$
6.

7. $\frac{15}{56}$ **8.** $\frac{32}{15}$ **9.** $\frac{3}{100}$ **10.** $\frac{14}{3}$
11. $\frac{3}{8}$ **12.** $\frac{8}{81}$ ft^2 **13.** $\frac{3}{40}$

Exercise Set 2.4, p. 120

1. $\frac{3}{5}$ **3.** $\frac{5}{8}$ **5.** $\frac{8}{11}$ **7.** $\frac{70}{9}$ **9.** $\frac{2}{5}$ **11.** $\frac{6}{5}$ **13.** $\frac{21}{4}$
15. $\frac{85}{6}$ **17.** $\frac{1}{6}$ **19.** $\frac{1}{40}$ **21.** $\frac{2}{15}$ **23.** $\frac{4}{15}$ **25.** $\frac{9}{16}$ **27.** $\frac{14}{39}$
29. $\frac{7}{100}$ **31.** $\frac{49}{64}$ **33.** $\frac{1}{1000}$ **35.** $\frac{182}{285}$ **37.** $\frac{3}{8}$ cup **39.** $\frac{21}{32}$
41. $\frac{12}{25}$ m^2 **43.** $\frac{7}{16}$ L **45.** **D$_W$** **47.** 204 **48.** 700
49. 3001 **50.** 204 R 8 **51.** 8 thousands
52. 8 millions **53.** 8 ones **54.** 8 hundreds **55.** 3
56. 81 **57.** 50 **58.** 6399 **59.** $\frac{71,269}{180,433}$ **61.** $\frac{56}{1125}$

Margin Exercises, Section 2.5, pp. 122–126

1. $\frac{8}{16}$ **2.** $\frac{30}{50}$ **3.** $\frac{52}{100}$ **4.** $\frac{200}{75}$ **5.** $\frac{12}{9}$ **6.** $\frac{18}{24}$ **7.** $\frac{90}{100}$
8. $\frac{9}{45}$ **9.** $\frac{56}{49}$ **10.** $\frac{1}{4}$ **11.** $\frac{5}{6}$ **12.** 5 **13.** $\frac{4}{3}$ **14.** $\frac{7}{8}$
15. $\frac{89}{78}$ **16.** $\frac{8}{7}$ **17.** $\frac{1}{4}$ **18.** $\frac{7}{24}$ **19.** $\frac{37}{80}$
20. $\frac{20}{100} = \frac{1}{5}$; $\frac{42}{100} = \frac{21}{50}$; $\frac{8}{100} = \frac{2}{25}$; $\frac{16}{100} = \frac{4}{25}$; $\frac{14}{100} = \frac{7}{50}$
21. = **22.** ≠

Calculator Corner, p. 125

1. $\frac{14}{15}$ **2.** $\frac{7}{8}$ **3.** $\frac{138}{167}$ **4.** $\frac{7}{25}$

Exercise Set 2.5, p. 127

1. $\frac{5}{10}$ **3.** $\frac{20}{32}$ **5.** $\frac{27}{30}$ **7.** $\frac{28}{32}$ **9.** $\frac{20}{48}$ **11.** $\frac{51}{54}$ **13.** $\frac{75}{45}$
15. $\frac{42}{132}$ **17.** $\frac{1}{2}$ **19.** $\frac{3}{4}$ **21.** $\frac{1}{5}$ **23.** 3 **25.** $\frac{3}{4}$ **27.** $\frac{7}{8}$
29. $\frac{6}{5}$ **31.** $\frac{1}{3}$ **33.** 6 **35.** $\frac{1}{3}$ **37.** $\frac{4}{75}$ **39.** $\frac{45}{112}$ **41.** =
43. ≠ **45.** = **47.** ≠ **49.** = **51.** ≠ **53.** =
55. ≠ **57.** **D$_W$** **59.** 4992 ft^2; 284 ft **60.** $928
61. 11 **62.** 32 **63.** 186 **64.** 2737 **65.** 5 **66.** 89
67. 3520 **68.** 9001 **69.** $\frac{137}{149}$ **71.** $\frac{2}{5}$; $\frac{3}{5}$
73. No. $\frac{262}{704} \neq \frac{135}{373}$ because $262 \cdot 373 \neq 704 \cdot 135$.

Margin Exercises, Section 2.6, p. 130

1. $\frac{7}{12}$ **2.** $\frac{1}{3}$ **3.** 6 **4.** $\frac{5}{2}$ **5.** 14 lb

Exercise Set 2.6, p. 131

1. $\frac{1}{3}$ **3.** $\frac{1}{8}$ **5.** $\frac{1}{10}$ **7.** $\frac{1}{6}$ **9.** $\frac{27}{10}$ **11.** $\frac{14}{9}$ **13.** 1
15. 1 **17.** 1 **19.** 1 **21.** 2 **23.** 4 **25.** 9 **27.** 9
29. $\frac{26}{5}$ **31.** $\frac{98}{5}$ **33.** 60 **35.** 30 **37.** $\frac{1}{5}$ **39.** $\frac{9}{25}$
41. $\frac{11}{40}$ **43.** $\frac{5}{14}$ **45.** $\frac{5}{8}$ in. **47.** 30 mph
49. 625 addresses **51.** $\frac{1}{3}$ cup **53.** $115,500
55. 160 mi **57.** Food: $9000; housing: $7200; clothing: $3600; savings: $4000; taxes: $9000; other expenses: $3200
59. **D$_W$** **61.** 35 **62.** 85 **63.** 125 **64.** 120
65. 4989 **66.** 8546 **67.** 6498 **68.** 6407 **69.** 4673
70. 5338 **71.** $\frac{129}{485}$ **73.** $\frac{1}{12}$ **75.** $\frac{1}{168}$

Margin Exercises, Section 2.7, pp. 135–139

1. $\frac{5}{2}$ **2.** $\frac{7}{10}$ **3.** $\frac{1}{9}$ **4.** 5 **5.** $\frac{8}{7}$ **6.** $\frac{8}{3}$ **7.** $\frac{1}{10}$ **8.** 100
9. 1 **10.** $\frac{14}{15}$ **11.** $\frac{4}{5}$ **12.** 32 **13.** 320 loops
14. 252 mi

Translating for Success, p. 140

1. C **2.** H **3.** A **4.** N **5.** O **6.** F **7.** I **8.** L
9. D **10.** M

Exercise Set 2.7, p. 141

1. $\frac{6}{5}$ **3.** $\frac{1}{6}$ **5.** 6 **7.** $\frac{3}{10}$ **9.** $\frac{4}{5}$ **11.** $\frac{4}{15}$ **13.** 4 **15.** 2
17. $\frac{1}{8}$ **19.** $\frac{3}{7}$ **21.** 8 **23.** 35 **25.** 1 **27.** $\frac{2}{3}$ **29.** $\frac{9}{4}$
31. 144 **33.** 75 **35.** 2 **37.** $\frac{3}{5}$ **39.** 315
41. 75 times **43.** 32 pairs **45.** 24 bowls **47.** 16 L
49. 288 km; 108 km **51.** $\frac{1}{16}$ in. **53.** **D$_W$**
55. associative **56.** factors **57.** prime
58. denominator **59.** additive **60.** reciprocals
61. whole **62.** equation **63.** $\frac{9}{19}$ **65.** 36 **67.** $\frac{3}{8}$

Concept Reinforcement, p. 144

1. True **2.** False **3.** True **4.** True **5.** False
6. True **7.** True **8.** False

Summary and Review: Chapter 2, p. 144

1. 1, 2, 3, 4, 5, 6, 10, 12, 15, 20, 30, 60
2. 1, 2, 4, 8, 11, 16, 22, 44, 88, 176
3. 8, 16, 24, 32, 40, 48, 56, 64, 72, 80
4. Yes **5.** No **6.** Prime **7.** Neither **8.** Composite
9. $2 \cdot 5 \cdot 7$ **10.** $2 \cdot 3 \cdot 5$ **11.** $3 \cdot 3 \cdot 5$ **12.** $2 \cdot 3 \cdot 5 \cdot 5$
13. $2 \cdot 2 \cdot 2 \cdot 3 \cdot 3 \cdot 3 \cdot 3$ **14.** $2 \cdot 3 \cdot 5 \cdot 5 \cdot 5 \cdot 7$
15. 4344, 600, 93, 330, 255,555, 780, 2802, 711
16. 140, 182, 716, 2432, 4344, 600, 330, 780, 2802
17. 140, 716, 2432, 4344, 600, 780 **18.** 2432, 4344, 600
19. 140, 95, 475, 600, 330, 255,555, 780
20. 4344, 600, 330, 780, 2802 **21.** 255,555, 711
22. 140, 600, 330, 780 **23.** Numerator: 2; denominator: 7
24. $\frac{3}{5}$ **25.** $\frac{7}{6}$ **26.** $\frac{2}{7}$ **27.** (a) $\frac{3}{5}$; (b) $\frac{5}{3}$; (c) $\frac{3}{8}$ **28.** 0
29. 1 **30.** 48 **31.** 6 **32.** $\frac{2}{3}$ **33.** $\frac{1}{4}$ **34.** 1 **35.** 0
36. $\frac{2}{5}$ **37.** 18 **38.** 4 **39.** $\frac{1}{3}$ **40.** Not defined

41. Not defined   **42.** $\frac{11}{23}$ **43.** $\frac{2}{7}$ **44.** $\frac{39}{40}$ **45.** $\frac{32}{225}$
46. $\frac{3}{100}$; $\frac{8}{100} = \frac{2}{25}$; $\frac{10}{100} = \frac{1}{10}$; $\frac{15}{100} = \frac{3}{20}$; $\frac{21}{100}$; $\frac{43}{100}$ **47.** $\ne$ **48.** $=$
49. $\ne$ **50.** $=$ **51.** $\frac{3}{2}$ **52.** 56   **53.** $\frac{5}{2}$ **54.** 24   **55.** $\frac{2}{3}$
56. $\frac{1}{14}$ **57.** $\frac{2}{3}$ **58.** $\frac{1}{22}$ **59.** $\frac{3}{20}$ **60.** $\frac{10}{7}$ **61.** $\frac{5}{4}$ **62.** $\frac{1}{3}$
63. 9   **64.** $\frac{36}{47}$ **65.** $\frac{9}{2}$ **66.** 2   **67.** $\frac{11}{6}$ **68.** $\frac{1}{4}$ **69.** $\frac{9}{4}$
70. 300   **71.** 1   **72.** $\frac{4}{9}$ **73.** $\frac{3}{10}$ **74.** 240   **75.** 9 days
76. 1000 km   **77.** $\frac{1}{3}$ cup; 2 cups   **78.** $15   **79.** 60 bags
80. 256,000,000 metric tons
81. D_W To simplify fraction notation, first factor the numerator and the denominator into prime numbers. Examine the factorizations for factors common to both the numerator and the denominator. Factor the fraction, with each pair of like factors forming a factor of 1. Remove the factors of 1, and multiply the remaining factors in the numerator and in the denominator, if necessary.
82. D_W Taking $\frac{1}{2}$ of a number is equivalent to multiplying the number by $\frac{1}{2}$. Dividing by $\frac{1}{2}$ is equivalent to multiplying by the reciprocal of $\frac{1}{2}$, or 2. Thus taking $\frac{1}{2}$ of a number is not the same as dividing by $\frac{1}{2}$.
83. D_W $9432 = 9 \cdot 1000 + 4 \cdot 100 + 3 \cdot 10 + 2 \cdot 1 = 9(999 + 1) + 4(99 + 1) + 3(9 + 1) + 2 \cdot 1 = 9 \cdot 999 + 9 \cdot 1 + 4 \cdot 99 + 4 \cdot 1 + 3 \cdot 9 + 3 \cdot 1 + 2 \cdot 1$. Since 999, 99, and 9 are each a multiple of 9, $9 \cdot 999$, $4 \cdot 99$, and $3 \cdot 9$ are multiples of 9. This leaves $9 \cdot 1 + 4 \cdot 1 + 3 \cdot 1 + 2 \cdot 1$, or $9 + 4 + 3 + 2$. If $9 + 4 + 3 + 2$, the sum of the digits, is divisible by 9, then 9432 is divisible by 9.
84. $a = 11{,}176$; $b = 9887$ **85.** 13, 11, 101, 37

Test: Chapter 2, p. 147

1. [2.1a] 1, 2, 3, 4, 5, 6, 10, 12, 15, 20, 25, 30, 50, 60, 75, 100, 150, 300   **2.** [2.1c] Prime   **3.** [2.1c] Composite
4. [2.1d] $2 \cdot 3 \cdot 3$ **5.** [2.1d] $2 \cdot 2 \cdot 3 \cdot 5$ **6.** [2.2a] Yes
7. [2.2a] No   **8.** [2.2a] No   **9.** [2.2a] Yes
10. [2.3a] Numerator: 4; denominator: 5   **11.** [2.3a] $\frac{3}{4}$
12. [2.3a] $\frac{3}{7}$ **13.** [2.3a] **(a)** $\frac{336}{497}$; **(b)** $\frac{161}{497}$ **14.** [2.3b] 26
15. [2.3b] 1   **16.** [2.3b] 0   **17.** [2.5b] $\frac{1}{2}$ **18.** [2.5b] 6
19. [2.5b] $\frac{1}{14}$ **20.** [2.3b] Not defined
21. [2.3b] Not defined   **22.** [2.5b] $\frac{1}{4}$ **23.** [2.5b] $\frac{2}{3}$
24. [2.5c] $=$ **25.** [2.5c] $\ne$ **26.** [2.6a] 32   **27.** [2.6a] $\frac{3}{2}$
28. [2.6a] $\frac{5}{2}$ **29.** [2.6a] $\frac{1}{10}$ **30.** [2.6a] $\frac{2}{9}$ **31.** [2.7a] $\frac{8}{5}$
32. [2.7a] 4   **33.** [2.7a] $\frac{1}{18}$ **34.** [2.7b] $\frac{3}{10}$ **35.** [2.7b] $\frac{8}{5}$
36. [2.7b] 18   **37.** [2.7b] $\frac{18}{7}$ **38.** [2.7c] 64   **39.** [2.7c] $\frac{7}{4}$
40. [2.6b] 4375 students   **41.** [2.7d] $\frac{3}{40}$ m   **42.** [2.7d] 5 qt
43. [2.6b] $\frac{3}{4}$ in.   **44.** [2.6b] $\frac{15}{8}$ tsp   **45.** [2.6b] $\frac{7}{48}$ acre
46. [2.6a], [2.7b] $\frac{7}{960}$ **47.** [2.7c] $\frac{7}{5}$

CHAPTER 3

Margin Exercises, Section 3.1, pp. 150–155

1. 45   **2.** 40   **3.** 30   **4.** 24   **5.** 10   **6.** 80   **7.** 40
8. 360   **9.** 864   **10.** 2520   **11.** $2^3 \cdot 3^2 \cdot 5 \cdot 7$, or 2520
12. $2^3 \cdot 5$, or 40; $2^3 \cdot 3^2 \cdot 5$, or 360; $2^5 \cdot 3^3$, or 864   **13.** 18

14. 24   **15.** 36   **16.** 210   **17.** 600   **18.** 3780
19. 600

Exercise Set 3.1, p. 156

1. 4   **3.** 50   **5.** 40   **7.** 54   **9.** 150   **11.** 120
13. 72   **15.** 420   **17.** 144   **19.** 288   **21.** 30
23. 105   **25.** 72   **27.** 60   **29.** 36   **31.** 900   **33.** 48
35. 50   **37.** 143   **39.** 420   **41.** 378   **43.** 810
45. 2160   **47.** 9828   **49.** Every 60 yr   **51.** Every 420 yr
53. D_W **55.** 90 days   **56.** 704 performances
57. 33,135   **58.** 6939   **59.** $\frac{2}{3}$ **60.** $\frac{8}{7}$ **61.** 18,900
63. 5 in. by 24 in.

Margin Exercises, Section 3.2, pp. 158–161

1. $\frac{4}{5}$ **2.** 1   **3.** $\frac{1}{2}$ **4.** $\frac{3}{4}$ **5.** $\frac{5}{6}$ **6.** $\frac{29}{24}$ **7.** $\frac{5}{9}$ **8.** $\frac{413}{1000}$
9. $\frac{197}{210}$ **10.** $\frac{65}{72}$ **11.** $\frac{9}{10}$ mi

Exercise Set 3.2, p. 162

1. 1   **3.** $\frac{3}{4}$ **5.** $\frac{3}{2}$ **7.** $\frac{7}{24}$ **9.** $\frac{3}{2}$ **11.** $\frac{19}{24}$ **13.** $\frac{9}{10}$
15. $\frac{29}{18}$ **17.** $\frac{31}{100}$ **19.** $\frac{41}{60}$ **21.** $\frac{189}{100}$ **23.** $\frac{7}{8}$ **25.** $\frac{13}{24}$
27. $\frac{17}{24}$ **29.** $\frac{3}{4}$ **31.** $\frac{437}{500}$ **33.** $\frac{53}{40}$ **35.** $\frac{391}{144}$ **37.** $\frac{5}{6}$ lb
39. $\frac{23}{12}$ mi   **41.** 690 kg; $\frac{14}{23}$ cement; $\frac{5}{23}$ stone; $\frac{4}{23}$ sand; 1
43. $\frac{5}{8}$"   **45.** $\frac{13}{12}$ lb   **47.** D_W **49.** 210,528
50. 4,194,000   **51.** 3,387,807   **52.** 352,350
53. 537,179   **54.** 5   **55.** 84   **56.** 510,314
57. 21,468,755   **58.** 33,112,603   **59.** 12 tickets
60. $\frac{3}{64}$ acre   **61.** $\frac{4}{15}$; $320

Margin Exercises, Section 3.3, pp. 165–168

1. $\frac{1}{2}$ **2.** $\frac{3}{8}$ **3.** $\frac{1}{2}$ **4.** $\frac{1}{12}$ **5.** $\frac{13}{18}$ **6.** $\frac{1}{2}$ **7.** $\frac{9}{112}$ **8.** $<$
9. $>$ **10.** $>$ **11.** $>$ **12.** $<$ **13.** $\frac{1}{6}$ **14.** $\frac{11}{40}$
15. $\frac{5}{24}$ mi

Translating for Success, p. 169

1. J   **2.** E   **3.** D   **4.** B   **5.** I   **6.** N   **7.** A   **8.** C
9. L   **10.** F

Exercise Set 3.3, p. 170

1. $\frac{2}{3}$ **3.** $\frac{3}{4}$ **5.** $\frac{5}{8}$ **7.** $\frac{1}{24}$ **9.** $\frac{1}{2}$ **11.** $\frac{9}{14}$ **13.** $\frac{3}{5}$ **15.** $\frac{7}{10}$
17. $\frac{17}{60}$ **19.** $\frac{53}{100}$ **21.** $\frac{26}{75}$ **23.** $\frac{9}{100}$ **25.** $\frac{13}{24}$ **27.** $\frac{1}{10}$
29. $\frac{1}{24}$ **31.** $\frac{13}{16}$ **33.** $\frac{31}{75}$ **35.** $\frac{13}{75}$ **37.** $<$ **39.** $>$
41. $<$ **43.** $<$ **45.** $>$ **47.** $>$ **49.** $<$ **51.** $\frac{1}{15}$
53. $\frac{2}{15}$ **55.** $\frac{1}{2}$ **57.** $\frac{5}{12}$ hr   **59.** $\frac{19}{24}$ cup
61. $\frac{1}{4}$ of the business   **63.** $\frac{11}{20}$ lb   **65.** D_W **67.** 1
68. Not defined   **69.** Not defined   **70.** 4   **71.** $\frac{4}{21}$
72. $\frac{3}{2}$ **73.** 21   **74.** $\frac{1}{32}$ **75.** 17 days   **76.** 9 cups
77. $\frac{14}{3553}$ **79.** $\frac{21}{40}$ km   **81.** $\frac{19}{24}$ **83.** $\frac{145}{144}$ **85.** $>$
87. *Day 1*: Cut off $\frac{1}{7}$ of bar and pay him. *Day 2*: Cut off $\frac{2}{7}$ of the bar. Trade him for the $\frac{1}{7}$. *Day 3*: Give him back the $\frac{1}{7}$.

Day 4: Trade him the $\frac{4}{7}$ for his $\frac{3}{7}$. *Day 5*: Give him the $\frac{1}{7}$ again. *Day 6*: Trade him the $\frac{2}{7}$ for the $\frac{1}{7}$. *Day 7*: Give him the $\frac{1}{7}$ again. This assumes that he does not spend parts of the gold bar immediately.

Margin Exercises, Section 3.4, pp. 173–176

1. $1\frac{2}{3}$ **2.** $2\frac{3}{4}$ **3.** $8\frac{3}{4}$ **4.** $12\frac{2}{3}$ **5.** $\frac{22}{5}$ **6.** $\frac{61}{10}$ **7.** $\frac{29}{6}$
8. $\frac{37}{4}$ **9.** $\frac{62}{3}$ **10.** $2\frac{1}{3}$ **11.** $1\frac{1}{10}$ **12.** $18\frac{1}{3}$ **13.** $807\frac{2}{3}$
14. $134\frac{23}{45}$

Calculator Corner, p. 176

1. $1476\frac{1}{6}$ **2.** $676\frac{4}{9}$ **3.** $800\frac{51}{56}$ **4.** $13{,}031\frac{1}{2}$ **5.** $51{,}626\frac{9}{11}$
6. $7330\frac{7}{32}$ **7.** $134\frac{1}{15}$ **8.** $2666\frac{130}{213}$ **9.** $3571\frac{51}{112}$
10. $12\frac{169}{454}$

Exercise Set 3.4, p. 177

1. $\frac{57}{4}, \frac{27}{4}, \frac{9}{4}$ **3.** $3\frac{5}{8}, 2\frac{3}{4}$ **5.** $\frac{17}{3}$ **7.** $\frac{13}{4}$ **9.** $\frac{81}{8}$ **11.** $\frac{51}{10}$
13. $\frac{103}{5}$ **15.** $\frac{59}{6}$ **17.** $\frac{73}{10}$ **19.** $\frac{13}{8}$ **21.** $\frac{51}{4}$ **23.** $\frac{43}{10}$
25. $\frac{203}{100}$ **27.** $\frac{200}{3}$ **29.** $\frac{279}{50}$ **31.** $3\frac{3}{5}$ **33.** $4\frac{2}{3}$ **35.** $4\frac{1}{2}$
37. $5\frac{7}{10}$ **39.** $7\frac{4}{7}$ **41.** $7\frac{1}{2}$ **43.** $11\frac{1}{2}$ **45.** $1\frac{1}{2}$
47. $7\frac{57}{100}$ **49.** $43\frac{1}{8}$ **51.** $108\frac{5}{8}$ **53.** $618\frac{1}{5}$ **55.** $40\frac{4}{7}$
57. $55\frac{1}{51}$ **59.** $\mathbf{D_W}$ **61.** 45,800 **62.** 45,770 **63.** $\frac{8}{15}$
64. $\frac{21}{25}$ **65.** $\frac{16}{27}$ **66.** $\frac{583}{669}$ **67.** 18 **68.** $\frac{5}{2}$ **69.** $\frac{1}{4}$
70. $\frac{2}{5}$ **71.** 24 **72.** 49 **73.** $\frac{2560}{3}$ **74.** $\frac{4}{3}$ **75.** $237\frac{19}{541}$
77. $8\frac{2}{3}$ **79.** $52\frac{2}{7}$

Margin Exercises, Section 3.5, pp. 180–184

1. $7\frac{2}{5}$ **2.** $12\frac{1}{10}$ **3.** $13\frac{7}{12}$ **4.** $1\frac{1}{2}$ **5.** $3\frac{1}{6}$ **6.** $3\frac{5}{18}$
7. $3\frac{2}{3}$ **8.** $232\frac{3}{20}$ mi **9.** $4\frac{5}{6}$ ft **10.** $354\frac{23}{24}$ gal

Exercise Set 3.5, p. 185

1. $28\frac{3}{4}$ **3.** $185\frac{7}{8}$ **5.** $6\frac{1}{2}$ **7.** $2\frac{11}{12}$ **9.** $14\frac{7}{12}$ **11.** $12\frac{1}{10}$
13. $16\frac{5}{24}$ **15.** $21\frac{1}{2}$ **17.** $27\frac{7}{8}$ **19.** $27\frac{13}{24}$ **21.** $1\frac{3}{5}$
23. $4\frac{1}{10}$ **25.** $21\frac{17}{24}$ **27.** $12\frac{1}{4}$ **29.** $15\frac{3}{8}$ **31.** $7\frac{5}{12}$
33. $13\frac{3}{8}$ **35.** $11\frac{5}{18}$ **37.** $5\frac{3}{8}$ yd **39.** $7\frac{5}{12}$ lb **41.** $6\frac{5}{8}$ in.
43. $2\frac{7}{8}$ in., $4\frac{7}{8}$ in. **45.** $19\frac{1}{16}$ in. **47.** $95\frac{1}{5}$ mi **49.** $36\frac{1}{2}$ in.
51. $20\frac{1}{8}$ in. **53.** $78\frac{1}{12}$ in. **55.** $3\frac{4}{5}$ hr **57.** $28\frac{3}{4}$ yd
59. $7\frac{3}{8}$ ft **61.** $1\frac{9}{16}$ in. **63.** $\mathbf{D_W}$ **65.** 16 packages
66. 286 cartons; 2 oz left over **67.** Yes **68.** No
69. No **70.** Yes **71.** No **72.** Yes **73.** Yes
74. Yes **75.** $\frac{10}{13}$ **76.** $\frac{1}{10}$ **77.** $8568\frac{786}{1189}$ **79.** $5\frac{3}{4}$ ft

Margin Exercises, Section 3.6, pp. 190–193

1. 20 **2.** $1\frac{7}{8}$ **3.** $12\frac{4}{5}$ **4.** $8\frac{1}{3}$ **5.** 16 **6.** $7\frac{3}{7}$ **7.** $1\frac{7}{8}$
8. $\frac{7}{10}$ **9.** $227\frac{1}{2}$ mi **10.** 20 mpg **11.** $240\frac{3}{4}$ ft²

Calculator Corner, p. 194

1. $\frac{7}{12}$ **2.** $\frac{11}{10}$ **3.** $\frac{35}{16}$ **4.** $\frac{3}{10}$ **5.** $10\frac{2}{15}$ **6.** $1\frac{1}{28}$ **7.** $10\frac{11}{15}$
8. $2\frac{91}{115}$

Translating for Success, p. 195

1. O **2.** K **3.** F **4.** D **5.** H **6.** G **7.** L **8.** E
9. M **10.** J

Exercise Set 3.6, p. 196

1. $22\frac{2}{3}$ **3.** $2\frac{5}{12}$ **5.** $8\frac{1}{6}$ **7.** $9\frac{31}{40}$ **9.** $24\frac{91}{100}$ **11.** $975\frac{4}{5}$
13. $6\frac{1}{4}$ **15.** $1\frac{1}{5}$ **17.** $3\frac{9}{16}$ **19.** $1\frac{1}{8}$ **21.** $1\frac{8}{43}$ **23.** $\frac{9}{40}$
25. 45,000 beagles **27.** About 4,500,000 **29.** $62\frac{1}{2}$ ft²
31. $13\frac{1}{3}$ tsp **33.** $343\frac{3}{4}$ lb **35.** 68°F
37. About 1,800,750
39. *Cake*: $1\frac{1}{8}$ cups all-purpose flour, $\frac{3}{8}$ cup sugar, $\frac{3}{8}$ cup cold butter, $\frac{3}{8}$ cup sour cream, $\frac{1}{4}$ teaspoon baking powder, $\frac{1}{4}$ teaspoon baking soda, $\frac{1}{2}$ egg, $\frac{1}{2}$ teaspoon almond extract; *filling*: $\frac{1}{2}$ package (4 ounces) cream cheese, $\frac{1}{8}$ cup sugar, $\frac{1}{2}$ egg, $\frac{3}{8}$ cup peach preserves, $\frac{1}{4}$ cup sliced almonds; *cake*: 9 cups all-purpose flour, 3 cups sugar, 3 cups cold butter, 3 cups sour cream, 2 teaspoons baking powder, 2 teaspoons baking soda, 4 eggs, 4 teaspoons almond extract; *filling*: 4 packages (8 ounces each) cream cheese, 1 cup sugar 4 eggs, 3 cups peach preserves, 2 cups sliced almonds **41.** 15 mpg **43.** 4 cu ft
45. $16\frac{1}{2}$ servings **47.** $35\frac{115}{256}$ sq in. **49.** $59{,}538\frac{1}{8}$ sq ft
51. $\mathbf{D_W}$ **53.** divisor, quotient, dividend **54.** common
55. composite **56.** divisible, divisible
57. multiplications, divisions, additions, subtractions
58. addends **59.** numerator **60.** reciprocal
61. $360\frac{60}{473}$ **63.** $35\frac{57}{64}$ **65.** $\frac{4}{9}$ **67.** $1\frac{4}{5}$

Margin Exercises, Section 3.7, pp. 201–204

1. $\frac{1}{2}$ **2.** $\frac{3}{10}$ **3.** $20\frac{2}{3}$, or $\frac{62}{3}$ **4.** $9\frac{7}{8}$ in. **5.** $\frac{5}{9}$ **6.** $\frac{31}{40}$
7. $\frac{27}{56}$ **8.** 0 **9.** 1 **10.** $\frac{1}{2}$ **11.** 1
12. 12; answers may vary **13.** 32; answers may vary
14. 27; answers may vary **15.** 15; answers may vary
16. 1; answers may vary **17.** 1,000,000; answers may vary
18. $22\frac{1}{2}$ **19.** 132 **20.** 37

Exercise Set 3.7, p. 205

1. $\frac{1}{24}$ **3.** $\frac{2}{5}$ **5.** $\frac{4}{7}$ **7.** $\frac{59}{30}$, or $1\frac{29}{30}$ **9.** $\frac{3}{20}$ **11.** $\frac{211}{8}$, or $26\frac{3}{8}$
13. $\frac{7}{16}$ **15.** $\frac{1}{36}$ **17.** $\frac{3}{8}$ **19.** $\frac{37}{48}$ **21.** $\frac{25}{72}$ **23.** $\frac{103}{16}$, or $6\frac{7}{16}$
25. $2\frac{41}{128}$ lb **27.** $7\frac{23}{50}$ sec **29.** $\frac{17}{6}$, or $2\frac{5}{6}$ **31.** $\frac{8395}{84}$, or $99\frac{79}{84}$
33. 0 **35.** 0 **37.** $\frac{1}{2}$ **39.** $\frac{1}{2}$ **41.** 0 **43.** 1 **45.** 6
47. 12 **49.** 19 **51.** 6 **53.** 12 **55.** 16 **57.** 3
59. 13 **61.** 2 **63.** $1\frac{1}{2}$ **65.** $\frac{1}{2}$ **67.** $271\frac{1}{2}$ **69.** 3
71. 100 **73.** $29\frac{1}{2}$ **75.** $\mathbf{D_W}$ **77.** 3402 **78.** 1,038,180
79. 59 R 77 **80.** 348 **81.** 783 **82.** $\frac{8}{3}$ **83.** $\frac{3}{8}$
84. Prime: 5, 7, 23, 43; composite: 9, 14; neither: 1
85. 16 people **86.** 43 mg

87. (a) $13 \cdot 9\frac{1}{4} + 8\frac{1}{4} \cdot 7\frac{1}{4}$; **(b)** $\frac{2881}{16}$, or $180\frac{1}{16}$ in²; **(c)** Multiply before adding. **89.** $a = 2, b = 8$ **91.** The largest is $\frac{4}{3} + \frac{5}{2} = \frac{23}{6}$.

Concept Reinforcement, p. 209

1. True **2.** True **3.** False **4.** True **5.** True **6.** False

Summary and Review: Chapter 3, p. 209

1. 36 **2.** 90 **3.** 30 **4.** 1404 **5.** $\frac{63}{40}$ **6.** $\frac{19}{48}$ **7.** $\frac{25}{12}$ **8.** $\frac{891}{1000}$ **9.** $\frac{1}{3}$ **10.** $\frac{1}{8}$ **11.** $\frac{5}{27}$ **12.** $\frac{11}{18}$ **13.** > **14.** > **15.** $\frac{19}{40}$ **16.** $\frac{2}{5}$ **17.** $\frac{15}{2}$ **18.** $\frac{67}{8}$ **19.** $\frac{13}{3}$ **20.** $\frac{75}{7}$ **21.** $2\frac{1}{3}$ **22.** $6\frac{3}{4}$ **23.** $12\frac{3}{5}$ **24.** $3\frac{1}{2}$ **25.** $877\frac{1}{3}$ **26.** $456\frac{5}{23}$ **27.** $10\frac{2}{5}$ **28.** $11\frac{11}{15}$ **29.** $10\frac{2}{3}$ **30.** $8\frac{1}{4}$ **31.** $7\frac{7}{9}$ **32.** $4\frac{11}{15}$ **33.** $4\frac{3}{20}$ **34.** $13\frac{3}{8}$ **35.** 16 **36.** $3\frac{1}{2}$ **37.** $2\frac{21}{50}$ **38.** 6 **39.** 12 **40.** $1\frac{7}{17}$ **41.** $\frac{1}{8}$ **42.** $\frac{9}{10}$ **43.** $4\frac{1}{4}$ yd **44.** $177\frac{3}{4}$ in² **45.** $50\frac{1}{4}$ in²

46. *Serving 2:* $\frac{1}{8}$ cup extra-virgin olive oil, $\frac{3}{4}$ pound fresh red snapper fillets, $\frac{1}{6}$ cup kalamata olives, $1\frac{1}{4}$ tablespoons capers, $\frac{1}{2}$ cup canned tomatoes, $1\frac{1}{2}$ tablespoons chopped shallots, $\frac{1}{4}$ tablespoon fresh rosemary leaves, $\frac{1}{4}$ tablespoon minced garlic, $\frac{1}{6}$ cup white wine; *serving 12:* $\frac{3}{4}$ cup extra-virgin olive oil, $4\frac{1}{2}$ pounds fresh red snapper fillets, 1 cup kalamata olives, $7\frac{1}{2}$ tablespoons capers, 3 cups canned tomatoes, 9 tablespoons chopped shallots, $1\frac{1}{2}$ tablespoons fresh rosemary leaves, $1\frac{1}{2}$ tablespoons minced garlic, 1 cup white wine **47.** $1\frac{73}{100}$ in. **48.** 24 lb **49.** About $69\frac{3}{8}$ kg **50.** $8\frac{3}{8}$ cups **51.** $63\frac{2}{3}$ pies; $19\frac{1}{3}$ pies **52.** 1 **53.** $\frac{7}{40}$ **54.** 3 **55.** $\frac{77}{240}$ **56.** $\frac{1}{2}$ **57.** 0 **58.** 1 **59.** 7 **60.** 10 **61.** 2 **62.** $28\frac{1}{2}$

63. **DW** It might be necessary to find the least common denominator before adding or subtracting. The least common denominator is the least common multiple of the denominators. **64.** **DW** Suppose that a room has dimensions $15\frac{3}{4}$ ft by $28\frac{5}{8}$ ft. The equation $2 \cdot 15\frac{3}{4} + 2 \cdot 28\frac{5}{8} = 88\frac{3}{4}$ gives the perimeter of the room, in feet. Answers may vary. **65.** 12 min **66.** $\frac{6}{3} + \frac{5}{4} = 3\frac{1}{4}$

Test: Chapter 3, p. 212

1. [3.1a] 48 **2.** [3.1a] 600 **3.** [3.2a] 3 **4.** [3.2a] $\frac{37}{24}$ **5.** [3.2a] $\frac{921}{1000}$ **6.** [3.3a] $\frac{1}{3}$ **7.** [3.3a] $\frac{1}{12}$ **8.** [3.3a] $\frac{77}{120}$ **9.** [3.3c] $\frac{15}{4}$ **10.** [3.3c] $\frac{1}{4}$ **11.** [3.3b] > **12.** [3.4a] $\frac{7}{2}$ **13.** [3.4a] $\frac{79}{8}$ **14.** [3.4a] $4\frac{1}{2}$ **15.** [3.4a] $8\frac{2}{9}$ **16.** [3.4b] $162\frac{7}{11}$ **17.** [3.5a] $14\frac{1}{5}$ **18.** [3.5a] $14\frac{5}{12}$ **19.** [3.5b] $4\frac{7}{24}$ **20.** [3.5b] $6\frac{1}{6}$ **21.** [3.6a] 39 **22.** [3.6a] $4\frac{1}{2}$ **23.** [3.6b] 2 **24.** [3.6b] $\frac{1}{36}$ **25.** [3.6c] About 105 kg **26.** [3.6c] 80 books **27.** [3.5c] **(a)** 3 in.; **(b)** $4\frac{1}{2}$ in. **28.** [3.3d] $\frac{1}{16}$ in. **29.** [3.7a] $6\frac{11}{36}$ ft **30.** [3.7a] $3\frac{1}{2}$ **31.** [3.7a] $\frac{3}{4}$

32. [3.7b] 0 **33.** [3.7b] 1 **34.** [3.7b] 4 **35.** [3.7b] $18\frac{1}{2}$ **36.** [3.7b] 16 **37.** [3.7b] $1214\frac{1}{2}$ **38.** [3.1a] **(a)** 24, 48, 72; **(b)** 24 **39.** [3.3b], [3.5c] Rebecca walks $\frac{17}{56}$ mi farther.

Cumulative Review: Chapters 1–3, p. 214

1. [3.3d] **(a)** $\frac{1}{48}$ in.; **(b)** $\frac{1}{12}$ in. **2.** [2.7d] 61 **3.** **(a)** [3.5c] $14\frac{13}{24}$ mi; **(b)** [3.6c] $4\frac{61}{72}$ mi **4.** [3.6c], [3.5c] **(a)** $142\frac{1}{4}$ ft²; **(b)** 54 ft **5.** [1.8a] 31 people **6.** [1.8a] $108 **7.** [2.6b] $\frac{2}{5}$ tsp; 4 tsp **8.** [3.6c] 39 lb **9.** [3.6c] 16 pieces **10.** [3.2b] $\frac{33}{20}$ mi **11.** [1.1a] 5 **12.** [1.1b] 6 thousands + 7 tens + 5 ones **13.** [1.1c] Twenty-nine thousand, five hundred **14.** [2.3a] $\frac{5}{16}$ **15.** [1.2a] 899 **16.** [1.2a] 8982 **17.** [3.2a] $\frac{5}{12}$ **18.** [3.5a] $8\frac{1}{4}$ **19.** [1.3b] 5124 **20.** [1.3b] 4518 **21.** [3.3a] $\frac{5}{12}$ **22.** [3.5b] $1\frac{1}{6}$ **23.** [1.5a] 5004 **24.** [1.5a] 293,232 **25.** [2.6a] $\frac{3}{2}$ **26.** [2.6a] 15 **27.** [3.6a] $7\frac{1}{3}$ **28.** [1.6b] 715 **29.** [1.6b] 56 R 11 **30.** [3.4b] $56\frac{11}{45}$ **31.** [3.7a] $\frac{1377}{100}$, or $13\frac{77}{100}$ **32.** [2.7b] $\frac{4}{7}$ **33.** [3.6b] $7\frac{1}{3}$ **34.** [1.4a] 38,500 **35.** [3.1a] 72 **36.** [2.2a] No **37.** [2.1a] 1, 2, 4, 8, 16 **38.** [3.3b] > **39.** [2.5e] = **40.** [3.3b] < **41.** [2.5b] $\frac{4}{5}$ **42.** [2.3b] 0 **43.** [2.5b] 32 **44.** [3.4a] $\frac{37}{8}$ **45.** [3.4a] $5\frac{2}{3}$ **46.** [1.7b] 93 **47.** [3.3c] $\frac{5}{9}$ **48.** [2.7c] $\frac{12}{7}$ **49.** [1.7b] 905 **50.** [3.7b] 1 **51.** [3.7b] $\frac{1}{2}$ **52.** [3.7b] 0 **53.** [3.7b] 30 **54.** [3.7b] 1 **55.** [3.7b] 42 **56.** [2.1a, b, c, d], [2.2a]
Factors of 68: 1, 2, 4, 17, 34, 68
Factorization of 68: $2 \cdot 34$, or $2 \cdot 2 \cdot 17$
Prime factorization of 68: $2 \cdot 2 \cdot 17$
Numbers divisible by 6: 12, 54, 72, 300
Numbers divisible by 8: 8, 16, 24, 32, 40, 48, 64, 864
Numbers divisible by 5: 70, 95, 215
Prime numbers: 2, 3, 17, 19, 23, 31, 47, 101
57. [2.6b] (d) **58.** [2.7d] (a) **59.** [3.6c] (a) **60.** [3.6c] (a) **61.** [3.2a] **(a)** $\frac{1}{2}, \frac{2}{3}, \frac{3}{4}, \frac{4}{5}$; **(b)** $\frac{9}{10}$ **62.** [2.1c] 2003

CHAPTER 4

Margin Exercises, Section 4.1, pp. 219–224

1. Eighty and thirty-one hundredths; seventy-seven and forty-three hundredths **2.** Two and six thousand seven hundred sixty-seven hundred-thousandths **3.** Two hundred forty-five and eighty-nine hundredths **4.** Thirty-four and sixty-four ten-thousandths **5.** Thirty-one thousand, seventy-nine and seven hundred sixty-four thousandths **6.** $\frac{896}{1000}$ **7.** $\frac{2378}{100}$ **8.** $\frac{56,789}{10,000}$ **9.** $\frac{19}{10}$ **10.** 7.43 **11.** 0.406 **12.** 6.7089 **13.** 0.9 **14.** 0.057 **15.** 0.083 **16.** 4.3 **17.** 283.71 **18.** 456.013 **19.** 2.04 **20.** 0.06 **21.** 0.58 **22.** 1 **23.** 0.8989 **24.** 21.05

25. 2.8   **26.** 13.9   **27.** 234.4   **28.** 7.0   **29.** 0.64
30. 7.83   **31.** 34.68   **32.** 0.03   **33.** 0.943   **34.** 8.004
35. 43.112   **36.** 37.401   **37.** 7459.355   **38.** 7459.35
39. 7459.4   **40.** 7459   **41.** 7460   **42.** 7500   **43.** 7000

Exercise Set 4.1, p. 225

1. Sixty-three and five hundredths   **3.** Twenty-six and fifty-nine hundredths   **5.** Eight and thirty-five hundredths
7. Eighty-six and eighty-nine hundredths   **9.** Thirty-four and eight hundred ninety-one thousandths
11. $\frac{83}{10}$ **13.** $\frac{356}{100}$ **15.** $\frac{4603}{100}$ **17.** $\frac{13}{100,000}$ **19.** $\frac{10,008}{10,000}$
21. $\frac{20,003}{1000}$ **23.** 0.8   **25.** 8.89   **27.** 3.798   **29.** 0.0078
31. 0.00019   **33.** 0.376193   **35.** 99.44   **37.** 3.798
39. 2.1739   **41.** 8.953073   **43.** 0.58   **45.** 0.91
47. 0.001   **49.** 235.07   **51.** $\frac{4}{100}$ **53.** 0.4325   **55.** 0.1
57. 0.5   **59.** 2.7   **61.** 123.7   **63.** 0.89   **65.** 0.67
67. 1.00   **69.** 0.09   **71.** 0.325   **73.** 17.002
75. 10.101   **77.** 9.999   **79.** 800   **81.** 809.473
83. 809   **85.** 34.5439   **87.** 34.54   **89.** 35   **91.** D_W
93. 6170   **94.** 6200   **95.** 6000
96. $2 \cdot 2 \cdot 2 \cdot 2 \cdot 5 \cdot 5 \cdot 5$, or $2^4 \cdot 5^3$
97. $2 \cdot 3 \cdot 3 \cdot 5 \cdot 17$, or $2 \cdot 3^2 \cdot 5 \cdot 17$ **98.** $2 \cdot 7 \cdot 11 \cdot 13$
99. $2 \cdot 2 \cdot 2 \cdot 7 \cdot 7 \cdot 11$, or $2^3 \cdot 7^2 \cdot 11$
101. 2.000001, 2.0119, 2.018, 2.0302, 2.1, 2.108, 2.109
103. 6.78346   **105.** 0.03030

Margin Exercises, Section 4.2, pp. 228–232

1. 10.917   **2.** 34.2079   **3.** 4.969   **4.** 3.5617
5. 9.40544   **6.** 912.67   **7.** 2514.773   **8.** 10.754
9. 0.339   **10.** 0.5345   **11.** 0.5172   **12.** 7.36992
13. 1194.22   **14.** 4.9911   **15.** 38.534   **16.** 14.164
17. 2133.5
18. The "balance forward" column should read:
   $3078.92
   2738.23
   2659.67
   2890.47
   2877.33
   2829.33
   2868.91
   2766.04
   2697.45
   2597.45

Calculator Corner, p. 230

1. 317.645   **2.** 506.553   **3.** 17.15   **4.** 49.08   **5.** 4.4
6. 33.83   **7.** 454.74   **8.** 0.99

Exercise Set 4.2, p. 233

1. 334.37   **3.** 1576.215   **5.** 132.560   **7.** 50.0248
9. 40.007   **11.** 977.955   **13.** 771.967   **15.** 8754.8221
17. 49.02   **19.** 85.921   **21.** 2.4975   **23.** 3.397
25. 8.85   **27.** 3.37   **29.** 1.045   **31.** 3.703   **33.** 0.9902
35. 99.66   **37.** 4.88   **39.** 0.994   **41.** 17.802

43. 51.13   **45.** 32.7386   **47.** 4.0622   **49.** 11.65
51. 384.68   **53.** 582.97   **55.** 15,335.3
57. The balance forward should read:
   $ 9704.56
     9677.12
   10,677.12
   10,553.17
   10,429.15
   10,416.72
   12,916.72
   12,778.94
   12,797.82
     9997.82
59. D_W **61.** 35,000   **62.** 34,000   **63.** $\frac{1}{6}$ **64.** $\frac{34}{45}$
65. 6166   **66.** 5366   **67.** $16\frac{1}{2}$ servings   **68.** $60\frac{1}{5}$ mi
69. 345.8

Margin Exercises, Section 4.3, pp. 237–240

1. 529.48   **2.** 5.0594   **3.** 34.2906   **4.** 0.348   **5.** 0.0348
6. 0.00348   **7.** 0.000348   **8.** 34.8   **9.** 348   **10.** 3480
11. 34,800   **12.** 3,700,000   **13.** 6,100,000,000
14. 2,700,000,000   **15.** 1569¢   **16.** 17¢   **17.** $0.35
18. $5.77

Calculator Corner, p. 239

1. 48.6   **2.** 6930.5   **3.** 142.803   **4.** 0.5076   **5.** 7916.4
6. 20.4153

Exercise Set 4.3, p. 241

1. 60.2   **3.** 6.72   **5.** 0.252   **7.** 0.522   **9.** 237.6
11. 583,686.852   **13.** 780   **15.** 8.923   **17.** 0.09768
19. 0.782   **21.** 521.6   **23.** 3.2472   **25.** 897.6
27. 322.07   **29.** 55.68   **31.** 3487.5   **33.** 50.0004
35. 114.42902   **37.** 13.284   **39.** 90.72   **41.** 0.0028728
43. 0.72523   **45.** 1.872115   **47.** 45,678   **49.** 2888¢
51. 66¢   **53.** $0.34   **55.** $34.45   **57.** 258,700,000,000
59. 748,900,000   **61.** D_W **63.** $11\frac{1}{5}$ **64.** $\frac{35}{72}$ **65.** $2\frac{7}{15}$
66. $7\frac{2}{15}$ **67.** 342   **68.** 87   **69.** 4566   **70.** 1257
71. 87   **72.** 1176 R 14   **73.** $10^{21} = 1$ sextillion
75. $10^{24} = 1$ septillion

Margin Exercises, Section 4.4, pp. 244–250

1. 0.6   **2.** 1.5   **3.** 0.47   **4.** 0.32   **5.** 3.75   **6.** 0.25
7. (a) 375; **(b)** 15   **8.** 4.9   **9.** 12.8   **10.** 15.625
11. 12.78   **12.** 0.001278   **13.** 0.09847   **14.** 67.832
15. 0.78314   **16.** 1105.6   **17.** 0.04   **18.** 0.2426
19. 593.44   **20.** 5967.5 m

Calculator Corner, p. 247

1. 14.3   **2.** 2.56   **3.** 200   **4.** 0.75   **5.** 20   **6.** 0.064
7. 15.7   **8.** 75.8

Exercise Set 4.4, p. 251

1. 2.99 **3.** 23.78 **5.** 7.48 **7.** 7.2 **9.** 1.143
11. 4.041 **13.** 0.07 **15.** 70 **17.** 20 **19.** 0.4
21. 0.41 **23.** 8.5 **25.** 9.3 **27.** 0.625 **29.** 0.26
31. 15.625 **33.** 2.34 **35.** 0.47 **37.** 0.2134567
39. 21.34567 **41.** 1023.7 **43.** 9.3 **45.** 0.0090678
47. 45.6 **49.** 2107 **51.** 303.003 **53.** 446.208
55. 24.14 **57.** 13.0072 **59.** 19.3204 **61.** 473.188278
63. 10.49 **65.** 911.13 **67.** 205 **69.** \$1288.36
71. \$206.34 billion **73.** D_W **75.** $\frac{6}{7}$ **76.** $\frac{7}{8}$ **77.** $\frac{19}{73}$
78. $\frac{19}{73}$ **79.** $2 \cdot 2 \cdot 3 \cdot 3 \cdot 19$, or $2^2 \cdot 3^2 \cdot 19$
80. $2 \cdot 3 \cdot 3 \cdot 3 \cdot 3$, or $2 \cdot 3^4$ **81.** $3 \cdot 3 \cdot 223$, or $3^2 \cdot 223$
82. $5 \cdot 401$ **83.** $15\frac{1}{8}$ **84.** $5\frac{7}{8}$ **85.** 6.254194585
87. 1000 **89.** 100

Margin Exercises, Section 4.5, pp. 255–259

1. 0.8 **2.** 0.45 **3.** 0.275 **4.** 1.32 **5.** 0.4 **6.** 0.375
7. $0.1\overline{6}$ **8.** $0.\overline{6}$ **9.** $0.\overline{45}$ **10.** $1.\overline{09}$ **11.** $0.\overline{428571}$
12. 0.7; 0.67; 0.667 **13.** 0.8; 0.81; 0.808 **14.** 6.2; 6.25;
6.245 **15.** 0.510 **16.** 24.2 mpg **17.** 12.1 million
digital cameras **18.** 0.72 **19.** 0.552 **20.** 9.6575

Exercise Set 4.5, p. 260

1. 0.23 **3.** 0.6 **5.** 0.325 **7.** 0.2 **9.** 0.85 **11.** 0.375
13. 0.975 **15.** 0.52 **17.** 20.016 **19.** 0.25 **21.** 1.16
23. 1.1875 **25.** $0.2\overline{6}$ **27.** $0.\overline{3}$ **29.** $1.\overline{3}$ **31.** $1.1\overline{6}$
33. $0.\overline{571428}$ **35.** $0.91\overline{6}$ **37.** 0.3; 0.27; 0.267
39. 0.3; 0.33; 0.333 **41.** 1.3; 1.33; 1.333 **43.** 1.2; 1.17;
1.167 **45.** 0.6; 0.57; 0.571 **47.** 0.9; 0.92; 0.917
49. 0.2; 0.18; 0.182 **51.** 0.3; 0.28; 0.278 **53.** (a) 0.429;
(b) 0.75; (c) 0.571; (d) 1.333 **55.** 15.8 mpg
57. 17.8 mpg **59.** 15.2 mph **61.** \$24.5625; \$24.56
63. \$3.734375; \$3.73 **65.** \$59.875; \$59.88 **67.** 11.06
69. 8.4 **71.** $417.51\overline{6}$ **73.** 0 **75.** 2.8125 **77.** 0.20425
79. 317.14 **81.** 0.1825 **83.** 18 **85.** 2.736
87. D_W **89.** 21 **90.** $238\frac{7}{8}$ **91.** 10 **92.** $\frac{43}{52}$
93. $50\frac{5}{24}$ **94.** $30\frac{7}{10}$ **95.** $1\frac{1}{2}$ **96.** $14\frac{13}{24}$ **97.** $1\frac{1}{24}$ cups
98. $1\frac{33}{100}$ in. **99.** $0.\overline{142857}$ **101.** $0.\overline{428571}$
103. $0.\overline{714285}$ **105.** $0.\overline{1}$ **107.** $0.\overline{001}$

Margin Exercises, Section 4.6, pp. 264–266

1. (b) **2.** (a) **3.** (d) **4.** (b) **5.** (a) **6.** (d) **7.** (b)
8. (c) **9.** (b) **10.** (b) **11.** (c) **12.** (a) **13.** (c)
14. (c)

Exercise Set 4.6, p. 267

1. (d) **3.** (c) **5.** (a) **7.** (c) **9.** 1.6 **11.** 6 **13.** 60
15. 2.3 **17.** 180 **19.** (a) **21.** (c) **23.** (b) **25.** (b)
27. $1800 \div 9 = 200$ posts; answers may vary **29.** D_W
31. repeating **32.** multiple **33.** distributive
34. solution **35.** multiplicative **36.** commutative
37. denominator; multiple **38.** divisible; divisible
39. Yes **41.** No **43.** (a) $+, \times$; (b) $+, \times, -$

Margin Exercises, Section 4.7, pp. 270–276

1. \$2.5 billion **2.** 199.1 lb **3.** \$51.26 **4.** \$368.75
5. 96.52 cm^2 **6.** \$1.33 **7.** 28.6 mpg **8.** \$716,667
9. \$158,760

Translating for Success, p. 277

1. I **2.** C **3.** N **4.** A **5.** G **6.** B **7.** D **8.** O
9. F **10.** M

Exercise Set 4.7, p. 278

1. \$17.8 billion **3.** \$19.15 **5.** 102.8°F
7. \$64,333,333.33 **9.** Area: 8.125 cm^2; perimeter: 11.5 cm
11. 22,691.5 mi **13.** 20.2 mpg **15.** \$30
17. 11.9752 ft^3 **19.** 78.1 cm **21.** 28.5 cm **23.** 2.31 cm
25. 876 calories **27.** \$1171.74 **29.** 227.75 ft^2
31. 0.362 **33.** \$53.04 **35.** 2152.56 yd^2 **37.** 10.8¢
39. \$906.50 **41.** 5.665 billion **43.** 1.4°F
45. \$266,791 **47.** \$165,565 **49.** \$1,131,429
51. D_W **53.** 6335 **54.** $\frac{31}{24}$ **55.** $6\frac{5}{6}$ **56.** $\frac{23}{15}$ **57.** $\frac{1}{24}$
58. 2803 **59.** $\frac{2}{15}$ **60.** $1\frac{5}{6}$ **61.** $\frac{129}{251}$ **62.** $\frac{5}{16}$ **63.** $\frac{13}{25}$
64. $\frac{25}{19}$ **65.** 28 min **66.** $7\frac{1}{5}$ min **67.** 186 calories
68. 30 calories **69.** \$17.28

Concept Reinforcement, p. 285

1. False **2.** True **3.** True **4.** False **5.** True

Summary and Review: Chapter 4, p. 285

1. 6,590,000 **2.** 6,900,000 **3.** Three and
forty-seven hundredths **4.** Thirty-one thousandths
5. Twenty-seven and eleven hundred-thousandths
6. Seven millionths **7.** $\frac{9}{100}$ **8.** $\frac{4561}{1000}$ **9.** $\frac{89}{1000}$ **10.** $\frac{30,227}{10,000}$
11. 0.034 **12.** 4.2603 **13.** 27.91 **14.** 867.006
15. 0.034 **16.** 0.91 **17.** 0.741 **18.** 1.041 **19.** 17.4
20. 17.43 **21.** 17.429 **22.** 17 **23.** 574.519
24. 0.6838 **25.** 229.1 **26.** 45.551 **27.** 29.2092
28. 790.29 **29.** 29.148 **30.** 70.7891 **31.** 12.96
32. 0.14442 **33.** 4.3 **34.** 0.02468 **35.** 7.5 **36.** 0.45
37. 45.2 **38.** 1.022 **39.** 0.2763 **40.** 1389.2
41. 496.2795 **42.** 6.95 **43.** 42.54 **44.** 4.9911
45. \$15.52 **46.** 1.9 lb **47.** \$912.68 **48.** \$307.49
49. 14.5 mpg **50.** (a) 102.6 lb; (b) 14.7 lb **51.** 272
52. 216 **53.** 4 **54.** \$125 **55.** 2.6 **56.** 1.28
57. 2.75 **58.** 3.25 **59.** $1.1\overline{6}$ **60.** $1.\overline{54}$ **61.** 1.5
62. 1.55 **63.** 1.545 **64.** \$82.73 **65.** \$4.87
66. 2493¢ **67.** 986¢ **68.** 1.8045 **69.** 57.1449
70. 15.6375 **71.** $41.537\overline{3}$
72. D_W Multiply by 1 to get a denominator that is a power
of 10:

$$\frac{44}{125} = \frac{44}{125} \cdot \frac{8}{8} = \frac{352}{1000} = 0.352.$$

We can also divide to find that $\frac{44}{125} = 0.352$.
73. D_W Each decimal place in the decimal notation
corresponds to one zero in the power of ten in the fraction

notation. When the fractions are multiplied, the number of zeros in the denominator of the product is the sum of the number of zeros in the denominators of the factors. So the number of decimal places in the product is the sum of the number of decimal places in the factors.
74. (a) $2.56 \times 6.4 \div 51.2 - 17.4 + 89.7 = 72.62$;
(b) $(11.12 - 0.29) \times 3^4 = 877.23$
75. $\frac{1}{3} + \frac{2}{3} = 0.33333333\ldots + 0.66666666\ldots$
  $= 0.99999999\ldots$
Therefore, $1 = 0.99999999\ldots$ because $\frac{1}{3} + \frac{2}{3} = 1$.
76. $2 = 1.\overline{9}$ **77.** $a = 5, b = 9$

Test: Chapter 4, p. 288

1. [4.3b] 8,900,000,000 **2.** [4.3b] 3,756,000
3. [4.1a] Two and thirty-four hundredths
4. [4.1a] One hundred five and five ten-thousandths
5. [4.1b] $\frac{91}{100}$ **6.** [4.1b] $\frac{2769}{1000}$ **7.** [4.1b] 0.074
8. [4.1b] 3.7047 **9.** [4.1b] 756.09 **10.** [4.1b] 91.703
11. [4.1c] 0.162 **12.** [4.1c] 0.078 **13.** [4.1c] 0.9
14. [4.1d] 6 **15.** [4.1d] 5.68 **16.** [4.1d] 5.678
17. [4.1d] 5.7 **18.** [4.2a] 0.7902 **19.** [4.2a] 186.5
20. [4.2a] 1033.23 **21.** [4.2b] 48.357 **22.** [4.2b] 19.0901
23. [4.2b] 152.8934 **24.** [4.3a] 0.03 **25.** [4.3a] 0.21345
26. [4.3a] 73,962 **27.** [4.4a] 4.75 **28.** [4.4a] 30.4
29. [4.4a] 0.19 **30.** [4.4a] 0.34689 **31.** [4.4a] 34,689
32. [4.4b] 84.26 **33.** [4.2c] 8.982 **34.** [4.7a] $314.99
35. [4.7a] 28.3 mpg **36.** [4.7a] $6572.45
37. [4.7a] $181.93 **38.** [4.7a] 58.24 million passengers
39. [4.6a] 198 **40.** [4.6a] 4 **41.** [4.5a] 1.6
42. [4.5a] 0.88 **43.** [4.5a] 5.25 **44.** [4.5a] 0.75
45. [4.5a] $1.\overline{2}$ **46.** [4.5a] $2.\overline{142857}$ **47.** [4.5b] 2.1
48. [4.5b] 2.14 **49.** [4.5b] 2.143 **50.** [4.3b] $9.49
51. [4.4c] 40.0065 **52.** [4.4c] 384.8464 **53.** [4.5c] 302.4
54. [4.5c] 52.339$\overline{4}$ **55.** [4.7a] $35
56. [4.1b, c] $\frac{2}{3}, \frac{5}{7}, \frac{15}{19}, \frac{11}{13}, \frac{17}{20}, \frac{13}{15}$

CHAPTER 5

Margin Exercises, Section 5.1, pp. 292–295

1. $\frac{5}{11}$, or 5:11 **2.** $\frac{57.3}{86.1}$, or 57.3:86.1 **3.** $\frac{6\frac{3}{4}}{7\frac{2}{5}}$, or $6\frac{3}{4}:7\frac{2}{5}$

4. $\frac{739}{12}$ **5.** $\frac{12}{14}$ **6.** $\frac{71}{214.1}; \frac{214.1}{71}$ **7.** $\frac{38.2}{56.1}$ **8.** $\frac{205}{278}, \frac{278}{205}, \frac{278}{483}$
9. 18 is to 27 as 2 is to 3 **10.** 3.6 is to 12 as 3 is to 10
11. 1.2 is to 1.5 as 4 is to 5 **12.** $\frac{9}{16}$

Exercise Set 5.1, p. 296

1. $\frac{4}{5}$ **3.** $\frac{178}{572}$ **5.** $\frac{0.4}{12}$ **7.** $\frac{3.8}{7.4}$ **9.** $\frac{56.78}{98.35}$ **11.** $\frac{8\frac{3}{4}}{9\frac{5}{6}}$ **13.** $\frac{4}{1}$

15. $\frac{356}{100,000}; \frac{173}{100,000}$ **17.** $\frac{93.2}{1000}$ **19.** $\frac{190}{547}; \frac{547}{190}$ **21.** $\frac{60}{100}; \frac{100}{60}$
23. $\frac{2}{3}$ **25.** $\frac{3}{4}$ **27.** $\frac{12}{25}$ **29.** $\frac{7}{9}$ **31.** $\frac{2}{3}$ **33.** $\frac{14}{25}$ **35.** $\frac{1}{2}$
37. $\frac{3}{4}$ **39.** $\frac{478}{213}; \frac{213}{478}$ **41.** $\mathbf{D_W}$ **43.** $=$ **44.** $\neq$ **45.** $\neq$
46. $=$ **47.** 50 **48.** 9.5 **49.** 14.5 **50.** 152
51. $6\frac{7}{20}$ cm **52.** $17\frac{11}{20}$ cm **53.** $\frac{30}{47}$ **55.** 1:2:3

Margin Exercises, Section 5.2, pp. 300–301

1. 5 mi/hr, or 5 mph **2.** 12 mi/hr, or 12 mph
3. $\frac{89}{13}$ km/h, or 6.85 km/h **4.** 1100 ft/sec **5.** 4 ft/sec
6. $\frac{121}{8}$ ft/sec, or 15.125 ft/sec **7.** $\frac{34\text{ home runs}}{92\text{ strikeouts}} \approx$
0.370 home run per strikeout **8.** $\frac{714\text{ home runs}}{1330\text{ strikeouts}} \approx$
0.537 home run per strikeout; Babe Ruth's rate is approximately 0.167 higher **9.** 7.45¢/oz
10. 24.143¢/oz; 25.9¢/oz; 24.17¢/oz; the 7-oz package has the lowest unit price

Exercise Set 5.2, p. 302

1. 40 km/h **3.** 7.48 mi/sec **5.** 24 mpg **7.** 23 mpg
9. $\frac{32,270\text{ people}}{0.75\text{ sq mi}}$; about 43,027 people/sq mi
11. 25 mph; 0.04 hr/mi **13.** About 18.3 points/game
15. 0.623 gal/ft^2 **17.** 186,000 mi/sec **19.** 124 km/h
21. 25 beats/min **23.** 19.185¢/oz; 15.709¢/oz; 25.4 oz
25. 11.5¢/oz; 13.833¢/oz; 16 oz
27. 18.174¢/oz; 15.275¢/oz; 34.5 oz
29. 10.5¢/oz; 11.607¢/oz; 12.475¢/oz; 12.484¢/oz; 18 oz
31. 8.58¢/oz; 5.29¢/oz; 5.245¢/oz; 5.263¢/oz; 200 fl oz
33. $\mathbf{D_W}$ **35.** 1.7 million **36.** $37\frac{1}{2}$ servings
37. 30 tests **38.** 8.9 billion **39.** 109.608 **40.** 67,819
41. 5833.56 **42.** 466,190.4
43. 6-oz: 10.83¢/oz; 5.5-oz: 10.91¢/oz

Margin Exercises, Section 5.3, pp. 307–310

1. Yes **2.** No **3.** No **4.** Yes **5.** No **6.** Yes
7. 14 **8.** $11\frac{1}{4}$ **9.** 10.5 **10.** 2.64 **11.** 10.8
12. $\frac{125}{42}$, or $2\frac{41}{42}$

Calculator Corner, p. 310

1. Left to the student **2.** Left to the student **3.** 27.5625
4. 25.6 **5.** 15.140625 **6.** 40.03952941
7. 39.74857143 **8.** 119

Exercise Set 5.3, p. 311

1. No **3.** Yes **5.** Yes **7.** No **9.** 0.61; 0.66; 0.69; 0.66; the completion rates (rounded to the nearest hundredth) are the same for Brees and Roethlisberger
11. 45 **13.** 12 **15.** 10 **17.** 20 **19.** 5 **21.** 18
23. 22 **25.** 28 **27.** $9\frac{1}{3}$ **29.** $2\frac{8}{9}$ **31.** 0.06 **33.** 5
35. 1 **37.** 1 **39.** 14 **41.** $2\frac{3}{16}$ **43.** $\frac{51}{16}$, or $3\frac{3}{16}$
45. 12.5725 **47.** $\frac{1748}{249}$, or $7\frac{5}{249}$ **49.** $\mathbf{D_W}$ **51.** quotient
52. sum **53.** average **54.** dollars, cents
55. subtrahend **56.** terminating **57.** commutative
58. cross products **59.** Approximately 2731.4
61. (a) Ruth: 1.863 strikeouts per home run; Schmidt: 3.436 strikeouts per home run; (b) Schmidt

Margin Exercises, Section 5.4, pp. 314–318

1. 445 calories **2.** 15 gal **3.** 8 shirts **4.** 38 in. or less
5. 9.5 in. **6.** 2074 deer

Translating for Success, p. 319

1. N **2.** I **3.** A **4.** K **5.** J **6.** F **7.** M **8.** B
9. G **10.** E

Exercise Set 5.4, p. 320

1. 11.04 hr **3.** 880 calories **5.** 177 million, or
177,000,000 **7.** 9.75 gal **9.** 175 bulbs **11.** 2975 ft^2
13. 450 pages **15.** (a) 23.63445 British pounds;
(b) \$16,450.56 **17.** (a) 21,206 Japanese yen; (b) \$29.99
19. (a) About 112 gal; (b) 3360 mi **21.** 60 students
23. 13,500 mi **25.** 120 lb **27.** 64 gal **29.** 100 oz
31. 954 deer **33.** 58.1 mi **35.** (a) 56 games; (b) about
2197 points **37.** D$_W$ **39.** Neither **40.** Composite
41. Prime **42.** Composite **43.** Prime
44. $2 \cdot 2 \cdot 2 \cdot 101$, or $2^3 \cdot 101$ **45.** $2 \cdot 2 \cdot 7$, or $2^2 \cdot 7$
46. $2 \cdot 433$ **47.** $3 \cdot 31$ **48.** $2 \cdot 2 \cdot 5 \cdot 101$, or $2^2 \cdot 5 \cdot 101$
49. 17 positions **51.** 2150 earned runs **53.** CD player:
\$150; receiver: \$450; speakers: \$300

Margin Exercises, Section 5.5, pp. 325–328

1. 15 **2.** 24.75 ft **3.** 7.5 ft **4.** 21 cm **5.** 29 ft

Exercise Set 5.5, p. 329

1. 25 **3.** $\frac{4}{3}$, or $1\frac{1}{3}$ **5.** $x = \frac{27}{4}$, or $6\frac{3}{4}$; $y = 9$ **7.** $x = 7.5$;
$y = 7.2$ **9.** 1.25 m **11.** 36 ft **13.** 7 ft **15.** 100 ft
17. 4 **19.** $10\frac{1}{2}$ **21.** $x = 6$; $y = 5.25$; $z = 3$ **23.** $x = 5\frac{1}{3}$,
or $5.\overline{3}$; $y = 4\frac{2}{3}$, or $4.\overline{6}$; $z = 5\frac{1}{3}$, or $5.\overline{3}$ **25.** 20 ft **27.** 152 ft
29. D$_W$ **31.** \$59.81 **32.** 9.63 **33.** 679.4928
34. 2.74568 **35.** 27,456.8 **36.** 0.549136 **37.** 0.85
38. 1.825 **39.** 0.909 **40.** 0.843 **41.** 13.75 ft
43. 1.25 cm **45.** 3681.437 **47.** $x = 0.4$; $y \approx 0.35$

Concept Reinforcement, p. 333

1. True **2.** True **3.** False **4.** False **5.** True

Summary and Review: Chapter 5, p. 333

1. $\frac{47}{84}$ **2.** $\frac{46}{1.27}$ **3.** $\frac{83}{100}$ **4.** $\frac{0.72}{197}$ **5.** (a) $\frac{12,480}{16,640}$, or $\frac{3}{4}$;
(b) $\frac{16,640}{29,120}$, or $\frac{4}{7}$ **6.** $\frac{3}{4}$ **7.** $\frac{9}{16}$ **8.** 26 mpg **9.** 6300 rpm
10. 0.638 gal/ft^2 **11.** 0.72 serving/lb **12.** 4.33¢/tablet
13. 14.173¢/oz **14.** 1.329¢/sheet; 1.554¢/sheet;
1.110¢/sheet; 6 big rolls **15.** 6.844¢/oz; 5.188¢/oz;
5.609¢/oz; 5.539¢/oz; 48 oz **16.** No **17.** No **18.** 32
19. 7 **20.** $\frac{1}{40}$ **21.** 24 **22.** \$4.45 **23.** 351 circuits
24. (a) 202 Euros; (b) \$61.88 **25.** 832 mi **26.** 27 acres
27. Approximately 3,293,558 kg **28.** 6 in.
29. Approximately 2096 lawyers **30.** $x = \frac{14}{3}$, or $4\frac{2}{3}$

31. $x = \frac{56}{5}$, or $11\frac{1}{5}$; $y = \frac{63}{5}$, or $12\frac{3}{5}$ **32.** 40 ft
33. $x = 3$; $y = 9$; $z = \frac{15}{2}$, or $7\frac{1}{2}$
34. D$_W$ In terms of cost, a low faculty-to-student ratio is
less expensive than a high faculty-to-student ratio. In terms
of quality of education and student satisfaction, a high
faculty-to-student ratio is more desirable. A college
president must balance the cost and quality issues.
35. D$_W$ Leslie used 4 gal of gasoline to drive 92 mi. At the
same rate, how many gallons would be needed to travel
368 mi? **36.** 105 min, or 1 hr 45 min
37. $x = 4258.5$; $z \approx 10{,}094.3$ **38.** Finishing paint: 11 gal;
primer: 16.5 gal

Test: Chapter 5, p. 336

1. [5.1a] $\frac{85}{97}$ **2.** [5.1a] $\frac{0.34}{124}$ **3.** [5.1b] $\frac{9}{10}$ **4.** [5.1b] $\frac{25}{32}$
5. [5.2a] 0.625 ft/sec **6.** [5.2a] $1\frac{1}{3}$ servings/lb
7. [5.2a] 22 mpg **8.** [5.2b] About 7.765¢/oz
9. [5.2b] 11.182¢/oz; 7.149¢/oz; 8.389¢/oz; 6.840¢/oz;
263 oz **10.** [5.3a] Yes **11.** [5.3a] No **12.** [5.3b] 12
13. [5.3b] 360 **14.** [5.3b] 42.1875 **15.** [5.3b] 100
16. [5.4a] 1512 km **17.** [5.4a] 4.8 min **18.** [5.4a] 525 mi
19. [5.5a] 66 m **20.** [5.4a] (a) 3498.75 Hong Kong dollars;
(b) \$102.25 **21.** [5.4a] About 86,151 arrests
22. [5.5a] $x = 8$; $y = 8.8$ **23.** [5.5b] $x = 8$; $y = 8$; $z = 12$
24. [5.4a] 5888

Cumulative Review: Chapters 1–5, p. 338

1. [1.6b], [4.3b], [4.4a] (a) \$252,000,000; (b) \$0.252 billion;
(c) \$25,200,000; (d) \$45,487.36 **2.** [5.2a] 22 mpg
3. [4.2a] 513.996 **4.** [3.5a] $6\frac{3}{4}$ **5.** [3.2a] $\frac{7}{20}$
6. [4.2b] 30.491 **7.** [4.2b] 72.912 **8.** [3.3a] $\frac{7}{60}$
9. [4.3a] 222.076 **10.** [4.3a] 567.8 **11.** [3.6a] 3
12. [4.4a] 43 **13.** [1.6b] 899 **14.** [2.7b] $\frac{3}{2}$
15. [1.1b] 3 ten thousands + 7 tens + 4 ones
16. [4.1a] One hundred twenty and seven hundredths
17. [4.1c] 0.7 **18.** [4.1c] 0.8
19. [2.1d] $2 \cdot 2 \cdot 2 \cdot 2 \cdot 3 \cdot 3$, or $2^4 \cdot 3^2$ **20.** [3.1a] 140
21. [2.3a] $\frac{5}{8}$ **22.** [2.5b] $\frac{5}{8}$ **23.** [4.5c] 5.718
24. [4.5c] 0.179 **25.** [5.1a] $\frac{0.3}{15}$ **26.** [5.3a] Yes
27. [5.2a] 55 m/sec **28.** [5.2b] 11.769¢/oz; 9.344¢/oz;
9.728¢/oz; 6.357¢/oz; 7.002¢/oz; 28-oz Joy
29. [5.3b] 30.24 **30.** [4.4b] 26.4375 **31.** [2.7c] $\frac{8}{9}$
32. [5.3b] 128 **33.** [4.2c] 33.34 **34.** [3.3c] $\frac{76}{175}$
35. [2.6b] 390 cal **36.** [5.4a] (a) 1338.7 Rand; (b) \$336.89
37. [4.7a] 976.9 mi **38.** [5.4a] 7 min **39.** [3.5c] $2\frac{1}{4}$ cups
40. [2.7d] 12 doors **41.** [4.2b], [2.7d] (a) 40,200 yr;
(b) answers may vary **42.** [1.8a] (a) \$360,000;
(b) \$144,000,000; (c) \$1,728,000,000
43. [4.7a], [5.2a] 42.2025 mi **44.** [4.7a] 132 orbits
45. [2.1c] (d) **46.** [5.2a] (b) **47.** [1.2b] (b)
48. [5.5a] $10\frac{1}{2}$ ft

CHAPTER 6

Margin Exercises, Section 6.1, pp. 342–345

1. $\frac{70}{100}$; $70 \times \frac{1}{100}$; 70×0.01 **2.** $\frac{23.4}{100}$; $23.4 \times \frac{1}{100}$; 23.4×0.01
3. $\frac{100}{100}$; $100 \times \frac{1}{100}$; 100×0.01 **4.** 0.34   **5.** 0.789
6. 0.06625   **7.** 0.18   **8.** 0.0008   **9.** 24%   **10.** 347%
11. 100%   **12.** 32.1%   **13.** 25.3%

Calculator Corner, p. 343

1. 0.14   **2.** 0.00069   **3.** 0.438   **4.** 1.25

Exercise Set 6.1, p. 346

1. $\frac{90}{100}$; $90 \times \frac{1}{100}$; 90×0.01 **3.** $\frac{12.5}{100}$; $12.5 \times \frac{1}{100}$; 12.5×0.01
5. 0.67   **7.** 0.456   **9.** 0.5901   **11.** 0.1   **13.** 0.01
15. 2   **17.** 0.001   **19.** 0.0009   **21.** 0.0018   **23.** 0.2319
25. 0.14875   **27.** 0.565   **29.** 0.09; 0.58   **31.** 0.44
33. 0.36   **35.** 47%   **37.** 3%   **39.** 870%   **41.** 33.4%
43. 75%   **45.** 40%   **47.** 0.6%   **49.** 1.7%   **51.** 27.18%
53. 2.39%   **55.** 26%; 38%   **57.** 17.7%   **59.** 21.5%
61. $\mathbf{D_W}$ **63.** $33\frac{1}{3}$ **64.** $37\frac{1}{2}$ **65.** $9\frac{3}{8}$ **66.** $18\frac{9}{16}$
67. $5\frac{11}{14}$ **68.** $111\frac{2}{3}$ **69.** $0.\overline{6}$ **70.** $0.\overline{3}$ **71.** $0.8\overline{3}$
72. $1.41\overline{6}$ **73.** $2.\overline{6}$ **74.** 0.9375

Margin Exercises, Section 6.2, pp. 350–352

1. 25%   **2.** 62.5%, or $62\frac{1}{2}$%   **3.** $66.\overline{6}$%, or $66\frac{2}{3}$%
4. $83.\overline{3}$%, or $83\frac{1}{3}$%   **5.** 57%   **6.** 76%   **7.** $\frac{3}{5}$ **8.** $\frac{13}{400}$
9. $\frac{2}{3}$
10.

FRACTION NOTATION	$\frac{1}{5}$	$\frac{5}{6}$	$\frac{3}{8}$
DECIMAL NOTATION	0.2	$0.83\overline{3}$	0.375
PERCENT NOTATION	20%	$83.\overline{3}$%, or $83\frac{1}{3}$%	$37\frac{1}{2}$%

Calculator Corner, p. 350

1. 52%   **2.** 38.46%   **3.** 110.26%   **4.** 171.43%
5. 59.62%   **6.** 28.31%

Calculator Corner, p. 353

1. 30.54; 1.31%   **2.** 32.05; 1.20%   **3.** 34.47; 1.19%
4. 26.47; 1.00%   **5.** 11.98; 4.32%   **6.** 17.52; 0.89%

Exercise Set 6.2, p. 354

1. 41%   **3.** 5%   **5.** 20%   **7.** 30%   **9.** 50%
11. 87.5%, or $87\frac{1}{2}$%   **13.** 80%   **15.** $66.\overline{6}$%, or $66\frac{2}{3}$%
17. $16.\overline{6}$%, or $16\frac{2}{3}$%   **19.** 18.75%, or $18\frac{3}{4}$%

21. 81.25%, or $81\frac{1}{4}$%   **23.** 16%   **25.** 5%   **27.** 34%
29. 40%; 18%   **31.** 22%   **33.** 5%   **35.** 9%   **37.** $\frac{17}{20}$
39. $\frac{5}{8}$ **41.** $\frac{1}{3}$ **43.** $\frac{1}{6}$ **45.** $\frac{29}{400}$ **47.** $\frac{1}{125}$ **49.** $\frac{203}{800}$
51. $\frac{176}{225}$ **53.** $\frac{711}{1100}$ **55.** $\frac{3}{2}$ **57.** $\frac{13}{40,000}$ **59.** $\frac{1}{3}$ **61.** $\frac{2}{25}$
63. $\frac{3}{5}$ **65.** $\frac{1}{50}$ **67.** $\frac{7}{20}$ **69.** $\frac{47}{100}$
71.

FRACTION NOTATION	DECIMAL NOTATION	PERCENT NOTATION
$\frac{1}{8}$	0.125	12.5%, or $12\frac{1}{2}$%
$\frac{1}{6}$	$0.1\overline{6}$	$16.\overline{6}$%, or $16\frac{2}{3}$%
$\frac{1}{5}$	0.2	20%
$\frac{1}{4}$	0.25	25%
$\frac{1}{3}$	$0.\overline{3}$	$33.\overline{3}$%, or $33\frac{1}{3}$%
$\frac{3}{8}$	0.375	37.5%, or $37\frac{1}{2}$%
$\frac{2}{5}$	0.4	40%
$\frac{1}{2}$	0.5	50%

73.

FRACTION NOTATION	DECIMAL NOTATION	PERCENT NOTATION
$\frac{1}{2}$	0.5	50%
$\frac{1}{3}$	$0.\overline{3}$	$33.\overline{3}\%$, or $33\frac{1}{3}\%$
$\frac{1}{4}$	0.25	25%
$\frac{1}{6}$	$0.1\overline{6}$	$16.\overline{6}\%$, or $16\frac{2}{3}\%$
$\frac{1}{8}$	0.125	12.5%, or $12\frac{1}{2}\%$
$\frac{3}{4}$	0.75	75%
$\frac{5}{6}$	$0.8\overline{3}$	$83.\overline{3}\%$, or $83\frac{1}{3}\%$
$\frac{3}{8}$	0.375	37.5%, or $37\frac{1}{2}\%$

75. D_W **77.** 70 **78.** 5 **79.** 400 **80.** 18.75
81. 23.125 **82.** 25.5 **83.** 4.5 **84.** $8\frac{3}{4}$ **85.** $33\frac{1}{3}$
86. $37\frac{1}{2}$ **87.** $83\frac{1}{3}$ **88.** $20\frac{1}{2}$ **89.** $43\frac{1}{8}$ **90.** $62\frac{1}{6}$
91. $18\frac{3}{4}$ **92.** $7\frac{4}{9}$ **93.** $\frac{18}{17}$ **94.** $\frac{209}{10}$ **95.** $\frac{203}{2}$ **96.** $\frac{259}{8}$
97. $11.\overline{1}\%$ **99.** $257.\overline{46317}\%$ **101.** $0.01\overline{5}$
103. $1.04\overline{142857}$

Margin Exercises, Section 6.3, pp. 358–361

1. $12\% \times 50 = a$ **2.** $a = 40\% \times 60$ **3.** $45 = 20\% \times t$
4. $120\% \times y = 60$ **5.** $16 = n \times 40$ **6.** $b \times 84 = 10.5$
7. 6 **8.** \$35.20 **9.** 225 **10.** \$50 **11.** 40%
12. 12.5%

Calculator Corner, p. 362

1. 1.2 **2.** \$5.04 **3.** 48.64 **4.** \$22.40 **5.** 0.0112
6. \$29.70 **7.** 450 **8.** \$1000 **9.** 2.5% **10.** 12%

Exercise Set 6.3, p. 363

1. $y = 32\% \times 78$ **3.** $89 = a \times 99$ **5.** $13 = 25\% \times y$
7. 234.6 **9.** 45 **11.** \$18 **13.** 1.9 **15.** 78%
17. 200% **19.** 50% **21.** 125% **23.** 40 **25.** \$40
27. 88 **29.** 20 **31.** 6.25 **33.** \$846.60 **35.** D_W

37. $\frac{9}{100}$ **38.** $\frac{179}{100}$ **39.** $\frac{875}{1000}$, or $\frac{7}{8}$ **40.** $\frac{125}{1000}$, or $\frac{1}{8}$
41. $\frac{9375}{10,000}$, or $\frac{15}{16}$ **42.** $\frac{6875}{10,000}$, or $\frac{11}{16}$ **43.** 0.89 **44.** 0.07
45. 0.3 **46.** 0.017 **47.** \$800 (can vary); \$843.20
49. \$10,000 (can vary); \$10,400 **51.** \$1875

Margin Exercises, Section 6.4, pp. 366–368

1. $\dfrac{12}{100} = \dfrac{a}{50}$ **2.** $\dfrac{40}{100} = \dfrac{a}{60}$ **3.** $\dfrac{130}{100} = \dfrac{a}{72}$ **4.** $\dfrac{20}{100} = \dfrac{45}{b}$
5. $\dfrac{120}{100} = \dfrac{60}{b}$ **6.** $\dfrac{N}{100} = \dfrac{16}{40}$ **7.** $\dfrac{N}{100} = \dfrac{10.5}{84}$ **8.** \$225
9. 35.2 **10.** 6 **11.** 50 **12.** 30% **13.** 12.5%

Exercise Set 6.4, p. 369

1. $\dfrac{37}{100} = \dfrac{a}{74}$ **3.** $\dfrac{N}{100} = \dfrac{4.3}{5.9}$ **5.** $\dfrac{25}{100} = \dfrac{14}{b}$ **7.** 68.4
9. 462 **11.** 40 **13.** 2.88 **15.** 25% **17.** 102%
19. 25% **21.** 93.75% **23.** \$72 **25.** 90 **27.** 88
29. 20 **31.** 25 **33.** \$780.20 **35.** D_W **37.** 8
38. 4000 **39.** 8 **40.** 2074 **41.** 100 **42.** 15
43. $8.0\overline{4}$ **44.** $\frac{3}{16}$, or 0.1875 **45.** $\frac{43}{48}$ qt **46.** $\frac{1}{8}$ T
47. \$1134 (can vary); \$1118.64

Margin Exercises, Section 6.5, pp. 372–377

1. About 9.5% **2.** 14,560,000 workers **3. (a)** \$1475;
(b) \$38,350 **4. (a)** \$9218.75; **(b)** \$27,656.25
5. About 2.9% **6.** About 76.6%

Translating for Success, p. 378

1. J **2.** M **3.** N **4.** E **5.** G **6.** H **7.** O **8.** C
9. D **10.** B

Exercise Set 6.5, p. 379

1. About 13,247 wild horses **3.** 3 years: \$21,080;
5 years: \$17,680 **5.** Overweight: 176.4 million people;
obese: 73.5 million people **7.** Acid: 20.4 mL;
water: 659.6 mL **9.** About 1808 miles
11. About 39,867,000 people **13.** 36.4 correct;
3.6 incorrect **15.** 95 items **17.** 25%
19. 166; 156; 146; 140; 122 **21.** 8% **23.** 20%
25. About 86.5% **27.** \$30,030 **29.** \$16,174.50;
\$12,130.88 **31.** About 27% **33.** 34.375%, or $34\frac{3}{8}\%$
35. (a) 7.5%; **(b)** 879,675 **37.** 71% **39.** \$1560
41. 80% **43.** 98,775; 18.0% **45.** 799,065; 14.8%
47. 4,550,688; 38.1% **49.** \$36,400 **51.** 40% **53.** D_W
55. $2.\overline{27}$ **56.** 0.44 **57.** 3.375 **58.** $4.\overline{7}$ **59.** 0.92
60. $0.8\overline{3}$ **61.** 0.4375 **62.** 2.317 **63.** 3.4809
64. 0.675 **65.** About 5 ft 6 in. **67.** $83\frac{1}{3}\%$

Margin Exercises, Section 6.6, pp. 385–389

1. \$48.50; \$717.45 **2.** \$5.39; \$140.14 **3.** 6% **4.** \$999
5. \$5628 **6.** 12.5%, or $12\frac{1}{2}\%$ **7.** \$1675 **8.** \$180; \$360
9. 20%

Exercise Set 6.6, p. 390

1. $19.53 **3.** $2.65 **5.** $16.39; $361.39 **7.** 5%
9. 4% **11.** $2000 **13.** $800 **15.** $719.86 **17.** 5.6%
19. $2700 **21.** 5% **23.** $980 **25.** $5880 **27.** 12%
29. $420 **31.** $30; $270 **33.** $2.55; $14.45
35. $125; $112.50 **37.** 40%; $360 **39.** $30; 16.7%
41. $549; 36.4% **43.** ^{D}W **45.** ^{D}W **47.** 18 **48.** $\frac{22}{7}$
49. $265.62\overline{5}$ **50.** $1.11\overline{3}$ **51.** $0.\overline{5}$ **52.** $2.\overline{09}$ **53.** $0.91\overline{6}$
54. $1.\overline{857142}$ **55.** $2.\overline{142857}$ **56.** $1.58\overline{3}$
57. 4,030,000,000,000 **58.** 5,800,000 **59.** 42,700,000
60. 6,090,000,000,000 **61.** $2.69
63. He bought the plaques for 166\frac{2}{3}$ + $250, or 416\frac{2}{3}$, and sold them for $400, so he lost money.

Margin Exercises, Section 6.7, pp. 394–397

1. $301 **2.** $225.75 **3.** (a) $33.53; (b) $4833.53
4. $2376.20 **5.** $7690.94

Calculator Corner, p. 397

1. $16,357.18 **2.** $12,764.72

Exercise Set 6.7, p. 398

1. $8 **3.** $84 **5.** $113.52 **7.** $925 **9.** $671.88
11. (a) $147.95; (b) $10,147.95 **13.** (a) $80.14;
(b) $6580.14 **15.** (a) $46.03; (b) $5646.03 **17.** $441
19. $2802.50 **21.** $7853.38 **23.** $99,427.40
25. $4243.60 **27.** $28,225.00 **29.** $9270.87
31. $129,871.09 **33.** $4101.01 **35.** $1324.58 **37.** ^{D}W
39. reciprocals **40.** divisible by 6 **41.** additive
42. unit rate **43.** perimeter **44.** divisible by 3
45. prime **46.** proportional **47.** 9.38%

Margin Exercises, Section 6.8, pp. 402–406

1. (a) $97; (b) interest: $86.40; amount applied to principal: $10.60; (c) interest: $55.17; amount applied to principal: $41.83; (d) At 13.6%, the principal was decreased by $31.23 more than at the 21.3% rate. The interest at 13.6% is $31.23 less than at 21.3%. **2.** (a) Interest: $91.78; amount applied to principal: $229.22; (b) $58; (c) $4080
3. Interest: $843.94; amount applied to principal: $135.74
4. (a) Interest: $844.69; amount applied to principal: $498.64; (b) $88,799.40; (c) The Sawyers will pay $110,885.40 less in interest with the 15-yr loan than with the 30-yr loan.
5. (a) Interest: $701.25; amount applied to principal: $548.89; (b) $72,025.20; (c) The Sawyers will pay $16,774.20 less in interest with the 15-yr loan at 5$\frac{1}{2}$% than with the 15-yr loan at 6$\frac{5}{8}$%.

Exercise Set 6.8, p. 407

1. (a) $98; (b) interest: $86.56; amount applied to principal: $11.44; (c) interest: $51.20; amount applied to principal: $46.80; (d) At 12.6%, the principal is decreased by $35.36 more than at the 21.3% rate. The interest at 12.6% is $35.36 less than at 21.3%. **3.** (a) Interest: $125.14; amount applied to principal: $312.79; (b) $51.24; (c) $7991.60, $11,504, $3512.40 **5.** (a) Interest: $854.17; amount applied to principal: $155.61; (b) $199,520.80; (c) new principal: $163,844.39; interest: $853.36; amount applied to principal: $156.42 **7.** (a) Interest: $854.17; amount applied to principal: $552; (b) $89,110.60; (c) The Martinez family will pay $110,410.20 less in interest with the 15-yr loan than with the 30-yr loan. **9.** $99,917.71; $99,834.94 **11.** $99,712.04; $99,422.15 **13.** $149,882.75; $149,764.79 **15.** $199,382.07; $198,760.41
17. (a) $2395, $21,555; (b) $52.09, $401.97; (c) $239.88
19. (a) $595; $11,305; (b) interest: $87.61; amount applied to principal: $273.47; (c) $1693.88 **21.** ^{D}W **23.** ^{D}W
25. 17.5, or $\frac{35}{2}$ **26.** 28 **27.** 100 **28.** 56.25, or $\frac{225}{4}$
29. $\frac{66,875}{36}$, or approximately 1857.64 **30.** 787.69
31. 71.81 **32.** 17.5, or $\frac{35}{2}$ **33.** 56.25, or $\frac{225}{4}$
34. $\frac{66,875}{36}$, or approximately 1857.64

Concept Reinforcement, p. 410

1. True **2.** False **3.** True **4.** False

Summary and Review: Chapter 6, p. 410

1. 56% **2.** 1.7% **3.** 37.5% **4.** 33.$\overline{3}$%, or 33$\frac{1}{3}$%
5. 0.735 **6.** 0.065 **7.** $\frac{6}{25}$ **8.** $\frac{63}{1000}$
9. $30.6 = p \times 90$; 34% **10.** $63 = 84\% \times n$; 75
11. $y = 38\frac{1}{2}\% \times 168$; 64.68 **12.** $\frac{24}{100} = \frac{16.8}{b}$; 70
13. $\frac{42}{30} = \frac{N}{100}$; 140% **14.** $\frac{10.5}{100} = \frac{a}{84}$; 8.82
15. 223 students; 105 students **16.** 42% **17.** 2500 mL
18. 12% **19.** 93.15 **20.** $14.40 **21.** 5% **22.** 11%
23. $42; $308 **24.** $42.70; $262.30 **25.** $2940
26. Approximately 18.4% **27.** $36 **28.** (a) $394.52;
(b) $24,394.52 **29.** $121 **30.** $7727.26 **31.** $9504.80
32. (a) $129; (b) interest: $100.18; amount applied to principal: $28.82; (c) interest: $70.72; amount applied to principal: $58.28; (d) At 13.2%, the principal is decreased by $29.46 more than at the 18.7% rate. The interest at 13.2% is $29.46 less than at 18.7%.
33. ^{D}W No; the 10% discount was based on the original price rather than on the sale price.
34. ^{D}W A 40% discount is better. When successive discounts are taken, each is based on the previous discounted price rather than on the original price. A 20% discount followed by a 22% discount is the same as a 37.6% discount off the original price.
35. 19.5% increase **36.** 66$\frac{2}{3}$% **37.** $168

Test: Chapter 6, p. 413

1. [6.1b] 0.064 **2.** [6.1b] 38% **3.** [6.2a] 137.5%
4. [6.2b] $\frac{13}{20}$ **5.** [6.3a, b] $a = 40\% \cdot 55$; 22
6. [6.4a, b] $\frac{N}{100} = \frac{65}{80}$; 81.25% **7.** [6.5a] 400 passengers;
575 passengers **8.** [6.5a] About 539 at-bats

9. [6.5b] 50.$\overline{90}$%   **10.** [6.5a] 5.5%   **11.** [6.6a] $16.20; $340.20   **12.** [6.6b] $630   **13.** [6.6c] $40; $160
14. [6.7a] $8.52   **15.** [6.7a] $5356   **16.** [6.7b] $1110.39
17. [6.7b] $11,580.07   **18.** [6.5b] Registered nurses: 2.9, 26.1%; post-secondary teachers: 0.6, 37.5%; food preparation and service workers: 2.0, 20%; restaurant servers: 2.1, 0.4   **19.** [6.6c] $275, about 14.1%
20. [6.8a] $119,909.14; $119,817.72
21. [6.6b] $194,600   **22.** [6.6b], [6.7b] $2546.16

CHAPTER 7

Margin Exercises, Section 7.1, pp. 418–423

1. 75   **2.** 54.9   **3.** 81   **4.** 19.4   **5.** 37   **6.** 34 mpg
7. 2.5   **8.** 94   **9.** 17   **10.** 17   **11.** 91   **12.** $3700
13. 67.5   **14.** 45   **15.** 34, 67   **16.** No mode exists.
17. (a) 17 g; (b) 18 g; (c) 19 g
18. Wheat A: average stalk height ≈ 25.21 in.; wheat B: average stalk height ≈ 22.54 in.; wheat B is better.

Calculator Corner, p. 420

1. 285.5   **2.** 75; 54.9; 81; 19.4   **3.** 202.$\overline{3}$

Exercise Set 7.1, p. 424

1. Average: 21; median: 18.5; mode: 29
3. Average: 21; median: 20; modes: 5, 20
5. Average: 5.2; median: 5.7; mode: 7.4
7. Average: 239.5; median: 234; mode: 234
9. Average: 23.$\overline{8}$; median: 15; mode: 1   **11.** 31 mpg
13. 2.7   **15.** Average: $8.19; median: $8.49; mode: $6.99
17. 90   **19.** 263 days
21. Bulb A: average time = 1171.25 hr; bulb B: average time ≈ 1251.58 hr; bulb B is better   **23.** DW   **25.** 196
26. $\frac{4}{9}$ **27.** 1.96   **28.** 1.999396   **29.** 225.05
30. 126.0516   **31.** $\frac{3}{35}$ **32.** $\frac{14}{15}$ **33.** 118.75%
34. 68.75%   **35.** 51.2%   **36.** 97.81%   **37.** 182
39. 10 home runs   **41.** 58

Margin Exercises, Section 7.2, pp. 427–430

1. Zone (Men's Menu)   **2.** Both Ornish (Eat More, Weigh Less) and Zone (Men's Menu) have 17 servings of fruits and vegetables   **3.** Ornish (Eat More, Weigh Less)
4. About 43 g   **5.** About 24.5 g   **6.** 22 g
7. Average: about 9.3 g; median: 7 g; mode: 7 g
8. 20 calories   **9.** Yes   **10.** 560 mg   **11.** 24%
12. 14 g   **13.** 2100 rhinos   **14.** There are twelve times as many black rhinos as Sumatran rhinos, or 3300 more.
15. 3537 rhinos; answers may vary
16. 795 cups; answers may vary
17. 750 cups; answers may vary
18. 1830 cups; answers may vary

Exercise Set 7.2, p. 431

1. 483,612,200 mi   **3.** Neptune   **5.** All
7. 11 Earth diameters   **9.** Average: 27,884.$\overline{1}$ mi; median: 7926 mi; no mode exists   **11.** 92°   **13.** 108°
15. 3   **17.** 90° and higher   **19.** 30% and higher
21. 50%   **23.** 1940: 1976; 1980: 3849; 94.8%
25. 1920; 3186; 1266   **27.** 1.0 billion   **29.** 2070
31. 1650 and 1850   **33.** 3 billion; 75%   **35.** Africa
37. 475,000 gal   **39.** 325,000 gal   **41.** DW
43. Cabinets: $13,444; countertops: $4033.20; appliances: $2151.04; fixtures: $806.64
44. Cabinets: $3597.55; countertops: $1276.55; labor: $2901.25; flooring: $696.30   **45.** $\frac{6}{25}$ **46.** $\frac{9}{20}$
47. $\frac{6}{125}$ **48.** $\frac{8}{125}$ **49.** $\frac{531}{1000}$ **50.** $\frac{873}{1000}$ **51.** 1   **52.** $\frac{1}{50}$
53.

Coffee Consumption

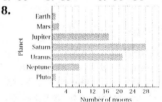

Margin Exercises, Section 7.3, pp. 436–441

1. About 77 million   **2.** NASCAR   **3.** NFL, NBA, and MLB
4. 60   **5.** 85+   **6.** 60–64   **7.** Yes
8.

9. Month 7, June   **10.** Months 1 and 2, December and January, months 4 and 5, March and April, months 6 and 7, May and June, and months 11 and 12, October and November
11. Month 2, January, and month 8, July   **12.** $900
13. 40 yr   **14.** $1300
15.

Exercise Set 7.3, p. 442

1. 190 calories **3.** 1 slice of chocolate cake with fudge frosting **5.** 1 cup of premium chocolate ice cream
7. About 120 calories **9.** About 920 calories
11. About 28 lb **13.** 1970: $11,000; 2002: $58,000; $47,000; 427% **15.** 1970: $6000; 2002: $25,000; $19,000; 317% **17.** $4000 **19.** $11,000
21.

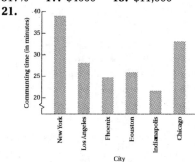

23. Indianapolis **25.** 28.73 min **27.** 1995 and 1996, 1996 and 1997, 1998 and 1999 **29.** 51% **31.** $3.9 billion
33. 30.4 yd **35.** 1988 and 1995
37.

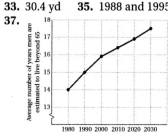

39. 25%0 **41.** 10.1% **43.** 1995 and 1996
45. About 308 murders **47.** 14.1% **49.** D_W
51. natural **52.** add; divide **53.** simple
54. marked price; rate of discount; discount; sale price
55. compound **56.** repeating **57.** distributive
58. commutative
59.

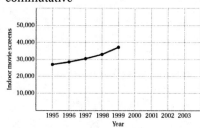

Using the line through the points for 1996 and 1998 (instead of a line through the point for 1999) probably gives more realistic estimates of the number of movie screens for the years 2000, 2001, and 2003. 2000: 37,500; 2001: 40,000; 2003: 44,500. Answers may vary.

Margin Exercises, Section 7.4, pp. 448–449

1. Spaying or neutering **2.** 87% **3.** $1122
4. 8% + 3%, or 11%

5.

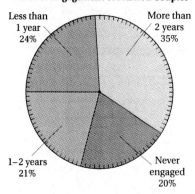

Times of Engagement of Married Couples

Translating for Success, p. 450

1. D **2.** B **3.** J **4.** K **5.** I **6.** F **7.** N **8.** E
9. L **10.** M

Exercise Set 7.4, p. 451

1. 17.1% **3.** About 613 students **5.** 86.1% **7.** Food
9. 14% **11.**

Holiday Baking: When Is It Done?

13.

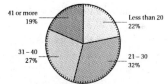

Weight Gain During Pregnancy

15.

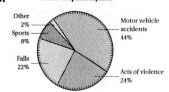

Causes of Spinal Injuries

17. D_W

Concept Reinforcement, p. 454

1. True **2.** False **3.** True **4.** True

Summary and Review: Chapter 7, p. 454

1. $32.25 **2.** $47.00 **3.** $20.95 **4.** $25.40 **5.** No
6. $19.75 **7.** 14,000 officers **8.** Los Angeles
9. Houston **10.** 12,500 **11.** 26 **12.** 11 and 17
13. 0.2 **14.** 700 and 800 **15.** $17 **16.** 20
17. $110.50; $107 **18.** 33 mpg **19.** 96

20. About 420 calories   **21.** About 440 calories
22. Big Bacon Classic   **23.** Plain Single   **24.** Plain Single
25. Chicken Club   **26.** About 50 calories
27. About 220 calories   **28.** Under 20   **29.** 12 accidents
30. 13 accidents per 100 drivers   **31.** 45–74
32. 11 accidents per 100 drivers   **33.** Under 20
34. 22%   **35.** 11%   **36.** 1600 travelers   **37.** 25%
38.

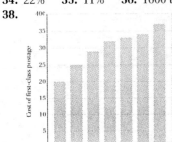

39.

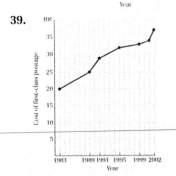

40. Battery A: average ≈ 43.04 hr; battery B:
average = 41.55 hr; battery A is better.   **41.** 38.5
42. 13.4   **43.** 1.55   **44.** 1840   **45.** $16.\overline{6}$ **46.** $321.\overline{6}$
47. 38.5   **48.** 14   **49.** 1.8   **50.** 1900   **51.** $17
52. 375   **53.** 3.1
54. ^{D}W The average, the median, and the mode are
"center points" that characterize a set of data. You might use
the average to find a center point that is midway between
the extreme values of the data. The median is a center point
that is in the middle of all the data. That is, there are as
many values less than the median than there are values
greater than the median. The mode is a center point that
represents the value or values that occur most frequently.
55. ^{D}W The equation could represent a person's average
income during a 4-yr period. Answers may vary.
56. $a = 316, b = 349$

Test: Chapter 7, p. 458

1. [7.2a] 179 lb   **2.** [7.2a] 111 lb   **3.** [7.2a] 5 ft, 3 in.;
medium frame   **4.** [7.2a] 5 ft, 11 in.; medium frame
5. [7.2b] Japan   **6.** [7.2b] United States
7. [7.2b] 800 pounds   **8.** [7.2b] 400 pounds
9. [7.1a] 49.5   **10.** [7.1a] 2.6   **11.** [7.1a] 15.5
12. [7.1b, c] 50.5; 52   **13.** [7.1b, c] 3; 1 and 3
14. [7.1b, c] 17.5; 17 and 18   **15.** [7.1a] 27 mpg
16. [7.1a] 76   **17.** [7.3c] 53%   **18.** [7.3c] 41%
19. [7.3c] 1967   **20.** [7.3c] 2006

21. [7.3b]

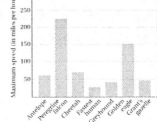

22. [7.2a], [7.3a] 197 mph   **23.** [7.2a], [7.3a] No; the
greyhound can run 14 mph faster than a human.
24. [7.2a], [7.3a] 89 mph   **25.** [7.2a], [7.3a] 61 mph
26. [7.4b]

27. [7.2a], [7.4a] Employee theft: $10.12 billion; shoplifting:
$7.521 billion; administrative error: $4.025 billion; vendor
fraud: $1.173 billion; other: $0.161 billion
28. [7.3b]

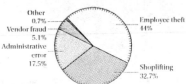

29. [7.3d]

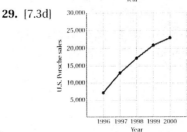

30. [7.1d] Bar A: average ≈ 8.417; bar B: average ≈ 8.417;
equal quality
31. [7.1a] 2.9   **32.** [7.1a, b] $a = 74, b = 111$

Cumulative Review: Chapters 1–7, p. 462

1. [4.3b] $46,600,000,000   **2.** [7.1a] 27 mpg
3. [1.1a] 5 hundreds   **4.** [1.9c] 128   **5.** [2.1a] 1, 2, 3, 4, 5,
6, 10, 12, 15, 20, 30, 60   **6.** [4.1d] 52.0   **7.** [3.4a] $\frac{33}{10}$
8. [4.3b] $2.10   **9.** [4.3b] $3,250,000,000,000
10. [5.3a] No   **11.** [3.5a] $6\frac{7}{10}$ **12.** [4.2a] 44.6351
13. [3.3a] $\frac{1}{3}$ **14.** [4.2b] 325.43   **15.** [3.6a] 15
16. [1.5a] 2,740,320   **17.** [2.7b] $\frac{9}{10}$ **18.** [3.4b] $4361\frac{1}{2}$
19. [5.3b] $9\frac{3}{5}$ **20.** [2.7c] $\frac{3}{4}$ **21.** [4.4b] 6.8
22. [1.7b] 15,312   **23.** [5.2b] 20.6 ¢/oz
24. [6.5a] 3324 students   **25.** [3.6c] $\frac{1}{4}$ yd   **26.** [2.6b] $\frac{3}{8}$ cup
27. [4.7a] 6.2 lb   **28.** [1.8a] 2572 billion kWh
29. [6.5a] 2.5%; 0.2%   **30.** [6.5b] About 4.1%

31. (a) [3.6c] 1870 sq yd; **(b)** [3.6c] 6400 sq yd; **(c)** [1.8a] 4530 sq yd **32.** [7.1a, b] $38.25; $38.25
33. [7.3b]

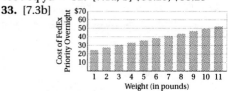

34. [7.3d]

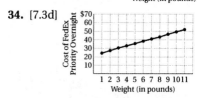

35. [3.2b], [3.3d] $\frac{1}{4}$ **36.** [5.4a] 1122 defective valves
37. [4.7a] $9.55 **38.** [6.6b] 7% **39.** [7.2a], [6.5a]
Clothing: $129.54; entertainment: $83.82; food: $83.82;
other: $83.82 **40.** [2.6b] $254; $127
41. [7.2a], [6.5a] Clothing: $44.064 billion;
entertainment: $28.512 billion;
food: $28.512 billion; other: $28.512 billion
42. [6.5b] 73% **43.** [6.5b], [7.1a] 12% decrease

CHAPTER 8

Margin Exercises, Section 8.1, pp. 466–469

1. 2 **2.** 3 **3.** $1\frac{1}{2}$ **4.** $2\frac{1}{2}$ **5.** 288 **6.** $8\frac{1}{2}$
7. 240,768 **8.** 6 **9.** $1\frac{5}{12}$ **10.** 8
11. $11\frac{2}{3}$, or $11.\overline{6}$ **12.** 5 **13.** 0.5
14. 288 **15.** 40,480 yd

Exercise Set 8.1, p. 470

1. 12 **3.** $\frac{1}{12}$ **5.** 5280 **7.** 108 **9.** 7 **11.** $1\frac{1}{2}$
13. 26,400 **15.** $5\frac{1}{4}$, or 5.25 **17.** $3\frac{1}{3}$ **19.** 37,488
21. $1\frac{1}{2}$ **23.** $1\frac{1}{4}$, or 1.25 **25.** 110 **27.** 2 **29.** 300
31. 30 **33.** $\frac{1}{36}$ **35.** 126,720 **37.** ᴰW **39.** $\frac{37}{400}$
40. $\frac{7}{8}$ **41.** $\frac{11}{40}$ **42.** $\frac{57}{100}$ **43.** 137.5%
44. $66.\overline{6}$%, or $66\frac{2}{3}$% **45.** 25% **46.** 43.75%
47. $\frac{373}{100,000}$; $\frac{100,000}{373}$ **48.** $\frac{29}{2000}$; $\frac{2000}{29}$ **49.** Length: 5400 in., or
450 ft; breadth: 900 in., or 75 ft; height: 540 in., or 45 ft

Margin Exercises, Section 8.2, pp. 473–477

1. 2 cm, or 20 mm **2.** 2.3 cm, or 23 mm **3.** 4.4 cm, or
44 mm **4.** cm **5.** km **6.** mm **7.** m **8.** cm
9. m **10.** 23,000 **11.** 400 **12.** 178 **13.** 9040
14. 7.814 **15.** 781.4 **16.** 0.967 **17.** 8,900,000
18. 6.78 **19.** 97.4 **20.** 0.1 **21.** 8.451

Exercise Set 8.2, p. 478

1. (a) 1000; **(b)** 0.001 **3. (a)** 10; **(b)** 0.1 **5. (a)** 0.01;
(b) 100 **7. (a)** 6700; **(b)** Substitute **9. (a)** 0.98;
(b) Multiply by 1 **11.** 8.921 **13.** 0.05666 **15.** 566,600

17. 4.77 **19.** 688 **21.** 0.1 **23.** 100,000 **25.** 142
27. 0.82 **29.** 450 **31.** 0.000024 **33.** 0.688 **35.** 230
37. 3.92 **39.** 180; 0.18 **41.** 278; 27.8 **43.** 48,440;
48.44 **45.** 4000; 400 **47.** 0.027; 0.00027 **49.** 442,000;
44,200 **51.** ᴰW **53.** 0.234 **54.** 0.0234 **55.** 13.8474
56. $80\frac{1}{2}$ **57.** 37.5% **58.** 62.5% **59.** $66.\overline{6}$%, or $66\frac{2}{3}$%
60. 20% **61.** 0.9 **62.** 0.108 **63.** 1.0 m **65.** 1.4 cm

Margin Exercises, Section 8.3, pp. 480–481

1. 91.4 **2.** 804.5 **3.** 1479.843 **4.** 913.912
5. 343.735 m **6.** 0.125

Exercise Set 8.3, p. 482

1. 100.65 **3.** 727.4394 **5.** 104.585 **7.** 289.62
9. 112.63 **11.** 9.14 **13.** 81.8896 **15.** 1250.061
17. 19.05 **19.** 1376.136 **21.** 0.51181
23.–33. Answers may vary, depending on the conversion
factor used.

	yd	cm	in.	m	mm
23.	0.2604	23.8	9.37006	0.238	238
25.	0.2361	21.59	$8\frac{1}{2}$	0.2159	215.9
27.	52.9934	4844	1907.0828	48.44	48,440
29.	4	365.6	144	3.656	3656
31.	0.000295	0.027	0.0106299	0.00027	0.27
33.	483.548	44,200	17,401.54	442	442,000

35. ᴰW **37.** 23,072,000,000,000 **38.** 25,100,000
39. 366,000,000 **40.** 585,000,000,000
41. 1 in. = 25.4 mm **43.** 21.3 mph

Margin Exercises, Section 8.4, pp. 484–488

1. 80 **2.** 4.32 **3.** 32,000 **4.** kg **5.** kg **6.** mg
7. g **8.** t **9.** 6200 **10.** 3.048 **11.** 77 **12.** 234.4
13. 6700 **14.** 0.001 **15.** 0.5 mg

Exercise Set 8.4, p. 489

1. 2000 **3.** 3 **5.** 64 **7.** 12,640 **9.** 0.1 **11.** 5
13. 26,000,000,000 lb **15.** 1000 **17.** 10
19. $\frac{1}{100}$, or 0.01 **21.** 1000 **23.** 10 **25.** 234,000
27. 5.2 **29.** 6.7 **31.** 0.0502 **33.** 8.492 **35.** 58.5
37. 800,000 **39.** 1000 **41.** 0.0034 **43.** 1000
45. 0.325 **47.** 125 mcg **49.** 0.875 mg; 875 mcg
51. 4 tablets **53.** 8 cc **55.** ᴰW **57.** $\frac{7}{20}$ **58.** $\frac{99}{100}$
59. $\frac{171}{200}$ **60.** $\frac{171}{500}$ **61.** $\frac{3}{8}$ **62.** $\frac{2}{3}$ **63.** $\frac{5}{6}$ **64.** $\frac{1}{6}$
65. 187,200 **66.** About 324 students **67.** $24.30
68. 12% **69.** 7500 sheets **70.** 46 test tubes, 2 cc left
over **71.** 144 packages **73. (a)** 109.134 g; **(b)** 9.104 g;
(c) Golden Jubilee: 3.85 oz; Hope: 0.321 oz

Margin Exercises, Section 8.5, pp. 493–495

1. 40 **2.** 20 **3.** mL **4.** mL **5.** L **6.** L **7.** 970
8. 8.99 **9.** 2.4 L **10. (a)** About 59.14 mL;
(b) about 0.059 L

Exercise Set 8.5, p. 496

1. 1000; 1000 **3.** 87,000 **5.** 0.049 **7.** 0.000401
9. 78,100 **11.** 320 **13.** 10 **15.** 32 **17.** 20
19. 14 **21.** 88

	gal	qt	pt	cups	oz
23.	1.125	4.5	9	18	144
25.	16	64	128	256	2048
27.	0.25	1	2	4	32
29.	0.1171875	0.46875	0.9375	1.875	15

	L	mL	cc	cm³
31.	2	2000	2000	2000
33.	64	64,000	64,000	64,000
35.	0.443	443	443	443

37. 2000 mL **39.** 0.32 L **41.** 59.14 mL **43.** 500 mL
45. 125 mL/hr **47.** 9 **49.** $\frac{1}{5}$ **51.** 6 **53.** 15
55. D_W **57.** 45.2% **58.** 99.9% **59.** 33.$\overline{3}$%, or $33\frac{1}{3}$%
60. 66.$\overline{6}$%, or $66\frac{2}{3}$% **61.** 55% **62.** 105% **63.** 88%
64. 8% **65.** $\frac{18.2}{79.3}; \frac{79.3}{18.2}$ **66.** $\frac{1}{4}; \frac{3}{4}$
67. 1.75 gal/week; 7.5 gal/month; 91.25 gal/year;
73,500,000 gal/day; 26,827,500,000 gal/year **69.** 0.21$\overline{3}$ oz

Margin Exercises, Section 8.6, pp. 499–501

1. 120 **2.** 1461 **3.** 1440 **4.** 1 **5.** 80°C **6.** 0°C
7. −20°C **8.** 80°F **9.** 100°F **10.** 50°F **11.** 176°F
12. 95°F **13.** 35°C **14.** 45°C

Calculator Corner, p. 501

1. 41°F **2.** 122°F **3.** 20°C **4.** 45°C

Exercise Set 8.6, p. 502

1. 24 **3.** 60 **5.** 365$\frac{1}{4}$ **7.** 0.05 **9.** 8.2 **11.** 6.5
13. 10.75 **15.** 336 **17.** 4.5 **19.** 56 **21.** 86,164.2 sec
23. 77°F **25.** 104°F **27.** 186.8°F **29.** 136.4°F
31. 35.6°F **33.** 41°F **35.** 5432°F **37.** 30°C
39. 55°C **41.** 81.$\overline{1}$°C **43.** 60°C **45.** 20°C **47.** 6.$\overline{6}$°C
49. 37°C **51. (a)** 136°F = 57.$\overline{7}$°C, 56$\frac{2}{3}$°C = 134°F;
(b) 2°F **53.** D_W **55.** compound **56.** ratio
57. median **58.** commission **59.** similar
60. mean **61.** composite **62.** subtrahend
63. About 0.03 yr **65.** About 31,688 yr **67.** 0.25

Margin Exercises, Section 8.7, pp. 505–506

1. 9 **2.** 45 **3.** 2880 **4.** 2.5 **5.** 3200 **6.** 1,000,000
7. 1 **8.** 28,800 **9.** 0.043 **10.** 0.678

Translating for Success, p. 507

1. E **2.** H **3.** O **4.** A **5.** G **6.** C **7.** M
8. I **9.** K **10.** N

Exercise Set 8.7, p. 508

1. 144 **3.** 640 **5.** $\frac{1}{144}$ **7.** 198 **9.** 396 **11.** 12,800
13. 27,878,400 **15.** 5 **17.** 1 **19.** $\frac{1}{640}$, or 0.0015625
21. 5,210,000 **23.** 140 **25.** 23.456 **27.** 0.085214
29. 2500 **31.** 0.4728 **33.** D_W **35.** $240 **36.** $212
37. (a) $484.11; **(b)** $15,984.11 **38. (a)** $209.59;
(b) $8709.59 **39. (a)** $220.93; **(b)** $6620.93
40. (a) $37.97; **(b)** $4237.97 **41.** 10.76 **43.** 1.67
45. 1876.8 m²

Concept Reinforcement, p. 510

1. False **2.** True **3.** True **4.** True **5.** False
6. False

Summary and Review: Chapter 8, p. 511

1. 2$\frac{2}{3}$ **2.** 30 **3.** 0.03 **4.** 0.004 **5.** 72 **6.** 400,000
7. 1$\frac{1}{6}$ **8.** 0.15 **9.** 218.8 **10.** 32.18 **11.** 10; 0.01
12. 305,000; 30,500 **13.** 112 **14.** 0.004 **15.** $\frac{4}{15}$, or 0.2$\overline{6}$
16. 0.464 **17.** 180 **18.** 4700 **19.** 16,140 **20.** 830
21. $\frac{1}{4}$, or 0.25 **22.** 0.04 **23.** 200 **24.** 30 **25.** 0.0007
26. 0.06 **27.** 1600 **28.** 400 **29.** 1.25 **30.** 50
31. 160 **32.** 7.5 **33.** 13.5 **34.** 60 **35.** 0.0302
36. 5.25 **37.** 6 mL **38.** 3000 mL **39.** 250 mcg
40. 80.6°F **41.** 23°F **42.** 20°C **43.** −12.$\overline{2}$°C
44. 36 **45.** 300,000 **46.** 14.375 **47.** 0.06
48. D_W The metric system was adopted by law in France in
about 1790, during the rule of Napoleon I.
49. D_W 1 gal = 128 oz, so 1 oz of water (as capacity) weighs
$\frac{8.3453}{128}$ lb, or about 0.0652 lb. An ounce of pennies weighs $\frac{1}{16}$ lb,
or 0.0625 lb. Thus an ounce of water (as capacity) weighs
more than an ounce of pennies. **50.** 17.66 sec

Test: Chapter 8, p. 513

1. [8.1a] 48 **2.** [8.1a] $\frac{1}{3}$ **3.** [8.2a] 6000 **4.** [8.2a] 0.87
5. [8.3a] 182.8 **6.** [8.3a] 1490.4 **7.** [8.2a] 5; 0.005
8. [8.2a] 1854.2; 185.42 **9.** [8.5a] 3.08 **10.** [8.5a] 240
11. [8.4a] 64 **12.** [8.4a] 8220 **13.** [8.4b] 3800
14. [8.4b] 0.4325 **15.** [8.4b] 2.2 **16.** [8.6a] 300
17. [8.6a] 360 **18.** [8.5a] 32 **19.** [8.5a] 1280
20. [8.5a] 40 **21.** [8.4c] 370 **22.** [8.6b] 35°C
23. [8.6b] 138.2°F **24.** [8.3a] 1.094; 100; 39.370; 1000
25. [8.3a] 36,377.2; 14,328; 363.772; 363,772
26. [8.5b] 2500 mL **27.** [8.4c] 1500 mcg
28. [8.5b] About 118.28 mL **29.** [8.7a] 1728
30. [8.7b] 0.0003 **31.** [8.3a] About 39.47 sec

CHAPTER 9

Margin Exercises, Section 9.1, pp. 516–518

1. 26 cm **2.** 46 in. **3.** 12 cm **4.** 17.5 yd **5.** $27\frac{5}{6}$ in.
6. 40 km **7.** 21 yd **8.** 31.2 km **9.** 70 ft; $346.50

Exercise Set 9.1, p. 519

1. 17 mm **3.** 15.25 in. **5.** 18 km **7.** 30 ft
9. 79.14 cm **11.** 88 ft **13.** 182 mm
15. 826 m; $6021.54 **17.** 122 cm **19.** (a) 228 ft;
(b) $1046.52 **21.** D_W **23.** $19.20 **24.** $96
25. 1000 **26.** 1331 **27.** 225 **28.** 484 **29.** 49
30. 64 **31.** 5% **32.** 11% **33.** 9 ft

Margin Exercises, Section 9.2, pp. 521–526

1. 8 cm² **2.** 56 km² **3.** $18\frac{3}{8}$ yd² **4.** 144 km²
5. 118.81 m² **6.** $12\frac{1}{4}$ yd² **7.** 43.8 cm² **8.** 12.375 km²
9. 96 m² **10.** 18.7 cm² **11.** 100 m² **12.** 88 cm²
13. 228 in²

Exercise Set 9.2, p. 527

1. 15 km² **3.** 1.4 in² **5.** $6\frac{1}{4}$ yd² **7.** 8100 ft² **9.** 50 ft²
11. 169.883 cm² **13.** $41\frac{2}{9}$ in² **15.** 484 ft²
17. 3237.61 km² **19.** $28\frac{57}{64}$ yd² **21.** 32 cm² **23.** 60 in²
25. 104 ft² **27.** 45.5 in² **29.** 8.05 cm² **31.** 297 cm²
33. 7 m² **35.** 1197 m² **37.** (a) About 8473 ft²;
(b) about $102 **39.** 630.36 ft² **41.** (a) 819.75 ft²;
(b) 10 gal; (c) $179.50 **43.** 80 cm² **45.** 675 cm²
47. 21 cm² **49.** 852.04 ft² **51.** D_W **53.** 234
54. 230 **55.** 336 **56.** 24 **57.** 0.724 **58.** 0.0724
59. 2520 **60.** 6 **61.** 28 **62.** $22\frac{1}{2}$ **63.** 12
64. 46,252.8 **65.** $33,597.91 **66.** $413,458.31
67. $641,566.26 **68.** $684,337.34 **69.** 16,914 in²

Margin Exercises, Section 9.3, pp. 532–536

1. 9 in. **2.** 5 ft **3.** 62.8 m **4.** 88 m **5.** 34.296 yd
6. $78\frac{4}{7}$ km² **7.** 339.62 cm² **8.** 12-ft–diameter flower
bed, by about 13.04 ft²

Exercise Set 9.3, p. 537

1. 14 cm; 44 cm; 154 cm² **3.** $1\frac{1}{2}$ in.; $4\frac{5}{7}$ in.; $1\frac{43}{56}$ in²
5. 16 ft; 100.48 ft; 803.84 ft² **7.** 0.7 cm; 4.396 cm;
1.5386 cm² **9.** 3 cm; 18.84 cm; 28.26 cm² **11.** 153.86 ft²
13. 2.5 cm; 1.25 cm; 4.90625 cm² **15.** 3.454 ft
17. 65.94 yd² **19.** 45.68 ft **21.** 26.84 yd **23.** 45.7 yd
25. 100.48 m² **27.** 6.9972 cm² **29.** 64.4214 in²
31. D_W **33.** 16 **34.** 289 **35.** 125 **36.** 64
37. 543 **38.** 0.00543 **39.** 41.01% **40.** $730
41. 10 cans **42.** 5 lb **43.** 3.1416
45. 3d; πd; circumference of one ball, since $\pi > 3$

Margin Exercises, Section 9.4, pp. 541–545

1. 12 cm³ **2.** 3087 in³ **3.** 128 ft³ **4.** 785 ft³
5. 67,914 m³ **6.** $91,989\frac{1}{3}$ ft³ **7.** 38.77272 cm³
8. 1695.6 m³ **9.** 528 in³ **10.** $83.7\overline{3}$ mm³

Calculator Corner, p. 544

1. Left to the student **2.** Left to the student

Exercise Set 9.4, p. 546

1. 768 cm³ **3.** 45 in³ **5.** 75 m³ **7.** $357\frac{1}{2}$ yd³
9. 803.84 in³ **11.** 353.25 cm³ **13.** 41,580,000 yd³
15. $4,186,666\frac{2}{3}$ in³ **17.** 124.72 m³ **19.** $1950\frac{101}{168}$ ft³
21. 113,982 ft³ **23.** 24.64 cm³ **25.** 4747.68 cm³
27. 367.38 m³ **29.** 143.72 cm³ **31.** 32,993,441,150 mi³
33. 646.74 cm³ **35.** 61,600 cm³ **37.** 5832 yd³
39. D_W **41.** 396 **42.** 3 **43.** 14 **44.** 253,440
45. 12 **46.** 335,808 **47.** 24 **48.** 14 **49.** 0.566
50. 13,400 **51.** About 57,480 in³ **53.** 9.425 L
55. The diameter of the earth at the equator is about
7930 mi. The diameter of the earth between the north and
south poles is about 7917 mi. If we use the average of these
two diameters (7923.5 mi), the volume of the earth is
$\frac{4}{3} \cdot \pi \cdot \left(\frac{7923.5}{2}\right)^3$, or about 260,000,000,000 mi³. **57.** 0.331 m³

Margin Exercises, Section 9.5, pp. 551–556

1. Angle DEF, angle FED, $\angle DEF$, $\angle FED$, or $\angle E$
2. Angle PQR, angle RQP, $\angle PQR$, $\angle RQP$, or $\angle Q$ **3.** 127°
4. 33° **5.** Right **6.** Acute **7.** Obtuse **8.** Straight
9. $\angle 1$ and $\angle 2$; $\angle 1$ and $\angle 4$; $\angle 2$ and $\angle 3$; $\angle 3$ and $\angle 4$
10. 45° **11.** 72° **12.** 5°
13. $\angle 1$ and $\angle 2$; $\angle 1$ and $\angle 4$; $\angle 2$ and $\angle 3$; $\angle 3$ and $\angle 4$
14. 142° **15.** 23° **16.** 90° **17.** (a) $\triangle ABC$;
(b) $\triangle ABC$, $\triangle MPN$; (c) $\triangle DEF$, $\triangle GHI$, $\triangle JKL$, $\triangle QRS$
18. Yes **19.** No **20.** (a) $\triangle DEF$; (b) $\triangle GHI$, $\triangle QRS$;
(c) $\triangle ABC$, $\triangle MPN$, $\triangle JKL$ **21.** 180° **22.** 64°

Exercise Set 9.5, p. 557

1. Angle GHI, angle IHG, $\angle GHI$, $\angle IHG$, or $\angle H$ **3.** 10°
5. 180° **7.** 130° **9.** Obtuse **11.** Acute **13.** Straight
15. Obtuse **17.** Acute **19.** Obtuse **21.** 79°
23. 23° **25.** 32° **27.** 61° **29.** 177° **31.** 41°
33. 95° **35.** 78° **37.** Scalene; obtuse **39.** Scalene;
right **41.** Equilateral; acute **43.** Scalene; obtuse
45. 46° **47.** 120° **49.** D_W **51.** three **52.** parallel
53. gram **54.** prime **55.** angle **56.** cents, dollars
57. perimeter **58.** multiplicative, additive
59. $m\angle 2 = 67.13°$; $m\angle 3 = 33.07°$; $m\angle 4 = 79.8°$;
$m\angle 5 = 67.13°$ **61.** $m\angle ACB = 50°$; $m\angle CAB = 40°$;
$m\angle EBC = 50°$; $m\angle EBA = 40°$; $m\angle AEB = 100°$;
$m\angle ADB = 50°$

Margin Exercises, Section 9.6, pp. 560–563

1. 81　**2.** 100　**3.** 121　**4.** 144　**5.** 169　**6.** 196
7. 225　**8.** 256　**9.** 289　**10.** 324　**11.** 400　**12.** 625
13. 3　**14.** 4　**15.** 11　**16.** 10　**17.** 9　**18.** 8
19. 18　**20.** 20　**21.** 15　**22.** 13　**23.** 1　**24.** 0
25. 2.236　**26.** 8.832　**27.** 12.961　**28.** $c = 13$
29. $a = \sqrt{75}$; $a \approx 8.660$　**30.** $b = \sqrt{120}$; $b \approx 10.954$
31. $a = \sqrt{175}$; $a \approx 13.229$　**32.** $\sqrt{424}$ ft ≈ 20.6 ft

Calculator Corner, p. 561

1. 6.6　**2.** 9.7　**3.** 19.8　**4.** 17.3　**5.** 24.9　**6.** 24.5
7. 121.2　**8.** 115.6　**9.** 16.2　**10.** 85.4

Translating for Success, p. 564

1. K　**2.** G　**3.** B　**4.** H　**5.** O　**6.** M　**7.** E
8. A　**9.** D　**10.** I

Exercise Set 9.6, p. 565

1. 10　**3.** 21　**5.** 25　**7.** 19　**9.** 23　**11.** 100
13. 6.928　**15.** 2.828　**17.** 4.243　**19.** 2.449
21. 3.162　**23.** 8.660　**25.** 14　**27.** 13.528
29. $c = \sqrt{34}$; $c \approx 5.831$　**31.** $c = \sqrt{98}$; $c \approx 9.899$
33. $a = 5$　**35.** $b = 8$　**37.** $c = 26$　**39.** $b = 12$
41. $b = \sqrt{1023}$; $b \approx 31.984$　**43.** $c = 5$
45. $\sqrt{250}$ m ≈ 15.8 m　**47.** $\sqrt{8450}$ ft ≈ 91.9 ft
49. $h = \sqrt{500}$ ft ≈ 22.4 ft
51. $\sqrt{211,200,000}$ ft $\approx 14,532.7$ ft　**53.** $\sqrt{832}$ ft ≈ 28.8 ft
55. **D**w　**57.** 1000　**58.** 100　**59.** 100,000　**60.** 10,000
61. $208　**62.** $11.25　**63.** $115.02　**64.** $994,274.04
65. $1,686,435.46　**67.** The areas are the same.
69. Length: 36.6 in.; width: 20.6 in.

Concept Reinforcement, p. 569

1. False　**2.** True　**3.** True　**4.** False　**5.** True
6. False

Summary and Review: Chapter 9, p. 570

1. 23 m　**2.** 4.4 m　**3.** 228 ft; 2808 ft²　**4.** 36 ft; 81 ft²
5. 17.6 cm; 12.6 cm²　**6.** 60 cm²　**7.** 35 mm²
8. 22.5 m²　**9.** 29.64 cm²　**10.** 88 m²　**11.** $145\frac{5}{9}$ in²
12. 840 ft²　**13.** 8 m　**14.** $\frac{14}{11}$ in., or $1\frac{3}{11}$ in.　**15.** 14 ft
16. 20 cm　**17.** 50.24 m　**18.** 8 in.　**19.** 200.96 m²
20. $5\frac{1}{11}$ in²　**21.** 1038.555 ft²　**22.** 93.6 m³
23. 193.2 cm³　**24.** 31,400 ft³　**25.** 33.493 cm³
26. 4.71 in³　**27.** 942 cm³　**28.** 26.28 ft²; 20.28 ft
29. 54°　**30.** 180°　**31.** 140°　**32.** 90°　**33.** Acute
34. Straight　**35.** Obtuse　**36.** Right　**37.** 49°
38. 136°　**39.** 60°　**40.** Scalene　**41.** Right　**42.** 8
43. 9.110　**44.** $c = \sqrt{850}$; $c \approx 29.155$
45. $b = \sqrt{51}$; $b \approx 7.141$　**46.** $c = \sqrt{89}$ ft; $c \approx 9.434$ ft
47. $a = \sqrt{76}$ cm; $a \approx 8.718$ cm　**48.** About 28.8 ft
49. About 44.7 ft　**50.** About 85.9 ft

51. **D**w See the volume formulas listed at the beginning of the Summary and Review Exercises for Chapter 9.
52. **D**w Volume of two spheres, each with radius r: $2\left(\frac{4}{3}\pi r^3\right) = \frac{8}{3}\pi r^3$; volume of one sphere with radius $2r$: $\frac{4}{3}\pi(2r)^3 = \frac{32}{3}\pi r^3$. The volume of the sphere with radius $2r$ is four times the volume of the two spheres, each with radius r: $\frac{32}{3}\pi r^3 = 4 \cdot \frac{8}{3}\pi r^3$.　**53.** 100 ft²
54. 7.83998704 m²　**55.** 42.05915 cm²

Test: Chapter 9, p. 574

1. [9.1a], [9.2a] 32.82 cm; 65.894 cm²
2. [9.1a], [9.2a] $19\frac{1}{2}$ in.; $23\frac{49}{64}$ in²　**3.** [9.2b] 25 cm²
4. [9.2b] 12 m²　**5.** [9.2b] 18 ft²　**6.** [9.3a] $\frac{1}{4}$ in.
7. [9.3a] 9 cm　**8.** [9.3b] $\frac{11}{14}$ in.　**9.** [9.3c] 254.34 cm²
10. [9.3d] 65.46 km; 103.815 km²　**11.** [9.4a] 84 cm³
12. [9.4e] 420 in³　**13.** [9.4b] 1177.5 ft³
14. [9.4c] 4186.$\overline{6}$ yd³　**15.** [9.4d] 113.04 cm³
16. [9.5a] 90°　**17.** [9.5a] 35°　**18.** [9.5a] 180°
19. [9.5a] 113°　**20.** [9.5b] Right　**21.** [9.5b] Acute
22. [9.5b] Straight　**23.** [9.5b] Obtuse　**24.** [9.5e] 35°
25. [9.5d] Isosceles　**26.** [9.5d] Obtuse
27. [9.5c] Complement: 25°; supplement: 115°
28. [9.6a] 15　**29.** [9.6b] 9.327　**30.** [9.6c] $c = 40$
31. [9.6c] $b = \sqrt{60}$; $b \approx 7.746$　**32.** [9.6c] $c = \sqrt{2}$; $c \approx 1.414$　**33.** [9.6c] $b = \sqrt{51}$; $b \approx 7.141$
34. [9.6d] About 15.8 m　**35.** [8.1a], [9.2a] 2 ft²
36. [8.1a], [9.2b] 1.875 ft²　**37.** [8.1a], [9.4a] 0.65 ft³
38. [8.1a], [9.4d] 0.033 ft³　**39.** [8.1a], [9.4b] 0.055 ft³

Cumulative Review: Chapters 1–9, p. 577

1. [4.3b] 1,500,000　**2.** [8.1a], [8.3a] $437\frac{1}{3}$ yd; about 400 m
3. [7.3c] 236 in 1993 and 1995　**4.** [7.3c] 258 in 2000
5. [7.1a, b, c] Average: 243.375; median: 239.5; mode: 236
6. [7.1a] 249.5　**7.** [7.1a] 237.25; the average over the years 1993–1996 is 12.25 lower than the average over the years 1997–2000.　**8.** [6.5b] About 8.4%
9. [8.5b] 56 mg　**10.** [9.4e] 93,750 lb　**11.** [3.5a] $4\frac{1}{6}$
12. [4.5c] 49.2　**13.** [4.2b] 87.52　**14.** [1.6b] 1234
15. [1.9d] 2　**16.** [1.9c] 1565　**17.** [4.1b] $\frac{1209}{1000}$
18. [6.2b] $\frac{17}{100}$　**19.** [3.3b] <　**20.** [2.5c] =　**21.** [8.4a] $\frac{3}{8}$
22. [8.6b] 59　**23.** [8.5a] 87　**24.** [8.6a] $\frac{3}{20}$　**25.** [8.7a] 27
26. [8.2a] 0.17　**27.** [8.4c] 2.437　**28.** [8.3a] 8870.01
29. [8.5a] 9.51　**30.** [5.3b] $14\frac{2}{5}$　**31.** [5.3b] $4\frac{2}{7}$
32. [4.4b] 113.4　**33.** [3.3c] $\frac{1}{8}$　**34.** [9.1a], [9.2b] 380 cm; 5500 cm²　**35.** [9.1a], [9.2b] 32.3 ft; 56.55 ft²
36. [9.3a, c] 70 in.; 3850 in²
37. [9.4c] 179,666$\frac{2}{3}$ in³　**38.** [7.1a] 99
39. [1.8a] 528 million pets　**40.** [6.7a] $84
41. [6.7b] $22,376.03　**42.** [9.6d] 17 m　**43.** [6.6a] 6%
44. [3.5c] $2\frac{1}{8}$ yd　**45.** [4.7a] $37.42
46. [5.2b] The 8-qt box　**47.** [2.6b] $\frac{7}{20}$ km　**48.** [9.5e] 30°
49. [9.5d] Isosceles　**50.** [9.5d] Obtuse
51. [9.3c] Area of a circle of radius 4 ft: $16 \cdot \pi$ ft²;
[9.2a] Area of a square of side 4 ft: 16 ft²;
[9.3b] Circumference of a circle of radius 4 ft: $8 \cdot \pi$ ft;
[9.4d] Volume of a cone with radius of base 4 ft and height

8 ft: $\frac{128}{3} \cdot \pi$ ft^3; [9.2a] Area of a rectangle of length 8 ft and width 4 ft: 32 ft^2; [9.2b] Area of a triangle with base 4 ft and height 8 ft: 16 ft^2; [9.4c] Volume of a sphere of radius 4 ft: $\frac{4^4}{3} \cdot \pi$ ft^3; [9.4b] Volume of a right circular cylinder with radius of base 4 ft and height 8 ft: 128 $\cdot \pi$ ft^3; [9.1a] Perimeter of a square of side 4 ft: 16 ft; [9.1a] Perimeter of a rectangle of length 8 ft and width 4 ft: 24 ft   **52.** [8.1a], [9.4e] 272 ft^3 **53.** [8.1a], [9.4b] 94,200 ft^3 **54.** [8.1a], [9.4a] 1.342 ft^3 **55.** [9.4b, c] 1204.260429 ft^3; about 22,079,692.8 ft, or 4181.76 mi

CHAPTER 10

Margin Exercises, Section 10.1, pp. 583–587

1. 8; −5   **2.** 125; −50   **3.** The integer −3 corresponds to the decrease in the stock value.
4. −10; 148   **5.** −120; 50; −80
6.

7.

8.

9. −0.375   **10.** −0.5$\overline{4}$ **11.** 1.$\overline{3}$ **12.** <   **13.** <
14. >   **15.** >   **16.** >   **17.** <   **18.** <   **19.** >
20. 8   **21.** 0   **22.** 9   **23.** $\frac{2}{3}$ **24.** 5.6

Exercise Set 10.1, p. 588

1. −34,000,000   **3.** 24; −2   **5.** 950,000,000; −460
7. −34; 15   **9.**

11.

13. −0.875   **15.** 0.8$\overline{3}$ **17.** 1.1$\overline{6}$ **19.** 0.$\overline{6}$ **21.** −0.5
23. −8.28   **25.** >   **27.** <   **29.** <   **31.** <   **33.** >
35. <   **37.** >   **39.** <   **41.** <   **43.** <   **45.** 3
47. 18   **49.** 325   **51.** 3.625   **53.** $\frac{2}{3}$ **55.** $\frac{0}{4}$, or 0
57. D$_W$ **59.** 2 · 3 · 3 · 3, or 2 · 3^3
60. 2 · 2 · 2 · 2 · 2 · 2 · 3, or 2^6 · 3   **61.** 2 · 3 · 17
62. 2 · 2 · 5 · 13, or 2^2 · 5 · 13
63. 2 · 2 · 2 · 2 · 3 · 3 · 3, or 2^5 · 3^3
64. 2 · 2 · 3 · 3 · 13, or 2^2 · 3^2 · 13   **65.** 18   **66.** 72
67. 96   **68.** 72   **69.** 1344   **70.** 252   **71.** >   **73.** =
75. −100, −8$\frac{7}{8}$, −8$\frac{5}{8}$, −$\frac{67}{8}$, −5, 0, 1^7, |3|, $\frac{14}{4}$, 4, |−6|, 7

Margin Exercises, Section 10.2, pp. 590–593

1. −3   **2.** −3   **3.** −5   **4.** 4   **5.** 0   **6.** −2   **7.** −11
8. −12   **9.** 2   **10.** −4   **11.** −2   **12.** 0   **13.** −22
14. 3   **15.** 0.53   **16.** 2.3   **17.** −7.7   **18.** −6.2
19. −$\frac{2}{9}$ **20.** −$\frac{19}{20}$ **21.** −58   **22.** −56   **23.** −14
24. −12   **25.** 4   **26.** −8.7   **27.** 7.74   **28.** $\frac{8}{9}$ **29.** 0

30. −12   **31.** −14; 14   **32.** −1; 1   **33.** 19; −19
34. 1.6; −1.6   **35.** −$\frac{2}{3}$; $\frac{2}{3}$ **36.** $\frac{9}{8}$; −$\frac{9}{8}$ **37.** 4   **38.** 13.4
39. 0   **40.** −$\frac{1}{4}$

Calculator Corner, p. 593

1. 2   **2.** 13   **3.** −15   **4.** −8   **5.** −3.3   **6.** −13.4

Exercise Set 10.2, p. 594

1. −7   **3.** −4   **5.** 0   **7.** −8   **9.** −7   **11.** −27
13. 0   **15.** −42   **17.** 0   **19.** 0   **21.** 3   **23.** −9
25. 7   **27.** 0   **29.** 45   **31.** −1.8   **33.** −8.1   **35.** −$\frac{1}{5}$
37. −$\frac{8}{7}$ **39.** −$\frac{3}{8}$ **41.** −$\frac{29}{35}$ **43.** −$\frac{11}{15}$ **45.** −6.3
47. $\frac{7}{16}$ **49.** 39   **51.** 50   **53.** −1093   **55.** −24
57. 26.9   **59.** −9   **61.** $\frac{14}{3}$ **63.** −65   **65.** $\frac{5}{3}$ **67.** 14
69. −10   **71.** D$_W$ **73.** 357.5 ft^2 **74.** 45.51 ft^2
75. 54,756 mi^2 **76.** 1.4196 mm^2 **77.** 66.97 ft^2
78. 7976.1 m^2 **79.** All positive   **81.** −640,979
83. Negative

Margin Exercises, Section 10.3, pp. 596–598

1. −10   **2.** 3   **3.** −5   **4.** −1   **5.** 2   **6.** −4   **7.** −2
8. −11   **9.** 4   **10.** −2   **11.** −6   **12.** −16   **13.** 7.1
14. 3   **15.** 0   **16.** $\frac{3}{2}$ **17.** Three minus eleven; −8
18. Twelve minus five; 7   **19.** Negative twelve minus negative nine; −3   **20.** Negative twelve point four minus ten point nine; −23.3   **21.** Negative four-fifths minus negative four-fifths; 0   **22.** −9   **23.** −$\frac{6}{5}$ **24.** 12.7
25. 214°F higher

Exercise Set 10.3, p. 599

1. −4   **3.** −7   **5.** −6   **7.** 0   **9.** −4   **11.** −7
13. −6   **15.** 0   **17.** 11   **19.** −14   **21.** 5   **23.** −7
25. −5   **27.** −3   **29.** −23   **31.** −68   **33.** −73
35. 116   **37.** −2.8   **39.** −$\frac{1}{4}$ **41.** $\frac{1}{12}$ **43.** −$\frac{17}{12}$ **45.** $\frac{1}{8}$
47. 19.9   **49.** −9   **51.** −0.01   **53.** −2.7   **55.** −3.53
57. −$\frac{1}{2}$ **59.** $\frac{6}{7}$ **61.** −$\frac{41}{30}$ **63.** −$\frac{1}{156}$ **65.** 37
67. −62   **69.** 6   **71.** 107   **73.** 219   **75.** Down 3 ft
77. −3°   **79.** 20,602 ft   **81.** −$85   **83.** 100°F
85. D$_W$ **87.** 96.6 cm^2 **88.** 2 · 3 · 5 · 5 · 5, or 2 · 3 · 5^3
89. 108   **90.** 125.44 km^2 **91.** 64   **92.** 125
93. 8 cans   **94.** 288 oz   **95.** True   **97.** True
99. True   **101.** True

Margin Exercises, Section 10.4, pp. 602–603

1. 20; 10; 0; −10; −20; −30   **2.** −18   **3.** −100   **4.** −80
5. −$\frac{5}{9}$ **6.** −30.033   **7.** −$\frac{7}{10}$ **8.** −10; 0; 10; 20; 30
9. 12   **10.** 32   **11.** 35   **12.** $\frac{20}{63}$ **13.** $\frac{2}{3}$ **14.** 13.455
15. −30   **16.** 30   **17.** −32   **18.** −$\frac{8}{3}$ **19.** −30
20. −30.75   **21.** −$\frac{5}{3}$ **22.** 120   **23.** −120   **24.** 6

Exercise Set 10.4, p. 604

1. -16 **3.** -24 **5.** -72 **7.** 16   **9.** 42   **11.** -120
13. -238 **15.** 1200   **17.** 98   **19.** -12.4 **21.** 24
23. 21.7   **25.** $-\frac{2}{5}$ **27.** $\frac{1}{12}$ **29.** -17.01 **31.** $-\frac{5}{12}$
33. 420   **35.** $\frac{2}{7}$ **37.** -60 **39.** 150   **41.** $-\frac{2}{45}$
43. 1911   **45.** 50.4   **47.** $\frac{10}{189}$ **49.** -960 **51.** 17.64
53. $-\frac{5}{784}$ **55.** -756 **57.** -720 **59.** $-30,240$
61. **D**W   **63.** isosceles   **64.** acute
65. complementary   **66.** simple   **67.** unit
68. mode   **69.** rectangle   **70.** square root
71. **(a)** One must be negative and one must be positive.
(b) Either or both must be zero. **(c)** Both must be negative
or both must be positive.

Margin Exercises, Section 10.5, pp. 606–611

1. -2 **2.** 5   **3.** -3 **4.** 9   **5.** -6 **6.** $-\frac{30}{7}$ **7.** Not
defined   **8.** 0   **9.** $\frac{3}{2}$ **10.** $-\frac{4}{5}$ **11.** $-\frac{1}{3}$ **12.** -5
13. $\frac{1}{5.78}$ **14.** $-\frac{7}{2}$
15.

NUMBER	OPPOSITE	RECIPROCAL
$\frac{2}{3}$	$-\frac{2}{3}$	$\frac{3}{2}$
$-\frac{5}{4}$	$\frac{5}{4}$	$-\frac{4}{5}$
0	0	Undefined
1	-1	1
-4.5	4.5	$-\frac{1}{4.5}$

16. $\frac{4}{5}\cdot\left(-\frac{5}{3}\right)$ **17.** $5\cdot\left(-\frac{1}{8}\right)$ **18.** $-10\cdot\left(\frac{1}{7}\right)$ **19.** $-\frac{2}{3}\cdot\frac{7}{4}$
20. $-5\cdot\left(\frac{1}{7}\right)$ **21.** $-\frac{20}{21}$ **22.** $-\frac{12}{5}$ **23.** $\frac{16}{7}$ **24.** -7
25. $-3.4°$F per minute   **26.** -1237 **27.** 8   **28.** 381
29. -12

Translating for Success, p. 612

1. I   **2.** C   **3.** F   **4.** L   **5.** B   **6.** O   **7.** A   **8.** D
9. H   **10.** M

Exercise Set 10.5, p. 613

1. -6 **3.** -13 **5.** -2 **7.** 4   **9.** -8 **11.** 2
13. -12 **15.** -8 **17.** Not defined   **19.** -9 **21.** $-\frac{7}{15}$
23. $\frac{1}{13}$ **25.** $-\frac{9}{8}$ **27.** $\frac{5}{3}$ **29.** $\frac{9}{14}$ **31.** $\frac{9}{64}$ **33.** -2
35. $\frac{11}{13}$ **37.** -16.2 **39.** Not defined   **41.** $-54°$C
43. $12.71   **45.** 32 m below sea level   **47.** 44.3%
49. -5.1% **51.** -7 **53.** -7 **55.** -334 **57.** 14
59. 1880   **61.** 12   **63.** 8   **65.** -86 **67.** 37   **69.** -1
71. -10 **73.** -67 **75.** -7988 **77.** -3000 **79.** 60
81. 1   **83.** 10   **85.** $-\frac{13}{45}$ **87.** $-\frac{4}{3}$ **89.** **D**W
91. $2\cdot2\cdot2\cdot2\cdot2\cdot2\cdot3\cdot5$, or $2^6\cdot3\cdot5$
92. $5\cdot5\cdot41$, or $5^2\cdot41$ **93.** 665   **94.** 320   **95.** 1710

96. 4%
97.

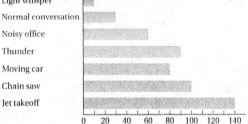

99. -159 **101.** Negative   **103.** Negative

Concept Reinforcement, p. 616

1. True   **2.** False   **3.** True   **4.** True   **5.** False
6. True

Summary and Review: Chapter 10, p. 616

1. -45; 72   **2.** 38   **3.** 7.3   **4.** $\frac{5}{2}$ **5.** -0.2 **6.** -1.25
7. $-0.8\overline{3}$ **8.** $-0.41\overline{6}$ **9.** $-0.\overline{27}$
10.
11.
12. $<$ **13.** $>$ **14.** $>$ **15.** $<$ **16.** -3.8 **17.** $\frac{3}{4}$
18. 34   **19.** 5   **20.** $\frac{8}{3}$ **21.** $-\frac{1}{7}$ **22.** -10 **23.** -3
24. $-\frac{7}{12}$ **25.** -4 **26.** -5 **27.** 4   **28.** $-\frac{7}{5}$
29. -7.9 **30.** 54   **31.** -9.18 **32.** $-\frac{2}{7}$ **33.** -210
34. -7 **35.** -3 **36.** $\frac{3}{4}$ **37.** 40.4   **38.** -62 **39.** -5
40. 2   **41.** -180 **42.** 8-yd gain   **43.** $-\$130$
44. $4.64 per share   **45.** $18.95
46. **D**W Yes; the numbers 1 and -1 are their own
reciprocals: $1\cdot1=1$ and $-1(-1)=1$.
47. **D**W We know that $a+(-a)=0$, so the opposite of $-a$
is a. That is, $-(-a)=a$.
48. 403 and 397   **49.** 12 and -7
50. **(a)** $-7+(-6)+(-5)+(-4)+(-3)+(-2)+$
$(-1)+0+1+2+3+4+5+6+7+8=8$; **(b)** 0
51. -1; Consider reciprocals and pairs of products of
negative numbers.
52. $-\frac{5}{8}$ **53.** -2.1

Test: Chapter 10, p. 619

1. [10.1d] $<$ **2.** [10.1d] $>$ **3.** [10.1d] $>$ **4.** [10.1d] $<$
5. [10.1c] -0.125 **6.** [10.1c] $-0.\overline{4}$ **7.** [10.1c] $-0.\overline{18}$
8. [10.1e] 7   **9.** [10.1e] $\frac{9}{4}$ **10.** [10.1e] -2.7
11. [10.2b] $-\frac{2}{3}$ **12.** [10.2b] 1.4   **13.** [10.2b] 8
14. [10.1b]
15. [10.5b] $-\frac{1}{2}$ **16.** [10.5b] $\frac{7}{4}$ **17.** [10.3a] 7.8
18. [10.2a] -8 **19.** [10.2a] $\frac{7}{10}$ **20.** [10.3a] 10
21. [10.3a] -2.5 **22.** [10.3a] $\frac{7}{8}$ **23.** [10.4a] -48

24. [10.4a] $\frac{3}{16}$ **25.** [10.5a] -9 **26.** [10.5c] $\frac{3}{4}$
27. [10.5c] -9.728 **28.** [10.5e] 109 **29.** [10.3b] 14°F higher **30.** [10.3b] Up 15 pts **31.** [10.5d] 16,080
32. [10.5d] About 0.9429°C each minute
33. [10.1e], [10.3a] 15 **34.** [10.3b] 2385 m
35. (a) [10.3a] $-4, -9, -15$; **(b)** [10.3a] $-2, -6, -10$;
(c) [10.3a] $-18, -24, -31$; **(d)** [10.5c] $-0.25, 0.125, -0.0625$

CHAPTER 11

Margin Exercises, Section 11.1, pp. 622–628

1. 64 **2.** 28 **3.** 60; -27.2 **4.** 192 ft^2 **5.** -25
6. 16 **7.**

Value	$1 \cdot x$	x
$x = 3$	3	3
$x = -6$	-6	-6
$x = 4.8$	4.8	4.8

8.

Value	$2x$	$5x$
$x = 2$	4	10
$x = -6$	-12	-30
$x = 4.8$	9.6	24

9.

Value	$5(x + y)$	$5x + 5y$
$x = 6, y = 7$	65	65
$x = -3, y = 4$	5	5
$x = -10, y = 5$	-25	-25

10. 90; 90 **11.** 64; 64 **12.** 14; 14 **13.** 30; 30
14. 12; 12 **15.** $5x$; $-4y$; 3 **16.** $-4y$; $-2x$; $3z$
17. $3x - 15$ **18.** $5x + 5$ **19.** $\frac{5}{4}x - \frac{5}{4}y + 5$
20. $-2x + 6$ **21.** $-5x + 10y - 20z$ **22.** $6(z - 2)$
23. $3(x - 2y + 3)$ **24.** $2(8a - 18b + 21)$
25. $-4(3x - 8y + 4z)$ **26.** $3x$ **27.** $6x$ **28.** $-8x$
29. $0.59x$ **30.** $3x + 3y$ **31.** $-4x - 5y - 7$
32. $\frac{1}{10}x + \frac{7}{9}y - \frac{2}{3}$

Calculator Corner, p. 623

1. 51 **2.** 98 **3.** -6 **4.** -19 **5.** 9 **6.** 12
7. 52; 52 **8.** 156; 156 **9.** 228; 228 **10.** 84; 84

Exercise Set 11.1, p. 629

1. 42 **3.** 3 **5.** -1 **7.** 6 **9.** -20 **11.** 240; 240
13. 160; 160 **15.** $2b + 10$ **17.** $7 - 7t$ **19.** $30x + 12$
21. $7x + 28 + 42y$ **23.** $-7y + 14$ **25.** $45x + 54y - 72$
27. $\frac{3}{4}x - \frac{9}{4}y - \frac{3}{2}z$ **29.** $-3.72x + 9.92y - 3.41$
31. $2(x + 2)$ **33.** $5(6 + y)$ **35.** $7(2x + 3y)$

37. $5(x + 2 + 3y)$ **39.** $8(x - 3)$ **41.** $4(8 - y)$
43. $2(4x + 5y - 11)$ **45.** $6(-3x - 2y + 1)$, or
$-6(3x + 2y - 1)$ **47.** $19a$ **49.** $9a$ **51.** $8x + 9z$
53. $-19a + 88$ **55.** $4t + 6y - 4$ **57.** $8x$ **59.** $5n$
61. $-16y$ **63.** $17a - 12b - 1$ **65.** $4x + 2y$
67. $\frac{39}{20}x + \frac{1}{2}y + 12$ **69.** $0.8x + 0.5y$ **71.** D_W
73. 30 yd; 94.2 yd; 706.5 yd^2 **74.** 16.4 m; 51.496 m;
211.1336 m^2 **75.** 19 mi; 59.66 mi; 283.385 mi^2
76. 4800 cm; 15,072 cm; 18,086,400 cm^2 **77.** 10 mm;
62.8 mm; 314 mm^2 **78.** 132 km; 828.96 km; 54,711.36 km^2
79. 2.3 ft; 14.444 ft; 16.6106 ft^2 **80.** 5.15 m; 32.342 m;
83.28065 m^2 **81.** $q(1 + r + rs + rst)$

Margin Exercises, Section 11.2, pp. 631–632

1. (a) $2 + \boxed{-2} = 0$; **(b)** 9 **2.** -5 **3.** 13.2 **4.** -6.5

Exercise Set 11.2, p. 633

1. 4 **3.** -20 **5.** -14 **7.** 7 **9.** -26 **11.** -18
13. 15 **15.** -14 **17.** 2 **19.** 20 **21.** -6 **23.** $\frac{7}{3}$
25. $-\frac{7}{4}$ **27.** $\frac{41}{24}$ **29.** $-\frac{1}{20}$ **31.** 5.1 **33.** 12.4 **35.** -5
37. $1\frac{5}{6}$ **39.** $-\frac{10}{21}$ **41.** D_W **43.** -11 **44.** $-\frac{1}{24}$
45. -34.1 **46.** -1.7 **47.** 5 **48.** $-\frac{31}{24}$ **49.** 5.5
50. 8.1 **51.** 24 **52.** $-\frac{5}{12}$ **53.** 283.14 **54.** -15.68
55. 8 **56.** $-\frac{16}{15}$ **57.** -14.3 **58.** -4.9 **59.** 342.246
61. $-\frac{26}{15}$ **63.** -10 **65.** $-\frac{5}{17}$

Margin Exercises, Section 11.3, pp. 635–637

1. 15 **2.** $-\frac{7}{4}$ **3.** -18 **4.** 10 **5.** $-\frac{4}{5}$ **6.** 7800
7. -3 **8.** 28

Exercise Set 11.3, p. 638

1. 6 **3.** 9 **5.** 12 **7.** -40 **9.** 5 **11.** -7 **13.** -6
15. 6 **17.** -63 **19.** 36 **21.** -21 **23.** $-\frac{3}{5}$ **25.** $-\frac{3}{2}$
27. $\frac{9}{2}$ **29.** 7 **31.** -7 **33.** 8 **35.** 15.9 **37.** -50
39. -14 **41.** D_W **43.** 62.8 ft; 20 ft; 314 ft^2
44. 75.36 cm; 12 cm; 452.16 cm^2 **45.** 8000 ft^3
46. 31.2 cm^3 **47.** 53.55 cm^2 **48.** 64 mm^2 **49.** 68 in^2
50. 38.25 m^2 **51.** -8655 **53.** No solution
55. No solution

Margin Exercises, Section 11.4, pp. 640–646

1. 5 **2.** 4 **3.** 4 **4.** 39 **5.** $-\frac{3}{2}$ **6.** -4.3 **7.** -3
8. 800 **9.** 1 **10.** 2 **11.** 2 **12.** $\frac{17}{2}$ **13.** $\frac{8}{3}$
14. $-\frac{43}{10}$, or -4.3 **15.** 2 **16.** 3 **17.** -2 **18.** $-\frac{1}{2}$

Calculator Corner, p. 646

1. Left to the student **2.** Left to the student

Exercise Set 11.4, p. 647

1. 5   **3.** 8   **5.** 10   **7.** 14   **9.** −8   **11.** −8   **13.** −7
15. 15   **17.** 6   **19.** 4   **21.** 6   **23.** −3   **25.** 1
27. −20   **29.** 6   **31.** 7   **33.** 2   **35.** 5   **37.** 2
39. 10   **41.** 4   **43.** 0   **45.** −1   **47.** $-\frac{4}{3}$ **49.** $\frac{2}{5}$
51. −2   **53.** −4   **55.** $\frac{4}{5}$ **57.** $-\frac{28}{27}$ **59.** 6   **61.** 2
63. 6   **65.** 8   **67.** 1   **69.** 17   **71.** $-\frac{5}{3}$ **73.** −3
75. 2   **77.** $-\frac{51}{31}$ **79.** 2   **81.** $\mathbf{D_W}$ **83.** rational, zero
84. is greater than   **85.** one   **86.** absolute value
87. obtuse   **88.** equilateral   **89.** meter   **90.** factor
91. 2   **93.** −2   **95.** 8   **97.** 2 cm

Margin Exercises, Section 11.5, pp. 652–659

1. $x - 12$ **2.** $y + 12$, or $12 + y$ **3.** $m - 4$
4. $\frac{1}{2} \cdot p$ or $\frac{p}{2}$ **5.** $6 + 8x$, or $8x + 6$ **6.** $a - b$
7. $59\%x$, or $0.59x$ **8.** $xy - 200$ **9.** $p + q$ **10.** $62\frac{2}{3}$ mi
11. Jenny: 8 in.; Emma: 4 in.; Sarah: 6 in.   **12.** 587.8 mi
13. 30°, 90°, 60°   **14.** Second: 80; third: 89   **15.** $8400

Translating for Success, p. 660

1. B   **2.** H   **3.** G   **4.** N   **5.** J   **6.** C   **7.** L
8. E   **9.** F   **10.** D

Exercise Set 11.5, p. 661

1. $2x - 3$ **3.** $97\%y$, or $0.97y$ **5.** $5x + 4$, or $4 + 5x$
7. $\frac{1}{3}x$, or $240 - x$ **9.** 32   **11.** 305 ft   **13.** $4.29
15. 57   **17.** −12   **19.** $699\frac{1}{3}$ mi   **21.** First: 30 m;
second: 90 m; third: 360 m   **23.** Length: 94 ft; width: 50 ft
25. Length: 265 ft; width: 165 ft; area: 43,725 ft²
27. About 412.6 mi   **29.** First: 22.5°; second: 90°;
third: 67.5°   **31.** $350   **33.** $852.94   **35.** 12 mi
37. $36   **39.** Length: 48 ft; width: 14 ft   **41.** $\mathbf{D_W}$
43. $-\frac{47}{40}$ **44.** $-\frac{17}{40}$ **45.** $-\frac{3}{10}$ **46.** $-\frac{32}{15}$ **47.** 1.6
48. 409.6   **49.** −9.6   **50.** −41.6
51. $1863 = 1776 + (4s + 7)$ **53.** Length: 12 cm;
width: 9 cm   **55.** Half dollars: 5; quarters: 10; dimes: 20;
nickels: 60

Concept Reinforcement, p. 666

1. False   **2.** True   **3.** True   **4.** False   **5.** True

Summary and Review: Chapter 11, p. 666

1. 4   **2.** $15x - 35$ **3.** $-8x + 10$ **4.** $4x + 15$
5. $-24 + 48x$ **6.** $2(x - 7)$ **7.** $6(x - 1)$ **8.** $5(x + 2)$
9. $3(4 - x)$ **10.** $7a - 3b$ **11.** $-2x + 5y$ **12.** $5x - y$
13. $-a + 8b$ **14.** −22   **15.** 7   **16.** −192   **17.** 1
18. $-\frac{7}{3}$ **19.** 25   **20.** $\frac{1}{2}$ **21.** $-\frac{15}{64}$ **22.** 9.99   **23.** −8
24. −5   **25.** $-\frac{1}{3}$ **26.** 4   **27.** 3   **28.** 4   **29.** 16
30. 6   **31.** −3   **32.** −2   **33.** 4   **34.** $19\%x$, or $0.19x$
35. Length: 365 mi; width: 275 mi   **36.** $2117

37. 27 appliances   **38.** 35°, 85°, 60°   **39.** $220
40. $75,000   **41.** $138.95   **42.** Amazon: 6437 km;
Nile: 6671 km   **43.** $791   **44.** Width: 11 cm;
length: 17 cm   **45.** $\mathbf{D_W}$ The distributive laws are used to
multiply, factor, and collect like terms in this chapter.
46. $\mathbf{D_W}$ (a) $4 - 3x = 9$
$$3x = 9 \quad (1)$$
$$x = 3 \quad (2)$$

    1. 4 was subtracted on the left side but not on
the right side. Also, the minus sign preceding
$3x$ has been dropped.

    2. This step would give the correct result if the
preceding step were correct.

The correct steps are
$$4 - 3x = 9$$
$$-3x = 5 \quad (1)$$
$$x = -\frac{5}{3}. \quad (2)$$

(b) $2(x - 5) = 7$
$$2x - 5 = 7 \quad (1)$$
$$2x = 12 \quad (2)$$
$$x = 6 \quad (3)$$

    1. When a distributive law was used to remove
parentheses, x was multiplied by 2 but 5
was not.

    2. and 3. These steps would give the correct
result if the preceding step were correct.

The correct steps are
$$2(x - 5) = 7$$
$$2x - 10 = 7 \quad (1)$$
$$2x = 17 \quad (2)$$
$$x = \frac{17}{2}. \quad (3)$$

47. 23, −23   **48.** 20, −20

Test: Chapter 11, p. 669

1. [11.1a] 6   **2.** [11.1b] $18 - 3x$ **3.** [11.1b] $-5y + 5$
4. [11.1c] $2(6 - 11x)$ **5.** [11.1c] $7(x + 3 + 2y)$
6. [11.1d] $-5x - y$ **7.** [11.1d] $4a + 5b$ **8.** [11.2a] 8
9. [11.2a] 26   **10.** [11.3a] −6   **11.** [11.3a] 49
12. [11.4b] −12   **13.** [11.4a] 2   **14.** [11.4a] −8
15. [11.2a] $-\frac{7}{20}$ **16.** [11.4b] 2.5   **17.** [11.4c] 7
18. [11.4c] $\frac{5}{3}$ **19.** [11.5a] $x - 9$ **20.** [11.5b] Width: 7 cm;
length: 11 cm   **21.** [11.5b] About $240.7 billion
22. [11.5b] 3 m, 5 m   **23.** [11.5b] $880   **24.** [11.5b] 6
25. [11.5b] 25.625°   **26.** [10.1e], [11.4a] 15, −15
27. [11.5b] 60 tickets

Cumulative Review/Final Examination: Chapters 1–11, p. 671

1. [5.2b] Unit prices: 7.647¢/oz, 7.133¢/oz, 7.016¢/oz,
5.828¢/oz, 4.552¢/oz; brand E has the lowest unit price.
2. [4.1a] Seven and four hundred sixty-three thousandths
3. [9.3b], [9.4c] **(a)** 4400 mi; **(b)** about 1,437,333,333 mi³
4. [6.5a] $13,444   **5.** [6.5a] 15%   **6.** [6.5a] $2151.04
7. [6.5a] 30%   **8.** [6.5a] $537.76   **9.** [1.1a] 7

10. [1.1b] 7 thousands + 4 hundreds + 5 ones
11. [1.2a] 1012   **12.** [1.2a] 21,085   **13.** [3.2a] $\frac{5}{26}$
14. [3.5a] $5\frac{7}{9}$ **15.** [4.2a] 493.971   **16.** [4.2a] 802.876
17. [1.3b] 152   **18.** [1.3b] 674   **19.** [3.3a] $\frac{5}{24}$
20. [3.5b] $2\frac{17}{24}$ **21.** [4.2b] 19.9973   **22.** [4.2b] 34.241
23. [1.5a] 4752   **24.** [1.5a] 266,287   **25.** [3.6a] $4\frac{1}{12}$
26. [2.6a] $\frac{6}{5}$ **27.** [2.4a] 10   **28.** [4.3a] 259.084
29. [1.6b] 573   **30.** [1.6b] 56 R 10   **31.** [3.4b] $56\frac{5}{17}$
32. [2.7b] $\frac{3}{2}$ **33.** [3.6b] $\frac{7}{90}$ **34.** [4.4a] 39   **35.** [1.4a] 68,000
36. [4.1d] 0.428   **37.** [4.5b] 21.84   **38.** [2.2a] Yes
39. [2.1a] 1, 3, 5, 15   **40.** [3.1a] 800   **41.** [2.5b] $\frac{7}{10}$
42. [2.5b] 55   **43.** [3.4a] $3\frac{3}{5}$ **44.** [2.5c] $\neq$ **45.** [3.3b] $<$
46. [4.1c] 1.001   **47.** [1.4c] $>$ **48.** [2.3a] $\frac{3}{5}$
49. [4.1b] 0.037   **50.** [4.5a] 0.52   **51.** [4.5a] $0.\overline{8}$
52. [6.1b] 0.07   **53.** [4.1b] $\frac{463}{100}$ **54.** [3.4a] $\frac{29}{4}$ **55.** [6.2b] $\frac{2}{5}$
56. [6.2a] 85%   **57.** [6.1b] 150%   **58.** [1.7b] 555
59. [4.4b] 64   **60.** [2.7c] $\frac{5}{4}$ **61.** [5.3b] $76\frac{1}{2}$, or 76.5
62. [7.4b]

Number of Rounds of Golf Per Year

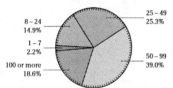

8 – 24 14.9%
25 – 49 25.3%
1 – 7 2.2%
50 – 99 39.0%
100 or more 18.6%

63. [7.3b]

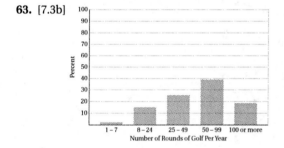

Percent
100
90
80
70
60
50
40
30
20
10

1 – 7 8 – 24 25 – 49 50 – 99 100 or more
Number of Rounds of Golf Per Year

64. [9.5e] 118°   **65.** [9.5d] Obtuse   **66.** [1.8a] $675
67. [1.8a] 65 min   **68.** [4.7a] $25.75   **69.** [4.7a] 485.9 mi
70. [1.8a] $8100   **71.** [1.8a] $783   **72.** [2.4c] $\frac{3}{10}$ km
73. [4.7a] $84.96   **74.** [5.4a] 13 gal   **75.** [6.7a] $150
76. [6.6b] 7%   **77.** [6.5b] 30,160   **78.** [7.1a, b, c] 28;
26; 18   **79.** [1.9b] 324   **80.** [1.9b] 400   **81.** [9.6a] 3
82. [9.6a] 11   **83.** [9.6b] 4.472   **84.** [8.1a] 12
85. [8.2a] 428   **86.** [8.6a] 72   **87.** [8.4b] 20
88. [8.4a] 80   **89.** [8.4b] 0.08   **90.** [8.5a] 8.19
91. [8.5a] 5   **92.** [9.6c] $c = \sqrt{50}$ ft; $c \approx 7.071$ ft
93. [9.1a], [9.2a] 25.6 m; 25.75 m^2 **94.** [9.2b] 25 in^2
95. [9.2b] 128.65 yd^2 **96.** [9.2b] 61.6 cm^2
97. [9.3a, b, c] 20.8 in.; 65.312 in.; 339.6224 in^2
98. [9.4a] 52.9 m^3 **99.** [9.4b] 803.84 ft^3
100. [9.4d] $267.94\overline{6}$ cm^3 **101.** [1.9c] 238   **102.** [1.9c] 172
103. [10.1e], [10.4a] 3   **104.** [10.2a] 14   **105.** [10.3a] $\frac{1}{3}$
106. [10.4a] 30   **107.** [10.4a] $-\frac{2}{7}$ **108.** [10.5a] -8
109. [11.4a] -5 **110.** [11.3a] 4   **111.** [11.4b] -8
112. [11.4c] $\frac{2}{3}$ **113.** [11.5a] $y + 17$, or $17 + y$
114. [11.5a] 38%x, or $0.38x$ **115.** [11.5b] $45
116. [11.5b] $1050   **117.** [11.5a] 50 m; 53 m; 40 m
118. [11.4b] 0   **119.** [11.4b] 2   **120.** [11.1d] (c)
121. [11.1c] (e)   **122.** [10.5c] (d)   **123.** [10.2a] (a)

Glossary

A

Absolute value The distance that a number is from 0 on the number line

Acute angle An angle whose measure is greater than 0° and less than 90°

Acute triangle A triangle in which all three angles are acute

Addend In addition, a number being added

Additive identity The number 0

Additive inverse A number's opposite; two numbers are additive inverses of each other if their sum is 0.

Algebraic expression An expression consisting of variables, constants, numerals, and operation signs

Angle A set of points consisting of two rays (half-lines) with a common endpoint (vertex)

Area The number of square units that fill a plane region

Arithmetic mean A center point of a set of numbers found by adding the numbers and dividing by the number of items of data; also called mean or average

Arithmetic numbers The whole numbers and the positive fractions

Associative law of addition The statement that when three numbers are added, regrouping the addends gives the same sum

Associative law of multiplication The statement that when three numbers are multiplied, regrouping the factors gives the same product

Average A center point of a set of numbers found by adding the numbers and dividing by the number of items of data; also called the arithmetic mean or mean

B

Bar graph A graphic display of data using bars proportional in length to the numbers represented

Base In exponential notation, the number being raised to a power

C

Celsius A temperature scale for metric measure

Circle graph A graphic means of displaying data using sectors of a circle; often used to show the percent of a quantity in different categories or to show visually the ratio of one category to another; also called a pie chart

Circumference The distance around a circle

Coefficient The numerical multiplier of a variable

Commutative law of addition The statement that when two numbers are added, changing the order in which the numbers are added does not affect the sum

Commutative law of multiplication The statement that when two numbers are multiplied, changing the order in which the numbers are multiplied does not affect the product

Commission A percent of total sales paid to a salesperson

Complementary angles Two angles for which the sum of their measures is 90°

Composite number A natural number, other than 1, that is not prime

Compound interest Interest paid on interest

Constant A known number

Cross products Given an equation with a single fraction on each side, the products formed by multiplying the left numerator and the right denominator, and the left denominator and the right numerator

D

Decimal notation A representation of a number containing a decimal point

Denominator The number below the fraction bar in a fraction

Diameter A segment that passes through the center of a circle and has its endpoints on the circle

Difference The result of subtracting one number from another

Digit A number 0, 1, 2, 3, 4, 5, 6, 7, 8, or 9 that names a place-value location

Discount The amount subtracted from the original price of an item to find the sales price

Distributive law of multiplication over addition The statement that multiplying a factor by the sum of two numbers gives the same result as multiplying the factor by each of the two numbers and then adding

Distributive law of multiplication over subtraction The statement that multiplying a factor by the difference of two numbers gives the same result as multiplying the factor by each of the two numbers and then subtracting

Dividend In division, the number being divided

G-1

Divisible   The number a is divisible by another number b if there exists a number c such that $a = b \cdot c$.

Divisor   In division, the number dividing another number

E

Equation   A number sentence that says that the expressions on either side of the equals sign, $=$, represent the same number

Equilateral triangle   A triangle in which all sides are the same length

Equivalent equations   Equations with the same solution set

Equivalent expressions   Expressions that have the same value for all allowable replacements

Even number   A number that is divisible by 2; that is, it has an even ones digit

Exponential notation   A representation of a number using a base raised to a power

Exponent   In expressions of the form a^n, the number n is an exponent. For n a natural number, a^n represents n factors of a.

F

Factor   *Verb:* to write an equivalent expression that is a product. *Noun:* a multiplier

Factorization   A number expressed as a product of natural numbers

Fahrenheit   A temperature scale for American measure

Fraction notation   A number written using a numerator and a denominator

H

Hypotenuse   In a right triangle, the side opposite the right angle

I

Identity property of 1   The statement that the product of a number and 1 is always the original number

Identity property of 0   The statement that the sum of a number and 0 is always the original number

Inequality   A mathematical sentence using $<, >, \leq, \geq$, or $\neq$.

Integers   The whole numbers and their opposites

Interest   A percentage of an amount invested or borrowed

Irrational number   A real number that cannot be named as a ratio of two integers

Isosceles triangle   A triangle in which two or more sides are the same length

L

Least common denominator (LCD)   The least common multiple of the denominators of two or more fractions

Least common multiple (LCM)   The smallest number that is a multiple of two or more numbers

Legs   In a right triangle, the two sides that form the right angle

Like terms   Terms that have exactly the same variable factors

Line graph   A graphic means of displaying data by connecting adjacent data points with line segments

M

Marked price   The original price of an item

Mean   A center point of a set of numbers found by adding the numbers and dividing by the number of items of data; also called the arithmetic mean or average

Median   In a set of data listed in order from smallest to largest, the middle number if there is an odd number of data items, or the average of the two middle numbers if there is an even number of data items

Minuend   The number from which another number is being subtracted

Mixed numeral   A number represented by a whole number and a fraction less than 1

Mode   The number or numbers that occur most often in a set of data

Multiple of a number   A product of the number and some natural number

Multiplicative identity   The number 1

Multiplicative inverses   Reciprocals; two numbers whose product is 1

N

Natural numbers   The counting numbers: 1, 2, 3, 4, 5, …

Numerator   The number above the fraction bar in a fraction

O

Obtuse angle   An angle whose measure is greater than $90°$ and less than $180°$

Obtuse triangle   A triangle in which one angle is an obtuse angle

Opposite   The opposite, or additive inverse, of a number a is written $-a$. Opposites are the same distance from 0 on the number line but on different sides of 0.

Original price   The price of an item before a discount is deducted

P

Parallelogram   A four-sided polygon with two pairs of parallel sides

Percent notation   A representation of a number as parts per 100

Perimeter   The sum of the lengths of the sides of a polygon

Pi (π)   The number that results when the circumference of a circle is divided by its diameter; $\pi \approx 3.14$, or 22/7

Pictograph   A graphic means of displaying data using pictorial symbols

Pie chart   A graphic means of displaying data using sectors of a circle; often used to show the percent of a quantity used in different categories or to show visually the ratio of one category to another; also called a circle graph

Polygon   A closed geometric figure with three or more sides

Prime factorization   A factorization of a composite number as a product of prime numbers

Prime number   A natural number that has exactly two different factors: itself and 1

Protractor   A device used to measure angles

Purchase price   The price of an item before sales tax is added

Pythagorean equation   The equation $a^2 + b^2 = c^2$, where a and b are the lengths of the legs of a right triangle and c is the length of the hypotenuse

Q

Quotient   The result when one number is divided by another

R

Radical sign   The symbol $\sqrt{}$

Radius   A segment with one endpoint on the center of a circle and the other endpoint on the circle

Rate   A ratio used to compare two different kinds of measure

Ratio   The quotient of two quantities

Rational number   A number that can be written in the form a/b, where a and b are integers and $b \neq 0$

Real numbers   All rational and irrational numbers

Reciprocal   A multiplicative inverse; two numbers are reciprocals if their product is 1

Rectangle   A four-sided polygon with four right angles

Right angle   An angle whose measure is 90°

Right triangle   A triangle that includes a right angle

Rounding   Approximating the value of a number; used when estimating

S

Sale price   The price of an item after a discount has been deducted

Sales tax   A tax added to the purchase price of an item

Scalene triangle   A triangle in which each side is a different length

Similar triangles   Triangles in which corresponding sides are proportional

Simple interest   A percentage of an amount P invested or borrowed for t years, computed by calculating principal × interest rate × time

Simplify   To rewrite an expression in an equivalent, abbreviated form

Solution of an equation   A replacement or substitution that makes an equation true

Sphere   The set of all points in space that are a given distance from a given point

Square   A four-sided polygon with four right angles and all sides of equal length

Square of a number   A number multiplied by itself

Square root of a number   A number that when multiplied by itself yields the given original number

Straight angle   An angle whose measure is 180°

Substitute   To replace a variable with a number

Subtrahend   In subtraction, the number being subtracted

Sum   The result in addition

Supplementary angles   Two angles for which the sum of their measures is 180°

T

Term   A number, a variable, or a product or a quotient of numbers and/or variables

Terminating decimal   A decimal that can be written using a finite number of decimal places

Total price   The sum of the purchase price of an item and the sales tax on the item

Trapezoid   A four-sided polygon with two parallel sides

Triangle   A three-sided polygon

U

Unit price   The ratio of price to the number of units; also called unit rate

Unit rate   The ratio of price to the number of units; also called unit price

V

Variable   A letter that represents an unknown number

Vertex   The common endpoint of the two rays that form an angle

W

Whole numbers   The natural numbers and 0: 0, 1, 2, 3, …

Photo Credits

xxxi, Michael St.–Andre   **6,** © Ed Quinn, CORBIS   **7,** Tony Stone/Getty   **8 (left),** © Jeff Greenberg/The Image Works; **(right),** © CLARO CORTES IV/Reuters/Corbis   **36,** © Kin Cheung/Reuters/Corbis   **38,** © Michael S. Yamshita/CORBIS   **69,** © Pete Saloutos/CORBIS   **72,** CORBIS   **84,** Tony Stone/Getty   **104 (top),** © Keith Dannemiller/CORBIS; **(bottom),** CORBIS   **107 (Kidman),** © Rufus F. Folkks/CORBIS; **(Berry),** © Eric Robert/CORBIS SYGMA; **(Dole),** © Reuters/CORBIS; **(Swank),** © Christy Bowe/CORBIS; **(Paltrow),** © Dusko Despotovic/Corbis; **(Roberts),** © Reuters/CORBIS; **(Feinstein),** © Roger Ressmeyer/CORBIS   **112,** © Ariel Skelley/ Corbis Stock Market   **113,** © LWA-JDC/CORBIS   **119,** © Laura Dwight/CORBIS   **128,** The Image Bank   **138,** © Bill Varie/CORBIS   **146 (left),** Greg Probst/Stone/ Getty; **(right),** © Craig Aurness/CORBIS   **163,** photodisc   **164,** © Ted Horowitz/ CORBIS   **171,** © Royalty-Free/Corbis   **177,** photodisc   **182,** J. P. Jenkins   **183,** © Joseph Sohm; ChromoSohm Inc./CORBIS   **184,** John Deere   **186,** © Anthony Redpath/CORBIS   **197 (left),** © Ted Spiegel/CORBIS; **(right),** © Royalty-Free/Corbis   **199,** photodisc   **202,** © Annie Griffiths Belt/CORBIS   **211,** CORBIS   **214 (left),** photodisc; **(right),** Karen Bittinger   **219 (left),** Plush Studios/Getty; **(right),** © Rick Rickman/NewSport   **225 (left),** Digital Vision/Getty; **(right),** © Sion Touhig/Corbis   **239,** Bettman/CORBIS   **257,** Mark Gibson, Digital Vision/Getty   **261,** Chuck Savage/ CORBIS   **262, 265, 268,** © Reuters/CORBIS   **276,** Think-stock/Getty   **285,** © Tom Nebbia/Corbis Stock Market   **286,** © Royalty-Free/Corbis   **292,** David Muench, CORBIS   **293,** © Matt A. Brown/NewSport   **294,** apwire photos   **296 (left),** © Royalty-Free/Corbis; **(right),** Albert J. Copley, photodisc   **297,** © Reuters/CORBIS   **300 (top),** Eyewire Collection; **(bottom),** © Reuters/CORBIS   **301,** Dick Morton   **303 (top),** © JOE GIZA/Reuters/Corbis; **(left),** © Royalty-Free/Corbis; **(right),** © Joe McDonald/CORBIS   **304,** Jeremy Woodhouse, Photodisc   **306 (top),** © Reuters/ CORBIS; **(bottom),** © Bil Janscha/Reuters/Corbis   **314,** Brian Spurlock   **315,** Buccina Studios, photodisc   **318,** Nicholas Devore III/Photographers Aspen   **321 (left),** Barry Rosenthal, FPG International; **(right),** Keith Brofsky, photodisc   **322 (left),** © Rob Lewine/CORBIS; **(right),** © Kevin Fleming, Corbis   **323 (left),** © Royalty-Free/Corbis; **(right),** © Chase Jarvis/CORBIS   **333,** Karen Bittinger   **334,** Dick Morton   **335 (top),** Patrick Clark, photodisc; **(bottom),** Phil Schermeister, Corbis   **339,** © Carl & Ann Purcell/CORBIS   **342,** photodisc   **343,** © Turbo/zefa/ CORBIS   **347, 348,** photodisc   **350,** © Guzelian Asadour/CORBIS   **359, 360, 361, 365, 372,** © Royalty-Free/CORBIS   **376,** Digital Vision   **379,** photodisc   **380,** © David H. Wells/CORBIS   **391,** Christopher Bissell, Stone/Getty Images   **401,** photodisc   **403, 404, 413,** © Royalty-Free/CORBIS   **418,** Hulton Archive/Getty Images   **419,** Reportage/Getty Images   **423,** Tom Stratmen   **425,** © Royalty-Free/ Corbis   **429,** Cincinnati Zoo & Botanical Garden, Photo, S. David Jenike   **430,** Stone/ Getty Images   **448,** © Larry Williams/CORBIS   **462,** © Reuters/CORBIS   **464,** FPG International   **480,** © Owen Franken/CORBIS   **488,** © Tom and Dee Ann McCarthy/ Corbis Stock Market   **489,** Digital Vision/photodisc   **491,** David Young-Wolff/ PhotoEdit   **492,** © Richard T. Nowitz/CORBIS   **498,** © Jonathan Blair/CORBIS   **503,** © Galen Rowell/Corbis   **509,** © Jeremy Woodhouse/photodisc   **512,** © Warren Morgan/CORBIS   **519,** © Michael Prince/CORBIS   **538,** © Nancy Dudley/Stock Boston   **548,** © Richard Cummins/CORBIS   **549,** Scott T. Baxer/photodisc   **550,** © 1988 Al Satterwhite   **577 (top),** © National Geographic Image Collection; **(bottom),** photodisc   **588,** © Buddy Mays/CORBIS   **600,** © Douglas Peebles/ CORBIS   **618,** Comstock Images   **653,** Appalachian Trail Conference   **662 (top),** EyeWire Collection; **(bottom left),** Kevin Horan, Tony Stone Images; **(bottom right),** © Ed Bock/CORBIS   **668,** © Warren Morgan/CORBIS   **676,** © ML Sinibaldi/The Stock Market

Index

Distributive laws, 33, 625, 626, 666
  and factoring, 627
  and multiplying, 33, 626
Dividend, 40
Divisibility, 92
  by 2, 98
  by 3, 99
  by 4, 101
  by 5, 100
  by 6, 99
  by 7, 101
  by 8, 101
  by 9, 100
  by 10, 100
  and simplifying fraction notation,
    124
Division
  by 0.1, 0.01, 0.001, and so on, 248
  by 10, 100, 1000, and so on, 247
  checking, 43, 44
  with decimal notation, 244–248
  definition, 41, 606
  dividend, 40
    of zero, 42, 607
  divisor, 40
  by estimate, multiply, and subtract,
    45
  estimating quotients, 265
  with fraction notation, 136, 194
  of integers, 606
  and LCMs, 154
  with mixed numerals, 191, 194
  of a number by itself, 42
  by one, 42
  by a power of ten, 247, 248
  by primes, 154
  quotient, 40, 41
  of real numbers, 606–609
  and reciprocals, 136, 608
  and rectangular arrays, 40
  related multiplication sentence, 41
  with remainders, 43
  as repeated subtraction, 40
  of whole numbers, 40, 47
  by zero, 42, 607
  of zero by a nonzero number, 42
Divisor, 40
Dollars, converting from/to cents, 240

E

Earned run average, 324
Effective yield, 400
Eight, divisibility by, 101
English system of measures, *see*
    American system of measures
Equality of fractions, test for, 126
Equation, 26, 52
  checking solutions, 54, 632, 646
  equivalent, 631
  false, 26
  percent, 358

Pythagorean, 561
solution of, 52
solving, 52, 53, 55, 138, 167, 231,
    248, 631, 635, 640. *See also*
    Solving equations.
translating to, 58
true, 25, 358
Equilateral triangle, 556
Equivalent, decimal, 352
Equivalent equations, 631
Equivalent expressions, 624
Equivalent, fraction, 352
Equivalent fractions, 122
Equivalent numbers, 122
Equivalent, percent, 352
Estimate, multiply, and subtract, in
    division, 45
Estimating. *See also* Rounding.
  with decimal notation, 264
  differences, 26, 264
  in division process, 45
  with fraction notation, 203
  with mixed numerals, 204
  products, 35, 265
  quotients, 265
  sums, 25, 264
  wildlife populations, 318
Evaluating
  algebraic expressions, 622, 623
  exponential notation, 76
Even number, 98
Expanded notation, 3
Exponent, 75
Exponential notation, 75
  on a calculator, 76
  evaluating, 76
  and LCMs, 153
Expressions
  algebraic, 622
  equivalent, 624
  evaluating, 622, 623
  factoring, 627
  multiplying, 626
  simplifying, 76
  terms, 626
  value of, 622

F

Factor, 90, 92. *See also* Factoring;
    Factorization; Factors.
Factor tree, 95
Factoring, 90
  algebraic expressions, 627
Factorization
  of natural numbers, 91
  prime, 93
    and LCMs, 151, 152
Factorization method, 152, 154
Factors, 31, 90. *See also* Factor.
  and sums, 97
Fahrenheit temperature, 500

False equation, 26
False inequality, 26
Familiarize, 58, 653
Five, divisibility by, 100
Fluid ounce, 493
Foot, 466
Four, divisibility by, 101
Fraction equivalent, 352
Fraction notation, 104. *See also*
    Fractions.
  addition, 158, 159, 194
  converting
    from/to decimal notation, 220,
      221, 255
    from/to mixed numerals, 173,
      174
    from/to percent notation,
      349–351
  and decimal notation together, 259
  denominator, 104
  in division, 136, 194
  estimation with, 203
  multiplication using, 115, 116, 129,
    194
  numerator, 104
  for one, 108
  order, 167
  order of operations, 201
  and percent notation, 343
  for rational numbers, 584
  for ratios, 107
  simplest, 123
  simplifying, 123, 125
  subtraction, 165, 194
  for whole numbers, 108, 109
  for zero, 108
Fractions, 104. *See also* Fraction
    notation.
  clearing, 643
  equivalent, 122
  estimation with, 203
  improper, 106, 176
  multiplication by a whole number,
    115
  multiplicative identity, 122
  reciprocals, 135
  test for equality, 126

G

Gallon, 493
GPA, 419
Grade point average, 419
Gram, 484
Graph
  bar, 417, 436
  circle, 448
  line, 417, 438
  of a number, 584
  picture, 416, 429
Greater than (>), 26, 586

Number line, addition on, 590
Numbers
 arithmetic, 218
 composite, 93
 digits, 2
 equivalent, 122
 even, 98
 expanded notation, 3
 graphing, 584
 integers, 582
 irrational, 585
 natural, 3, 90
 nonnegative rational, 218
 palindrome, 146
 periods, 2, 4
 place-value, 2
 prime, 93
 ratio, 292
 rational, 583, 584
  nonnegative, 218
 real, 586
 signs of, 593
 standard notation, 3
 whole, 3
 word names, 4
Numerals, mixed, 173. *See also* Mixed
  numerals.
Numerator, 104

O

Obtuse angle, 553
Obtuse triangle, 556
One
 division by, 42
 fraction notation for, 108
 identity property, 624
 multiplying by, 467, 476, 484, 493,
  499, 505
Ones period, 2
Operations, order of, 76, 78, 201, 249
Opposite, 582, 592, 593
 and subtraction, 597
Order
 in decimal notation, 223
 in fraction notation, 167
 of operations, 76, 78, 201, 249, 610
 of real numbers, 586
 of whole numbers, 26
Original price, 388
Ounce, 493

P

Palindrome prime, 146
Paragraph presentation of data, 416
Parallelogram, 522
 area, 523, 569
Parentheses, 76
 equations containing, 645
 in multiplication, 31

within parentheses, 79
Percent, *see* Percent notation
Percent equation, 358
Percent equivalent, 352
Percent notation, 342, 343
 converting
  from/to decimal notation,
   343–345
  from/to fraction notation,
   349–352
 in pie charts, 342, 448
 solving problems involving,
  359–362, 365–368, 371–377
Percent of decrease, 374, 375
Percent of increase, 374, 376
Perimeter, 11, 516
 rectangle, 517, 569
 square, 517, 569
Periods, 2, 4
Pi (π), 533
 on a calculator, 544
Pictographs, 416, 429
Picture graphs, 416, 429
Pie chart, 448
Pint, 493
Pitch of a screw, 132
Pixels, 70
Place value, 2, 218
Polygon, 516
Positive integers, 582
Pound, 484
Power, 75
Power of ten
 dividing by, 247, 248
 multiplying by, 238
Price
 marked, 388
 original, 388
 purchase, 385
 sale, 388
 total, 385
 unit, 300
Price-earnings ratio, 353
Prime factorization, 93
 in finding LCMs, 151, 152
 in simplifying fractions, 124
Prime numbers, 93
 division by, 155
 palindrome, 146
Principal, 394
Principles
 addition, 631, 666
 multiplication, 635, 666
Problem solving, 58, 653. *See also*
  Index of Applications.
Products, 31. *See also* Multiplication.
 cross, 307, 308
 estimating, 35, 265
Proportional, 306. *See also*
  Proportions.
Proportions, 306

and geometric shapes, 325, 327
 and similar triangles, 325
 solving, 307, 308, 310
 used in solving percent problems,
  365
Protractor, 552
Purchase price, 385
Pythagoras, 562
Pythagorean equation, 561, 569
Pythagorean theorem, 561

Q

Quadrillion, 243
Quality points, 419
Quart, 493
Quintillion, 243
Quotient, 40, 41
 estimating, 265
 as a mixed numeral, 175
 zeros in, 46

R

Radical sign ($\sqrt{}$), 560
Radius, 532, 569
Rate, 299
 commission, 387
 of discount, 388
 interest, 394
 sales tax, 385
 unit, 300
Ratio, 107, 292
 and circle graphs, 448
 notation, 292
 percent as, 343
 price-earnings, 353
 and proportion, 309
 as a rate, 299
 simplifying, 294
Rational numbers, 583, 584
 and decimal notation, 585
 and fraction notation, 584
 graphing, 584
 nonnegative, 218
Rays, 551
Real-number system, 586
 and absolute value, 587
 and addition, 590, 591
 additive inverses, 592
 and division, 606–609
 integers, 582
 and multiplication, 602, 603
 opposites, 592, 593
 and order, 586
 and order of operations, 610
 rational numbers, 583, 584
 and subtraction, 596
Reciprocal, 135, 607
 and division, 136, 608
 of a fraction, 135

equilateral, 556
isosceles, 556
obtuse, 556
right, 556, 561
scalene, 556
similar, 625
sum of angle measures, 556, 569
Trillion, 239
Trillions period, 2
True equation, 26
True inequality, 26
Truncating, 227
Two, divisibility by, 98

U

Unit angle, 551
Unit cube, 541
Unit price, 300
Unit rate, 300
Unit segment, 466

V

Value of an expression, 622
Variable, 622
substituting for, 622

Vertex, 551
Volume
of a circular cone, 544, 569
of a circular cylinder, 543, 569
of a rectangular solid, 541, 569
of a sphere, 543, 569

W

Week, 499
Weight, 484, 510. *See also* Mass.
Whole numbers, 3
addition, 9, 12
division, 40, 47
expanded notation, 3
fraction notation for, 108, 109
multiplication, 31, 35
by fractions, 115
order, 26
rounding, 22
standard notation, 3
subtraction, 15, 17, 18
word names for, 4
Wildlife population, estimating, 318
Word names
for decimal notation, 219
for whole numbers, 4

Y

Yard, 466
Year, 499
Yield
effective, 400
stock, 353

Z

Zero
addition of, 9, 591
divided by a nonzero number, 42, 607
division by, 42, 607
fraction notation for, 108
identity property, 591
in quotients, 46
reciprocal, 135